THE LIMITS OF JUDICIAL POWER

William Lasser.

THE LIMITS OF
JUDICIAL
POWER

The Supreme Court in American Politics

The University of North Carolina Press

Chapel Hill & London

© 1988 The University of North Carolina Press

Manufactured in the United States of America

The paper in this book meets the guidelines for permanence
and durability of the Committee on Production Guidelines
for Book Longevity of the Council on Library Resources.

92 91 90 89 88   5 4 3 2 1

Library of Congress Cataloging-in-Publication Data
Lasser, William.
The limits of judicial power.

Bibliography: p.
Includes index.
1. United States. Supreme Court—History.
2. Political questions and judicial power—United
States—History. I. Title.
KF8742.L38   1988   347.73'26'09   88-40141
347.3073509
ISBN 0-8078-1810-0 (alk. paper)
ISBN 0-8078-4233-8 (pbk.: alk. paper)

To Joseph and Shirley Lasser, with love

Contents

Acknowledgments

WRITING IS supposed to be a lonely profession, but my experience has been precisely the opposite. Throughout the long process of writing this book, I have been helped, encouraged, educated, critiqued, and supported by literally scores of people. I am grateful to all of them but must content myself with thanking only a few explicitly.

Several of my former professors continued to give invaluable support and advice. James Q. Wilson, now of UCLA, has remained a vital source of practical wisdom, scholarly advice, and professional support. Above all, he has the rare ability to push his students to their fullest potential, and his honest evaluations of my work were always appreciated. Others who have been of great help at various points in the completion of this project include R. Shep Melnick, Harry Hirsch, Walter Dean Burnham, Louis Menand III, and Al Sumberg. I thank all of them.

Several of my colleagues at Clemson University have provided encouragement and assistance. I am especially happy to have had the friendship of William F. Connelly, Jr., Susan and Bernie Duffy, Lois Duke, Leonard J. Greenspoon, John Johnson, Martin Slann, Steve Wainscott, and Dave Woodard. Charles W. Dunn was extremely helpful and supportive, not only reading and critiquing the manuscript but also making life easier in countless ways. Dean Robert A. Waller provided release time in 1986 to permit the completion of the manuscript, and I am grateful to him. Deborah Whitfield, Rita Pruitt, and Cathy Stowers have tolerated my jokes and contributed considerable support. The Clemson University Research Grants Committee provided generous financial assistance over several years.

Many other friends and colleagues should be recognized, either for providing specific assistance on the manuscript or for contributing to my education on the Court and on American politics. Among these are Louis Fisher, John Brigham, Sue Davis, Mary Thornberry, and Elder Witt.

Acknowledgments

Walter F. Murphy's 1985 seminar on the Supreme Court not only introduced me to several of these people but was itself a marvelous learning experience. William Leuchtenburg's reading of an early draft of the New Deal chapter was most appreciated. A number of friends from graduate school, including Ian Marsh, Eliot Cohen, Rob Vipond, Gina Feldberg, and Jim Stoner, all indulged my endless discussions of the *Dred Scott* case or the mystical depths of American politics. I am also much indebted to Neil Siegel for his encouragement and assistance and to Sherman L. Davis for his help on a range of matters.

I wish I could thank all the librarians and archivists who helped me on various matters. The Clemson librarians were particularly patient even when I was most bothersome, and I would like to thank in particular the Interlibrary Loan staff, especially Marian Withington, Julie Pennebaker, and Dale Simmons. I am also grateful for the financial support of the National Endowment for the Humanities, in the form of a Travel to Collections Grant (No. RY-2176-85) and a Summer Stipend (No. FT-26777-85) in 1985. Several individuals at the University of North Carolina Press have worked hard to create this book from the earliest query letter, and I am thankful especially to Paul Betz, Ron Maner, Lisa M. Dellwo, and Margaret Morse.

Finally, and most importantly, my family. It is impossible to measure the debt this book owes to my wife, Susan J. S. Lasser, who edited and critiqued the manuscript in its several forms. She endured countless explanations of obscure legal cases and never wavered in her love and support. Without her this book might have existed, but it would have been considerably less readable and its author would have been considerably less happy. Florence Shroder was always helpful and provided willing accommodations for research trips to Washington. I am also thankful to Ronald and Judith Lasser, and to my nephew, Avi, who would have helped if he were old enough to read.

To my parents, what can I say? See the dedication page.

THE LIMITS OF JUDICIAL POWER

I

Introduction

[The Supreme] Court of the modern era, like those of the past, has rendered a service of no small significance. From 1789 to the Civil War, the Court labored to establish a reasoned argument for the cause of union. From the war to 1937 it performed a similar function on behalf of laissez faire. Toward the end of each of these periods, the judges overstepped the practical boundaries of judicial power and endangered the place they had earned in the American system. Since 1937, the Court has striven to evolve a civil rights doctrine that will realize the promise of the American libertarian tradition, yet accord with the imperatives of political reality. . . . It would be a pity if the judges, having done so much, should now once more forget the limits that their own history so compellingly prescribes.
—*Robert G. McCloskey,* The American Supreme Court *(1960)*

THE MODERN COURT, McCloskey concluded in his landmark study, was in danger once again of overstepping the limits of its power and of endangering its place in the American system of government. In several cases, and especially in the desegregation cases of the mid-1950s, the Court had pushed forward at a rate that, to McCloskey, seemed "perilous and perhaps self-defeating." Surely, he warned, no purpose is served "when the judges seek the hottest political cauldrons of the moment and dive into the middle of them"; the clear lesson of the Court's history was that its "greatest successes have been achieved when it has operated near the margins rather than in the center of political controversy, when it has nudged and tugged the nation, instead of trying to rule it." If the modern Court refused to learn this lesson, McCloskey concluded, it risked repeating its greatest historical blunders.[1]

Instead of withdrawing to the sidelines of American politics in the years after 1960, however, the modern Supreme Court further intensified its political activity. Its decisions over the past twenty-five years have had a more pronounced impact on American politics and society than those of any other period in the nation's history. The Court moved beyond school desegregation to school integration and busing; banned organized prayer in the public schools; virtually transformed the nation's criminal justice system by imposing strict procedural requirements on state and local law enforcement officials; redrew the national political map by requiring legislative apportionment on the one person, one vote standard; and struck down state laws prohibiting abortion, at least in the first two trimesters of a woman's pregnancy. Even this list, impressive as it is, abbreviates the historical record; virtually every area of constitutional jurisprudence, from free speech to women's rights to capital punishment, has been transformed. Moreover, the Court has greatly expanded the scope of the remedies available to the federal judiciary, permitting the federal judiciary to engage in the direct supervision and management of federal prisons, local school districts, and hospitals.

The activism of the modern Court has generated considerable controversy and criticism. Critics of the Court have attacked it, sometimes viciously, for every one of these decisions. They have accused the justices of usurping the legitimate powers of Congress and the states, of meddling in the local affairs of the citizenry, of hostility to religion, and of contempt for democracy. Court decisions on abortion and school prayer have spawned virtual industries of opposition: abortion clinics have been bombed, threats have been made on the justices' lives, and in many places the school prayer decisions have been ignored altogether. Debate over new judicial appointments has turned angry and divisive, and hardly a single session of Congress passes without some attempt to reverse Court decisions by constitutional amendment or by statute.

McCloskey was not the only constitutional scholar to misjudge the prospects of the modern Court. Throughout its history the Court has consistently been treated as weak and vulnerable, forced to tread a thin line between using its power so boldly as to risk popular reprisal and acting so meekly as to abdicate its constitutional authority and responsibility. Even before the Constitution was ratified, the theme was set by Alexander Hamilton: the Court, he wrote, "is beyond comparison the weakest of the three departments of power; . . . it can never attack with success either of the other two, and . . . all possible care is requisite to enable it to defend itself against their attacks."[2]

This theme of weakness and vulnerability pervades the literature on the Supreme Court. "Judicial review runs so fundamentally counter to democratic theory," wrote Alexander Bickel in summing up the opinions of leading constitutional scholars, "that in a society which in all other respects rests on that theory, judicial review cannot ultimately be effective."[3] According to the traditional viewpoint, Congress has available a wide range of powers to check the Court and will not hesitate to use them. As the political scientist Walter Murphy has written, "Congress can increase the number of Justices, enlarge or restrict the Court's appellate jurisdiction, impeach and remove its members, or propose constitutional amendments either to reverse specific decisions or drastically alter the judicial role in American government. . . . A President to whom the nation looks for leadership can throw the moral authority of his office against that of the Court, just as can a senator, congressman, or governor."[4]

Even if there is no direct assault on the Court or the justices, it is argued, the very exercise of judicial power weakens the Court in the long run. "Since public antagonism, resistance, and retribution appear to have a spill-over effect," writes the legal scholar Jesse Choper, "if one or another of the Court's rulings sparks a markedly hostile reaction, then the likelihood that subsequent judgments will be rejected is greatly increased." The Court, Choper concludes, "in some principled fashion, must ration its power of invalidation."[5]

As the modern Court has expanded the reach of its powers, several of the justices have likewise taken up the theme that the Court's power is limited and must be exercised cautiously. Justice Powell, for example, wrote in 1974 that "the power recognized in *Marbury* v. *Madison* . . . is a potent one. . . . Were we to utilize this power as indiscriminately as is now being urged, we may witness efforts by the representative branches drastically to curb its use."[6] Justice Powell's concerns echo views that have been expressed on the Court for a long time; the second Justice Harlan, for example, repeatedly expressed disagreement with the Warren Court's predilection for expanding the reach of judicial power. "The powers of the federal judiciary will be adequate for the great burdens placed upon them only if they are employed prudently," he wrote in 1968. Felix Frankfurter, dissenting in the Warren Court's key reapportionment case, warned his brethren that "the Court's authority—possessed of neither the purse nor the sword—ultimately rests on sustained public confidence in its moral sanction. Such feeling must be nourished by the Court's complete detachment, in fact and in appearance, from political entanglements and by abstention from injecting itself into the clash of political forces in political settlements."[7] The remarks of Harlan and Frankfurter, in turn, reflect the views of Oliver Wendell Holmes, Learned Hand, and many others.[8]

Despite all of these warnings, the modern Court did not tone down its activism or shrink from the political arena. And yet, despite all of the controversy and criticism of the past thirty years, the Court is as powerful and effective today as at any time in its history. Its unprecedented activism, far from endangering its place in American politics, seems to have given the Court even more power. Its critics have been unable to reverse outright even one of the Court's controversial decisions, and the Court shows no signs of retreating from its activist approach to constitutional decision making. The justices, having ignored all of the advice proffered to the Court, have been rewarded instead of punished.

In fact, the Court has endured serious criticism and controversy throughout its history and, at least in the long run, has consistently survived and prospered. Despite the frequent characterization of the Court as weak and vulnerable, it has rarely faced a serious threat to its legitimacy or institutional integrity. The Court may be constantly at the "quiet of a storm-centre,"[9] as Oliver Wendell Holmes described it, but in only a handful of cases has the storm surrounding the Court grown into a tempest of fierce and apparently destructive power and led to a full-scale crisis for the Court. Studying these rare moments of crisis provides a unique perspective from which to analyze the limits of the Supreme Court's power and authority.

The first of these crisis periods occurred early in the Court's history, with the election of Thomas Jefferson to the presidency and the subsequent battle between the Jeffersonian Republicans and the Court, led by the Federalist John Marshall. During this period Marshall struggled to establish the Court as a powerful and effective institution of government while protecting the Court from the Republicans' onslaught. During the first decade of the nineteenth century, Marshall claimed for the Court the power to review acts of Congress and declare them unconstitutional, while parrying broad-based attacks on the Court, including threats of impeachment against himself and the other justices. The Court's ability to survive this first great crisis, and indeed to come out of that crisis with its authority firmly established, provided a foundation upon which it was able to build for the future.[10]

The few really great crises after the Marshall era come easily to mind: the infamous *Dred Scott* decision of 1857; the Reconstruction cases, which so alarmed the radical Republicans that they stripped the Court of its power to rule on the constitutionality of the Reconstruction Acts; and the New Deal crisis, which culminated in the ill-fated Court-packing plan of 1937. Because this study aims to understand the development of the Supreme Court's modern role, it begins not with the Jeffersonian era but with the *Dred Scott* case; while the Jeffersonian period is interesting in its own right and has been studied in depth, it would cast only limited light on the larger questions of this study.

The historical episodes examined below—*Dred Scott*, Reconstruction, and the New Deal—are the prime exhibits for those historians and political scientists who stress the Court's weakness and vulnerability. The futility and ultimate rejection of *Dred Scott*, Congress's domination of the Court during Reconstruction, and the events leading up to Franklin Roosevelt's Court-packing plan are seen as the outstanding examples of the Court's weakness, and are frequently brought forth as warnings to the modern Court. The mere fact that the Court was weak on these extraordinary occasions, however, does not close the matter. That the Court's views on slavery or on economic regulation were rejected hardly attests to the Court's weakness as an institution; the issues involved in these crises were not just any issues, but the most fundamentally divisive issues in the nation's history.

In analyzing both the historical Court and the modern Court, this study addresses two sets of questions. First, what do the crises of the past tell us about the Court's strengths and weaknesses as an institution? Do they reveal the Court as essentially weak and vulnerable? By what mechanism did the Court weather its most severe storms, and how can its survival be explained? Second, what does such a study of the Court's history tell us about the modern era? Did Court-watchers like McCloskey and others misjudge the danger to the modern Court because they misunderstood history, or because the modern era is fundamentally different from the past—or might it be both?

Beginning with *Dred Scott*, each of the Court's great episodes of crisis after the Marshall era is studied in detail: *Dred Scott*, the Reconstruction era, and the New Deal. In limiting the list to these three, many controversial and important cases have been deliberately excluded: the *Slaughterhouse Cases*, the *Civil Rights Cases* of 1883, the key economic cases of the 1890s, the segregation decision of 1896, *Lochner* v. *New York*, the *Child Labor Case*, the *Steel Seizure Case*, and countless others. However important and controversial these cases were (and many were not nearly as controversial as common knowledge suggests) none seriously approach *Dred Scott*, Reconstruction, and the New Deal in intensity, persistence, or fundamental importance. And it is by focusing on the Court in its most severe episodes of crisis that the limits of judicial power can be most clearly illuminated.

With these historical crises as a baseline of analysis, it becomes possible to understand the modern era in historical perspective. As in these past crises, the modern Court has been subjected to an enormous amount of criticism and has been the target of numerous attempts to modify its decisions or curb its power. Unlike the crises of the past, however, the controversy of the modern era shows no signs of abating, and the Court has shown few signs of reversing course. Only after a detailed analysis of both the historical crisis periods and the modern era will it be possible to determine why McCloskey and so many others underestimated the power of the modern Court. Was the historical Court's power greater than these analysts believed, or have the limits of judicial power expanded beyond their previous boundaries?

The answer, as the following pages will reveal, is yes to both questions. Historical analyses of the Court have traditionally underestimated the Supreme Court's power and overestimated the Court's vulnerability to damage from the political branches. Even when its decisions have been most controversial, the Supreme Court has enjoyed tremendous support as an institution. Even when they have vilified the Court and tried most strenuously to reverse particular decisions, the Court's opponents have rarely if ever sought to eliminate the Court as a potent force in American politics, at least in the long run. Rarely if ever have the Court's critics engaged in a fundamental attack on judicial power or questioned seriously the legitimacy of judicial review. Even in the midst of the *Dred Scott*, Reconstruction, and New Deal crises the Court's opponents lacked the will, the desire, and the ability to crush the Court. At best, they wanted and were able only to overturn, or convince the Court to overturn, one or a small number of particularly controversial decisions. Once they did so, the Court quickly reassumed its accustomed position, paradoxically strengthened by the very weakness of the arguments against it even at its weakest moments.

Moreover, the crises of the past turn out to be far more complex and entangled than is frequently assumed. In none of these cases did the Court's crisis occur in isolation. Instead, these Court crises were each part of a far larger crisis for the nation at large, and each can be understood only against this larger background. In each case, the Court had many enemies, but it also had allies. Sometimes it was simply caught in a crossfire between Congress and the president.

Thus the Court was far less weak and less vulnerable during these crises than McCloskey, Bickel, and many others assumed. And if these periods indeed represent the Court at its weakest and most vulnerable, it follows that the historical Court has had far more power and far more institutional capital than it has commonly been given credit for. Thus the Court entered the modern era not with a history of weakness, but of strength; not with a history of failure, but of success; not with reason to fear the results of judicial activism, but with reason to assume the vitality of its own power. Simply put, the record of the modern era is not an aberration, but a continuation of a long-established historical pattern.

There has been no shortage of discussion and commentary on what the legitimate and defensible limits of the Court's power ought to be. There has been far less analysis of what the Court's power has actually been. What has happened in the past need not be followed in the present, but the careful analysis of the past must inform any normative debate on the proper limits of judicial power. Unfortunately, far too much of the debate on judicial activism and restraint has progressed from the assumption that the Court is weak and vulnerable. Advocates of judicial restraint point to *Dred Scott* and the New Deal cases as arguments for caution. Advocates of judicial activism too often view the Court's weakness as a sort of insurance policy against an irresponsible Court. Others, perhaps trying to find a middle ground, long for a time when the Court's power seemed more limited and lament the apparent decline of political constraints.

In seeking out the limits of judicial power, this book adopts the advice of Justice Holmes: "a page of history is worth a volume of logic."[11] It is thus with the past that we must begin.

II

The Dred Scott *Case*

THE SUPREME COURT'S decision in the *Dred Scott* case was surely the most controversial decision in the Court's history. Abraham Lincoln, who had a great interest in the issues before the Court, called it "an astonisher in legal history." Chief Justice Hughes, whose own Court would be involved in political controversy, described the decision as a "self-inflicted wound." The decision brought down upon the Court a "tempest of malediction" that, temporarily at least, greatly damaged the Court's prestige and reduced its power.[1]

In many ways, the *Dred Scott* case is the prototype for the crises endured by the Supreme Court in later decades. As in later crises, the Court got into trouble by attempting to resolve a particularly sensitive, important, and divisive issue; the crisis, however, was short-lived and in the end presented no serious long-term threat to the Court's independence or autonomy. Along the way the Court played a major role in shaping and even catalyzing the larger national crisis of which *Dred Scott* was only one part. It is only in the context of that larger crisis that the decision can be properly understood.

I

Chief Justice Taney announced the Supreme Court's decision in *Dred Scott v. Sandford*[2] on 6 March 1857, exactly two days after the inauguration of James Buchanan as the fifteenth president of the United States. The case involved the claim for freedom of a slave named Dred Scott, who was at the time in the custody of his supposed master, John Sanford, a citizen of Missouri. Some years before, Scott's former master, John Emerson, had taken his slave with him to the state of Illinois and to the territory of

Wisconsin; slavery was prohibited in the former by the state constitution and in the latter by congressional statute. Scott's claim to freedom rested on the theory that, having lived for several years on free soil, he had become forever free. In response, Sanford pleaded (among his many arguments) that Congress had no power under the Constitution to prohibit slavery in any territory; if the Court accepted this claim, Scott's contention that he had lived in free territory would itself be undermined. Thus the question of the status of one alleged slave turned on a political issue of the highest importance: whether or not Congress had the power under the Constitution to regulate or prohibit slavery in the federal territories.

The problem of slavery in the territories had vexed the nation on and off for some eighty years, and almost continually since the Mexican War in the mid-1840s. In his 1857 inaugural address, however, President Buchanan belittled the territorial issue, noting that the only real issue in controversy concerned "a difference of opinion . . . in regard to the point of time when a people of a Territory shall decide this question [whether or not to allow slavery] for themselves." This interpretation was technically correct, since no one doubted the power of the people of a new state to exclude or condone slavery upon admission to the Union. Since the question of timing was precisely the issue in the upcoming *Dred Scott* case, Buchanan indicated that the question should be left to the Supreme Court, and to its resolution of the case he pledged his "cheerful" submission. He predicted optimistically that the question of slavery in the territories would thus be "speedily and finally settled."[3]

Buchanan's prediction was logical on the surface, but it was utterly unjustified from a practical point of view. The very question which Buchanan dismissed as one of mere timing had been at the heart of the presidential election of 1856, at least in the Northern states.[4] The question of slavery in the territories, moreover, was inseparably bound up with what historians now call the "sectional question." The conflict between the North and the South was based upon a complex dispute over the moral, economic, and social aspects of slavery itself; until the 1860s, however, it was expressed most often as a highly abstract legal question concerning the power of the federal government over the "domestic institutions" of the territories.[5]

That the sectional question was bound up with the question of slavery in the territories was no accident. The slavery issue had come up repeatedly

The Dred Scott *Case*

in the first half of the nineteenth century, and always within the context of the addition of new territories or of new states formed out of those territories. First the territory acquired in the Louisiana purchase had to be divided between slavery and freedom; this controversy was settled by the Compromise of 1820, which admitted Missouri as a slave state while prohibiting slavery in other territories north of latitude 36°30'. Then, twenty-five years later, the slavery problem erupted again, when the United States gained control over large tracts of formerly Mexican territory after the Mexican War. The controversy over the status of these new lands with respect to slavery set in motion the events that would lead within fifteen years to civil war.

The territorial issue became the central question in the growing sectional crisis. The addition of new slave states was important to the South in order to maintain the rough balance between free and slave states in the U.S. Senate. It was presumed on all sides that the Northern territories would be free, in line with the tradition of the Northwest Ordinance of 1787 (which barred slavery from the territories that now comprise the upper Midwest) and the Missouri Compromise. If the Southern territories could be turned into slave states, then the South would maintain its position of influence in the federal government. With the population of the North and West growing faster than that of the South, the Southern position in the House of Representatives and in the electoral college would weaken; only by maintaining its relative strength in the Senate could the South ensure that its interests would be protected.[6]

In the North, the territorial issue became the focus of the growing Free-Soil movement. The Free-Soil movement (also known as "political anti-slavery") was distinctly different from the older and more radical abolition movement. Abolitionists sought to "abolish slavery everywhere," whether by political action or by moral suasion. Some abolitionists, such as William Lloyd Garrison, viewed the U.S. Constitution as directly sanctioning slavery, and hence regarded it as a "covenant with death"; Garrison went so far as to stage a public burning of the document. Others, such as Alvan Stewart, Lysander Spooner, and William Goodell, argued that the Constitution in fact prohibited slavery and had been transformed into a bastion of slavery only through a perversion of its original intent. These men therefore demanded that the federal government abolish slavery in the states through congressional action.[7]

Neither of these abolitionist crusades had much appeal to the general public. The argument that the Constitution prohibited slavery even in the Southern states flew in the face of well-known facts, and the argument that the Constitution should be sacrificed to the abolitionist cause was too radical to be successful in a country where the Constitution was the object of constant and almost universal veneration. The Free-Soil movement was a deliberate attempt to chart a middle course. Led by Salmon P. Chase of Ohio, the Free-Soilers did not challenge slavery in the Southern states; instead, they concentrated only on the relationship between slavery and the federal government. They sought only "to divorce the National Government from Slavery; to prohibit slaveholding in places of exclusive national jurisdiction; to abolish the domestic slave trade . . . and in all proper and constitutional modes to discourage and discontinue the system of work without wages."[8]

The Free-Soil argument, developed largely by Chase, rested on the claim that slavery was an institution "wholly local in its existence and character." In order for a master-slave relationship to exist, it had to be created by local (or "municipal") law; states possessed the power to establish such a relationship, but Congress did not. Since the slave remained a slave only because of the force of state law, it followed that a slave who left the jurisdiction of a slave state became free: "The very moment a slave passes beyond the jurisdiction of the state," wrote Chase, " . . . he ceases to be a slave; not because any law or regulation of the state he enters confers freedom upon him, but because he *continues* to be a man and *leaves behind him* the law of force, which made him a slave."[9] Congress was nowhere granted the power to create the master-slave relationship or to condone it in any way; thus, as the Free-Soilers saw it, the federal government could not support slavery in any federal territory. Later, by the same reasoning, the Republicans would contest the constitutionality of the Fugitive Slave Law because it too involved the federal government in supporting the master-slave relationship.

By adopting this argument, the Free-Soilers were able to challenge the expansion of slavery while remaining supportive of the Constitution. Recognizing that the Constitution sanctioned the existence of slavery, the Free-Soil leaders had sought to limit slavery only so far as could be reconciled with the fundamental law of the land. Senator Seward, for example, claimed "no need, no purpose, no constitutional power, no duty" to abolish slavery in the slave states. He claimed only the "power to avert the extension of slavery in the territories of the Union," and added, "that is enough."[10] Abolitionists had often appealed to a moral law that transcended the Constitution, but this appeal had never been widely successful; the very success of the Republican Party after 1854, as against the failure of previous antislavery parties, can be traced to its limited policy goals and to its deliberate attempt to tie its platform to the Constitution. While Seward himself had proclaimed in 1850 that "there is a higher law than the Constitution," Republicans, including Seward, eschewed such sentiments after 1854.[11] As Lincoln asserted, the "chief and real purpose of the Republican Party is eminently conservative. It proposes nothing save and except to restore this government to its original tone in regard to the element of slavery, and there to maintain it."[12]

The Free-Soilers' arguments hit a responsive chord in much of the North. They appealed to moderate abolitionists who believed that slavery would eventually die out if it were constrained within narrow geographical limits.[13] They also appealed to Northerners who were indifferent to the fate of the slaves but who were amenable to a policy that would keep blacks out of the free North and West. Racial hostility was especially strong in the newer states and territories of the West, and antislavery caught on particularly strongly there.[14]

The event which brought all of the antislavery and abolition sentiment to a head was the enactment of the Kansas-Nebraska Act in 1854. That law, which had been led through Congress by Senator Stephen A. Douglas (D.-Ill.), organized the territories of Kansas and Nebraska (the latter at the time stretched from present-day Nebraska all the way to the Canadian border). The Kansas-Nebraska Act explicitly rejected the old Missouri Compromise line and replaced it with a provision that the people of the territories were to be left "perfectly free to form and regulate their domestic institutions in their own way, subject only to the Constitution of the United States."[15] Kansas and Nebraska—both of which lay entirely above the 36° 30' line of the Missouri Compromise—could now become slave states if their inhabitants so desired.

The Kansas-Nebraska Act provided a concrete issue that united the diverse antislavery movements. Anti-Nebraska parties (as they were called at the time) sprung up across the North and West to contest the 1854 elections, either independently or on fusion tickets. The Whig Party, which had welcomed both slavery and antislavery men under its umbrella, was bitterly divided and collapsed across the North. Conservative Whigs such as Ohio's Tom Corwin saw the anti-Nebraska activity as a mere pretext: "And do you not see," he complained, "how gladly it [the Kansas-Nebraska Act] was seized upon by those who have been trying to form a Northern Party for years?"[16] The new party took the name "Republican" and began looking forward to the 1856 election.

To the Republicans, the territorial issue was decidedly not a pretext; it was the very reason for the party's existence. Most Republicans saw the territories as the battleground for the struggle between the free peoples of the North and the "slave power" of the South. The slave power was viewed as the antithesis of the Republican Party, for it sought to extend slavery just as the Republicans sought to restrict it. Republicans believed that the presence of slavery in the territories of the West would make it impossible for Northerners to migrate there; the social systems of the North and South were not compatible, and thus Northerners would not be able to establish "populous, thriving villages and cities" because they would be choked off by the presence of slavery.[17] If the South had its way, the Republicans believed, the North and Midwest would become islands of freedom in a sea of slavery.

At first glance, though, it is not entirely clear why the Kansas-Nebraska Act was so repugnant to the thousands of Northerners who flocked to the new Republican Party. Republicans wished to exclude slavery from the territories; the Act did not do so explicitly, but it did provide a mechanism by which the people of a territory could prohibit slavery if they so desired. All of the Northern territories, and many of the Southern territories, were expected to be settled by men disposed against slavery. Why, then, did the Republicans assume that "popular sovereignty" would turn out to be a boon to slavery?

Republicans objected to the Kansas-Nebraska Act because Congress for the first time had failed to ban slavery outright in the Northern territories. In the past slavery had been allowed to exist in the South only as part of a compromise which outlawed slavery in the North; now the old policy had been rejected in favor of one regarded as a Southern policy of allowing slavery to exist everywhere. Chase saw the passage of the Kansas-Nebraska Act as a clear indication of the "immense, not to say overpowering influence, which slavery exerts over almost every act of government."[18] Republicans assumed in addition, as we have seen, that free Northerners could not coexist with slaveholders, and that no Northerners would migrate to Kansas and Nebraska to counteract the hordes of slaveholders the Republicans expected to overrun the new territories. Chase viewed the act "as part and parcel of an atrocious plot to exclude from a vast unoccupied region immigrants from the Old World, and free laborers from our own States, and convert it into a dreary region of despotism, inhabited by masters and slaves."[19]

Southerners, by contrast, accepted and supported the idea of popular sovereignty, but many did not view it as a neutral position between pro- and antislavery. The Kansas-Nebraska Act allowed the people to decide the question of slavery as they wished, "subject only to the Constitution of the United States." According to the radical Southern interpretation of the Constitution, best articulated by John C. Calhoun (D.-S.C.), Congress had no constitutional authority to pass any law which would prohibit citizens "from emigrating with their property, into any of the Territories of the United States." Calhoun began from the position that the several states "own jointly the territories"; therefore, he declared, it would be "utterly inconsistent with equality to pass measures which rob us of our share in the common property."[20] Because many Southerners who accepted the Kansas-Nebraska Act interpreted it as guaranteeing the existence of slavery in the territories, the potential for conflict between them and supporters of true popular sovereignty was always present.

The Free-Soilers and the Southern radicals held precisely opposite positions with respect to slavery in the territories. Free-Soilers (and later Republicans) argued that slavery could not exist in the federal territories; Southern radicals argued that slavery could not be prohibited in the territories. Neither view accorded with existing law or tradition. For the preceding eighty years, in fact, it had been assumed that Congress had discretion over the question of slavery in the territories. In some territories slavery was allowed; in others it was prohibited; in some the people were allowed to do as they wished.

The question which James Buchanan so optimistically called one only of timing was the fundamental issue of the day for the new Republican Party and for the increasingly militant and radical Southerners. The events of 1855 and 1856, in which proslavery and antislavery forces contended for control of Kansas, merely heightened the conflict. The presidential election of 1856 was fought against the backdrop of this civil war in Kansas, which to Republicans presented proof positive of the need to insist upon the absolute prohibition of slavery in the territories, and to many Southerners proved only that the Republicans were determined to ride roughshod over their "Southern rights."

The party platforms in 1856 reflected these concerns. Five of the nine provisions of the Republican platform dealt either with Kansas or with slavery in the territories; moreover, the platform pronounced it the duty of Congress to eliminate in the territories "those twin relics of barbarism— Polygamy and Slavery."[21] To all intents and purposes the Republican Party was a one-issue party, and that issue was not abolition but the prohibition of slavery in the federal territories. As the historian Allan Nevins concludes, the party "stood for opposition to slavery extension, and for little else." Its adherents not only did not deny the charge that the party was "an organization of but one idea," but actually reveled in it.[22] The Democratic Party platform merely pledged the party to support popular sovereignty, but left the precise definition of that phrase deliberately unclear. Douglas men could insist that it meant genuine choice; Southern extremists could read into it the Calhoun view that slavery was protected in all the territories.

By 1856—only two years after its formation—the Republican Party was the dominant political force in the North and West. The Whig Party was dead; nativist parties (such as the "Know-Nothings") were strong in only a few states; and the Democratic Party was held together by a tacit agreement to avoid a decision on the issue that mattered most. When James Buchanan took office in March 1857, he presided over a political system that in three short years had been utterly transformed. Its key feature was that it revolved around the very issue which the Supreme Court of the United States was to decide in *Dred Scott v. Sandford* two days later.

II

The *Dred Scott* decision has been the subject of so much historical and legal analysis that one can easily sympathize with the auditor of the Lincoln-Douglas debates who demanded that Lincoln "give us something besides Drid Scott [*sic*]."[23] The case had been originally argued in February 1856, but the Court's decision was delayed until the following year because the justices ordered reargument of certain key questions. This had the effect of postponing the decision until after the presidential election of 1856, perhaps because the Court was "reluctant to render such a controversial decision on the eve of a major political campaign."[24] The delay was bad news for the Republicans, since they assumed that the justices would not have hesitated unless they were about to make a broad proslavery decision; a decision upholding the tradition of congressional power over the territories or avoiding the political questions altogether, they believed, would have been uncontroversial. Also, the delay took away a powerful Republican campaign issue.

The case itself was and is hopelessly complex. Plaintiff Dred Scott was a slave putatively owned by one John F. A. Sanford. The case of *Dred Scott v. Sandford* was a suit for freedom in the form of an action for trespass, Scott claiming that he was not a slave but a free man and could not be held by Sanford against his will. Scott based his claim for freedom on the grounds that he had been taken by his master to live in both the free state of Illinois and the free territory of Wisconsin, which had been declared free soil by the Missouri Compromise. Because Scott was (or claimed to be) a citizen of Missouri, while Sanford was a citizen of New York, Scott brought his suit in federal court under the diversity jurisdiction.[25]

Scott's claim rested on the argument that a slave "once free" was "forever free"; this was essentially the argument of Lord Mansfield in *Somerset's Case*, an important British slavery case.[26] As interpreted by both Northern and Southern American courts, the *Somerset* doctrine came to mean that slaves could be taken onto free soil for temporary periods (this was known as "sojourning"), but that prolonged residence on free soil would result in permanent emancipation. The central political question raised by Scott's suit was whether the Wisconsin territory was indeed free—whether, in other words, Congress had the power under the Constitution to prohibit slavery in a federal territory. It was assumed that Illinois, as a sovereign state, had the power to outlaw slavery within its jurisdiction.

Both plaintiff and defendant agreed that Scott had been taken by his previous master, Dr. John Emerson, to Fort Armstrong, Illinois, where he lived and served his master from 1 December 1833 until 4 May 1836. At that point, Scott was taken by Emerson to Fort Snelling, in the Wisconsin territory, where he remained for almost two years. In April 1838, Scott and his new wife, Harriet (whom he had married at Fort Snelling), were taken to Louisiana, where slavery was permitted. They returned to the Wisconsin territory one more time, living with Emerson from October 1838 until May 1840, and then returned to Missouri. All together, Scott lived some two and a half years in a free state (Illinois) and a total of three and a half years in a free territory (Wisconsin).[27]

The first question in the case was whether the federal courts had jurisdiction to hear Scott's action for trespass against Sanford, who had inherited the slave according to Emerson's will. The federal courts have jurisdiction to hear suits brought by a citizen of one state against a citizen of another state; in order to accept Scott's case, the courts had to agree that Scott was indeed a citizen of some state other than New York. The question at the circuit court level, therefore, had been whether Scott was or could be a citizen of the state of Missouri. The circuit court accepted jurisdiction of the case on the grounds that "every person born in the United States and capable of holding property was a citizen having the right to sue in United States courts."[28] Thus if Scott were free he could hold property and could sue in federal court; if he were still a slave he could not hold property and could not sue. Since that issue was precisely the one the Court would have to decide if it took up the merits of the case, the circuit judge accepted jurisdiction.

The lower court's determination of the citizenship question was confusing enough, since it granted the right to sue in federal court to a free negro who was not a citizen "of a state." In Chief Justice Taney's opinion, the citizenship question turned into a legal, historical, and logical morass. The first question Taney addressed was whether free negroes were "*citizens of a State*, in the sense in which the word citizen is used in the Constitution of the United States."[29] Soon, however, Taney turned to whether the Constitution allows a state to make a free negro "a *citizen of the United States*, and endue him with the full rights of citizenship in every other state without their consent."[30] Taney continued: "Does the Constitution of the United States act upon him [a free negro] wherever he shall be made free under the laws of a State, and raised there to the rank of a citizen, and immediately clothe him with all the privileges of a citizen in every other State, and in its own courts? The Court think the affirmative of these propositions cannot be maintained. And if it cannot, the plaintiff in error [Scott] could not be a citizen of the State of Missouri, within the meaning of the Constitution of the United States, and, consequently, was not entitled to sue in its courts."[31]

Taney's distinction between a "citizen of a state" and a "citizen of the United States" is the key to his argument. The Constitution itself used both terms but defined neither one; Taney's treatment of the issue did little to clear up the matter.[32] The chief justice argued that no state can make a free negro eligible to sue in federal court, even if that state considers the negro to be a citizen. A state could presumably let free negroes sue in its own courts (that would not be a matter of federal concern), but it could not grant him a citizenship that would be recognized by the United States for the purposes of bringing a suit in federal court. Thus Scott was ineligible to sue in federal court; since *Dred Scott* v. *Sandford* was not a suit "between citizens of different States," the federal courts could not accept jurisdiction. Without reaching the merits of the case, Taney threw Scott out of court.

Taney's treatment of the citizenship question was unnecessary and confusing. It was also insensitive to the political realities of the day. Taney could have held, as the Court had held in similar cases, that the question of Scott's state citizenship was not a federal question, but one which had to be determined under Missouri law by Missouri courts. The Missouri courts had in fact decided that Scott was a slave and hence ineligible to sue. Instead, Taney held that no negro could ever be made a "citizen of the United States," and that even in those states where blacks were allowed the franchise and other privileges of citizenship they would not be recognized as citizens of a state by the federal courts. Taney's argument on the citizenship question was long-winded and vitriolic; it was against this portion of his opinion as well as his later argument on the territorial question that much of the Republicans' venom was directed.

Although Taney's treatment of the citizenship issue effectively disposed of the case, the Chief Justice went on to consider all of the substantive questions that the lower court had considered. To the non-lawyer it seems incredible that a judge would be justified in considering the substantive issues in a case in which he had refused jurisdiction, and indeed Taney's course of action was roundly criticized by lawyers and non-lawyers alike. Still, some have argued that Taney was correct in asserting that it was legitimate for him to review all of the errors made by the lower court, of which the jurisdictional error was only one. Whether or not it was an error in legal terms, the whole of Taney's opinion following the citizenship question, and much of the citizenship discussion itself, was a political error of the highest magnitude.[33]

Scott's contention that he had become free by virtue of his residence in the free state of Illinois was dismissed out-of-hand by Taney in a few paragraphs at the end of his opinion. In so dismissing one of Scott's two substantive claims, Taney relied heavily on the case of *Strader* v. *Graham*,[34] in which the Supreme Court held that the status of alleged slaves upon their return to a slave state from a free state depended on the laws of the slave state. The legal parallel between the *Strader* case and the *Dred Scott* case has been challenged, but the central fact is that Taney was unwilling to find for Scott on any grounds. Though he disregarded the *Strader* approach in his consideration of the territorial question, Taney invoked it to dispose of Scott's claims to freedom on the basis of his sojourn in Illinois.[35]

Thus we come to the central political question in the case: Was Scott "free in Missouri by reason of the stay in the territory of the United States hereinbefore mentioned"? It had been the Missouri Compromise, of course, which had "forever" prohibited slavery from the Wisconsin territory. In 1820, as part of the compromise by which Missouri had been admitted to the Union as a slave state, Congress had prohibited slavery in all the federal territories north of 36° 30′. Thus the Court faced another question: "whether Congress was authorized to pass this law under any of the power granted to it by the Constitution." If not, then the Compromise was unconstitutional, and "incapable of conferring freedom upon any one who is held as a slave under the laws of any one of the States."[36]

Taney began by admitting that the Constitution gives Congress the power to make "all needful rules and regulations respecting the territory or other property of the United States." He interpreted this grant of power narrowly, however, holding that Congress could acquire and regulate territory only "for the benefit of the people of the several States who created" the United States. Taney thus rejected John Marshall's famous dictum that asserted that in legislating for the territories Congress "exercises the combined powers of the General and of a State Government."[37] Taney ruled that Marshall's formulation held only in the particular context of the case in which it was articulated and did not have general applicability.

The Dred Scott *Case*

Instead of exercising "the combined powers of the General and of a State Government," wrote Taney, Congress could act in the territories merely as the "trustee" of the people of the United States and was "charged with the duty of promoting the interests of the whole people of the Union in the exercise of the powers specifically granted." When Congress sought to regulate the person and property of a citizen of the United States, its powers were strictly limited; unlike a state, which has residual or implied police powers, the federal government could exercise "no power over his [a citizen's] person or property beyond what . . . [the Constitution] confers, nor lawfully deny any right which is reserved." Moreover, since slaves were regarded as property under the Constitution, Taney viewed the Missouri Compromise as "an Act of Congress which deprives a citizen of the United States of his liberty or property, merely because he came himself or brought his property into a particular Territory of the United States, and who had committed no offense against the laws." It thus violated the Fifth Amendment's Due Process Clause.[38]

The *Dred Scott* case produced a total of eight opinions. Seven justices held that Dred Scott was still a slave; two (John McLean of Ohio and Benjamin R. Curtis of Massachusetts) dissented from the opinion of the Court and declared Scott a free man by virtue of his sojourn on free soil. Six justices declared the Missouri Compromise unconstitutional. Justice Samuel Nelson of Pennsylvania wrote a separate opinion holding that Scott's status depended entirely on the laws of Missouri, and that since he was a slave in the view of the Supreme Court of Missouri, he was a slave in the view of the Supreme Court of the United States. Of the six justices who voted to strike down the Missouri Compromise, five were from slave states—Taney of Maryland, John Catron of Tennessee, James M. Wayne of Georgia, Peter V. Daniel of Virginia, and John A. Campbell of Alabama. The sixth justice in the majority on the Missouri Compromise question was Robert C. Grier of Pennsylvania.

In striking down the Missouri Compromise, the Supreme Court did not rely on well-established or even obscure precedents; instead, it overturned existing precedent, creating new law to cope with the rising crisis over slavery. No judge, except Peter Daniel in *Prigg* v. *Pennsylvania*,[39] had ever suggested from the bench that Congress's power over the territories was less than the combined powers of the states and the federal government. Never in its thirty-four years of operation had any judge other than Daniel doubted the constitutionality of the Missouri Compromise; Congress had been selectively outlawing slavery in the federal territories since before the adoption of the federal Constitution. Taney's opinion in *Dred Scott* expressed a constitutional theory that had been invented relatively recently; though advocated by many Southerners before 1857 (and especially by John C. Calhoun), no American court and no institution of the federal government had ever endorsed so restrictive a view of federal power in this area. The *Dred Scott* decision violated both legal precedent and long-standing political tradition.

Moreover, Taney's opinion in the *Dred Scott* case changed the meaning of the Kansas-Nebraska Act dramatically. In an important dictum, Taney declared that since Congress could not exclude slavery from the territories, it could not authorize a territorial government to do so either.[40] Under this ruling, as Lincoln pointed out, popular sovereignty meant only that the people of a territory could vote to allow slavery if they wanted it; they could not vote "*not* to have it if they *do not* want it."[41] The Kansas-Nebraska Act's provision that the people of a territory were free to allow or exclude slavery "subject only to the Constitution of the United States" now took on a sinister meaning. To Republicans, Taney's *Dred Scott* opinion appeared to be the last act of a well-planned conspiracy that had been plotted since the passage of the Kansas-Nebraska Act.

III

In order to understand how the Taney Court came to make so radical a decision in the *Dred Scott* case, it is necessary to understand how the Court had previously handled the complex political and legal questions involving slavery. The slavery question had come before the Taney Court in various guises many times in the two decades that preceded its decision in the *Dred Scott* case. In 1841, *Groves* v. *Slaughter* presented the Court with a set of questions involving the interstate slave trade.[42] That same year, the case of *U.S.* v. *The Amistad* raised similar questions concerning the international slave trade.[43] A year later, *Prigg* v. *Pennsylvania* brought forward questions involving the constitutional implications of the fugitive slave act; similar questions arose also in the 1847 case of *Jones* v. *Van Zandt*.[44] Finally, in 1851, the Court was presented with a set of facts strikingly similar to those it would face six years later in the Dred Scott case, though here the plaintiffs had sojourned not in free territories but in free states.[45] In every one of these early slavery cases, the Supreme Court took a moderate stance, eschewing the political controversy it seemingly sought out in the *Dred Scott* case. Still, as early as the 1840s, the battle lines on the Court over the slavery issue could be clearly seen.

The Taney Court's first brush with the slavery controversy came in *Groves* v. *Slaughter*. The case involved the constitutionality of a provision of the Mississippi constitution prohibiting the importation of slaves into the state for sale. Groves had purchased some slaves in Mississippi but had defaulted on payment; he was sued and argued that he was not liable for payment because the sale itself had been illegal under the Mississippi constitution.

The question of whether a state could outlaw the importation of slaves or whether such a regulation was inconsistent with Congress's power to regulate "interstate and foreign commerce" was a difficult and contentious one. Rather than attempt to resolve so highly charged an issue, the Supreme Court disposed of the case in a way which avoided the difficult questions altogether. Justice Smith Thompson, writing for the Court, held simply that the Mississippi constitutional provision stipulating that "the introduction of slaves into this State . . . shall be prohibited, from and after the 1st day of May, 1833" was simply an instruction to the state legislature and was without independent force; without further legislation, the constitutional provision was not binding.[46] That Thompson wanted to avoid the sticky commerce and slavery issues is apparent from his strained reading of the state constitution and from his refusal to accept as settled law the Mississippi court's contrary interpretation of its own state constitution.[47]

Thompson's opinion expressed only the judgment of the Court, which was that the contract between Groves and Slaughter was valid. Only Justice Wayne joined Thompson's opinion, however; there were three separate concurrences, and there were two dissenting votes expressed without opinion.[48] The divisions within the majority in *Groves* are indicative of what was to come later in *Dred Scott*. Beneath the majority's refusal to take up the difficult slavery and commerce issues lay deep disagreements. Taney argued that each state "has a right to decide for itself, whether it will or will not allow . . . [slaves] to be brought within its limits, from another State, either for sale, or for any other purpose." State action in this area, he concluded, "cannot be controlled by Congress."[49] McLean reached the same conclusion, though he made it clear that his concern was to protect the right of free states to keep slaves outside their borders. McLean also contended that the Constitution regarded slaves as persons, not property; that their character as property is given to them only by the force of local law; and that states "cannot devest them of the leading and controlling quality of persons by which they are designated in the constitution."[50] Justice Henry Baldwin, at the proslavery extreme, contended that "slaves are property in every constitutional sense" and that, as such, their owners "are protected from any violations of the rights of property by congress, under the 5th amendment of the constitution."[51]

In the case of *The Amistad*, also in 1841, the Court was once again able to dispose of very difficult and divisive issues in a relatively uncontroversial way. The case involved a mutiny at sea aboard a Spanish slave ship. The vessel and the Africans on board were seized by the United States Navy. The United States government wanted to return them to their would-be masters, and the Africans sued to prevent such an action.

If the Africans were indeed slaves under the law, they would be considered "merchandise," and the United States was under a treaty obligation to return them to the Spanish. If, however, the Africans were by law free men, they were to be declared so and allowed to return to their homeland. The case thus raised the difficult questions of whether slavery could exist on the high seas, and whether the United States government could hold any men, even temporarily, as slaves. The antislavery lawyers who defended the Africans answered no to both questions, but Justice Story, writing for the Court, refused to take up either one. He resolved the case instead by holding that the burden of proof was on the government to show that the Africans were slaves. Absent conclusive proof to the contrary, the Africans were presumed to be free and were released. Though documents found aboard the ship seemed to indicate that the Africans were in fact slaves owned by the Spanish, Story dismissed the federal government's claims as inconclusive. The Court was united behind Story's opinion, with only Barbour dissenting, for reasons which he did not specify.

By far the most important slavery case to reach the Supreme Court prior to *Dred Scott* was the 1842 case of *Prigg* v. *Pennsylvania*. The dispute was fabricated by the states of Maryland and Pennsylvania to test the implications of the federal fugitive slave law. Pennsylvania, like several other Northern states, had a "personal liberty" law, which afforded recaptured runaway slaves various procedural guarantees ranging from jury trials to habeas corpus proceedings; the law included penalties for slave catchers who attempted to circumvent these statutory procedures. Pennsylvania and Maryland agreed to arrange the arrest and conviction of a Maryland slave catcher under the Pennsylvania personal liberty statute, and the case was hurried along to the U.S. Supreme Court. A fragmented Court produced seven opinions, which ranged across the political spectrum of the slavery controversy. The majority opinion, written by Justice Story, affirmed the constitutionality of the federal fugitive slave law, struck down the Pennsylvania statute as violating the federal Constitution and the federal statute, and affirmed the master's right to recapture his runaway slave in a state other than his own.

Justices Story, McLean, and Wayne held that a state could not pass a statute that assisted the federal government in the recapture of runaway slaves. For McLean this conclusion was an expression of his view that the Northern states should not involve themselves in the odious business of recapturing runaway slaves. (McLean added, in fact, that states could protect their free black citizens as long as they did not interfere with the capture of runaway slaves.) Wayne, however, reached this result because it left standing the federal protection of slave-owners' property rights. At the proslavery extreme, Chief Justice Taney argued that states were *required* to pass laws assisting the federal government in its slave-recapture efforts. Justice Thompson, in the center in this case, argued that states had discretion in deciding whether or not to assist the federal government.[52] Justice Peter Daniel agreed with Thompson's majority opinion, but added in dicta that Congress had no power to prohibit the importation of slaves into the federal territories—thus anticipating the *Dred Scott* decision by over fifteen years.

Jones v. *Van Zandt*, decided in 1847, involved another challenge to the federal fugitive slave law. Several slaves had escaped from their owner (Jones) and had fled from Kentucky to Ohio. The runaway slaves "when about twelve miles distant from their master's residence, were taken into a covered wagon by the defendant [Van Zandt] in the night, and driven with speed twelve or fourteen miles, so that one was never retaken."[53] *Jones* v. *Van Zandt* was an action for damages, as permitted by the fugitive slave law.

The case was decided during the heat of the slavery controversy that was ultimately resolved by the Compromise of 1850. With William Henry Seward and Salmon P. Chase arguing for Van Zandt, the case attracted widespread attention. Justice Levi Woodbury, writing for a unanimous Court, held for the slaveholder Jones; along the way he made a series of technical rulings concerning the application of the fugitive slave law. As for the constitutionality of the law, Woodbury simply announced that the Court would follow its holding in *Prigg* v. *Pennsylvania* that the law was constitutional. Woodbury, a New Hampshire Democrat, here expressed the essence of the Northern conservative viewpoint: "While the compromises of the Constitution exist, it is impossible to do justice to their requirements, or fulfill the duty incumbent on us towards all the members of the Union, under its provisions, without sustaining such enactments as that of the [fugitive slave] statute of 1793."[54] Woodbury's treatment of the issues in *Van Zandt* rejected the antislavery position of Chase and Seward without glorifying the extreme proslavery position. His diplomatic treatment of the case resulted in a Court united behind one opinion, a rarity for the Taney Court on issues involving slavery.

The final important slavery case before *Dred Scott* was *Strader* v. *Graham*, in 1851. Several Kentucky slaves had crossed over to Ohio and Indiana, with the permission of their master Graham, to work temporarily as musicians. After a return to Kentucky, they escaped to freedom. Strader assisted the slaves in their escape, and Graham sued Strader for damages as permitted by Kentucky law. Strader defended himself on the grounds that the runaways were no longer slaves because they had spent time on the free soil of Indiana and Ohio. Here, then, was a direct claim for the "once free, forever free" principle that would form the basis of Dred Scott's case six years later.

The opinion of the Court was written by Taney, who—in sharp contrast to the way he would handle *Dred Scott*—disposed of the case on narrow and unobjectionable grounds. The question of the status of the runaways was entirely a matter for decision by the state in which they currently resided, he wrote; whether or not they were free men, then, depended on the laws and courts of the state of Kentucky. The federal court, therefore, had to dismiss the suit for want of jurisdiction.

Taney's opinion was not as narrow and even-handed as the decision itself, however. He made an argument which some Northerners interpreted as hinting that he favored a ruling guaranteeing the rights of Southerners to take their property into free states. Taney added, in dicta, an argument that the Northwest Ordinance (which, passed by Congress in 1787 under the Articles of Confederation, "forever" outlawed slavery in the states of the Northwest) was of no legal effect.[55] McLean concurred in the result, agreeing with Taney's resolution of the case but noting that all of the Chief Justice's comments with respect to the Northwest Ordinance were "not in the case" and thus "extrajudicial."[56]

Looking at the Taney Court's record on slavery over the two decades prior to the *Dred Scott* decision, we see a deeply divided Court that managed, despite extreme views on both sides, to reach relatively moderate and uncontroversial decisions on a range of slavery-related issues. The Court affirmed Congress's power to pass laws regulating the interstate slave trade and providing for the recapture of runaway slaves, but it did not insist that Northern states actively participate in those activities. It shied away from the question of whether slaves attained freedom once they were taken to live on free soil, simply leaving the question of the status of alleged slaves to the state in which they happened to reside. It consistently affirmed the federal government's power and responsibility to protect the interests of slaveholders, but it did not go so far as to assert that free states had to respect those interests to the same degree. On the most pressing public issue of the 1840s and 1850s—the territorial question—the Court was silent, either by chance or by design. Although they were not presented with a case that squarely raised the territorial issue, rarely did any justice go out of his way to raise the issue in dicta. It is a fair judgment of the Taney Court prior to *Dred Scott* to conclude that, on the whole, it avoided controversy and extremism on the slavery question.

The Taney Court in 1857, then, can be summed up as follows. Taney, in particular, showed himself to be strongly proslavery. Wayne and Daniel, likewise, revealed a proslavery bias, especially in *Prigg* v. *Pennsylvania*. On the other side, Justice McLean was clearly antislavery. The other five justices were all disposed to avoid controversy. At the time of the *Dred Scott* decision, the moderate group included Samuel Nelson of New York, Robert Grier of Pennsylvania, Benjamin R. Curtis of Massachusetts, John Catron of Tennessee, and John A. Campbell of Alabama. Grier, Nelson, and Curtis were Northern conservatives who accepted the legal basis of slavery despite pressures to do otherwise; of the three, Curtis had most recently joined the Court and had expressed no judicial opinions on slavery from the high bench prior to the *Dred Scott* case. Before his appointment to the Supreme Court, however, Curtis had maintained a typical Northern conservative attitude: he accepted the existence of slavery in the Southern states and the validity of the fugitive slave law, but he refused any further concession.[57] Campbell was a Southerner who had freed his slaves and who spoke out against the worst abuses of the slave system and in favor of moderate reforms.[58] As for the territorial question, Campbell expressed the view in 1848 that Congress could allow or prohibit slavery as it saw fit.[59] When the *Dred Scott* case came up for decision, these five moderates would hold the balance of power.

IV

The *Dred Scott* case was officially docketed by the United States Supreme Court on 30 December 1854; in the period between that date and the Court's ultimate resolution of the controversy on 6 March 1857 the political issues involved in the case became increasingly urgent. The passage of the Kansas-Nebraska Act in 1854 had a paradoxical effect with respect to the central political question of the *Dred Scott* case—whether Congress had the power to regulate slavery in the federal territories. In one sense, the Kansas-Nebraska Act made the question moot, since Congress indicated in that act that it would not interfere with the existence or nonexistence of slavery in the territories. In political terms, however, the passage of the act and the resultant two years of intense political debate and of civil war in Kansas had transformed the issue into the most important political issue in the nation.

The Court heard arguments in the case in February 1856 but made little progress toward reaching a decision. On 12 May, therefore, the Court ordered a rehearing on two specific points, both relating to the jurisdiction of the federal courts over Dred Scott's case. The rehearing made it highly unlikely that the Court would reach a decision before the presidential election in November, an outcome which many at the time regarded as deliberate. There is no hard evidence on the subject, but Don E. Fehrenbacher seems justified in concluding that it is "likely . . . that some justices, at least, were reluctant to render such a controversial decision on the eve of a major political campaign."[60]

The reargument did not take place until mid-December. By that time the election was over and the political importance of the case was obvious. The second round of arguments, unlike the first, attracted huge crowds to the courtroom. Press coverage of the arguments was extensive, and the nation eagerly awaited the decision. The Court's consideration of the case was halted shortly after the second set of hearings, however, when Justice Daniel's wife died, and Daniel absented himself from Court business. The first postreargument conference on the case was not held until 14 February 1857; the Court's decision was announced less than three weeks later.

During those three weeks a great deal was taking place behind the scenes. At the first conference it became clear that the Court was divided along sectional lines. The five Southerners (Taney, Wayne, Daniel, Catron, and Campbell) voted to invalidate the Missouri Compromise; the four Northerners refused to do so. Two of them (McLean and Curtis) indicated their intention to uphold the Compromise; the other two (Nelson and Grier) indicated an unwillingness even to consider the question. Nelson and Grier persuaded their colleagues that discretion was the better part of valor, and the justices voted to avoid the political questions altogether. Nelson— a moderate Democrat who maintained a low profile—was assigned the opinion.[61]

By the first conference of the new term, then, the five Southerners had expressed a desire to strike down the Missouri Compromise. Nevertheless, the Southerners were unwilling to issue such a broad opinion, apparently for fear that the minority would be given a soapbox from which to make a strong antislavery statement.[62] Curtis indicated at that point that "the Court will not decide the question of the Missouri Compromise—a majority of the judges being of opinion that it is not necessary to do so."[63]

That Taney, Wayne, and Daniel adopted the extreme proslavery position is understandable, given their previous proslavery decisions and the enormous pressure of events as the sectional crisis mounted and the antislavery party gathered strength. Catron and Campbell, however, had shown no official proslavery inclination prior to the *Dred Scott* case. Campbell, as we have seen, was a moderate Southerner who had freed his own slaves and who had spoken out in favor of moderate reforms of the slave system. Under the pressure of events in 1856, however, Campbell took a hard proslavery stance. The disparity between his private views toward slavery and his public stance in *Dred Scott* prompted his biographer to speculate that Campbell "was partially proscribed from consistency and moderation by southern feelings. Certainly, the price of southern membership in the Union was rising, and perhaps Campbell was caught in the drift of southern expectations and pressure."[64] Still it should be noted that Campbell's concurring opinion was among the more moderate of the proslavery opinions: he did not ask whether free negroes could or could not become citizens of the United States, he did not speculate on the power of the people of a territory to exclude slavery, and he engaged in very little proslavery rhetoric.[65]

Catron's shift to the extreme proslavery side is interesting for three reasons. First, he displayed little if any proslavery bias in his previous decisions; in *Prigg*, for example, he concurred with the moderate opinion of the Court, whereas Taney expressed the extreme proslavery argument that states were required to assist the federal government in enforcing the fugitive slave law. Second, Catron was at the time of *Dred Scott* (and throughout the Civil War) a staunch Unionist.[66] Finally, Catron seems to have embraced the extreme proslavery position with all the passion of a recent convert: once he took the extreme position, he was a leader in the behind-the-scenes movement to have the Missouri Compromise struck down.

Just before the 14 February conference, President Buchanan had written to Catron to ascertain information about the upcoming decision, hoping to find out something that would be useful to him in preparing his inaugural address. Catron responded: "Some of the judges will not touch the question of power [of Congress to regulate slavery in the territories], others may, but that it will settle nothing, is my present opinion." On 19 February, however, Catron advised Buchanan that "a majority of my Brethren will be forced up to this point by two dissentients."[67]

In the meantime, Nelson had prepared his opinion of the Court, a moderate opinion holding for Sanford on the grounds that Scott's status depended only on Missouri law. He did not touch the territorial issue. At the same time, the five Southern justices seem to have decided that the opinion of the Court should address the territorial question, and they agreed that Taney should write the opinion. Catron's explanation for the shift in the Southern justices' strategy—that McLean and Curtis "forced" the majority to respond to their antislavery arguments—has been challenged.[68] It is clear, at the least, that many of the Southern justices wanted desperately to discuss the territorial issue; that many of the judges (Northern and Southern) felt a duty to try and resolve the difficult question the political branches had left to them; and that, in any event, there would have been concurring opinions by Wayne, Taney, or Daniel (or by some combination of the three) expressing the proslavery point of view. Despite their 14 February conference vote, the Southern justices and the two antislavery justices were not content to let the central political issue of the day pass them by.

To prevent a division of the Court along sectional lines, Catron wrote to Buchanan, asking the president to write to Grier and to try and persuade his fellow Pennsylvanian to join the Southern justices in striking down the Missouri Compromise. Buchanan did so, and on 23 February Grier informed the president: "On conversation with the Chief Justice I have agreed *to concur with him*."[69] Grier told the president that he and Wayne would try to get Catron, Campbell, and Daniel to join the chief justice in his opinion so as to present a unified front. "But," he added, "I fear some rather extreme views may be thrown out by some of our southern brethren."[70] Grier here reveals that he was grossly misinformed—either through ignorance or by the design of the Southern justices—about the tone and breadth of Taney's opinion, for Taney in the end turned out the most extreme proslavery opinion of all.

The final alignment showed Curtis and McLean emphatically upholding the constitutionality of the Missouri Compromise, Nelson expressing no opinion on the subject, and Grier and the five Southerners striking down the Compromise in four separate opinions. Among the Northerners, McLean and Nelson seem to have behaved in character, with McLean writing a radical antislavery opinion and Nelson expressing a more moderate view. Curtis's position was also consistent with his previous views, though it was perhaps expressed with more vehemence than might have been expected. In the year since the *Dred Scott* case had first been argued, Catron, Campbell, and Grier had all been persuaded to join the proslavery extremists. Indeed, even the proslavery trio of Taney, Wayne, and Daniel seem to have changed their views in the year before the decision, as in 1856 they were reluctant to involve themselves in what they realized was a sensitive political question. The events of 1856—in Kansas and on the campaign trail—had begun to polarize the nation and had already polarized the Supreme Court.

V

Republicans were well aware that the Supreme Court might make a broad proslavery decision in the *Dred Scott* case and had begun to prepare for the worst even before the decision was actually announced. The abolition papers especially had long since ceased to trust the Court and had been railing against it for several years prior to 1857; on the eve of the Dred Scott decision they simply stepped up their attacks. The *New York Tribune*, for example, observed in December 1856 that "our judicial decisions upon constitutional questions touching the subject of slavery are rapidly coming to be the enunciation of mere party dogmas; . . . in the process of time, if we continue a united people, what the law of the country and the Courts is, will depend upon the political ascendancy for the time being of the doctrines of freedom and slavery."[71] As word leaked out that the Court would invalidate the Missouri Compromise, the *Tribune's* correspondent in Washington commented that "it is very generally considered that the moral weight of such a decision would be about equal to that of a political stump speech of a slaveholder or doughface."[72]

Once the decision was handed down, Republicans responded swiftly and forcefully. The leading radical newspapers, such as the *Tribune*, were the most vociferous, but the responses of Republicans were extremely varied and served many different purposes. In the first few months after the decision, Republicans sought to discredit the Court's decision, but they tried to do so while maintaining their claim that they were holding to the constitutional ideals of the Founders. Republicans also used the *Dred Scott* case for their own partisan purposes in an effort to coalesce Northern antislavery sentiment in the wake of the partially but not completely successful presidential election campaign of 1856. The *Tribune*, again, was most explicit on this score: "It makes little difference to slavery whether it gets a decision in its favor now or after the public mind shall have time to cool. . . . But it would be best for anti-slavery that the decision should come now, while the popular heart is in a fused condition. . . . The Congress, the Court, and the Executive would then take their proper position of joint association, in the mind of the people, as confederates in the work of extending the intolerable nuisance of slavery."[73] The *New York Times*, a more moderate voice of Republicanism, saw the Court's decision as laying "the only solid foundation which has ever yet existed for an Abolition party."[74] Skillfully exploited by Republican orators and editors, the *Dred Scott* case was turned to the advantage of antislavery forces, providing a focus for Northern vituperation between presidential elections.

Some of the more extreme rhetoric, and some of the deliberate and patently unfair misrepresentations of Taney's opinion, can be attributed to this element of party politics. The Republicans took quotes from the opinion out of context and used them to full political advantage. In discussing the "state of public opinion" in the late eighteenth century, for example, Taney had written that negroes "had for more than a century been regarded as beings of an inferior order . . . and so far inferior, that they *had* no rights which the white man was bound to respect."[75] The Republicans took part of the above quotation out of context and changed the tense of the verb, claiming that Taney said the "negro *has* no rights which the white man was bound to respect."[76] This deliberate misrepresentation of the Chief Justice's statement made it a red flag to be waved in front of Northern antislavery men. Such rhetoric was at least partly intended to engender what one reporter called a "spirit of resistance and indignation, which shall wipe out this decision and all its results."[77]

The Court's decision was not simply a political bonanza for the Republicans; far from it. Almost immediately, their political opponents responded by challenging the Republicans' fidelity to the Constitution. The *New York Herald* declared that the decision "at a single blow shivers the anti-slavery platform of the late great Northern Republican party into atoms. . . . The supreme law is expounded by the supreme authority, and disobedience is rebellion, treason and revolution."[78] The *Pennsylvanian* echoed the refrain, accusing the Republicans of seeking to disrupt the Union: "Whoever now seeks to revive sectionalism arrays himself against the Constitution, and consequently against the Union."[79]

The problem, as Republicans saw it, was that "judicial tyranny is hard enough to resist under any circumstances, for it comes in the guise of impartiality and with the prestige of fairness."[80] Republicans thus turned their efforts to challenging the legitimacy of the decision while attempting all the while to remain faithful to the Constitution and to the Supreme Court as its final interpreter. One strategy they pursued was to deny that the *Dred Scott* decision was in fact a decision outlawing congressional regulation of slavery in the territories. The Republican logic was that since Taney had dismissed the case for lack of jurisdiction, the Supreme Court had no authority to examine the case on its merits; therefore, the Court's nullification of the Missouri Compromise was mere obiter dicta, unnecessary for the resolution of the case and hence not binding as precedent.[81] By declaring the Supreme Court's decision to be binding only on Dred Scott and his family, and then only for technical reasons, Republicans could undermine the impact of the decision without appearing to challenge the Supreme Court's legitimacy.

The obiter dicta argument was probably the most common charge leveled against the Court. It came in a variety of forms, the most colorful of which appeared, as expected, in the *Tribune*, which declared that the Court's opinion was "entitled to just so much moral weight as would be the judgment of a majority of those congregated in any Washington barroom."[82] Republican politicians routinely echoed this argument, if in less picturesque terms. Senator William P. Fessenden (R.-Me.), for example, parried charges that he had attacked the Supreme Court's decision by proclaiming that "they have made none: it is their opinion."[83] Senator Emory Pottle (R.-N.Y.) likewise considered the opinions of the justices to be "as binding . . . as if given by the same gentlemen at a political meeting, and no more so."[84] The obiter dicta argument became "the Republican battle cry in the war against the Dred Scott decision"; it was tailor-made to serve the Republicans' need to defend the constitutionality of their party platform and was at once plausible and effective.[85]

The obiter dicta argument did not explain why the justices had gone so far out of their way to decide a question they should never have taken up. To explain this, Republicans fell back on the charge that the Court was a tool of the slave power. "The Supreme Court certainly has shown itself quite as willing to enter the service of slavery as the most ultra friend of the institution could desire," said Congressman Cydnor B. Tompkins (R.-Ohio).[86] Tompkins's interpretation was mild; other Republicans added an element of conspiracy as well. Lincoln, for example, saw all the events from 1854 to 1857 as an "almost complete legal combination—piece of machinery, so to speak." He concluded: "We cannot absolutely known that all these exact adaptations are the result of preconcert. . . . [But] we find it impossible not to believe that Stephen and Franklin and Roger and James all understood one another from the beginning."[87] Moreover, Lincoln saw in the future the prospect of "another Supreme Court decision, declaring that the Constitution of the United States does not permit a *State* to exclude slavery from its limits."[88]

It was William Henry Seward, however, who provided the classic explication of the conspiracy theory. Seward, in charges repeated by Republicans everywhere, wove a story charging that Buchanan, before coming into office, "approached or was approached by the Supreme Court of the United States," as they were deliberating the *Dred Scott* case, which was on their docket "through some chance or by design." The Court "did not hesitate to please the incoming President" by declaring the Missouri Compromise unconstitutional; Chief Justice Taney whispered the news of the Court's upcoming decision to the new president on the inaugural platform, and Buchanan "announced (vaguely, indeed, but with satisfaction) the forthcoming extra-judicial exposition of the Constitution, and pledged his submission to it as authoritative and final."[89]

The conspiracy and slave power arguments were attacks on the members of the Supreme Court without being attacks on the Supreme Court itself. All six of the justices who joined with Taney in the result were open to criticism, but the Chief Justice, as leader of the Court and author of the leading opinion, was especially visible and vulnerable. Taney was lambasted for being dishonest and partisan; both were serious charges when leveled against a sitting judge, and Taney was deeply hurt by them.[90] Here again, Republicans played on common themes. "We have fallen upon evil times," said one congressman, "when a Chief Justice and a Chief Magistrate deliberately and officially utter what, seemingly, they must know to be untrue."[91] The *Tribune* characterized Taney's opinion as "subtle, ingenious, sophistical and false," calling it "the plea of a tricky lawyer and not the decree of an upright Judge."[92] Others denounced the justices collectively as "betrayers" of "liberty and law" and as "mere partisans."[93]

Another tactic employed by opponents of the decision was to attack Taney's opinion for its logical deficiencies, which were considerable. The opinion was criticized for "the anomalous character of its reasoning," scorned as "a perversion of all law, of all fact, and of all history," and condemned as being "so utterly at variance with all truth; so utterly destitute of all legal logic; so founded on legal error, and unsupported by anything like argument."[94] Reviews by lawyers and legal scholars were tamer in tone but just as critical of the reasoning behind the decision. Reviewers questioned "whether the Chief Justice really spoke for a majority of the Court, what the Court really decided, [and] how the justices aligned themselves on each specific issue."[95]

A final approach used to discredit the existing Supreme Court without attacking the institution itself was the argument that the Court's membership was heavily and unfairly weighted toward the slave states. The Court in this period was made up of nine members, one from each of nine judicial districts. Five of the districts represented slave states, while only four represented free states. The census of 1860, by contrast, indicated that approximately 60 percent of the population lived in the free-state circuits.[96] To redress this inequality, and of course to produce a Court which would be more amenable to antislavery interests, Seward proposed a mild Court reorganization bill in 1858, "so that the several States shall be represented . . . more nearly on the basis of their federal population," and so the administration of justice would be made "more speedy and efficient."[97] Though Seward's proposal addressed a real problem—the Northern judicial districts were simply too large—the partisan nature of the bill was obvious. Seward's presentation of the bill did not help matters, since he tied the court reorganization plan closely to the *Dred Scott* issue. The result was that the Southerners were able to deride the bill as merely an attempt to reform the Court's "political sentiments and practices."[98] Nonetheless, Seward's point was clear, and many picked up the argument that the Court's "sectional form" made it "necessarily the object of suspicion."[99]

By focusing their attacks on the decision of the Court, on the present membership of the Court, on the influences of the "slave power," and on the unrepresentative nature of the Court, Republicans were able to avoid direct attacks on judicial power per se. Their overriding concern was to paint themselves as defenders of the Constitution and of the status quo, and to depict the Court and its Southern supporters as "usurpers" and breakers of precedent. Thus Republicans attempted to align their views with those of the Founders and to cast the Court's decision as a "dangerous aggression" on the Constitution. The *New York Independent* denounced the Court's attempt "to foist this new and atrocious doctrine into the Constitution," this "vain attempt to change the law."[100] Congressman De Witt Clinton Leach (R.-Mich.) put the Republican claim most directly: "We ask only that the rights guaranteed to us . . . by the Constitution, and conceded to us during the earlier years of the Republic, be restored. We ask that the Constitution be interpreted in the same spirit in which it was made—that it be construed as the 'charter of liberty,' not as the bulwark of slavery."[101]

Republicans also cited earlier judicial decisions in an attempt to demonstrate the novelty of Taney's opinion. Over and over again Republicans claimed that the decisions of judges more eminent than Taney or any of his brethren had been ignored or overturned in *Dred Scott*. The Supreme Court, said the *Independent*, had been "blind to precedent."[102] This approach had the advantage of aligning the Republicans with eminent jurists of the past. Thus the Republicans were able to show their fidelity to the original interpretation of the Constitution (as they saw it) and to deflect the charge that they were radical opponents of judicial power. Most often quoted were Mansfield's *Somerset* opinion and the 1842 case of *Prigg* v. *Pennsylvania*.[103] Republicans cited these cases in support of their arguments that slavery could exist only by the positive force of "municipal law" and that slaves, "once free," were "forever free."

Despite their carefully constructed arguments the Republicans never achieved a satisfactory theoretical defense of their selective acceptance of judicial action. The most serious effort to establish such a theory was made by Lincoln, who wrestled with the problem for four years without ever really solving it. In his first statement after *Dred Scott*, Lincoln announced that the decisions of the Supreme Court, "when fully settled," should control "the general policy of the nation."[104] He deliberately left unclear what he meant by the phrase "when fully settled," though it was certain that the Court's decision did not end the matter.

Lincoln was also ambiguous in his debates with Douglas, preferring to put his opponent on the defensive rather than clarify his own position. Early in the summer of 1858, however, he had sketched out his views on the binding authority of Supreme Court decisions. Lincoln contended that a Court decision resolves the immediate question before the Court, and also indicates "that when a question comes up upon another person it will be so decided again, unless the court decides in another way"; unless, that is, "the court overrules its decision."[105] Then, citing Andrew Jackson's veto of the Bank of the United States recharter, Lincoln argued that "the

Supreme Court had no right to lay down a rule to govern a coordinate branch of the government."[106] Therefore, he concluded, Republicans "do not propose to be bound by" the *Dred Scott* decision "as a political rule."[107] The Court's decision clearly had to be accepted as regards Dred Scott himself, but Republicans could nevertheless work for a reversal.

Lincoln's position was full of holes, the largest of which was his absurdly narrow view of precedent. He struggled with this problem as late as his 1861 inaugural address, trying to reconcile his condemnation of the *Dred Scott* decision with his respect for judicial power. He concluded that if the policy of the nation on vital questions is to be "irrevocably fixed by the decisions of the Supreme Court, the instant they are made," then "the people will have ceased, to be their own rulers, having . . . practically resigned their government, into the hands of that eminent tribunal." In the next sentence, however, Lincoln showed the essential Republican ambiguity toward the Court: "Nor is there, in this view, any assault upon the court, or the judges."[108]

By pursuing these various strategies, Republicans sought to undermine the *Dred Scott* decision while maintaining their support for the concept of judicial power. This distinction was difficult to maintain in practice, however, and the onslaught against the *Dred Scott* decision and its authors was bound to spill over at times to a more general attack on the Supreme Court as an institution. Some Republicans, especially the radical abolition press, attacked the Court's action as violating the higher law of nature and of God; occasionally, there were even a few attacks on the Court as an antidemocratic institution.[109] Such remarks were rare, however, since they were politically dangerous, and since Republicans seemed to have a genuine respect for the idea of a free and independent judiciary despite their intense feeling that the contemporary Supreme Court had abused its power.

The Republicans' strategy of attacking the existing Court but not the Court as an institution constrained their choice of remedies. Their solution to the *Dred Scott* problem was to gain control of the White House and Senate, and to use the appointments process to reshape the Court in their own image. Alternatively, Republicans hoped the justices could be persuaded to change their minds, but there was little reason to think that such a hope was realistic. Lincoln advocated "so resisting" the decision "as to have it reversed if we can, and a new judicial rule established on the subject." Seward declared that the Republican goal was "to take the government out of unjust and unfaithful hands, and commit it to those which will be just and faithful."[110]

Reforming the Court through the appointment process and through the power of persuasion were the only remedies that were consistent with the Republicans' desire to present a conservative face to the nation. Amending the Constitution was impossible because almost half of the states were slave states, and three-quarters of the states were required to approve any amendment. Moreover, amendment was undesirable, since the Republicans contended that their party was in no way opposed to the Constitution as it then existed. Furthermore, any call for an amendment to the Constitution would have involved a tacit admission that Taney's interpretation of the Constitution had been correct—how could the Republicans argue that constitutional change was necessary when they argued that Taney's opinion was not justified under the Constitution as it was then written?

Eventually, the Supreme Court was reformed through the appointment process. Lincoln had three appointments to make by 1862. A very mild reorganization bill adding a tenth circuit, and therefore a tenth justice, gave him a fourth appointment in 1863.[111] The reorganization of 1863 was at least partially intended to give Lincoln an extra appointment, but it was also designed to address the long-standing problems of the rapidly growing Western circuits. Moreover, the addition of the tenth seat came at a time when the Court's resistance to the policy goals of the Republicans was at its lowest ebb; with the war raging, the Court had kept largely silent about slavery and other important political issues. Taney's death in 1864 gave Lincoln his fifth appointment and enabled him to fill the chief justiceship with a Republican, in this case Salmon P. Chase.[112]

VI

The *Dred Scott* decision had an effect on the Democratic Party as well as on the Republican. In traditional accounts of the period, the decision is said to have broken the Democrats in two; Taney's opinion and Lincoln's "shrewd exploitation of it in the Freeport debate of 1858 compelled Douglas to take a stand that alienated the South, disrupted the Democratic Party, and thus cleared the way for a Republican victory."[113] Charles Warren believed that "Chief Justice Taney elected Abraham Lincoln to the Presidency."[114] Chronologically at least, the splitting of the Democratic Party took place within a year of *Dred Scott*; the question is whether a causal relationship can be demonstrated.

To begin with, the unity of the Democratic Party before March 1857 has been exaggerated. The party was tied together by a common doctrine of popular sovereignty, but the Southern and Northern wings of the party placed very different interpretations on that slogan after the Kansas-Nebraska debate. Douglas advocated a genuine freedom of choice for the people of a territory throughout the territorial period; many Southerners, however, such as Robert Toombs (D.-Ga.), read popular sovereignty to require "protection to all persons and property on an equal basis throughout the territorial period," and believed that the Kansas-Nebraska Act allowed popular choice only upon application for statehood. Congressional debates from 1854 until 1857 reflected this split within the apparently united Democratic ranks.[115]

As the *Dred Scott* case neared decision, there was hope among Southern Democrats that their Northern colleagues would accept a Court decision vindicating the Southern position on popular sovereignty. Some Northerners, such as Congressman William English (D.-Ind.) made a similar assumption on the other side, hoping that the Southerners would accept the Northern position.[116] Buchanan's prediction that the *Dred Scott* decision would finally settle the territorial problem echoed the hopes of many Democrats on both sides of the Mason-Dixon line.

The gulf between the two wings of the Democratic Party was wider than men like Buchanan and English wanted to admit. Since both sides accepted the Kansas-Nebraska Act and paid lip service to popular sovereignty, the internal gulf seemed much smaller than that between the moderate Democrats and the Republicans. In reality, however, it was possible for the Democrats to maintain their veil of solidarity only so long as the meaning of popular sovereignty remained a vague question of abstract principles.

By declaring popular sovereignty as Douglas defined it to be unconstitutional, Taney's *Dred Scott* opinion raised the prospect of a confrontation between the two wings of the Democratic Party over the popular sovereignty issue. As Fehrenbacher points out, however, many Northern Democrats were pleased with the Supreme Court's decision in *Dred Scott* that negroes were ineligible for citizenship in the United States and regarded *congressional* intervention in the territories as bad policy in any event. Thus they joined their Southern colleagues in defending the Court against

Republican attacks and in denouncing the Republicans for those attacks. The popular sovereignty issue was thus suppressed for the moment in favor of party unity.[117]

What brought the popular sovereignty issue to a head was not the *Dred Scott* decision alone, but the combination of the Court's opinion and the Lecompton crisis of early 1858. This crisis grew out of the continuing struggle in Kansas to determine whether that territory would be admitted to the Union as a free state or as a slave state. The proslavery forces had met in constitutional convention in September 1857; antislavery men boycotted this convention because the electoral machinery was all in the hands of their opponents. The convention passed the Lecompton constitution and submitted it to the voters in December. The choice given to the voters consisted only in approving the constitution with a slavery provision or approving the constitution without a slavery provision; they could not reject the constitution outright. Moreover the constitution "without slavery" did not require the emancipation or removal of any slaves already in the territory, nor did it allow anyone to vote to eliminate slavery altogether.

With antislavery men again boycotting, the Lecompton constitution with slavery was approved by the Kansas electorate and was submitted to Congress in a formal application for statehood. The Congressional debate centered around Douglas, who opposed the admission of Kansas under the Lecompton constitution, and the Southerners, backed by the administration, who supported the application for statehood. The debate over the admission of Kansas in the winter and spring of 1857–58 "left a legacy of party disruption and sectional hatred from which the nation would not recover."[118] Neither, at least for some time, would the Democratic Party.

All the participants in the Lecompton debate were concerned about what would eventually happen to Kansas, but for very different reasons. To Northern Republicans, the actions of slavery supporters in the Kansas statehood movement showed that the South would stop at nothing in the attempt to create more slave states; Kansas thus appeared to be proof of the evils inherent in any policy other than direct congressional prohibition of slavery in the territories. To Douglas, approval of the Lecompton constitution would spell the death of the principle of popular sovereignty, a principle on which he had based much of his professional life. Douglas was in favor of self-determination for the territories at all stages of development, up to and including the application for statehood and the ratification of the new state constitution. The Southern attempt to impose slavery on an unwilling Kansas by underhanded means violated the popular sovereignty ideal and hence had to be resisted. To the Southerners, Kansas represented the last real hope of establishing a slave state in the foreseeable future. Kansas was a prize the South did not want to lose.

The *Dred Scott* case was never far from the center of the Lecompton controversy. Republicans now had a concrete and urgent reason to overturn the *Dred Scott* decision. The Lecompton constitution made it clear that congressional prohibition of slavery in the territories was a necessity, and such a prohibition could not be brought about until *Dred Scott* was overruled. The Southerners, feeling that they had somehow been cheated out of the practical benefits of the decision, constantly raised the *Dred Scott* issue. Specifically, they continually asked Douglas how he could reconcile his version of popular sovereignty with Chief Justice Taney's dictum that Congress could not delegate the power to prohibit slavery in a territory even to the people of that territory.

The bitter fight over Lecompton showed just how far apart the two wings of the Democratic Party really were. In fact, Douglas was as far from the Southern wing of his own party as he was from the Republicans. As the North and the South polarized over the question of slavery extension, the Republicans took the view that slavery had to be contained, while the South took the view that a sectional balance had to be maintained and could be maintained only by the addition of new slave states. Douglas, holding to the neutral principle of popular sovereignty, was caught in the middle.

The Lecompton debate blew apart the tenuous links between the Douglas wing of the Democratic Party and the Southern wing. As the debate progressed, it became clear that Douglas would not abandon his version of popular sovereignty, and that he would continue to insist on self-determination for the territories. Douglas's refusal to accept the argument that Taney's opinion had buried popular sovereignty alienated his Southern supporters. At the same time, his strong anti-Lecompton position temporarily allied him with the Republicans, and there was some talk in the spring of 1858 that a coalition between Douglas Democrats and the Republicans would be possible. But though Douglas never accepted the Southern view of popular sovereignty, he surely never accepted the Republican argument that Congress had the power and the duty to ban slavery from the territories. He was left without allies in the center of the American political battlefield.

The argument that Lincoln's exploitation of the *Dred Scott* issue forced Douglas to take a stand that alienated the Southern wing of the Democratic Party is not justified by the facts. Douglas's firm commitment to popular sovereignty during the congressional debates over the Lecompton constitution had already weakened his support in the South dramatically. For a short period from the settlement of the Lecompton issue through Congress's adoption of the English Bill, there was some chance that Douglas would let the issue lie and that the deep wounds within the Democratic ranks would be allowed to heal. But Douglas was bitterly opposed to the English Bill, which guaranteed popular sovereignty in Kansas (of which he of course approved), but which also made it impossible for Kansas to enter the Union with its current population except as a slave state; if the people of the territory voted to enter the Union as a free state (a course which they ultimately followed), they would have to wait until their population reached 90,000. Douglas regarded this settlement as a perversion of popular sovereignty; he led the forces of opposition to the English Bill in the Senate and ultimately voted against it.

Thus it is easy to understand why Douglas continued to oppose the English Bill even after it became law. The compromise measure was approved by Congress on 30 April 1858; on 9 July, after Douglas's return to Illinois at the close of the legislative session, he wasted no time in reviving the Lecompton issue. He declared that he had triumphed in the debate over the Lecompton constitution because he had resisted "to the utmost of my power the consummation of that fraud," and he denounced the English Bill. As the historian Robert Johannsen writes, Douglas's comments of 9 July "effectively closed the door to reconciliation with the administration."[119] The outpouring of Southern hostility toward Douglas at this point, well over a month before the debates with Lincoln were due to begin, supports the conclusion that it was Lecompton—and not Lincoln—that drove a wedge between Douglas and his Southern copartisans. As far as Southerners were concerned, after Douglas's 9 July speech it was: "Away with him to the tomb which he is digging for his political corpse."[120]

The debates with Lincoln did not create the split within the Democratic Party, but Lincoln's tactics in the debates neatly underscored the differences between the Southern and Northern Democrats. Lincoln did not force Douglas to make any new concessions or to adopt any new positions during the debate; Douglas simply reiterated views that he had held for some time. During the debate at Freeport, for example, Douglas made it clear that the principle of popular sovereignty could be made to override the Southerners' right to take their slaves with them into the federal territories. In the so-called "Freeport doctrine," Douglas indicated that the right of Southerners to hold slaves in the free territories was necessarily dependent on the existence of friendly police regulations, which a Free-Soil territorial legislature would be under no obligation to enact or enforce.

Here, then, was the crux of Douglas's disagreement with the Southern leadership. But the Freeport doctrine was not invented at Freeport; Douglas had clearly articulated it over a year before, as part of his ongoing attempt to reconcile popular sovereignty to Chief Justice Taney's opinion in the *Dred Scott* case. In a major speech in Chicago in June 1857, Douglas boldly defended the Court's decision, supported its invalidation of the Missouri Compromise, and managed to interpret Taney's opinion so as to make it compatible with popular sovereignty. The right of a master to hold a slave, Douglas said, anticipating almost word for word the Freeport doctrine, "necessarily remains a barren and worthless right, unless sustained, protected and enforced by appropriate police regulations and local legislation, prescribing adequate penalties for its violation. These regulations . . . can only be prescribed by the local legislatures. Hence the great principle of popular sovereignty is sustained and fully established by the authority of this decision."[121] This was a weak argument in 1857, and it remained a weak one in 1858. The key difference was this: whereas in 1857 the argument was part of an abstract debate over slavery, by 1858 it had been transformed into the key issue dividing Douglas and the Southern Democrats. When finally pushed to its limits by Lincoln, the Freeport doctrine was revealed to be the mere assertion of the principle that might makes right: popular sovereignty now meant only that what the people did not want, they would not have, legal niceties notwithstanding.

If the Democratic Party was hopelessly divided even before the Lincoln-Douglas debates, what then was the purpose of Lincoln's slashing and persistent attacks on Douglas's post–*Dred Scott* version of popular sovereignty? In the summer of 1858, Lincoln was trying to cope with a very difficult political situation within his own party. Douglas's fierce anti–

Lecompton stand had ingratiated him with many Republicans, since he had led the antislavery forces to victory over the proslavery forces in the battle over the Lecompton constitution. Some Republicans, in the heat of battle, dreamed of an alliance between Douglas and their own party, an alliance which was sure to capture the presidency in 1860. Horace Greeley and a few other Eastern Republicans even went so far as to suggest that Douglas be returned to the Senate in 1858 without Republican opposition.[122] This possibility created two problems for Lincoln. First, his personal ambitions for the presidency in 1860 would have been all but destroyed by Republican endorsement of Douglas and would have been greatly damaged even by tacit Republican endorsement of Douglas in the 1858 campaign for the Senate. Second, Lincoln's political and moral views toward slavery would have been severely compromised by such an alliance. Which of the two motives was predominant in Lincoln's mind has been the subject of considerable historical debate;[123] it is impossible to choose between them, however, and the attempt to make such a choice obscures the probable truth that Lincoln's actions in 1858 stemmed from a combination of motives, all leading in the same direction.

The personal and political differences between Douglas and Lincoln should not be minimized, as they are by those who argue that Lincoln's personal ambition alone caused him to adopt his strategy of opposing Douglas. Lincoln realized, as many Republicans did not, that Douglas's alliance with the antislavery forces was a marriage of convenience. Douglas and the Republicans had been united in one cause—that of defeating the Lecompton constitution—but their opposition to Lecompton was based on very different principles. Republicans opposed the Lecompton constitution because it was a slavery constitution; Douglas opposed it because it had not been adopted in a fair vote by the people. Douglas's argument in his 9 July 1858 speech in Chicago was not a new one: "I will be entirely frank with you. My object [in the Lecompton controversy] was to secure the right of the people of each State and of each Territory, North or South, to decide the question for themselves, to have slavery or not, as they choose; and my opposition to the Lecompton Constitution was not predicated upon the ground that it was a pro-slavery Constitution, nor would my action have been different had it been a Freesoil Constitution."[124] One would search in vain for any evidence that Douglas wavered from this position at any time during the Lecompton debate. He had staked his political career on the

THE LIMITS OF JUDICIAL POWER

principle of popular sovereignty, and held it to be of more importance than the slavery issue itself.

It is true that Lincoln's strategy of seeking and obtaining an unprecedented "nomination" for the Senate seat from the Republican caucus in the state house, and his decidedly nonmoderate "House Divided" speech of 16 June 1858, were calculated to remove the possibility of an alliance between Douglas and the Republicans.[125] The speech tried to paint Douglas as an actor in the Buchanan-Taney conspiracy detailed by Seward some months before and played up the differences between Douglas and the Republican Party. A man who was not seeking to run for the presidency might have downplayed his differences with Douglas, but that is not the point; the differences were real, and it is hard to conceive of a platform upon which Douglas and the Republicans could have agreed. Any endorsement of popular sovereignty, which would make slavery in the territories a possibility, was anathema to the Republicans, who had established their party specifically in response to the adoption of that principle in the Kansas-Nebraska Act; any platform which did not endorse popular sovereignty would have been unacceptable to Douglas.

In real terms, of course, the practical consequences of either stance would have led to free states in the West. The Western territories, as has been often pointed out, were not suitable for slave agriculture or for a slave economy, and the sheer numbers of Northern as compared to Southern settlers made it highly likely that all the territories would have eventually gone the way of Kansas. This outcome is clear with the hindsight of history, and it was clear to a few men at the time. But such a rational calculation was not at the heart of the dream that Douglas would ally himself with the Republican party. No Republican ever suggested an alliance based on an agreement that popular sovereignty was the proper principle under which to resolve the slavery question. The hope, instead—and it was never more than a hope—was that Douglas would change his mind and lead an antislavery ticket. Some Republicans even deluded themselves into thinking that Douglas's performance in the Lecompton debates was a manifestation of his conversion to antislavery.

It is of little help in understanding the historical situation in 1858 to suggest that an alliance between Douglas and the Republicans was a realistic possibility, for such an outcome would have required a dramatic change in the political views either of Douglas or of the Republican Party.

It is, of course, within the powers of imagination to suggest that Douglas might have changed his mind, abandoned popular sovereignty, and taken charge of the antislavery party. "There is evidence that Douglas was, in his private and personal thinking, an antislavery man," writes David M. Potter. He continues: "Thus, without much concern for the slaves, and without believing that the slavery issue was worth a political crisis, Douglas did regard the restriction of slavery as desirable, and thought of popular sovereignty as an effective device by which to restrict it without precipitating a constant running battle in Congress. For a man with sentiments such as these, the events of 1857 and 1858 might have been enough to cause a basic restructuring of his views." That, of course, is precisely the point: for Douglas to align himself with the Republicans would have required "a basic restructuring of his views," and there is no evidence that he was ever disposed to such a transformation. As Potter concludes, "Douglas . . . was deeply committed to certain attitudes which had become, with him, matters of principle."[126] Potter's suggestion that Douglas regarded the restriction of slavery as desirable, all other things being equal, is probably accurate. It is not at all accurate, however, to suggest that Douglas regarded popular sovereignty primarily as a tool to achieve antislavery ends, for he was prepared to defend popular sovereignty against all comers, from every side. A Douglas-Republican alliance can be posited only in the realm of counterfactual history, but it ultimately requires that Douglas not be Douglas or that the Republicans not be the Republicans.

Since many Republicans regarded an alliance with Douglas as a realistic possibility, Lincoln may well have calculated that it was politically wise for him to play up his differences with Douglas during the 1858 Senate campaign. His opposition to Douglas, while it might have accorded with his personal ambition, was not at all disingenuous. For Lincoln, Douglas's fatal flaw was that he "cared not whether slavery be voted down or up," if only in a political or public sense.[127]

Douglas won the election of 1858, but it was his last political victory. His description of the election reveals his isolated position: he had triumphed, he reported, "over the combined forces of Abolitionists and the federal office holders."[128] The break in the Democratic ranks was made irreparable in 1858 when Douglas was stripped of his chairmanship of the Committee on the Territories by the Democratic leadership of the Senate. In the end, Douglas made a desperate bid for the presidency in 1860 but could command only a fragment of his party. He died, a defeated and broken man, soon after the outbreak of the Civil War.

By giving legitimacy to the Calhoun view of Southern rights in the territories, the *Dred Scott* decision contributed to the radicalization of the Southern wing of the Democratic Party. To the South, as Fehrenbacher argues, "the sense of having won a victory without substance proved increasingly irritating." This feeling drove the South to embrace the Lecompton cause as passionately as it did and to reject Douglas's moderate position as thoroughly as the Republicans had rejected it four years earlier. The radicalization of the South and the consequent break with Douglas occurred before the Lincoln-Douglas debates; the positions of both Lincoln and Douglas in the 1858 Senate campaign only confirmed the impossibility of an alliance between Douglas and the Republicans or of a reconciliation between Douglas and the Southern Democrats.

VII

From late 1858 on, the South was increasingly concerned more with symbolism than with substance; Southerners sought to protect their view of "Southern rights" from attack by the North. Rather than proposing positive programs or seeking compromise, the South "became ever more ready to make issues on any and all aspects of slavery, and to devise doctrinal tests by which to measure the orthodoxy of northern Democrats."[129] When it became clear that the Republicans might capture the White House in 1860, Southerners turned to devising tests for them as well.

The most common test applied to both parties involved the rights of slaveholders in the territories. Here was an issue on which the South could claim the support of the Constitution and the Supreme Court, the issue over which they had broken with Douglas, and the issue which was most clearly in dispute between Democrats and Republicans.

The vague issue of "Southern rights" therefore became an assertion of "the unqualified right of the people of the slaveholding states to the protection of their property in the States [and] in the territories."[130] This was not a new position, but it was put to a new use. It fit well into the Southern strategy of attempting to purge Douglas and his followers from the party, since for years Douglas had taken the position that the people of a territory were not required to protect the property of slaveholders. And, of course, it was a useful weapon against the Republicans as well. Moreover, the territorial argument embodied a constitutional argument that was fully developed and had long been accepted in the South. Indeed, with just a little reinterpretation, Southerners could argue that the *Dred Scott* decision fully supported their claims, by holding it to be the duty of Congress or the territorial governments to promote and protect slave property. Thus the Southerners kept the *Dred Scott* case alive as a political issue throughout 1859 and 1860.

Both Republicans and Douglas Democrats were vulnerable to the charge that in opposing the *Dred Scott* decision they demonstrated their hostility to the South and their disloyalty to the Constitution.[131] In the rhetoric of the South, Douglas was as guilty as the Republicans of such disloyalty, but he defended himself along quite different lines. In a famous article in *Harper's Magazine*, Douglas argued that popular sovereignty was firmly grounded both in history and in constitutional law, a position which might have been tenable had it not been for the *Dred Scott* case.[132] While he cited the case at length in support of his argument, Douglas "made free use of ellipses . . . and at one point he transposed sentences in order to heighten the effect."[133] In 1860, Douglas took the position that *Dred Scott* barred Congress from prohibiting slavery in the territories and from authorizing the territorial governments to do so, but did not bar the people of a territory from prohibiting slavery on their own, independent of Congress. The Southern response was forceful and convincing: never before had Douglas or anyone else "pretended that if Congress did not have that power the Territory could have it."[134]

The Republicans were open to much broader salvos. They had shown themselves to be utterly opposed to the decision in *Dred Scott*, and the Southerners therefore charged them with opposing the rights of their section. Southerners agreed that the Republican Party was "hostile to State rights, and disloyal to the Constitution," as shown by "its openly avowed intention to keep the leading property interest of the South out of the common Territories." Republicanism was "a swelling wave . . . that threatens to engulf us all . . . destroying at once the Constitution and the Union." Northerners, they said, made "war not only upon the Supreme Court, but upon the constitutional rights of the South, when in conflict with their sentimentality."[135]

Republicans also came under fire for the highly publicized Northern resistance to federal attempts to enforce the provisions of the Fugitive Slave Law. Most famous was the case of Sherman Booth, a Wisconsin newspaper editor convicted in federal court for obstructing the enforcement of the law, only to be released on a writ of habeas corpus by the *state* Supreme Court. When the Supreme Court of the United States ordered Booth reimprisoned, he served a brief period and was then released by a Republican mob.[136] Southerners complained that "the trials in your Federal courts, growing out of the attempt to enforce the fugitive slave law, are the most outrageous and the most monstrous perversions of justice that are to be found on record."[137] Southerners routinely linked Republican refusal to enforce the Fugitive Slave Law, and their deliberate attempts to interfere with federal enforcement, with their refusal to respect the *Dred Scott* decision in the federal territories.

As it became clear to the South that the Republicans would take control of the White House in 1861, Southerners began to speak increasingly of secession. Their argument for secession was based on the claim that their rights would be violated by a Republican administration; Southerners regarded the Republican Party's refusal to respect *Dred Scott* as an indication that the Northern party was not fit to control the national government. Republican refusal to support the Supreme Court was evidence of their "reckless disregard of the Constitution and laws of the land," and was "an additional reason why we should fear the installment of that party in power in . . . the national Legislature."[138] Republican rejection of *Dred Scott* was almost grounds for secession by itself; as Representative John William Henderson Underwood (D.-Ga.) declared: "Obedience to the law of the land and the decision of our Supreme Court—justice and right. When this shall be heeded by the people of the North, I will then talk for the Union."[139]

Southern demands for Northern support of *Dred Scott* became even more intense as the South came to realize that the Court was its last line of defense against Republican encroachment, a realization that, in the words of Representative William E. Simms (D.-Ky.), "there is nothing now left between the South and her assailants, except the Democratic party of the northern States and the Constitution of the Federal Union as expounded by the Supreme Court." Southerners were aware of Republican plans to gain control of the Court and bemoaned the prospect that men like Taney, Catron, and Nelson would be replaced by Republican judges. "When that day comes," asked Senator Albert G. Brown (D.-S.C.), "what will become of the Dred Scott decision behind which I am asked to entrench myself? Sir, it will fade away as 'the baseless fabric of a vision.' "[140]

Faced with such attacks on their loyalty to the Constitution, but knowing that victory in the 1860 election was within reach if they could carry Pennsylvania and one other moderate antislavery state, the Republicans moved toward the political center as the 1860 campaign approached. They broadened their appeal by moderating their platform and by embracing a set of economic issues to go with their antislavery planks. At the Chicago convention, they rejected Seward, because he was too radical to carry the moderate Northern states, and turned to Lincoln, who had never advocated an appeal to higher law and who was therefore less vulnerable to the charge of being against the Constitution. As part of the Republican attempt to moderate their stance and undercut charges that the party was disloyal to the Constitution, attacks on the Supreme Court were softened during the campaign or dropped outright.

In an attempt to hold onto his position as front-runner for the Republican nomination, Seward responded to the pressure to move toward the center early in 1860, particularly in a famous Senate speech of 29 February. Seward presented his party as conservative and the Democrats as radicals who would break up the union simply because a Republican might be elected to the presidency. Significantly, Seward never once mentioned *Dred Scott* in this speech; the closest he came was a veiled reference to the American people as "the supreme tribunal to try and decide all political issues." Seward pledged that the Republican Party would be essentially conservative and engage in "no new transaction."[141]

The Republican trend toward moderation and away from direct attacks on the Supreme Court is also evident in the 1860 platform which, despite all the rhetoric of the preceding three years, contained not a single direct reference to the Supreme Court. Instead of attacking Taney, the platform attacked Buchanan for his attempted enforcement of the Fugitive Slave Law "through the intervention . . . of the federal courts." The platform denounced "the new dogma, that the Constitution of its own force carries slavery into any or all of the territories of the United States," as being "at variance with the explicit provisions of that instrument itself, with contemporaneous exposition, and with legislative and judicial precedents." Finally, it denied "the authority of Congress, of a territorial legislature, or of any individuals, to give legal existence to slavery in any territory of the United States." In general, the platform placed less stress on the territorial issue than had the 1856 platform and more stress on sundry economic proposals.[142]

Despite its moderation on certain key issues, the Republican party never wavered on slavery extension; after the election, Republicans rejected a compromise effort to reestablish the Missouri Compromise line and extend it westward. Significantly, however, they accepted a proposed constitutional amendment providing that the Constitution would never be amended to interfere with slavery in any state, though this move came too late to be a practical solution to what was already a secession crisis.[143]

The political struggle ended with the inauguration of Lincoln, and the military battle soon followed. After the election of Lincoln, the major question in the South was whether to secede immediately or to wait and see whether Lincoln the president would be as hostile to the South as, in their view, Lincoln the candidate had been. Lincoln's refusal to obey the Supreme Court's judgment in *Dred Scott* was taken by some as proof that he would violate his presidential oath to uphold the Constitution of the United States.[144] Even those who advised caution and advocated that the South not secede until Lincoln committed some overt act against the Constitution admitted that his record was not encouraging.[145]

As Lincoln observed in his first inaugural address, "One section of our country believes slavery is *right*, and ought to be expanded, while the other believes it is *wrong*, and ought not to be extended. This is the only substantial dispute."[146] That dispute—the same one that Chief Justice Taney had tried to settle four years before—would have to be settled not by lawyers, but by soldiers.

VIII

The crisis of the 1850s came to a head with the passage of the Kansas-Nebraska Act in 1854 and the consequent formation of the Republican Party and ended with the disruption of the Democratic Party and the election of Lincoln in 1860. The Supreme Court's decision in *Dred Scott* v. *Sandford* played an important role in the development of the crisis. In striking down the Missouri Compromise, the Court gave legitimacy to the extreme proslavery position on the territorial question and rendered illegitimate Stephen Douglas's version of popular sovereignty. As a result, the Court's decision was a major factor in bringing about the split in the Democratic Party which led to the Southern extremists' bolt from the 1860 convention.

The critical issue in the 1850s was the question of slavery in the territories, not the more general problem of slavery itself. The territorial question was the issue that spawned the Republican Party, in response to the Kansas-Nebraska Act; it was the central issue in the presidential campaign of 1856 and in the Lincoln-Douglas debates of 1858; and, ultimately, it was the issue over which the Democratic Party broke apart in 1860. The territorial question was above all a constitutional question, the same constitutional question decided by the Supreme Court in *Dred Scott*.

Before 1854, both major parties (Whig and Democratic) were committed to a compromise solution to the territorial problem, though such a compromise was difficult and always in need of modification. The Compromise of 1850 represents one attempt to solve the problem; in a way, the Kansas-Nebraska Act was another, since popular sovereignty, at least as originally conceived, was a middle-of-the-road position between repeal and affirmation of the Missouri Compromise. Douglas proposed popular sovereignty as a way of garnering Southern support for his Nebraska bill without adopting the Southern position on the territorial question. Immediately after he introduced the popular sovereignty provision, however, Southerners pushed him into conceding that his bill was in effect a repeal of the Compromise and into including explicit language to that effect in the bill itself. In theory, of course, popular sovereignty gave neither the Southern extremists nor the antislavery extremists what they wanted, since the status of the territories in question was left undetermined. In practice, Southerners regarded the bill as a victory, and antislavery men, as a betrayal.

Popular sovereignty—a policy which guaranteed nothing and which in effect sidestepped the difficult problem of whether to allow or exclude slavery by congressional mandate—was acceptable to a majority of the members of Congress in 1854. The Kansas-Nebraska Act, however, was the last compromise Congress would reach regarding the territorial question. Once antislavery Whigs and Democrats rejected the measure and formed the Republican Party, the first half of the realignment of the 1850s was completed: one of the major parties had been replaced by a new major party whose platform was based upon a polar position on the critical issue. For the realignment to be completed, the other party had to move toward the pole on the other side.

The process by which the Democratic Party was split into two sectional factions took some six years. Southerners were mollified by the victory of Buchanan in 1856 on a platform that was decidedly ambiguous on the territorial question. The platform stated simply that the party stood for "non-interference by Congress with slavery in state and territory or in the District of Columbia," a formulation which left unclear whether the people of a territory could or could not exclude slavery on their own.[147] Douglas said they could; the Southerners said they could not. The wording of the 1856 Democratic platform echoed the ambiguity of the Kansas-Nebraska Act on this very point: that act had left the people of the territories "perfectly free to form and regulate their domestic institutions in their own way, subject only to the Constitution of the United States." The last clause was open to interpretation; many Southerners interpreted the Constitution to bar any regulation of slavery in the territorial stage.

It is not correct to assert that the "process of party realignment reached completion in the presidential election of 1856," as David M. Potter, among others, argues.[148] It is true that if one looks only at the Republican Party's performance in the presidential elections of 1856 and 1860 there appears to be little change. Indeed, the Republican percentage of the presidential vote in 1856 is highly correlated with the Republican presidential vote in 1860.[149]

The difference between the 1856 and 1860 elections lies not in the Republican Party percentages, but in the rupture of the Democratic Party in the latter year. In 1856, though the Republicans had already moved to the antislavery pole, the Democrats were still united on an ambiguous platform. The key point is that in 1856 it was possible for the differences between Douglas and the Southerners to be patched over by the simple expedient of ambiguity. This is clear evidence that the party was not yet under the control of the proslavery extremists. In 1860, however, such ambiguity was no longer possible. As far as the Democratic Party was concerned, the realignment was not complete in 1856. Indeed, the correlation between the Democratic percentage of the total vote in 1856 and in 1860, even combining the votes of Douglas and Breckenridge, is much lower than the correlation of the Republican vote over the same two elections.[150]

The *Dred Scott* decision apparently had little effect on the strength and appeal of the Republican Party. Republican gains in the 1860 election as compared to 1856 came not in the most radical Northern states, which would have been most upset about the decision, but in the least radical states. The reason is simple: by 1856 the Republican Party had absorbed virtually all the antislavery elements in the radical Northern states but had not attracted more moderate voters in the less radical states. The moderation of the party platform in 1860 and the disruption of the Democratic Party led to increases in the Republican percentage of the vote in such moderate states as California, Illinois, Indiana, New Jersey, and Pennsylvania.[151] Significantly, the Republican percentage of the vote actually declined between 1856 and 1860 in Massachusetts and Vermont; in other states, the Republican gains were marginal at best.

The *Dred Scott* decision did have a major effect on the breakup of the Democratic Party, however. The disagreement between the Northern and Southern wings of the party could not be ignored after the *Dred Scott* decision and the Lecompton debate in 1858. It is impossible to say whether Lecompton would have had the same effect had there been no *Dred Scott* decision to precede it; such speculation cannot lead to meaningful results, especially since the *Dred Scott* issue was so intricately associated with the Lecompton controversy. Southerners had been arguing for some time that the events in Kansas and in the other territories were depriving them of their "Southern rights," and the *Dred Scott* decision only made them more sure that their rights were real and that they were being violated. Douglas's opposition to the Lecompton constitution further strengthened their feelings of isolation and frustration.

The decision had its most important effect on Douglas. In 1856, popular sovereignty represented a legitimate and plausible solution to the territorial problem. The problem of slavery in the territories was, as Douglas and others recognized, a temporary one; once all the territories had been populated and had applied for statehood, no one doubted that the people of those territories had the right to decide the slavery issue for themselves. Hence the short territorial phase represented the only difficult period. Furthermore, there were not that many more territories left to be organized;

once they were all admitted to the Union, the territorial issue would disappear. By 1856, however, half the nation would not accept any more new slave territories, and the other half would not accept any territories in which slavery was excluded by Congressional edict. The only middle ground left was therefore popular sovereignty, which, for all its defects, was a neat way of skirting the most difficult issue facing the nation.

Once the *Dred Scott* decision was handed down, however, Southerners no longer had any reason to accept Douglas's moderate position. In the first place, there was doubt as to whether popular sovereignty was constitutional. More important, the Supreme Court had endorsed (or at least seemed to have endorsed) the extreme Southern argument, that Southerners had a right to take their slave "property" into all the federal territories. Now the Southerners wanted not merely congressional noninterference in the territories but congressional protection of the slave system in the territories. Once the *Dred Scott* case had been decided and the popular sovereignty issue had come to a head in the Lecompton debate, any chance of holding the Southerners to a nonextremist course was eliminated.

The events of the 1850s can be viewed as a series of "triggering events," each of which intensified the sectional crisis and led, step by step, to the outbreak of military hostilities between the Confederacy and the Union. The Kansas-Nebraska Act, the *Dred Scott* case, John Brown's raid on the federal arsenal at Harper's Ferry, West Virginia, and a host of less important events, taken together, led to the Civil War. It is impossible to single out one of these and argue that it alone caused the breakup of the Democratic Party or the military confrontation.

The Supreme Court, for its part, recovered rapidly from the loss of prestige it suffered as a result of the *Dred Scott* case. As soon as the war ended, the Court began issuing important and in many cases controversial decisions; every such decision was obeyed and respected. The Court's rapid recovery was possible because, as Stanley Kutler argues, "the *idea* and *image* of the Court persisted with great vitality" throughout the period after the decision. At no time did the Republicans advocate the destruction of the Supreme Court; even Senator John Hale (R.-N.H.), who proposed that the existing Supreme Court be abolished, would have replaced it immediately with a new Supreme Court. Kutler draws a distinction between Republican attacks on the Court's decision in *Dred Scott* and "contemporary appraisals of the *institution*." The Court as an institution was not attacked; the *Dred Scott* decision and the current membership of the Court bore the brunt of the Republican offensive. The Republicans attacked neither the Court in the abstract nor the idea of judicial power.[152]

To be sure, the political crisis that followed *Dred Scott* had a negative effect on the Court's prestige in the short term. Its 1859 decision upholding federal enforcement of the Fugitive Slave Law was largely ignored by Northern authorities, and President Lincoln scoffed at an 1861 order by Taney that a Maryland secessionist be brought before him on a writ of habeas corpus. Taney himself felt that the Court would never "be restored to the authority and rank which the Constitution intended to confer on it."[153] The Republicans did not challenge the Court's decisions in areas not related to slavery or the war effort, however, and the Court continued to function on less highly charged issues. Once the Union's military victory made the slavery and wartime issues moot, it was easy and natural for the Court to resume its antebellum position. In some ways the Court emerged from its ordeal strengthened, for, despite all the criticism it suffered, its constitutional role had never been threatened.

One can say with reasonable certainty that the crisis of the 1850s was so deep-seated and the issue of slavery so emotional and divisive that the Supreme Court's attempt to resolve it was a political mistake of the highest magnitude. At the same time, however, it is an error to overstate the dangers that *Dred Scott* posed to the Court's independence and autonomy. *Dred Scott*, for all its defects, did not endanger the Court's place in American politics, nor was it a "calamity" for the Court in the long term. That the Court survived the *Dred Scott* crisis is no surprise; its Republican enemies consistently supported its authority to make constitutional decisions and made no effort to emasculate its legitimate powers. "The fact," wrote Robert McCloskey, "is that this wound, though grievous, was not fatal." In fact the wound, however acute, was highly localized and never presented any real threat to the Court's complete recovery.

III

Reconstruction and the Court

THE OUTBREAK of the Civil War shifted the conflict over slavery from the realm of law and politics to the arena of military battle. Under wartime conditions, the Supreme Court's role was naturally minimized, and the Court showed no great desire to allow itself to be drawn into struggles clearly beyond its capacity to win. From time to time opponents of the Lincoln administration would bring a case to the Court designed, at a minimum, to embarrass the administration and, if possible, to hinder the war effort. But the Court, perhaps chastened by *Dred Scott* or perhaps sensing the inadequacies of judicial power in wartime, consistently backed away. In 1863, for example, the Court permitted the Lincoln administration to continue its characterization of the war as a "domestic insurrection" yet allowed it, at the same time, to enjoy all the latitude that went with the practice of international warfare.[1] In 1864, similarly, the Court refused to consider the constitutionality of military trials of civilians in places where the civilian courts were open.[2] Little wonder, then, that Roger Taney feared the Court would never recover its strength and independence.

The secession of the Southern states, Lincoln's Emancipation Proclamation, and the eventual military occupation of the Confederacy raised constitutional and legal problems of such scope and significance, however, that the Court could hardly escape becoming involved once the war ended. In the first few years after the shooting stopped, the Court did indeed play a major role in shaping the nation's policy of Reconstruction.

The problems presented by Reconstruction fell into three broad categories. The first set involved questions of policy. What was to be done about the rebellious states, their property, their war debt, their leaders, and—

most difficult of all—their former slaves? On the one extreme were those who were now called "radical" Republicans, who were convinced that the Civil War had been fought primarily, if not exclusively, in order to eradicate slavery from the United States. On the other extreme were the Southern sympathizers who wanted a negotiated peace leaving matters as close as possible to what they had been before the war began. Finally, there was the middle ground sought by Lincoln: a difficult mixture of resoluteness in defense of the Union and a Reconstruction "with malice towards none, with justice for all."

A second aspect of Reconstruction was constitutional. The secession of the South raised new and complex constitutional issues ranging from the status of the ex-slaves to the status of the Southern states. Were the Southern states ever actually out of the Union? If so, did they immediately resume their status as component states of the Union, or did they have to be readmitted? What restrictions or limitations could be placed on the Southern states when they were allowed to resume their place in the national government? What limits did the Constitution place on the treatment of Southern prisoners and alleged traitors? The list of constitutional questions was seemingly endless, and they were critical, for the constitutional limitations on Reconstruction were taken seriously by all of the actors in the Reconstruction drama. That Reconstruction posed serious constitutional questions had implications not only for the Court's role but also for the determination of policy by Congress and the president.

Finally, Reconstruction must be considered as a problem in politics. The question of *who* would decide the answers to the many questions left undecided at war's end was perhaps as important as *what* would actually be decided. At bottom, Reconstruction politics boiled down to a controversy between Congress, controlled by the radical Republicans, and the White House, led first by Lincoln and then by the much less successful Andrew Johnson. Of course such a dichotomy oversimplifies the case, but it is at bottom correct. The courts, the states, the military, and the inter- and intraparty disputes of the period were all sideshows to the main event.

In the political war that raged along Pennsylvania Avenue in Washington, many were caught in the crossfire. The story of the Supreme Court during Reconstruction is largely the story of how the Court came to find itself in that crossfire, and how it managed to survive with minimal damage.

THE LIMITS OF JUDICIAL POWER

I

As the Civil War drew to a close, the two leading policy options for dealing with Reconstruction came to a head in the controversy over the Wade-Davis Bill in mid-1864. Until that time, the Lincoln administration had attempted to implement the so-called "Ten Per Cent" plan, under which loyalist governments would be recognized in captured Southern territory as soon as ten percent of the population agreed to take a loyalty oath to the Union and to take steps toward establishing a government. As an incentive, the plan offered amnesty to the vast majority of the citizenry in return for such participation. The Ten Per Cent plan was attempted in Louisiana, Arkansas, and Tennessee, but nowhere did it succeed in establishing governments that commanded the loyalty of the population at large.

With the Ten Per Cent plan generally agreed to be a failure, Benjamin Wade and Henry W. Davis (the former a Republican senator from Ohio, the latter a Know Nothing representative from Maryland) proposed what came to be known as the Wade-Davis Bill. The Wade-Davis plan differed from Lincoln's in the following particulars: first, while Lincoln had avoided pushing the Southerners on matters of race, the Wade-Davis bill specifically required the new governments to accept a state constitutional provision prohibiting slavery and guaranteeing "the freedom of all persons." Second, the plan required 50 percent of the 1860 voting population to swear oaths of loyalty before steps toward statehood could be taken. Third, the plan envisioned universal male suffrage. Fourth, delegates to the required state constitutional conventions had to swear not only that they would remain loyal to the union in the future, but that they had been loyal in the past; this was the so-called "ironclad" oath. Finally, and in some ways most importantly, the plan called for the president to appoint a civilian governor to oversee the Reconstruction process in each state. The civilian governors would replace the provisional military governors and would be subject to Senate confirmation.

The policy differences between the Wade-Davis Bill and the Lincoln administration's approach (that is, some modification of the obviously unworkable Ten Per Cent plan) were, as one historian suggests, "substantial, but not, seemingly, irreconcilable."[3] The Wade-Davis Bill, however, represented a critical shift in control over the Reconstruction process. At least relative to the wartime experience, the Wade-Davis plan would have shared control over Reconstruction between the White House and the Congress; prior to the Wade-Davis Bill, Reconstruction was largely a military (and hence executive) prerogative. The Wade-Davis Bill, in the words of the historian Herman Belz, "was definitely antiadministration, representing both political opposition to Lincoln and disagreement with his policy of reconstruction." The essential basis of the bill, Belz concludes, was "the fundamental jurisdictional conflict between the President and Congress over reconstruction."[4]

The key to this shift in control was the replacement of the military governors by civilian governors subject to Senate approval. Under the Constitution, the president is the "Commander in Chief of the Army and Navy of the United States."[5] Lincoln, like later wartime presidents, used his power as commander in chief greatly to expand the powers of his office. It was under this authority that Lincoln issued the Emancipation Proclamation, and it was by the same reasoning that the president asserted the power to control the Reconstruction of the vanquished Southern states. As long as policies were carried out by the military, it was apparent that those policies would be presidential policies. A major objective of the Wade-Davis Bill was therefore to govern "the rebel States *by law*, equalizing all before it"; by contrast, supporters of the congressional plan saw Lincoln's policy as committing the Southern states "to the lawless discretion of Military Governors and Provost Marshals."[6]

The policy differences between Lincoln and the congressional leadership centered around two issues: the extent to which former rebels would be permitted to take part in the government of the reconstructed states, and the extent to which the rights of the freedmen would be guaranteed.[7] Lincoln would have granted amnesty to any Southerner who agreed to take a loyalty oath, with the exception of military officers above the rank of colonel and high-ranking Confederate government officials. All those who received amnesty would then be legally permitted to participate in the Reconstruction of the individual states and in their future government. Congress would have banned from such participation not only those excluded by Lincoln but also all those who held office in rebel *state* governments, and would have further restricted the process of writing new state constitutions to those who could take the ironclad oath that they had *never* participated in the rebellion. The president and Congress also differed on the issue of the freedmen, as Belz explains: "Lincoln emphasized the necessity of educating and of guaranteeing the freedom of the former slaves, but he would allow the states to determine policy for achieving these goals. . . . Congress, on the other hand, proposed to support by legislation the Emancipation Proclamation and make it apply to those parts of the rebel states exempted from the President's original edict."[8]

Given these policy differences, Congress needed a way to ensure that the presidentially appointed governments in fact carried out its program and not the president's. The only available mechanism independent of the White House was the federal court system. It is therefore no coincidence that the federal courts were given an important role in the Wade-Davis scheme. If the administration did not vigorously protect the freedmen, the bill provided a remedy: "if any such persons or their posterity shall be restrained of liberty, under pretence of any claim to such service or labor, the courts of the United States shall, on *habeas corpus*, discharge them." In addition, the bill provided for criminal penalties to be imposed by the federal courts against those convicted of restraining the liberty of any person "with intent to be held or reduced to involuntary servitude or labor."[9]

Because of these differences, Lincoln refused to sign the Wade-Davis Bill; since Congress ended its 1863–64 session only days after passing the bill, this resulted in a pocket veto. A pocket veto does not require that the president return the bill in question to Congress "with his Objections," as the Constitution requires in the case of a conventional veto; nevertheless, perhaps because the 1864 presidential election was only four months away and his party was badly split by the fight over Reconstruction, Lincoln issued a "proclamation" on the Wade-Davis Bill. In this message the president explained that he had refused to accept the bill because he did not want to be "inflexibly committed to any single plan of restoration" and because he did not want to repudiate the steps toward Reconstruction already taken in Louisiana and Arkansas. He expressed the view that Congress could not constitutionally abolish slavery in the states by statute, but indicated that he was "at the same time sincerely hoping and expecting that a constitutional amendment abolishing slavery throughout the nation may be adopted." Despite his objections to the Wade-Davis Bill, Lincoln concluded, "I am fully satisfied with the system for restoration contained in the bill as one very proper plan for the loyal people of any State choosing to adopt it." If the plan envisioned by Wade-Davis were adopted by any state, Lincoln pledged, he would appoint *military* governors "with directions to proceed according to the bill."[10]

The Wade-Davis Proclamation was typically Lincolnesque in its ability to concede very little while at the same time appearing to offer conciliation and compromise. Wade and Davis themselves, still trying to unseat Lincoln, reacted strongly, accusing the president of "dictatorial usurpation" and of perpetrating "a studied outrage on the legislative authority of the people."[11] Lincoln's insistence on appointing military governors particularly annoyed the cosponsors of the congressional plan. On the whole, however, Lincoln's proclamation seemed to unite the Republican Party and played a role in assuring his reelection in November.[12]

The struggle over Wade-Davis was in many respects a harbinger of things to come. Wade-Davis had settled nothing. The major questions of policy—the fate of the freedmen, the treatment of rebels, and the status of the Southern states—were still undetermined. The critical question of who would control Reconstruction was also up in the air. And, finally, the constitutional questions that would certainly arise had hardly been dealt with.

Lincoln's reelection in November 1864 seemed to strengthen the president's hand. Though he still presided over a divided party and a divided nation, Lincoln now could claim a mandate from the people and appeared to have four years to work out the terms of peace. Lincoln's second inaugural address was short, eloquent, and moving, and though it said almost nothing about future policy, it set the tone for reunion: "With malice toward none; with charity for all; with firmness in the right as God gives us the right, let us strive to finish the work we are in; to bind up the nation's wounds, to care for him who shall have borne the battle, and for his widow, and his orphan—to do all which may achieve a just and a lasting peace among ourselves, and with all nations."[13]

Five weeks later, Lincoln would be killed by an assassin's bullet; Andrew Johnson would become president, and the political equation governing Reconstruction would be unpredictably and inescapably altered.

II

The year 1864 also brought a dramatic change for the Supreme Court of the United States: on 12 October, after a long illness, Chief Justice

Roger Brooke Taney died. Taney's death came less than a month before the conclusion of the difficult and uncertain presidential campaign, and Lincoln consequently put off filling the resulting vacancy until after the election. By November, two leading candidates for the position had emerged: Noah Swayne, already serving on the Court as an associate justice, and Salmon Portland Chase, Lincoln's former treasury secretary and a venerable Republican politician.[14]

Chase was the favorite of the radical Republicans, for whom he stood, in the words of Charles Sumner, as "an able, courageous, and determined friend of Freedom, who will never let Freedom suffer by concession or hesitation."[15] Chase's major backer was Senator Charles Sumner, who began to campaign for his man as soon as it became evident that Taney's health was deteriorating. As long as Taney lived, however, Lincoln remained noncommittal. When Taney at last died, Sumner and Chase stepped up their efforts on behalf of Lincoln's reelection bid, at least in part because of the open Court position.[16]

Swayne was the clear choice of the legal profession, led by Lincoln's close friend David Davis, himself an associate justice. Davis wrote Lincoln that Swayne "is a good lawyer, well grounded in the principles of the common law, but not a mere book Lawyer. . . . He has *good temper*, an important requisite, and unless my brother judges have changed since last winter, his appointment would be very agreeable to many of them. In no sense could his appointment be viewed as a political one, a consideration which should have great weight."[17] By contrast, Chase was regarded by many lawyers as a political hack who had not practiced law for many years and who would not leave politics behind when he assumed the bench. Lincoln's major objection to Swayne was that tradition opposed promoting a sitting justice to the chief justiceship.[18]

Chase, however, was the favorite of a large number of Abolitionists and radical Republicans. Throughout October and November, Chase's backers besieged Lincoln with letters urging the president to elevate his former treasury secretary to the Court. At the same time, two factors were working against Chase. First, he and the president did not always get along, personally or politically. Relations between the two men seemed to reach a low point in early 1864 when Chase, while still serving as treasury secretary, announced his candidacy for the presidency. Chase's supporters sought to help his cause by publishing an open letter declaring why their man ought to replace Lincoln as the Republican standard-bearer, but the ploy back-fired. "Both the people and the politicians regarded the cabinet member's candidacy as open disloyalty to his chief," writes the historian David Donald, "and the Chase boom quickly subsided."[19] A few months later, Lincoln and Chase fought over a patronage appointment, and Chase re-signed his treasury post.

Though there was no open display of animosity between the two men, it is clear that personal differences played some part in Chase's resignation and in the president's decision to accept it. One of Chase's supporters told the outgoing treasury secretary that the president had expressed "regret that our relations [i.e., between Lincoln and Chase] were not more free from embarrassment," adding that the president had come to feel "awkward" in his dealings with Chase and that the treasury secretary seemed "con-strained." When the same gentleman asserted that the president still felt a certain esteem for Chase and indeed planned to appoint him chief justice when Taney left the Court, Chase noted in his diary that "if such were the real feelings of Mr. Lincoln he would hardly have refused a personal interview when I asked it or have required me to consult local politics in the choice of an officer, whose character and qualifications were so vitally important to the Department."[20]

Lincoln's second major concern about his former treasury secretary was Chase's obvious desire to be president of the United States. Lincoln's concern was encouraged by the many lawyers and judges who wrote on behalf of Swayne, and Lincoln himself noted Justice Davis's concern that it was "best not to put a man on the bench who would still be aspiring to the Presidency."[21]

On 6 December, Lincoln put an end to all speculation by nominating Chase to be chief justice of the United States. The reasons behind the Chase nomination cannot be known with certainty, but Lincoln was surely aware that the nomination would improve his relations with the radicals and thus had great political value. At any rate, Lincoln's decision on the Chase nomination was consistent with his attempts in December and Janu-ary 1864–65 to reach a compromise with Congress over Reconstruction. The historian Willard King suggests that Lincoln was also moved by the argument that the appointment of Chase would be "magnanimous." Chase's supporters, King adds, "knew Lincoln—he could seldom resist his impulse to magniminity."[22] All that can be said with certainty about the

Chase nomination is that, as Charles A. Dana observed at the time, "That appointment was not made by the President with entire willingness."[23]

The Court over which Chase would preside was nearly as divided as the country itself. The early Chase Court consisted of nine associate justices in addition to the chief. Of the ten justices, five were appointed by Lincoln, five by previous presidents. Four were Republicans, six Democrats. John M. Wayne, now the senior associate, and John Catron, Democrat of Tennessee, were the Court's only Southerners. Nathan Clifford (Maine), Samuel Nelson (Pennsylvania), and Robert Grier (Pennsylvania) were moderate or conservative Northern Democrats. Besides Chase, Lincoln's appointees included pro-Union Democrat Stephen Field of California and Republicans Noah Swayne of Ohio, David Davis of Illinois, and Samuel F. Miller of Iowa. Of the six justices who had voted in the *Dred Scott* case to strike down the Missouri Compromise, only three remained on the Court.

It is widely assumed that with Chase's appointment Lincoln completed his reconstruction of the Court. With the appointment of Chase, it is true, Lincoln had appointed exactly half the Court and its chief. Nelson, moreover, though appointed earlier, had steered a middle course in *Dred Scott*, refusing to go along with Taney in the discussion or decision of difficult and divisive political questions. The historian Carl B. Swisher, expressing the traditional point of view, writes that "in terms of national politics the transition away from the Taney Court began with the election of Abraham Lincoln. . . . On the Court itself the transition came with the deaths of Justices Daniel and McLean and the resignation of Justice Campbell, and their replacement by Republicans with at least moderately abolitionist sympathies."[24] If the transition away from the Taney Court began with the election of Lincoln, it was surely confirmed with the death of Taney himself.

It is true that the five Lincoln appointees held the balance of power on the Court. But these five men were as different from each other as they were from their more senior brethren. The differences among them can be explained by Lincoln's method of selection: he looked first for men who were loyal to the Union, and second for men who would help him meet various personal and political obligations.[25] Such selection criteria practically guaranteed that the Lincoln appointees would be politically and personally diverse.

Chase alone could be classified as a "radical" Republican; the others, while staunchly pro-Union, were moderate Republicans (except Field, who was a Democrat). Davis was a close personal friend of the president and remained so until Lincoln's death. Swayne was a successful lawyer with solid connections among the Ohio Republican leadership; Miller was a leading Republican politician from Iowa. Field was chief justice of the state of California, and the brother of David Dudley Field of New York; the latter had played a role in securing the Republican nomination for Lincoln in 1860. Evidence that Lincoln did not look too deeply into his appointees' legal views can be found in Field's attitude toward the Legal Tender Act, the centerpiece of the Republican's scheme to finance the war. While chief justice of California, Field wrote an opinion denying the application of the Legal Tender Act to state and local taxes.[26]

The differences among the five Lincoln appointees reflected the differences in the larger world of Union politics as the war neared its end. Historians have rejected the idea that the Republican Party was neatly divided into well-defined "moderate" and "radical" factions; still, while the lines of division were not neat and were constantly shifting, the party was divided throughout the war years and afterwards. David H. Donald, for example, has shown that of the ninety-nine voting Republican congressmen in the Thirty-eighth Congress, fifty consistently voted the radical position on six key measures while forty-nine did not.[27]

The main line of division within the Republican party in the last years of the Lincoln presidency was over who would control the Reconstruction of the rebel states. Radical Republicans "favored congressional, rather than presidential, control over the Reconstruction process and . . . looked toward punitive action against the Southern rebels."[28] In general, it can also be said that the radicals were strongly committed to securing and protecting the rights of the freed blacks.

The other major set of issues dividing the Republican Party involved the civil liberties of civilians in the loyal states. Congress had accepted and ratified Lincoln's suspension of habeas corpus during the war, but many Republicans did so with reluctance, and a number spoke out against the most serious abuses. Attorney General Bates, referring to himself, wrote in dismay to a friend that "at least *one* member of the government did sometimes resist capricious power and the arbitrary domination of armed forces." So delicate was the question of military government and martial law that Congress decided to postpone a measure, introduced by Lyman Trumbull, to regulate and control martial law by statute. On the final vote, as Allan Nevins points out, "radical Republicans like Fessenden, Collamer, and Wade stood alongside balky conservatives like Bayard and Saulsbury."[29]

Once the war ended, the Supreme Court would be asked to decide cases dealing with these and other controversial issues. In such cases there was no single "Republican" position; on the contrary, these were issues which divided moderates and radicals throughout the war years. Furthermore, the political situation during the mid-1860s was inherently unstable, as the definitions of "moderate" and "radical" shifted and as new issues emerged. Though the Court was now in many respects Lincoln's Court, it was not and could not be a mere rubber stamp for his or any other "Republican" position on Reconstruction measures. All that was certain was that the Court would often find itself in the middle not only of interparty but of intraparty strife in the last half of the tumultuous 1860s.

III

The Supreme Court's first brush with the issues of Reconstruction did not come until 1866. The 1864–65 term, like the 1863–64 term, was relatively quiet, giving Chase some time to settle in as chief justice. The calm of 1864 and 1865 would soon give way to a maelstrom; the case of *Ex Parte Milligan* would plunge the Supreme Court back into the political arena it had largely avoided since *Dred Scott*.

Ex Parte Milligan[30] involved the constitutionality of military trials of civilians in areas where the civil courts were still open. The issue of military trials had been a gnawing one throughout the war years, but the Court, perhaps sensing its own weakness, managed to avoid the issue as long as the war lasted.[31] When the war ended, the Court at last took up the issue.

Lambdin P. Milligan, a civilian resident of Indiana, had been arrested in 1864 on charges of disloyalty and of giving "aid and comfort to the rebels." He was tried by a military commission, according to the procedures set out by President Lincoln in 1862. He was found guilty and, on 21 October

1864, sentenced to death. In May 1865, Milligan petitioned the United States circuit court for the district of Indiana, asking to be discharged from military custody and "either turned over to the proper civil tribunal, to be proceeded against according to the law of the land, or to be discharged from custody altogether." Milligan pointed out that he was a citizen of a loyal state; that at the time of his arrest the civilian courts of the United States were open and functioning there; and that, though given the opportunity, a civilian grand jury had declined to bring charges against him. He asserted that the "military commission had no jurisdiction to try him upon the charges preferred, or upon any charges whatever."[32]

The Supreme Court heard arguments in *Ex Parte Milligan* on 5 to 13 March 1866. Appearing for the government were the attorney general of the United States, James Speed; Henry Stanberry, who would replace Speed as attorney general in July 1866, and who would later defend Andrew Johnson during his impeachment trial; and Benjamin F. Butler, a radical Republican who would be one of Johnson's chief accusers at the impeachment. Appearing on behalf of Milligan were David Dudley Field, the brother of Supreme Court justice Stephen Field; James A. Garfield, war hero, Republican congressman from Ohio, and later president of the United States; and Jeremiah S. Black, formerly Buchanan's attorney general. Counsel on both sides were distinguished not only for their prominence and legal ability, but also for their divided political and partisan loyalties. In particular, it should be noted, there were Republicans on both sides of the case, a reflection of the long standing division in the party over the Lincoln administration's alleged disregard of civil rights and due process of law.

The oral arguments in *Milligan* attracted considerable attention. Justice Davis's wife, perhaps reflecting her husband's long-standing opposition to the military trial of civilians, wrote her son in March 1866 that the *Milligan* case "is considered the most important case *ever* brought before the court."[33] The *New York Times* correspondent covering the oral arguments wrote that "the case involves one of the most important questions that has been submitted to the Court since its organization."[34] The oral arguments were also given extensive coverage in the Democratic press.[35]

On 3 April 1866, the last day of the Court's term, Chief Justice Chase announced the result in *Milligan*. The majority of the Court held

1. That on the facts stated . . . a writ of *habeas corpus* ought to be issued. . . .

2. That . . . Milligan ought to be discharged from custody. . . .

3. That . . . the military commission . . . had no jurisdiction legally to try and sentence [Milligan]. . . . [36]

The opinions of the justices were not handed down until the opening of the next term, in December 1866. Though it was apparent in April that there would be some dissent from the opinion of the Court, it was not yet clear how many justices would dissent or on what grounds.[37]

The Court's April announcement of the result in *Milligan*—in sharp contrast to the reading of the opinions eight months later—attracted very little attention from Republicans. Some Democratic papers rejoiced at what they called the "vindication" of the Democratic Party. The *New York World*, for example, beamed that "the principles of the Democratic Party stand the test of time."[38] The Republican press, however, raised little if any outcry at the time the result was announced and, in fact, showed little interest in the case. Historians who have canvassed the press reaction to *Milligan* can indeed cite many examples of criticism of the Court by the Republican press and politicians, but they come almost entirely from December, when the full opinions of the Court in the *Milligan* case were finally released, or afterward.[39] In April, it is clear, the Court's announcement "occasioned no great outcry."[40] There was, in short, no reason at that time to suspect that the *Milligan* decision would provoke the kind of response engendered by the release of the opinions eight months later.

Why did the Republicans' reaction to the announcement of the *Milligan* decision differ so sharply from their reaction to the Court's full opinion a few months later? Historians have responded to this question in a number of ways. Some simply ignore the issue, analyzing the Republican response to the reading of the opinions while failing to report the corresponding indifference to the original announcement of the decision.[41] Others explain the mystery by suggesting that Republicans paid little attention to *Milligan* in April because, as Charles Warren points out, "on this date, the Court confined itself to a mere announcement of its judgment, without setting forth its reasoning."[42] Presumably it was the Court's reasoning, and not the decision itself, that caused the outcry. Such a hypothesis is unpersuasive, however, for the difference in response to the Milligan announcement in

April and the opinion in December cannot be explained away simply by claiming that the country did not understand the significance of the decision until the Court's reasoning was made clear. American politicians are not known for comprehending the subtleties and fine points of legal decisions; one need only look to the response to *Dred Scott* to appreciate this. Surely, if the Court's opinion had been of great importance to the Republicans in April, they would have at least begun to speculate on the reasoning behind the Court's decision; in fact, the issues involved were clear from the briefs and arguments before the Court.

Another explanation rests on the changing political terrain between April and December. Willard King, in his biography of Justice Davis, argues that the April announcement occasioned "no great outcry" because "at that time the quarrel between the Radicals and President Johnson over reconstruction had been in its early stages. By December, however, when Davis and Chase delivered their opinions, this battle had been joined."[43] In April, echoes Stanley Kutler, "the hostility between President Johnson and Congress was still in an embryonic state and the battle over Reconstruction had not been fully joined; more important, the mere statement that there was no military jurisdiction surely touched sympathetic and responsive chords in the political and legal communities."[44]

King and Kutler are assuredly on the right track. At the same time, it is not enough to state simply that the battle between Congress and the president had not yet been joined in April. In fact, to argue that by April the tension between Johnson and the congressional leaders was in an "embryonic" stage understates the tension between the two branches at the time of Chase's announcement of the *Milligan* result. King and Kutler are correct, however, in pointing to the changing political situation between April and December in an effort to explain the Republican responses to *Milligan*, and it is to the general contours of Reconstruction politics that we must now turn.

IV

By the time Chief Justice Chase announced the result in *Ex Parte Milligan* on 3 April 1866, the break between Andrew Johnson and the congressional radicals was almost complete. The historian Eric McKitrick writes, "The critical period of President Johnson's relations with Congress may be said to have terminated on April 6, 1866, with the successful repassage of the Civil Rights Bill over the President's veto."[45] Though McKitrick's selection of 6 April as the key date is somewhat arbitrary, it is clear that the early months of 1866 do indeed represent a "critical period" in the relations between the legislative and executive branches and in the shaping of the future course of Reconstruction. The days surrounding the Court's 3 April announcement of the *Milligan* result were among the most critical days of all.

Between April and December 1865, the year before the *Milligan* announcement, Congress was not in session, and President Johnson carried out his own plan of Reconstruction. When Congress reconvened in December, the tensions between Johnson and the congressional Republicans became evident. Still, though Johnson's performance in the months since Lincoln's assassination had disappointed many radicals, the majority of Republican congressmen seemed willing to negotiate with the president and work out an acceptable compromise.

The vehicle for congressional negotiation with the White House was to be the Joint Committee on Reconstruction, a special committee of fifteen appointed to "inquire into the condition of the States which formed the so-called Confederate States of America, and report whether they or any of them are entitled to be represented in either House of Congress."[46] Though the radical Republican Thaddeus Stevens (R.-Pa.) was a member of the committee, its overall composition revealed a "strong moderate balance." As William Pitt Fessenden (R.-Me.), the chairman of the committee, wrote of Johnson in December 1865, "I am disposed and ready to support him to the best of my ability."[47]

By the following April the political balance in Washington had been transformed. Johnson had destroyed any chance of compromise by consistently refusing to support congressional measures that sought a middle ground. The two key congressional proposals were the Freedmen's Bureau Bill and the Civil Rights Bill, both of which Johnson vetoed in the spring of 1866. The president's vetoes made it clear that Johnson would insist on Reconstruction on his own terms, which by then were unacceptable to both the radical and moderate wings of the Republican Party. The Senate, still hoping for compromise, refused to override Johnson's veto of the Freedmen's Bureau Bill in February; its override of the Civil Rights veto on 6

April was a clear indication that the possibility of compromise was all but gone.

The central purpose of both the Freedmen's Bureau Bill and the Civil Rights Bill was to protect the former slaves. Though by law slavery had been ended by the Thirteenth Amendment, in reality Southern blacks were still far from free. Under President Johnson's Reconstruction policy, "provisional" governments had been established across the South. These new governments—composed largely of former Confederate officers and political leaders—immediately enacted "Black Codes" designed to control the now-free black population. Though the codes varied from state to state, all treated the Negro race as inferior and withheld rights and privileges that were the birthright of the white population.[48] The existence of the codes was deeply annoying to many Northerners and especially to the radical Republicans in Congress. Many saw in the codes an unofficial but effective return to the slave system.

Hence the need for federal protection of the freedmen. Republicans approached the problem from two directions at once. One possibility was to offer the freedmen the protection of the Union army, guaranteeing at least minimal rights through the force of arms. A second possibility was to leave the task of protecting the freedmen to the federal judges, who could be authorized if necessary to supersede the process of the state courts. The second alternative was more appealing, since it offered a permanent solution based on law instead of a temporary remedy based on force. For many reasons, however, the first alternative was more practical. For one thing, the federal judiciary was not yet functioning in many of the Southern states. For another, it was not yet clear that the South would accept the rule of law unless the federal courts could count on the support of Union troops.

Very early in the first session of the Thirty-ninth Congress, moderate Republicans moved to provide military protection for the freedmen by means of what became known as the Freedmen's Bureau Bill. On 5 January 1866, Senator Lyman Trumbull (R.-Ill.) introduced a bill "to enlarge the powers of the Freedmen's Bureau," an agency which had been set up a year before to provide economic, medical, and educational relief for former slaves and other refugees.[49] Trumbull's bill would have extended the life of the agency indefinitely; originally, the bureau was to go out of existence one year after the end of hostilities. The bill would have expanded the bureau and given it jurisdiction over refugees and freedmen in all parts of the United States, not only in the South. It would have expanded the agency's relief and educational programs, and would have allowed the bureau to purchase land for the use of the freedmen and for the building of schools and asylums.[50]

More importantly, Trumbull's bill would have authorized the Freedmen's Bureau to provide direct protection for any person denied rights guaranteed by law. The language of the proposed statute was broad:

Whenever in any State or district in which the original course of judicial proceedings has been interrupted by the rebellion, and wherein, in consequence of any State or local law, ordinance, police or other regulation, custom, or prejudice, any of the civil rights or immunities belonging to white persons . . . are refused or denied to Negroes . . . refugees, or any other persons, on account of race, color, or any previous condition of slavery . . . except as a punishment for crime . . . it is to be the duty of the President of the United States, through the commissioner [of the Freedmen's Bureau], to extend military protection and jurisdiction over all cases affecting such persons so discriminated against.[51]

Any person accused of such discrimination was to be tried before "the officers and agents" of the bureau, and, if convicted, could be sentenced to a fine of $1,000 and imprisonment for one year. The bureau also would have been given authority to try "all cases affecting negroes, mullattoes, freedmen, refugees, or other persons who are discriminated against." These quasi-judicial powers were to be conferred on the Freedmen's Bureau only in states where "the ordinary course of judicial proceedings has been interrupted by the rebellion."

Congressional support for the Freedmen's Bureau Bill was predicated on the Republicans' rejection of Johnson's provisional state governments and on their general distaste for the Black Codes promulgated by those governments. These developments, combined with the president's rejection of military rule as inappropriate in peacetime, had dramatically altered the political situation. Whereas Congress had rejected the idea of military rule in the debate over Wade-Davis, they now embraced it as preferable to the continuation of the unsupervised provisional governments. Furthermore, there was genuine hope in early 1866 that relations with the White House could be improved once Johnson and the Congress began to negotiate over Reconstruction policy; after all, such an opportunity had existed only since Congress's return for its December 1865 session. "We are confident that there is no necessary incompatibility between the views and purposes of Congress and those of the President," wrote the *New York Tribune* in January. "And," the paper continued, "we feel sure that frank, earnest, kindly conferences between the Capitol and the White-House [*sic*] will speedily and almost certainly remove any obstacles which may seem to exist to a cordial and thorough cooperation."[52]

Peaceful coexistence between the two political branches was not to be. The Senate passed the Freedmen's Bureau Bill on 25 January, and the House concurred on 6 February. Every Republican in the Senate, and almost every Republican in the House, voted in favor. It was assumed that the president would sign the bill, perhaps exacting as a price the readmission of his home state of Tennessee. On 19 February, however, Johnson vetoed the Freedmen's Bureau Bill and sent a stiff and unconciliatory message to the Senate. He told the Senate that the bill was unnecessary, expensive, dangerous, unconstitutional, and unfair. He objected that the power of the military tribunals established in the bill was unlimited and that "from these arbitrary tribunals there lies no appeal, no writ of error to any of the courts" of the United States. A vote to override Johnson's veto failed by two votes in the Senate.[53]

With Johnson's veto of the Freedmen's Bureau Bill, Congress turned to a consideration of the second measure introduced by Trumbull, a bill "to protect all persons in the United States in their civil rights, and furnish the means of their vindication."[54] Even after Johnson's veto of the Freedmen's Bill, and even after the president made an embarassing drunken speech denouncing the Joint Reconstruction Committee (calling that body "an irresponsible central directory" and accusing Sumner and others of plotting to "incite assassination"), all hope for compromise was not yet gone. If Johnson could be persuaded to sign the Civil Rights Bill, Congress's main goals could be satisfied even without the Freedmen's Bureau Bill. The latter, after all, was intended only as a stopgap measure and was to have effect, in the words of Trumbull, only "until peace shall be firmly established and the civil tribunals of the country shall be restored with an assurance that they may peacefully enforce the laws without opposition."[55] The Civil Rights Bill, intended as a permanent guarantee of civil freedoms, was by far the more important measure in the long run.

There was, moreover, no reason to think that Johnson would look negatively on the Civil Rights Bill. Unlike the Freedmen's Bureau Bill, the Civil Rights Bill established no large bureaucracy; depended on civil rather than military rule; was intended to be permanent, for wartime and peacetime; and was to cover the entire country rather than only the South. Though Johnson had hinted in his veto message that he objected in principle to the passage of important legislation before the Southern representatives were seated, it seemed unlikely he would push that argument to such an extreme as to endanger the Civil Rights Bill.

As ultimately enacted, the Civil Rights Act of 1866 declared that all citizens (including, of course, the former slaves)

> shall have the same right in every State and Territory of the United States to make and enforce contracts, to sue, be parties, and give evidence, to inherit, purchase, lease, sell, hold, and convey real personal property, and to full and equal benefit of all laws and proceedings for the security of person and property as is enjoyed by white citizens, and shall be subject to like punishment, pains, and penalties, and to none other, any law, statute, ordinance, regulation, or custom to the contrary notwithstanding.[56]

The bill made it a federal crime for any person "under cover of law" to subject "any inhabitant of any State or Territory to the deprivation of any right secured or protected by this act"; gave the the district courts of the United States jurisdiction, "exclusively of the courts of the several States," over "all crimes and offenses committed against the provisions of this act"; and gave the federal courts concurrent jurisdiction in "any cause, civil or criminal" which affects persons "who are denied or cannot enforce their rights in the State courts." The law authorized the president to use the army and navy to enforce the act and gave the right of final appeal to the Supreme Court of the United States "upon all questions of law arising in any cause under the provisions of this act."[57]

By emphasizing the differences between the Freedmen's Bureau Bill and the Civil Rights Bill, some congressional leaders still held out the possibility of a compromise with the president, but the tone of the congressional position was hardening. Senator John Sherman, for example, declared that he was prepared to support the president, despite the Freedmen's Bureau veto, if Johnson stood in support of the freedmen's rights. "As long as he stands by that declaration," Sherman said, "I will not quarrel with him about the means." But, warned Sherman, "Let him fail to do that, and I will denounce him as freely and as bitterly as any Senator on this floor."[58] The Civil Rights Bill, approved by the Senate on 2 February and by the House on 13 March, was "generally approved as moderate and sensible," writes McKitrick, "and most of Johnson's supporters hoped he would sign it."[59] Sherman, again, held out the possibility of accord with the White House: "If he sign it," said Sherman of the Civil Rights bill, "it will be a solemn pledge of the law-making power of the nation that the negroes shall have secured to them all these natural and inalienable rights. I believe the President will sign it."[60]

Sherman was wrong; on 27 March 1866, Johnson sent the Senate a message vetoing the Civil Rights Bill. Now breaking irrevocably with the congressional Republicans, Johnson told the Senate that "the details of the bill seem fraught with evil." He complained that through this bill Congress threatened to convert "the State judge into a mere ministerial officer, bound to decree according to the will of Congress"; that the bill would make it impossible for the states to discriminate against the Negro race in any way, including in their social relations with whites; and that the bill would "foment discord between the two races." Though Johnson pledged to "cheerfully cooperate with Congress in any measure that may be necessary for the protection of the civil rights of the freedmen . . . in conformity with the provisions of the Federal Constitution," his veto seemed to signal the end to any chance for normal relations between the legislative and executive branches.[61]

On 2 April, to complete his utter rejection of Congress's policy, Johnson issued a proclamation declaring that "the insurrection which heretofore existed" in the Southern states "is at an end, and is henceforth to be so regarded." In the same message, Johnson stated that "standing armies, military occupation, martial law, military tribunals, and the suspension of the privilege of *habeas corpus* are, in time of peace dangerous to public liberty, incompatible with the individual rights of the citizen, contrary to the genius and spirit of our free institutions, and exhaustive of the natural resources, and ought not, therefore, to be sanctioned or allowed except in cases of actual necessity."[62] On 6 April, the Senate repassed the Civil Rights Act over Johnson's veto. On 9 April, the House followed suit.

Johnson's opposition to the Civil Rights Act, expressed in constitutional terms, gave new urgency to the ongoing debates over what would become the Fourteenth Amendment. Because a number of constitutional problems remained unsolved, some form of constitutional amendment to go beyond the Thirteenth (which formally abolished slavery) had been under consideration since late 1865. Central among them was the question of representation for the Southern states; slaves had been counted as three-fifths of free persons for the purpose of representation, and many Republicans sought to tie voting rights for the freedmen to the increase in the Southern delegation in the House of Representatives that would come from counting them in full. Also left unsettled were the Confederate and U.S. war debt and the eligibility of Confederate activists for federal offices.

Another key aspect of the debate over the Fourteenth Amendment centered around the Civil Rights Bill. Some Republican congressmen, though supportive of the bill, were concerned that Congress lacked constitutional authority to pass the measure. Jonathan Bingham (R.-Ohio) was the leading exponent of this position, even to the point of voting against the Civil Rights Act. Thus Bingham proposed that the Constitution be amended to guarantee both due process of law and the equal protection of the laws to all persons under the jurisdiction of the United States.[63] Others supported such an amendment out of fear that even if the Civil Rights Act were constitutional, its provisions could be repealed by a later Congress. The Fourteenth Amendment passed Congress in June 1866, but its incorporation into the Constitution would be delayed by some two years as Congress fought with Johnson over the status of the Southern states.

Congress's actions in early 1866, though moving away from military rule, did not contemplate an end to the military's involvement in Reconstruction; the Civil Rights act specifically provided that all officials "appointed to execute any warrant or process" under the act had "authority to summon and call to their aid . . . such portion of the land and naval forces of the United States . . . as may be necessary to the performance of the duty with which they are charged."[64] Still, combined with the president's proclamation ending the state of hostilities, the Civil Rights Act reduced the army to the role of carrying out the orders of the federal judges and other civilian officials. On 9 April, Assistant Adjutant General Edward D.

Townsend cautioned the commander of the military district of Georgia that "it is not expedient . . . to resort to military tribunals in any case where justice can be attained through the medium of civil authority."[65] Later, the commander of the Louisiana district interpreted Townsend's order to mean, in the words of the historian James E. Sefton, that "military power was to be used when necessary to enforce federal court processes but unnecessary interference with civil authority was barred."[66] General George H. Thomas, commander of the military district of Tennessee, wrote that the order "virtually denies to the Military all supervision of the civil [power] . . . or the right to enforce their orders, where they in any degree collide with the decision of a civil Magistrate."[67] As the *New York World* put it, "The department intrusted by the [Civil Rights] bill with the enforcement of its provisions is not the Executive but the Judiciary."[68]

In April 1866, then, the idea of military Reconstruction seemed all but dead. The president had declared all hostilities at an end and had vetoed the Freedmen's Bureau Bill partly on the grounds that military rule over the South was no longer appropriate. Congress, in response, made the Civil Rights Act the centerpiece of its Reconstruction program. Instead of the army, the federal courts would enforce the freedmen's newly acquired rights. Congress would eventually return to military Reconstruction when it met for the second session of the Thirty-ninth Congress in December 1866. In the spring of that year, however, for a brief period, military Reconstruction took a back seat.

In the midst of all this political activity, on 3 April, the Supreme Court announced its decision in *Ex Parte Milligan*. There is little wonder that the announcement was largely ignored by the Republicans. The nation was preoccupied; military rule had just been denounced by the only man who had the power to impose it, and the freedmen's security had just been placed solidly in the hands of the civilian courts of the United States rather than those of the military. The Court's announcement was perhaps of historical interest, but it had almost no relevance to the political realities facing the nation in April 1866.

V

The *Milligan* opinion was not read until 17 December 1866, just days after the opening of the second session of the Thirty-ninth Congress and barely a month after the congressional elections of 1866. The elections constituted a sort of referendum on the Fourteenth Amendment and on congressional Reconstruction policy and brought to a head the growing tension between the president and the congressional leadership. The results of the voting spelled a clear defeat for Johnson and made it clear that the congressional Republicans would be in charge of setting Reconstruction policy. Just what Congress's Reconstruction policy would look like, and precisely what conditions would have to be met by the Southern states prior to read-mission, were for the moment up in the air.

Because the second session of the Thirty-ninth Congress ended with the enactment of a whole set of radical Reconstruction measures, it is easy to overestimate the influence of the radicals as the session began. "Though eager for new and harsher measures to impose upon the South," writes David Donald, "veteran radical leaders were unsure of their strength dur-ing the early part of the new session, and their less experienced followers vainly 'waited month after month for some of these old and experienced legislators to bring forward something upon the subject of reconstruc-tion.' "[69] "Stevens, Sumner, [John] Broomall [R.-Pa.], and other radical congressmen were determined from the beginning of the session to impose a program of radical reconstruction on the South," echoes Eric McKitrick, but beyond this general sentiment there was little agreement on what shape the policy should take. Stevens favored confiscation of property, while the others favored "a minimum program of universal Negro suffrage and wide disenfranchisement of ex-Confederates," neither of which had been se-cured by the Fourteenth Amendment.[70] All the radicals did agree on was "that the existing state governments in the South—with the exception of Tennessee's—must be set aside and replaced for the time being by direct federal rule." As the session wore on, "direct federal rule" came to mean military rule.

The radicals' position in the Thirty-ninth Congress was strengthened in the first few months of the new session by a series of events that drew attention to the inadequacy of Johnson's policy and intensified the North-ern appetite for harsher measures against the ex-rebel states. With the single exception of Tennessee, the provisional Johnson governments all rejected the Fourteenth Amendment; at the same time, reports of "steady persecutions of Unionists and Negroes in the South" came with increased frequency and occupied the attention of the Northern press.[71] To these events was added the release of the Supreme Court's opinion in *Milligan*, and it is in this context that the Republicans' response to *Milligan* must be understood.

Justice Davis's opinion in *Milligan* is short and eloquent and is justly regarded as "one of the bulwarks of American liberty."[72] For Davis, the legal questions were simple and straightforward. "The Constitution of the United States is a law for rulers and people, equally in war and peace, and covers with the shield of its protection all classes of men, at all times, and under all circumstances."[73] The Constitution places the judicial power "in one Supreme Court and in such inferior courts as the Congress may from time to time ordain and establish"; "certainly no part of the judicial power of the country was conferred" on the military commission which tried Milligan, Davis wrote. Thus "one of the plainest constitutional provisions was . . . infringed when Milligan was tried by a court not ordained and established by Congress, and not composed of judges appointed during good behavior."[74] Nor was Milligan's trial justified under the "laws and usages of war," for at the time of his arrest and trial in Indiana "the Federal authority was always unopposed, and its courts always open to hear criminal accusations and redress grievances." Martial law can be properly applied, Davis concluded, only if "in foreign invasion or civil war, the courts are actually closed, and it is impossible to administer criminal justice according to law," and then only "on the theatre of active military operations, where war really prevails" and only until the civilian courts are reinstated.[75]

Chief Justice Chase concurred with the result reached by Davis but entered a separate opinion. Joined by Justices Wayne, Swayne, and Miller, Chase argued that the military commission in question lacked the authority to try and convict Milligan, but only because the commission was not authorized to do so by Congress. Chase then set out the core of his disagreement with the majority:

The [majority] opinion . . . asserts not only that the military commission held in Indiana was not authorized by Congress, but that it was not in the power of Congress to authorize it, from which it may be thought to follow that Congress has no power to indemnify those officers who composed the commission against liability in civil courts for acting as members of it.

We cannot agree to this.[76]

In the view of the minority, Congress could authorize the trial of civilians by military courts during time of actual war; "where peace exists," they were careful to point out, "the laws of peace must prevail."[77]

At the beginning of his majority opinion, Justice Davis expressed his view of the Court's responsibility in the *Milligan* case as compared to its resolution of cases during the war, such as *Ex Parte Vallandingham*: "During the late wicked Rebellion, the temper of the times did not allow that calmness in deliberation and discussion so necessary to a correct conclusion of a purely judicial question. *Then*, considerations of safety were mingled with the exercise of power; and feelings and interests prevailed which are happily terminated. *Now* that the public safety is assured, this question, as well as all others, can be discussed and decided without passion or the admixture of any element not required to form a legal judgment."[78] Despite Davis's assessment of the political situation at the time his opinion was read, however, the *Milligan* decision was not received in an atmosphere of "calmness in deliberation and discussion." Instead, the *Milligan* decision set off what Davis himself called a "political tempest."[79]

The Republicans' December response to *Milligan* was predicated on three factors, one practical, one speculative, and one political. Practically, there was legitimate concern that the Court's decision meant that the quasi-military freedmen's courts established for the protection of the newly freed slaves were now unconstitutional. Whereas in April these courts seemed dead anyway, the victim of Johnson's veto, in December the situation was different. In July, Congress had passed a new Freedmen's Bureau Bill, and this time the Republicans had the votes to override Johnson's veto. In December, therefore, the freedmen's courts were operating to protect the rights of the ex-slaves, and the Court's decision threatened their existence.

Concern over the freedmen's courts was legitimate. The second Freedmen's Bureau Act provided for military jurisdiction over various offenses "whenever . . . the ordinary course of judicial proceedings has been interrupted by the rebellion";[80] it was possible, though by no means necessary, to read Davis's opinion so as to outlaw such trials, at least in peacetime. (One counterargument was to suggest that the civil courts were not in fact functional in the Southern states, thus making military trials necessary; in light of President Johnson's declaration ending the hostilities and establishing provisional civil governments, however, such an argument was shaky at best.) Republican fears were heightened when, shortly after *Milligan*, Johnson ordered the release of a prisoner who had been convicted by a Freedmen's Bureau court. Later, Johnson frustrated efforts by General Oliver Howard, commissioner of the Bureau, to present a case to the Supreme Court to clarify *Milligan* and permit the Bureau's courts to operate.[81] Commented the *New York Herald*: "The President insists that the decision applies as well to Virginia as Indiana, and eager to please the blood-hounds of the Old Dominion, he orders the dismissal of a military tribunal engaged in trying the murderer of a black man. . . . The President will not wait, but wishes with unseemly haste to issue his order to all departmental commanders on rebel soil *to respect the decision of the Court*." The Republicans' fear, according to the *Boston Daily Advertiser*, was that the Court's decision "overthrows the Freedmen's Bureau, and renders the Army wholly powerless in the South."[82]

A second factor which made *Milligan* less palatable to the Republicans than it had been in April was political. When the Thirty-ninth Congress reconvened in December 1866, two things were clear. First, the Democrats' only hope in stopping Reconstruction was a strategy of "deadlock"; that is, instead of pursuing a positive program of their own, they were constrained to attempt to prevent the enactment of any Republican program. Above all, this meant exploiting the obvious gulf between Johnson and the congressional radicals and making sure that the gulf was never narrowed. Second, the Republican party was itself divided into at least three groups: a radical wing, which insisted on putting the South under military rule and reorganizing the Southern state governments; a moderate group, which regarded the Fourteenth Amendment as an offer of terms to the South and was thus inclined away from further measures; and another group that was prepared to consider the Fourteenth Amendment an offer of terms but which was unwilling to "hold the offer open indefinitely in the face of Southern intransigence."[83]

Careful exploitation of *Milligan* by both the Democrats and the radicals was useful, therefore, in moving the moderates one way or the other— either toward Johnson, in which case Congress would be deadlocked, or toward the radicals, in which case the radical program would be enacted.

The Democrats could use the *Milligan* decision as the South had used *Dred Scott*: by insisting that any compromise involving military rule violated the Constitution, they hoped to strengthen Johnson's position, divide the Republicans, and eliminate the middle ground—the result, they hoped, would be no policy at all. The radicals, on the other hand, could use *Milligan* to discredit Johnson's position, pushing the moderates in their direction and altering the balance of power. They followed Lincoln's actions toward *Dred Scott* by denouncing *Milligan* as part of a conspiracy by Johnson, the Democratic Party, and the Supreme Court to frustrate Reconstruction and bolster the South.

Finally, the decision engendered fear that the Supreme Court would interfere with the future course of Reconstruction. The *Indianapolis Journal*, for example, warned that the decision was "clearly a forerunner of other decisions looking to a defeat of Republican ascendancy and to a restoration of Southern domination."[84] Fears of judicial interference with radical Reconstruction increased in direct proportion to the degree of radicalism espoused by a given critic of the Court. The *Washington Chronicle*, at the radical pole, declared that "time and reflection have only served to strengthen the conviction of the partisan character of the decision and the apprehension that it is the precursor of other decisions in the interest of unrepentant treason in the support of an apostate President."[85]

At first glance, it is not clear why the radical position of military Reconstruction had suddenly become a congressional rather than an executive policy. As events would make clear, however, military Reconstruction was accompanied by an attempt by Congress to take control of the army from the president and vest it in General Ulysses S. Grant, whom they in turn sought to control by statute. This attempt to circumvent the Commander-in-Chief Clause of the Constitution was necessary to resolve Congress's problem of seeking to punish the South through military rule despite their virtually complete estrangement from the White House. By early 1867, military Reconstruction had become a purely congressional policy, not an executive one, and *Milligan* was therefore a threat to Congress's power, not the president's.[86]

It is in this context that the Republican reaction to *Milligan* must be understood. The Republicans' attacks on the Court were indeed sharp, but they were motivated more by the exigencies of the ever-changing political situation than by a deep or fundamental hostility toward the Supreme Court. Moreover, the Republicans' comments did not occur in isolation; they were part and parcel of an ongoing debate in which the Democrats used *Milligan* for their own purposes as well. Finally, it is a mistake to assume that Republican hostility toward the Court lasted for a long time; in fact, after the passage of the Reconstruction Act of 1867 in March, attacks on the Court dropped off considerably. They would resurface, under very different circumstances, in 1868.[87]

Faced with a Court decision that threatened both their existing and projected Reconstruction program, the Republicans sought to narrow the scope and to undermine the legitimacy of the decision. As after *Dred Scott*, the Republicans argued that much of Davis's argument was obiter dicta and therefore not binding on the Court in the future. In particular, the Court decided in *Milligan* that the military trial there in question had not been authorized by Congress; therefore, the Court's holding that Milligan's trial would have been illegal even if authorized by the legislature was mere hypothetical speculation. It is true, James F. Wilson (R.-Iowa) conceded, that the Court denied Congress the power to authorize military trials in cases such as Milligan's. "But," he added, "this is a piece of judicial impertinence which we are not bound to respect. No such question was before the Court in the Milligan case, and that tribunal wandered beyond the record in treating of it."[88] Lyman Trumbull tried similarly to narrow the impact of *Milligan*: "Military commissions are just as legal as courts-martial, where they were properly authorized. There has been no decision that you cannot try a person by military commission. The decision was that a particular military commission in a certain State, under the particular circumstances of that case, was not authorized to try the party, but military commissions in the disloyal States have never been pronounced to be illegal."[89]

Other tactics used by the Republicans to combat the potential impact of *Milligan* included claiming that the decision was wrong: "That Congress could authorize such [military] trials . . . I have no doubt at all," said Thaddeus Stevens. "That part of the opinion of the Supreme Court is, I ought not to say absurd, but I think clearly erroneous."[90] They also argued that the condition of national emergency or the principles of international law justified extreme measures, no matter what the lawyers might say:

"The Supreme Court," as Henry J. Raymond (R.-N.Y.) put it, "has declared that the Constitution as interpreted by that court is and must be the supreme law alike for rulers and people under all circumstances and at all times, in peace and war. . . . Now, for all practical purposes in the ordinary movements and operations of government this is well enough. . . . But as an absolute statement of the nature and residence of national sovereignty I cannot accept it."⁹¹

The Democrats, at the same time, took advantage of the Republicans' discomfiture by charging that the Republicans were deliberately ignoring the Supreme Court. At first, the Democrats reacted to *Milligan* merely by praising the decision for establishing the ancient right of habeas corpus as constitutionally sacred, ratifying the position espoused by the Democrats throughout the war years. "It is both a triumphant vindication of the Democratic party and a happy augury of the future," said the *New York World*. "This decision on a matter which was the main topic of controversy between the Democratic Party and its opponents during the war," the paper continued, "is the final judgment of the law, as it will be the verdict of history, that the obloquy heaped upon Democrats for their opposition to the arbitrary exertion of authority was undeserved."⁹² Within a few weeks, however, Democrats began to focus more on the implications of the decision for the future of Reconstruction. Basing their argument on a particular reading of the *Milligan* decision and on their own predictions of how the Court would act in pending cases, the Democrats asserted that the proposed Reconstruction acts were unconstitutional and would be nullified by the Supreme Court. Said the *National Intelligencer*: "The Supreme Court has decided military commissions for civilians to be unconstitutional. It will, in our judgment, decide that no State can so get out of the Union as, under the Constitution, to be relieved of the obligation or deprived of the right of representation in the Congress of the United States. . . . We believe that it will decide against the folly of undertaking to convert one of the original thirteen States into a Territory."⁹³ "Now that the Supreme Court has come to the rescue of the Constitution," said a Richmond paper, "the future is lighted with signs of good cheer."⁹⁴

As the debate progressed, the Democrats became more direct in their attacks on the Court issue. Michael C. Kerr (D.-Ind.), for example, commenting on Bingham's views on Congress's powers, accused the Republicans of attempting to use their power "to govern this country without the aid of the unrepresented States, the Constitution, or the Supreme Court."[95] Augustus Brandegee (R.-Conn.), though a Republican, assailed the radicals for trying to "impeach the President of the United States, paralyze the arm of the Supreme Court, and of the judiciary generally."[96] "Do gentlemen believe," asked William E. Finck (D.-Ohio), "that they have the least shadow of authority to attempt to close the doors of the judicial department of this Government, so that the Supreme Court of the United States cannot examine the sentence or order made by one of these petty military tribunals which are to be set up over the lives, liberty, and property of the people of ten of these States?"[97]

The Republicans responded to these charges in two ways. First, they defended the legality and propriety of their policies. Their most common argument—and one with some force—was that the *Milligan* decision did not conclusively decide whether military Reconstruction in the South was constitutional or not. The Reconstruction Act itself, as ultimately passed, began with the explicit declaration that there were "no legal State governments or adequate protection for life or property in the rebel States," language inspired most likely by Davis's statement in *Milligan* that "if, in foreign invasion or civil war, the courts are actually closed, and it is impossible to administer criminal justice according to law, *then*, on the theatre of active military operations, where war really prevails, there is a necessity to furnish a substitute for the civil authority."[98] In the same vein, the Republicans' insistence that military reconstruction was only a temporary expedient was perhaps motivated by Davis's argument that "if this [military] government is continued *after* the courts are reinstated, it is a gross usurpation of power."[99] Indeed, the argument that *Milligan* did not prohibit military Reconstruction was not at all farfetched; Davis himself, writing in February, noted that "not a word [was] said in the opinion about reconstruction, & the power is conceded in insurrectionary States."[100]

The Republicans also invoked various Supreme Court decisions and dicta in defense of Republican Reconstruction policy. While debating the Tenure of Office Act (which greatly restricted the president's power to dismiss executive officials), Thomas Williams (R.-Pa.) declared that the decisions of the Supreme Court "have a direct bearing" on the constitutionality of that bill, "and so far as they do go they tend to sustain the constitutionality and correctness of this bill."[101] Such arguments were not particularly novel; many of the same arguments were made by the Republicans after *Dred Scott*. The important point is not whether these arguments are new or persuasive, or even whether they are plausible. What is important is that the Republicans attempted to reconcile their policies to the decisions of the Court at all.

Finally, as after *Dred Scott*, the Republicans focused much of their fire on particular individual justices, rather than on the Court as an instutition. Above all, they attacked David Davis. "This two-faced opinion of Mr. Justice Davis is utterly inconsistent with the deciding facts of the war, and therefore utterly preposterous," cried the *New York Tribune*. "These antediluvian Judges seem to forget that the war was an appeal from the Constitution to the sword. . . . This constitutional twaddle of Mr. Justice Davis will no more stand the fire of public opinion than the Dred Scott decision." "The hearts of traitors will be glad," wrote the *Washington Chronicle*, "by the announcement that treason, vanquished upon the battlefield and hunted from every other retreat, has at last found a secure shelter in the bosom of the Supreme Court." The decision, concluded the *Independent*, "will be treated as a mere partisan harangue, unseemly, because of the source whence it emanated . . . a sorry attempt of five not very distinguished persons to express themselves as profound jurists, whereas they have only succeeded in proving themselves to be very poor politicians."[102]

A set of important cases decided just after *Milligan* also caused some controversy. Known as the *Test Oath Cases*, these cases (*Ex Parte Garland* and *Cummings* v. *Missouri*) involved the constitutionality of loyalty oaths imposed by Congress and the states as a condition for entry to various professions. The particular cases that went to the Supreme Court involved a congressional oath for lawyers seeking to practice in the federal courts, and a state oath for clergymen.[103] The Court held both of these unconstitutional, by identical five-to-four majorities. The problem, the majority concluded, was that such an oath constituted an ex post facto law; Congress and the state in question had imposed a punishment in excess of what was provided by law at the time the act of rebellion was committed.

Reaction to the *Test Oath Cases* was mixed. The cases should not be regarded as reflecting simply a Republican-Democrat split; in fact, the opinions were complicated and cut across existing political lines. Justice Davis, for example, though the author of the *Milligan* decision, dissented in the *Test Oath Cases*. As it turned out, Republicans were not wholly aghast at the *Test Oath* outcome; as Charles Fairman concluded, "What was lost in *Garland* was no more than Thad Stevens and many other Republicans wanted to concede." Still, like *Milligan*, the *Test Oath Cases* raised the spectre of judicial interference with the Reconstruction Acts, and in the mood of early 1867 the Court was left open for numerous attacks and substantial criticism.[104]

Congress's actual response to *Milligan*, aside from rhetoric, was minimal. What was important to the radicals was not to punish the Supreme Court for its decision, but rather to ensure the enactment and then defend the constitutionality of the Reconstruction Acts. Much has been made of scattered comments denouncing the Court and of a bill introduced in the House in January by Thomas Williams that would have required a unanimous decision by the Supreme Court before a state or federal law could be invalidated. Veiled or explicit threats against the Court were made by a handful of congressmen and senators; Jonathan Bingham went so far as to threaten that Congress might "sweep away at once their appellate jurisdiction in all cases, and leave the tribunal without even color or appearance of authority for their wrongful intervention" if the Court dared to interfere with the process of ratification of the Fourteenth Amendment.[105] Alternatively, he suggested, the people might by constitutional amendment "defy judicial usurpation by annihilating the usurpers in the abolition of the tribunal itself."[106] There are a handful of other remarks during the session that present such threats, but they are rare and in no way reflect the dominant attitude of the Republicans toward the Court.[107] Certainly, Bingham's rhetoric was extreme even for the radicals.

One additional action by Congress has been widely viewed as evidence of Republican hostility to the Court: in July 1866, Congress decreased the size of the Supreme Court from ten to seven. Congress's action negated an 1863 law which increased the Court from nine to ten, largely to effect necessary reform of the judicial circuit system.[108] The 1866 reform, as described in the traditional way by Charles Warren, reflected a determination by the Senate "to curb the President in every move" and revealed Congress's unwillingness to let Johnson make "further appointments to the Bench."[109] In fact, however, the 1866 reduction of the Court shows nothing of the kind.

As Stanley Kutler has conclusively argued, the contention that the 1866 reduction shows hostility to the Court (or, for that matter, to Johnson) fails for a number of reasons. First, as we have seen, the Republicans were not yet angry at the Supreme Court, which did not announce its opinion in the *Milligan* case until December. Second, Johnson, far from vetoing the bill, signed it, apparently without reservation. (Furthermore, Johnson could have pocket vetoed the bill, thus killing it, but chose instead to sign it.) Third, there is evidence that the justices themselves—particularly Chase—actively supported the measure. Unquestionably, the Court bill of 1866 passed with little controversy, with no apparent hostility to the Court or the president, and for reasons totally independent of the upcoming controversy over *Milligan*.[110]

In fact, at the same time that the Republicans were trying to ignore, explain away, or get around the *Milligan* decision—and at the same time that a few Republicans were denouncing the Court for being a tool of the Copperheads—overall Republican policy continued to stress the importance of the federal courts. The Fourteenth Amendment, like the 1866 Civil Rights Act, was designed for judicial enforcement. The Freedmen's Bureau Bill, though largely self-enforcing through the Freedmen's courts, also relied on judicial support. Several of the new acts passed by the Fortieth Congress also called upon the federal judiciary to help in the process of Reconstruction.

The first session of the Fortieth Congress passed several laws designed to strengthen the authority of the federal courts. One bill expanded the jurisdiction of the federal courts to allow any litigant in a suit "between a citizen of the State in which the suit is brought and a citizen of another State, and the matter in dispute exceeds the sum of five hundred dollars" to remove such case to the federal circuit court upon the filing of an affidavit "that he has reason to and does believe that, from prejudice or local influence he will not be able to obtain justice in such State court."[111]

Also passed during this session was an act amending the Judiciary Act of 1789 to permit an appeal to the United States Supreme Court in cases involving writs of habeas corpus. Prior to the passage of this act, habeas corpus cases could reach the Supreme Court only through a circuitous and inconvenient route involving an appeal by writ of certiorari. The process—known as "habeas corpus aided by certiorari"—dated back to the days of Chief Justice Marshall but was of dubious legality. On 5 February 1867, Congress remedied the situation by approving a bill granting direct appeals to the Supreme Court in habeas corpus cases. The statute provided in part:

That the several courts of the United States, and the several justices and judges of such courts . . . shall have power to grant writs of habeas corpus in all cases where any person may be restrained of his or her liberty in violation of the Constitution, or of any treaty or law of the United States. . . . From the final decision of any judge, justice, or court, inferior to the circuit court, an appeal may be taken to the circuit court of the United States for the district in which said cause is heard, and from the judgment of said circuit court to the Supreme Court of the United States.[112]

"The immediate concern" of the Congress in passing this amendment, writes the historian Charles Fairman, "was to enforce the grant Congress had made by a resolution to encourage enlistments, in 1865: where a slave volunteered, his wife and children should be free." Before the passage of the 1867 act, writes Fairman, "the federal judiciary had no authority to issue writs of habeas corpus" in such cases.[113]

Several other measures respecting the federal courts were enacted or at least considered by the second session of the Thirty-ninth Congress. Near the end of the session, Congress approved an act which permitted appeals and writs of error to be brought to the Supreme Court from the decisions of lower federal courts even if, because of the rebellion, the time limit for bringing such appeals had already expired. Senator Ira Harris (R.-N.Y.) explained the purpose of this bill to the Senate as follows: "Suppose a judgment rendered in the circuit court at New Orleans just before the breaking out of the rebellion, and the party against whom it was rendered desired to take an appeal from that judgment. The State of Louisiana was in the possession of the rebels. How could a party bring an appeal under those circumstances? Now, after we have acquired possession of that rebel territory an appeal is brought, but objection is taken that the appeal is brought too late; . . . Now, this bill is intended to validate that appeal."[114] Except for a minor objection by Senator Trumbull, which was resolved by amendment, the bill engendered no real debate.

In 1867, as earlier, the radical Republicans revealed their willingness to rely on the federal judiciary for the enforcement of their program. Throughout the Reconstruction debates, their concern was not to lessen the power of the federal courts but to negate the power of the state courts. In accomplishing this objective, they moved cautiously and within the established framework of federal constitutional law. As it turned out, the expansion of the power of the federal courts—and the easing of the process by which habeas corpus cases could be brought to the Supreme Court—would come back to haunt the radicals. Eventually, these acts were used to bring cases to the High Court that threatened the existence of the Reconstruction Acts, and the radicals would respond by repealing the 1867 amendment to the Judiciary Act. It is that repeal which constitutes the best argument for the radicals' alleged hostility toward the Supreme Court. In weighing the radicals' attitude toward the Court, however, it is well to recall the spirit in which the 1867 amendment was passed in the first place.

VI

Congress passed the first Reconstruction Act on 20 February 1867. The "Military Reconstruction Act," as it is known, divided the South into military districts and provided for military government with or without the assistance of the civilian courts, at the discretion of the military commanders. To gain readmission to the Union and thus bring an end to military government, a state had to form a constitution through a convention of delegates elected by adult males regardless of color; the new constitution had to be approved by Congress; the state had to approve the Fourteenth Amendment; and that amendment had to have become a part of the Constitution of the United States. President Johnson promptly vetoed the act, and it was repassed over his veto, becoming law on 2 March 1867.[115]

The Military Reconstruction Act was passed in the final days of the expiring Thirty-ninth Congress, part of the usual crush of end-of-session legislation. The bill was the result of complicated negotiation and compromise and was far from perfect or complete. Both the overall effect of the bill and the meaning of particular provisions were unclear even to those most involved in the legislative process. It would therefore be necessary to provide subsequent measures to clarify ambiguities and provide guidance as to how the bill was to be enforced. Normally, Congress would not have met again until December 1867. In January, however, Congress had passed a law authorizing the new Fortieth Congress to meet immediately upon the final adjournment of the old Congress.[116] (It was generally assumed that "supplemental" Reconstruction measures would be passed by the new

Congress, and that these would be even more radical than the original Military Reconstruction Act. Fear of more radical legislation was one of the reasons that Johnson actively vetoed the Reconstruction Bill, allowing it to be passed over his veto, rather than killing the bill outright by exercising a pocket veto.[117]

Congress's willingness in February 1867 to place Reconstruction under the control of the army stands in marked contrast to its refusal to accept military government in the Wade-Davis debates a few years earlier. The difference, this time, was that the radicals took definite steps to insulate the military from the power of the president. First, in a rider to the military appropriations act of 2 March 1867, Congress forbade the president from dismissing Ulysses S. Grant as commanding general of the army or reassigning him outside the District of Columbia without the approval of the Senate. Moreover, all presidential orders to the army were to be transmitted through the secretary of war (Stanton) and the commanding general. Then, on the same day, Congress passed the Tenure of Office Act, which required the president to obtain Senate approval for the dismissal of any officer appointed with the consent of the Senate. The Tenure of Office Act was intended both to limit Johnson's patronage opportunities and, by a late amendment to the bill, to wrest control of the cabinet from the executive. In particular, it was thought, Congress wanted to guarantee Stanton's tenure as war secretary. Johnson vetoed the Tenure of Office Act, contending that the bill "conflicts, in my judgment, with the Constitution of the United States."[118] The president also expressed his opposition to that part of the Army Appropriations Act which, as he put it, "virtually deprives the President of his constitutional functions as Commander-in-Chief of the Army" as well as to the provision disbanding the militias of the Southern states. Because of the importance of the appropriations contained in the act, though, Johnson felt compelled to sign the whole package. He did take the extraordinary step of returning the signed bill to the House of Representatives with his objections.[119]

Military Reconstruction would have been unthinkable without the radicals' belief that both Grant and Stanton were on their side, and it would have been decidedly risky if they had not somehow tried to cut the War Department and the army from Johnson's executive power. Grant was of particular importance, both because of his power and influence within the army and because of his presidential prospects, which were considerable. As a military officer, Grant shied away from public political pronouncements; privately, though, he made his political views and ambitions known. It was known that, although at first supportive of Johnson's Reconstruction policy, Grant had moved toward the radicals at precisely the same moment Johnson moved away from them. As time went on, Grant played an increasingly active role in political affairs. Ultimately, he played a major role in the process of drafting the Military Reconstruction Bill.[120] Stanton had been quietly distrustful of Johnson ever since the president had taken power in 1865, and, it appears, the feeling was mutual. For some time it had been an open secret that Johnson wanted Stanton to resign, but the war secretary refused to take the hint. By early 1867, Stanton was the only member of the cabinet offering resistance to Johnson's policies.[121]

Events throughout the rest of 1867 merely served to exacerbate the already existing tensions between the president and the congressional radicals. As the situation developed, Grant and Stanton became the focal points around which the controversy revolved. First the Thirty-ninth Congress, just before adjournment, overrode Johnson's vetoes of the Reconstruction Bill and the Tenure of Office Act. Then the new Congress proceeded to pass the first of several supplemental Reconstruction Acts. The original act, though calling for conventions in the Southern states to draw up new state governments, did nothing actively to bring these state governments into existence, providing only that those states which failed to form acceptable new governments would remain under military rule. From the Southern point of view, inaction seemed the best stategy, at least for the moment. Accepting the terms of the Reconstruction Act might have been worse than continuing to live under military government; and, in any event, there was always the possibility that the Supreme Court would declare the act unconstitutional. In that event, the South might well be stuck with new governments they could have avoided.

The 23 March supplemental act ordered the army commanders in the South to take the initiative and begin the process of registering voters and calling conventions. This bill too was passed only over Johnson's veto. At that point, Congress recessed, but only after making provision for a special summer session, to be held if necessary in July. Meanwhile, Congress left enforcement of the Reconstruction Acts to the army and to Johnson, whom they continued to watch with suspicion.

The district commanders all imposed military rule with a gentle hand, at least at first. All left the existing state governments (set up, it will be recalled, under Johnson's Reconstruction plan) intact, and relations between the commanding generals and the Southern leadership are described by at least one historian as "cordial."[122] In the district comprising Louisiana and Texas, General Sheridan took a somewhat firmer stance, eventually going as far as to remove various state and local officials in an attempt to strengthen the military's position.

Two related questions of great importance then came to the surface. The first involved the relationship between the provisional governments established by Johnson and the military governments set up by the Reconstruction Acts. In most districts the two coexisted more or less peacefully, but in Sheridan's district especially the question was gaining in significance. The second was perhaps more fundamental: Who ultimately controlled Reconstruction—the president or the military? Again the question came to a head in Sheridan's district, where friends of the administration sought the president's help in extending the deadline for voter registration, in the hope of improving their position in the upcoming election.

With Congress out of session, Johnson asked Attorney General Stanberry for his opinion on these and other questions. Stanberry responded in June, arguing that the military and civilian governments were intended by Congress to coexist, with the military taking charge only of basic police functions. The power to "abolish, modify, control, or supersede" the civilian governments, expressed in the first Reconstruction Act, was interpreted by Stanberry to be "reserved to Congress, not delegated to the military commanders."[123] As for the second question, it was clear that any attempt by Johnson to enforce Stanberry's opinion would in fact constitute an answer to the question of who controlled Reconstruction.

The Stanberry opinions were discussed within the Cabinet, with Stanton, as expected, objecting to the attorney general's conclusions. There is reason to believe that the military commanders would have carried out a direct order from the president to enforce the Stanberry opinions. Instead, Johnson issued orders to Grant, suggesting that certain parts of the opinions be enforced but avoiding the most controversial issues. In any event, Grant interpreted the president's orders as purely advisory.

At this point Congress reconvened, quickly reversing Stanberry's opinions by means of a third Reconstruction Act passed on 19 July. Congress strengthened the powers of the military commanders by specifically authorizing them to "suspend or remove from office . . . any officer or person holding or exercising, or professing to hold or exercise, any civil or military office or duty in such district."[124] The act also gave the general of the army the same power and declared "that no district commander . . . or any of the officers or appointees acting under them, shall be bound in his action by any opinion of any civil officer of the United States."[125]

Once Congress adjourned, matters went from bad to worse. On 5 August 1867, Johnson requested Stanton's resignation. When Stanton refused to resign, Johnson suspended him from office, pursuant to the Tenure of Office Act, and appointed Grant as war secretary. Grant accepted the position, creating some temporary confusion as to where the general stood on Reconstruction. All doubts were dispelled when, in September, Johnson dismissed Sheridan from his command and Grant responded with a strong protest that quickly became public. Then, Johnson issued a broad amnesty proclamation that sought to circumvent the "ironclad" oath required by Congress of all voters in the third Reconstruction Act.

Congress reconvened on 21 November 1867, following a state and local election season in which the Democrats made broad gains in many Northern states. Though the congressional balance of power was not directly affected by the election returns, there was a general feeling that the political tide had turned toward moderation. In such an atmosphere, any attempt by the radicals to impeach Johnson was impossible, and on 7 December the House voted overwhelmingly to defeat the latest in a series of efforts to remove him.[126]

Any chance for an easing of tension between the president and the Republicans in Congress immediately disappeared after the impeachment effort failed. Johnson, instead of moving toward Congress, moved away from them. He denounced the Republican Reconstruction program as unconstitutional, accused his opponents of attempting to impose black rule over the South, and declared his determination to resist any law that would do "immediate and irreparable injury to the organic structure of the Government."[127] With presidential-congressional relations again turning bitter, Johnson officially notified the Senate of his suspension of Stanton; the Senate, fearful that concurrence in the suspension of Stanton would create a situation in which the office of the secretary of war would remain vacant, eventually rejected efforts at compromise and disapproved of Johnson's action. Stanton thus was reinstated. The Stanton controversy forced Grant to choose between loyalty to his chief and to his party; given his obvious presidential ambitions, the choice was not difficult. Grant turned his office back to Stanton, who resolved to remain as war secretary until his successor was approved by the Senate. A few days later Johnson dismissed Stanton outright, now ignoring the Tenure of Office Act altogether, and appointed General Lorenzo Thomas. Stanton refused to turn over the office (literally, as Stanton barricaded himself in his office and refused to admit Thomas). The result was that the president recognized Thomas as war secretary ad interim and permitted him to attend cabinet meetings, while Congress (and Grant) continued to recognize Stanton instead.

The Stanton-Grant-Thomas affair was enough to add new momentum to the radicals' drive to impeach Johnson. Specifically, Johnson's opponents could now accuse the president of failing to execute the laws, in that Johnson had deliberately and consciously refused to obey the commands of the Tenure of Office Act. On 24 February 1868, the House of Representatives formally adopted a resolution declaring "That Andrew Johnson, President of the United States, be impeached of high crimes and misdemeanors in office." A committee was appointed to draw up formal charges.

Five days later the committee returned with ten specific articles of impeachment (an eleventh was added later by the House). The articles of impeachment were clearly intended to present specific charges against Johnson, avoiding the broader areas of disagreement between the president and his congressional opponents. All ten of the original articles dealt with the affairs of 21–22 February, accusing Johnson, among other things, of ignoring the Tenure of Office Act; of attempting to appoint Stanton's successor without seeking Senate approval; of illegally attempting to "seize, take and possess the property of the United States in the War Department"; and of a succession of similar acts growing out of the same incident. The eleventh article accused Johnson of declaring that the Thirty-ninth Congress "was not a Congress of the United States . . . but, on the contrary, was a Congress of only part of the States." This last article cited Johnson's embarrassing 1866 speech in which, while drunk, he lashed out individually and collectively at members of the Congress.

The narrowness of the charges should not mask the larger issues that divided Johnson from his congressional opponents. The charges, including those in the last article, were framed "in such a way as to avoid difficulties in the procuring of evidence . . . and to insure the success of the prosecution before the bar of the Senate."[128] The subsequent debates, both in the House and at the Senate trial, reveal the broader nature of the Republicans' grievances. Representative Luke Poland (R.-Vt.) summed up the attitude of the House when, after discussing the merits of the impeachment charges, he said: "There are involved in the consideration of this question far higher and more important consequences than by whom the duties of War Secretary shall be performed. . . . All this becomes insignificant when we look at the principle involved in this violation of the law by the President. It is now to be decided whether the people, by their Representatives in Congress, are to make and establish the laws by which this country is to be governed, or whether they may be set at naught and defied by the Chief Magistrate of the nation."[129] Johnson's main line of defense, as it had been all along, was that the laws passed by Congress with respect to Reconstruction and related matters were unconstitutional, and that it was both his right and duty to refuse to enforce such laws as would contravene the Constitution of the United States.

As the Senate prepared to try Andrew Johnson on the charges brought forward by the House of Representatives, this much was clear: the Tenure of Office Act was only symbolic of the larger controversy between the White House and the Congress. The question, boiled down to its essence, was whether Congress had an untrammeled right to force the president to obey laws which he regarded as unconstitutional. The formal charges concerning the dismissal of Stanton were inextricably bound up with the broader issues of Reconstruction. As one Senator put it, "The issue here today is the same which prevails throughout the country. . . . It is between two paramount ideas, each struggling for supremacy. One is, that the war to suppress the rebellion was right and just on our part. . . . The other idea is, that the rebellion was not sinful, but was right; that those engaged in it forfeited no rights, civil or political, and have a right to take charge of their State governments and be restored in their representation in Congress just as if there had been no rebellion and nothing had occurred."[130]

VII

In the midst of the growing tension between Johnson and the congressional Republicans, the president's supporters found hope from another quarter: the United States Supreme Court. William H. McCardle, the editor of the *Vicksburg Times*, had been arrested by federal military authorities for disturbing the peace and for inciting "insurrection, disorder, and violence" in connection with certain editorials published in the newspaper in late 1867. Prior to his scheduled military trial, McCardle brought a habeas corpus action in federal district court; the judge ruled against him. McCardle then took advantage of the newly passed statute permitting appeals to the U.S. Supreme Court from adverse judgments in habeas corpus cases. That law, it will be recalled, was passed in order to protect blacks and federal military officers from the actions of state officials.

McCardle filed his appeal on 23 December 1867. A preliminary hearing—to determine whether the Supreme Court should take the case—was held on 17 January 1868. On that day the Court ruled that a hearing should be held and set a date in early March for arguments. Oral arguments on the merits were held on 2, 3, 4, and 9 March 1868.

From the point of view of the congressional Republicans, the timing of McCardle's appeal could not have been worse. *Ex Parte McCardle* directly raised the question of the constitutionality of the Military Reconstruction Act, a question which the Republicans were quite anxious to avoid. Though they knew that various parts of the Reconstruction program were of dubious constitutionality, the Republicans wanted to keep the plan in place until the ex-rebel states would be compelled to rejoin the Union on the Republicans' terms. By the same token, opponents of congressional Reconstruction knew that if the Court was to help them, it had to do so quickly. By the end of the summer of 1868, all but four of the ex-Confederate states had been readmitted, making the question of Reconstruction moot everywhere but Texas, Georgia, Mississippi, and Virginia. Indeed, once the Fourteenth Amendment was ratified (in July 1868), the legal problems of Reconstruction became moot everywhere.

Hence the Court's decision to take up McCardle's case threatened to ruin congressional Reconstruction just at the point where it seemed to be working. The process of calling conventions and electing delegates was already under way in most states, and the end was in sight. If the Court ruled adversely on the Reconstruction questions, all would be for nought. Moreover, and perhaps more immediately, the Republicans had an additional problem with the *McCardle* case: it came just as the process of impeaching Andrew Johnson was finally getting under way.

Both the specific charge brought against Johnson and the more general opposition to the president rested on the claim that he had ignored or flouted the Constitution of the United States. Equally important, Johnson's defense rested on his contention that his actions were not only not inconsistent with the Constitution but were required in fulfillment of his duty to preserve, protect, and defend it. Johnson's opposition to the various Reconstruction measures, as well as of such auxiliary acts as the Tenure of Office Act and the Command of the Army Bill, was based on constitutional grounds. A decision by the Supreme Court that the Reconstruction acts were unconstitutional would all but derail the impeachment effort; the Court, in effect, would be saying that Johnson had been right all along and the Republicans wrong.

Johnson and his supporters, well aware of this and anxious anyway to kill the congressional Reconstruction program before it finished its task, took every opportunity to test Reconstruction legislation in the courts. Most well known are the cases of *Ex Parte McCardle* and *Georgia* v. *Stanton*, but there were other attempts. One little known example, involving General Lorenzo Thomas, Johnson's choice to replace Stanton as war secretary, is recalled by Gideon Welles: "On Wednesday, Gen. T.[Thomas] appeared before Judge C.[Cartter, the Chief Justice of the Supreme Court for the District of Columbia] and gave himself up to be imprisoned. His object was to sue out a writ of *habeas corpus*, and get the case before the Supreme Court, who would, without doubt declare the tenure-of-office act unconstitutional. This neither the radicals, Stanton, nor Cartter wanted. They knew the law is unconstitutional, and that the Court will so decide when[ever?] the law comes under their action. This being the case, Cartter, who had been in such haste to arrest Gen. Thomas, after [hearing?] and evidence, released him."[131] Other cases involving the constitutionality of various parts of the Republican reconstruction program include *Mississippi* v. *Johnson, Ex Parte Yerger*, and *Georgia* v. *Grant*.[132]

The Johnson supporters were not at all choosy in their attempts to get the Reconstruction legislation into court. General Thomas, for example, was clearly attempting to litigate the constitutionality of the Tenure of Office Act. McCardle and the various states were making direct challenges to the Reconstruction Act itself. This diversity of lawsuits is not surprising, given that the various pieces of legislation were interrelated both legally and politically. Any one lawsuit would likely raise issues involving several aspects of the Reconstruction legislation; whether in dicta or in the actual resolution of the case at hand, the Supreme Court might well comment on different parts of the legislation or on the various theories of constitutionalism espoused by the Republicans. An adverse decision in any one area, therefore, could easily impact not only on Reconstruction generally but on the impeachment as well.

On 12 March 1868, just a few days after the completion of the oral arguments in *McCardle*, Rep. Robert C. Schenck (R.-Ohio) rose in the House to offer a bill to permit appeals to the Supreme Court in cases involving civil suits against a collector of internal revenue. The Senate had passed the bill the day before. To this technical and obscure amendment to the Judiciary Act of 1789, James F. Wilson (R.-Iowa) offered another amendment:

> Sec. 2. *And be it further enacted*, That so much of the act approved February 5, 1867, entitled, "An act to amend an act to establish the judicial courts of the United States, approved September 24, 1789," as authorizes an appeal from the judgment of a circuit court to the Supreme Court of the United States, or the exercise of any such jurisdiction by said Supreme Court on appeals which have been or may hereafter be taken, be, and the same is hereby, repealed.[133]

The bill, with Wilson's amendment, was passed without debate in the House and was sent back to the Senate. Later the same day, the Senate reconsidered the bill as amended by the House. Senator Charles R. Buckalew (D.-Pa.) now objected, observing of the amendment, "I observe that it is a very important amendment. I do not know what the effect of it is."[134] He asked for a postponement but was brushed aside, with Senator George H. Williams (R.-Ore.) declaring that the amendment "explains itself."

On 14 March, the House Democrats suddenly realized what had happened. Benjamin M. Boyer (D.-Pa.) told his colleagues that the amendment in question had passed the House without debate "solely because it was introduced in a manner calculated to deceive and to disarm suspicion of its real design and effect." Boyer, by now stating the obvious, noted that the amendment was intended "to repeal the jurisdiction of the Supreme Court" in the McCardle case.[135] The ensuing debate was hot and acrimonious, occupying several days. Finally, on 25 March, President Johnson vetoed the bill and returned it to the Senate, again claiming that the bill was both unconstitutional and unsound policy.[136] The Senate repassed the bill on 26 March, and it became law on the twenty-eighth when repassed by the House. Only in the last round was the bill was fully debated.

Thus the Court had several weeks in which they could have tendered a decision in *McCardle*, defeating the congressional Republicans by handing down the decision before the veto override. The case had been fully argued earlier in the month; the Court could have even handed down its judgment in the case (as it had two years before in *Milligan*) and postponed delivery of the formal opinions. Instead, the Court decided to wait, postponing decision until Congress had had a chance to act on the proposal to take away its jurisdiction in the case. "It would not have become the Supreme Court to *hasten* their decision of an appeal for the purpose of getting ahead of the legislation of Congress," wrote Chase in a private letter. "It would have been, as we thought, an indecency to run a race in the exercise of *that* jurisdiction with the legislature." Whether Congress could in fact constitutionally "*oust* an appeal already taken and perfected," Chase wrote, "is another question."[137] The Court, with Chase away at the impeachment trial, decided to carry over argument on that question until the next term. Justices Field and Grier entered a public dissent to the Court's decision to delay action. "This case was fully argued in the beginning of the month," Grier wrote. "It is a case that involves the liberty and rights not only of the appellant, but of millions of our fellow citizens. The country and the parties had a right to expect that it would receive the solemn and immediate attention of this Court."[138] More than a year later, however, Chase, writing for the Court, upheld Congress's right to "make exceptions" to the Court's appellate jurisdiction, even after a case had already been appealed and argued.[139]

Congress's response to the *McCardle* case was extraordinary. Never before had Congress succeeded in disabling the Court from performing its power of judicial review.[140] Extraordinary circumstances call for extraordinary remedies, however. The possibility that the Court would strike down at a single blow not only the Reconstruction Act but also the impeachment effort was too much for the Republicans to bear.

From the Republicans' perspective, the removal of the Court's jurisdiction in the *McCardle* case was logical and appropriate. For one thing, as Stanley Kutler points out, "As the *McCardle* case moved to the Supreme Court, a rising chorus of opinion maintained that the justices would invalidate the Reconstruction Acts." This "self-fulfilling prophecy . . . became indistinguishable from fact," Kutler concludes. It hardly makes sense to argue that this action was "misguided" or "misconceived" solely because, in fact, there is (and was) considerable doubt as to how the Court would have acted if it had reached the merits of the constitutionality of the Reconstruction Acts.[141]

Even if their action in stripping the Court of its appellate jurisdiction was itself struck down as unconstitutional, the Radical Republicans would still have won the day. In fact, the Republicans could have counted it a victory even if the Reconstruction Acts were struck down, so long as the Court's action took place after the passage of the Fourteenth Amendment and after the impeachment trial. What mattered most to the congressional Republicans was delay. A Court decision on the merits of the Reconstruction Acts had to be put off until after the impeachment trial, after the ratification of the Fourteenth Amendment and the readmission of at least the bulk of Southern states, and after the presidential election in the fall. The removal of the Court's jurisdiction in *McCardle* was sure to produce, at a minimum, a hearing on what the legal effect of the congressional action was. The Court was scheduled to adjourn in early April. Thus, it would seem, Congress's action would accomplish the goal of putting off any court action until at least December.

The Court, in the end, managed to steer clear of either repudiating the Republican Reconstruction plan or condoning it. Instead, Chase put off a decision in *McCardle* until after another round of arguments and then upheld Congress's power to withdraw jurisdiction from the Court even in a pending case. Writing for the Court in 1869, Chase wrote: "We are not at liberty to inquire into the motives of the legislature. We can only examine into its power under the Constitution; and the power to make exceptions to the appellate jurisdiction of this court is given by express words."[142] "Jurisdiction is the power to declare the law," Chase concluded, "and when it ceases to exist, the only function remaining to the court is that of announcing the fact and dismissing the cause."[143]

On 26 May 1868 the Senate acquitted Andrew Johnson of "high crimes and misdemeanors" by a single vote. Over the summer, the Fourteenth Amendment became a part of the Constitution, and all but four of the ex-rebel states were readmitted to the Union. Ulysses S. Grant, as expected, was elected president of the United States in November. The most critical period of Reconstruction, for the Court and the country, was over.

VIII

Just how severe was the crisis faced by the Supreme Court in the late 1860s? For traditional historians, whose views reigned unchallenged for almost a hundred years, the answer was simple. "Never has the Supreme Court been treated with such ineffable contempt," wrote the historian Claude G. Bowers of the Reconstruction Court, "and never has that tribunal so often cringed before the clamor of the mob."[144] "Although, from 1861 to 1870, the Court had consistently upheld the authority of the National Government," wrote Charles Warren, "it was destined to become the object of the most serious and determined attack by the very political party which favored such extension of National power."[145]

The traditional view has been challenged, most notably by Stanley Kutler. "To be sure, the Supreme Court encountered almost unprecedented hostility in the fifteen years following Dred Scott," writes Kutler. Yet, according to Kutler, this observation by itself does not tell the whole story:

> The Republican party . . . should be measured by what it actually did, not by what a few of its members said or proposed. With regard to the Supreme Court there was a great deal of sound and fury, but it signified only the disaffection and dissatisfaction of a limited group within the party. The majority rebuffed repeated attempts to punish the Court or curtail its powers.
>
> The temporary withdrawal of jurisdiction in the *McCardle* case stands as the only exception to this behavior. The congressional action cannot be justified; it can, however, be understood.[146]

The view that the Court played only a passive role in Reconstruction, Kutler concludes, "however persistent, is open to challenge."[147]

The traditional view of the Court in Reconstruction seems correct only during the war years. After the debacle of *Ex Parte Merryman*, the Court stayed mostly on the sidelines until after the shooting stopped. In the *Prize Cases*, the Court smoothed the way for the administration's attempt to treat the Confederates as both rebels and enemies, depending on what suited its purposes. In *Ex Parte Vallandingham*, the Court deferred consideration of the controversial question of military trials. Contrary to the traditional view, however, during the war the Court was the subject of relatively little debate or discussion on any side; it was surely not the object of vehement or vituperative criticism.

Once the war ended, the Court resumed its accustomed role. In *Ex Parte Milligan*, military trials of civilians in areas where the civilian courts were open were struck down. Surely, as Robert G. McCloskey suggests, "this is not the Court of the wartime years, smarting under the lash of criticism that had immediately followed *Dred Scott*, modestly forbearing from interference in the great affairs of state."[148] At the same time, however, the *Milligan* Court was not so brave as some would suggest. At the time the decision was announced, the case was of little practical importance and, in any event, the Republican Party had long been divided over the question of military trials of civilians. It was only after the idea of military Reconstruction became a real possibility that the *Milligan* decision assumed real political importance.

With decisions such as *Milligan* and the *Test Oath Cases*, then, the Court was willing to participate in the controversial business of postwar politics. With *Ex Parte McCardle*, however, the situation changed. The Republican attacks became more sweeping; the issues before the Court were not only important but were the central issues facing the country; moreover, Congress was now under the firm control of radical Republicans who had shown themselves willing to impeach the president and to strike a direct blow at the Court's power. The extent and nature of the crisis surrounding the Court's aborted consideration of the constitutionality of the Reconstruction Acts should not be underestimated.

As the impeachment crisis drew closer, the Republicans in command of the House and Senate stepped up their attacks on the Court and began to consider alternatives that had previously been either rejected or never proposed in the first place. Early in the second session of the Fortieth Congress, Senator Trumbull (R.-Ill.) introduced a bill reducing the number of justices needed for a quorum in the Supreme Court from six to five. With the Court having been reduced already from nine to eight, and with it scheduled to be reduced to seven upon the next death or resignation,[149] the bill was necessary, according to Senator Reverdy Johnson (D.-Md.), because "the court was very near being without a quorum to-day, and the probability is, in the present condition of things, that it may often be without a quorum during the present session."[150] That bill passed the Senate immediately, without debate.

When the bill reached the House, the judiciary committee added an amendment providing that "no cause pending before the Supreme Court of the United States which involves the action or effect of any law of the United States shall be decided adversely to the validity of such law without the concurrence of two-thirds of all the members of said court."[151] To this amendment, Thomas Williams offered a substitute that would have required a unanimous decision by the Supreme Court before a federal statute could be invalidated.

Such a law, whether requiring unanimity or only a two-thirds majority, was necessary, Williams said, "to defend the legislative power, which is the true sovereign power of the nation."[152] "The rights of the people of this country are to be respected," declared Jonathan Bingham (R.-Ohio), "and those whom they send to this Congress are clothed by the Constitution to compel even the Supreme Court to respect those rights, and to that end, if need be, to reduce that court to a single person, if you please, and thereby compel unanimity at least in a decision which may deny the people's rights and limit the people's laws."[153] Wilson, defending his two-thirds requirement, argued that his bill was "a conservative measure. . . . We are simply declaring that the Supreme Court of the United States shall not have legislative power without the concurrence of two-thirds of its members. That body makes law when it decides a case. It makes law from which there is no appeal except in that indirect way which goes to the people at the ballot-box. And it is not merely a legislative rule but an organic rule which is established by the Supreme Court by the decisions which it utters; and it is our duty . . . to protect the people and to protect the Government against an accidental creation of organic law by that court."[154] The Wilson amendment passed the House by a vote of 116 to 39 on that same day, but it was held up in the Senate, either because the Republicans feared that even a two-thirds requirement would be insufficient to save the Reconstruction

Acts (as the Democrats and, later, Charles Warren suggested) or because the Senate was influenced by moderate Republican opinion.[155] Eventually, the bill was buried in the judiciary committee.

Despite a great deal of rhetoric in January and February, nothing came of these proposals (and others) to curb the Court. One reason, as Kutler points out, is that the Republicans "were unable . . . to agree on any legislation to prevent an unfavorable court decision . . . so long as they felt no need to react against an obvious transgression on the part of the judiciary."[156] Even the outbreaks of rhetorical hostility against the Court were episodic, rising to the surface only when the threat of imminent action by the Court was felt. Wilson's two-thirds proposal, for example, was prompted by what Wilson described as "an apprehension that the country will suffer by any delay [in the consideration of his amendment]. It is said that there is a case now depending in the Supreme Court of the United States on which this question may be ruled to-day or to-morrow."[157]

Nonetheless, it is apparent from the debate over the Wilson proposal that the Republicans in Congress were prepared to protect their Reconstruction program from judicial assault if and when the threat materialized in concrete form. When a few weeks later the Court announced that it would hear *Ex Parte McCardle*, and when a decision in that case was indeed imminent, the Republicans lost no time in reacting. The Republicans' strategy in trying to pass a bill withdrawing the Court's appellate jurisdiction in McCardle's case was, at first, to avoid debate altogether by sneaking the bill past a confused and slumbering opposition. When that approach failed, and especially after Johnson's veto of the measure, the Republicans were forced to debate the bill on the merits. Here again the radicals' rhetoric was strident and sweeping. Said Representative Robert Schenck (R.-Ohio): "I have lost confidence in the Supreme Court of the United States. Is not that plain enough? I believe they usurp power whenever they dare to undertake to settle questions purely political."[158] "When we are told day by day that the majority of the court had practically made up its judgment . . . to infringe [*sic*] upon the political power of Congress and declare the laws for the government of the rebel States in every respect unconstitutional," said Wilson, "it was our duty to intervene."[159] Furthermore, Wilson told one Democratic opponent, "The gentleman cannot hope that the majority of the House, possessing the legislative power of the Government with the majority in the Senate, will yield, on any misconstruction of law or any political subterfuge, the right to settle into a condition of peace and repose this country, reorganize the rebel States upon just, firm, and abiding foundations, and restore them to the Union."[160] "If the McCardle case falls," Wilson said, "the country may have escaped the danger of another political decision by a majority of the Supreme Court."[161]

By the spring of 1868, the Republicans were acting on a theory of government that was conducive to its assault on the independence of the Supreme Court. It was nothing less than a theory of legislative sovereignty. As *Harper's Weekly* expressed the argument a year earlier, "The President, by the Constitution, is made a co-ordinate but not a co-equal branch of government. So, also, is the Supreme Court. But Congress, or the Legislative branch, is wisely made the chief and superior branch. The Executive and Judiciary are 'checks and balances' only. The Constitution, in giving Congress power to remove the President by impeachment and to reorganize the Supreme Court by increasing the number of judges, establishes the necessary final supremacy of the Legislature."[162]

Moreover, events had conspired to make the Republicans less deferential to constitutional tradition and to the Constitution itself than they had been only a few years before. When it seemed that the Civil Rights Bill might be struck down as unconstitutional, the Republican response was to incorporate its provisions into the Fourteenth Amendment, thus insulating its provisions from judicial attack. Between 1865 and 1869, the Constitution was amended three times; taken together, the Civil War amendments represent the most truly fundamental alterations of the Constitution of 1787 by formal amendment in two hundred years of American history. In an atmosphere conducive to such changes, it is not surprising that at least some Republicans found it easy to speak of fundamental changes with respect to the powers of the three branches—and that some of this spilled over into attacks on the Court.

Finally, and most immediately, the assault on the Court was provoked by the radicals' growing disaffection with Johnson. Relations between the legislative and executive branches had so deteriorated by 1868 that the impeachment and conviction of the president was almost accomplished; when it seemed possible that the Court might interfere with the impeachment effort by declaring one or more radical acts unconstitutional, the radicals' response was swift and direct.

At the same time, several factors acted to mitigate the dangers to the Supreme Court from the radical Republicans. First, though the radicals feared what a court decision might do to their program and to the impeachment effort, they had no tangible grounds upon which to criticize the Court; after all, with respect to Reconstruction, the Court had hitherto done nothing except avoid making a decision. The Court's actions in *Milligan* and the *Test Oath Cases*, while provoking considerable criticism, did not give rise to viable attempts to curb the court. The *Milligan* case, despite its importance for the future of Reconstruction, was favored by many Republicans, who had long been averse to military trials, while the *Test Oath Cases* were simply not of the same level of importance as an all-embracing anti–Reconstruction Act decision would have been. As far as Reconstruction itself was concerned, the Court had not actually done anything.

A second mitigating factor was the extreme speed with which the crisis dissipated. The Court's willingness to lay the decision in *McCardle* over to the next term put the Court out of the public spotlight for a time; by the time the Court reassembled in December, Johnson had been acquitted and then defeated in his bid for the Democratic nomination; the Fourteenth Amendment had become a part of the Constitution; and the bulk of the Southern states had been readmitted to the Union. In its acute stage, the court crisis lasted only a matter of weeks.

Third, the Republicans had no fundamental objection to judicial power. They objected only when the judicial power threatened the impeachment effort or congressional Reconstruction policy. There is a fine line to be drawn here, for the Republicans' rhetoric, especially in early 1868, seemed to indicate a preference for a system of legislative sovereignty, in which, of course, judicial review has no place. Yet these words are belied by the Republicans' consistent support of the federal judiciary and of the United States Supreme Court throughout the postwar years. The Republicans, advocating a broad extension of federal power over the Southern states, knew the courts would be a valuable ally. Their dependence on federal judicial enforcement of the Civil Rights Act presaged a dependence on federal judicial enforcement of the Fourteenth Amendment. In fact, ironically, the jurisdictional legislation repealed by the court-curbing act of 1868 was designed specifically to permit the federal courts (and the Supreme Court) to protect federal officials and blacks from the vicissitudes of

Southern justice. John Marshall had for decades shown that the federal judiciary was the natural ally of federal power, and the Republicans had not forgotten that lesson.

Fourth, some of the hostility that might have been directed against the Court was directed instead against Andrew Johnson. The main lines of interbranch conflict throughout the postwar years were drawn between Congress and the White House, not between Congress and the courts. Surely the coincidence of the start of the impeachment and the passage of the anti-Court bill cannot be easily dismissed.

Finally, the Reconstruction period was made easier for the Supreme Court by its own actions, especially those of Chief Justice Chase. If in *Dred Scott* the Court administered a self-inflicted wound, in Reconstruction the Court helped to protect itself from injury. Chase's decision to avoid "running a race" with Congress over the jurisdictional issue in *McCardle*, and his graceful retreat a year later when the opinions were released, diffused the crisis before it could escalate to a dangerous level. Although it would be incorrect to describe the Court as timid during these years, it would not be incorrect to say that the Court exercised discretion and avoided foolhardiness. At no time during Reconstruction did the Court make an antiradical decision on an issue of central importance at the time, *Ex Parte Milligan* not excepted. The Court, perhaps, had learned its lesson from *Dred Scott*. It would be several generations before it would make a similar mistake.

IV

The Supreme Court and the New Deal

THE SUPREME COURT played a central role in the political struggles of the 1930s. Over a two-year period beginning in 1935 the Court waged a bitter war with President Franklin D. Roosevelt over the constitutionality of the New Deal recovery and reform program. During this period the Court struck down no fewer that a dozen pieces of New Deal legislation, including some of Roosevelt's most important and cherished programs. The Court's attempt to stop the New Deal and to defend its own view of the Constitution led to a popular referendum over the New Deal in the 1936 election, a referendum which Roosevelt won by an unprecedented margin. Armed with such a mandate, Roosevelt challenged the Court directly with his infamous "Court-packing" plan in 1937; the plan itself was immensely unpopular, but in the end the Court reversed itself and gave its stamp of approval to the New Deal.

Once again the Court had brought intense criticism and controversy down upon itself by attempting to resolve an issue that was as important and as divisive as the issues involved in the *Dred Scott* and Reconstruction crises. Once again, the Court survived. Contained within the story of the Court's confrontation with Franklin D. Roosevelt, and its ultimate survival, is the heart of the story of the New Deal itself.

I

Franklin D. Roosevelt was elected to the presidency in November 1932 on a distinctly moderate platform. During the campaign he had attacked Herbert Hoover's administration for being "the greatest spending administration in peacetime in all our history" and had promised to balance the federal budget. He promised to help the farmer through the current agricultural crisis but insisted that he would spend no additional government money. His position on the tariff question was virtually indistinguishable from Hoover's, though Roosevelt's was somewhat ambiguous. He even attacked the Republicans for wanting "to center control of everything in Washington as rapidly as possible."[1]

There were hints of progressivism in the Roosevelt campaign as well. Despite all his rhetoric against government spending, he promised not to hesitate in spending enough money to remedy "starvation and dire need on the part of any of our citizens." He advocated what became the Civilian Conservation Corps and backed government regulation of Wall Street and of private utilities. He hinted at the need for government cooperation with industry and for economic planning.[2]

It was not in substance but in style that Roosevelt appeared more activist than Hoover. He flew to Chicago immediately after being nominated to run for president to accept his party's call, breaking a long-standing tradition by actually addressing the convention. "Let it . . . be symbolic that in doing so I broke tradition," he told the delegates. "Let it be from now on the task of our Party to break foolish traditions." Roosevelt had "an infectious smile," a "warm, mellow voice" and an "obvious ease with crowds"— and, most important, he projected an image not of defeat but of inspiring optimism.[3] By 1932, America was ready for a change, ready for a new face in the White House. In November, the voters gave Roosevelt a landslide victory, with almost 60 percent of the popular vote and almost 90 percent of the electoral vote. Still, Roosevelt's great victory did not necessarily translate into a clear policy mandate, for, as Senator Burton K. Wheeler (D.-Mont.) told presidential adviser Rexford Tugwell, the 1932 election "was a vote against Hoover" more than a clear vote for Roosevelt.[4]

By March 4, 1933—Inauguration Day—the American economy had reached its lowest point. Roosevelt took office in the middle of a banking crisis, with unemployment estimated at over fifteen million; the gross national product was less than half of what it had been before the stock market crash of 1929; and the nation was emerging from an unusually cold and desperate winter. In his inaugural address, the new president told the nation what it already knew: "Values have shrunken to fantastic levels; taxes have risen; our ability to pay has fallen; government of all kinds is faced by serious curtailment of income; the means of exchange are frozen in the currents of trade; farmers find no markets for their products; the savings of many years in thousands of families has gone." Something had to be done, said Roosevelt: "The nation asks for action, and action now." Still, the President was not specific as to what actions he would take, declaring only that his goal was to "put people to work" and that he would call the Seventy-third Congress into special session to deal with the banking crisis.[5]

Over the next one hundred days, Roosevelt led the special session through a period of unprecedented legislative activity. Between March and June, Congress enacted a spate of bills designed to ameliorate the economic situation. Among these were the "three pillars of the New Deal": the National Industrial Recovery Act (NIRA), which authorized the president to set up and enforce "codes of fair competition" for all industries engaged in interstate commerce; the Agricultural Adjustment Act (AAA), which provided much-needed relief to farmers by imposing production controls through marketing agreements and processing taxes; and the Economy Act, which slashed ordinary government expenditures. In addition, the special session passed the Emergency Banking Act, fulfilling the purpose for which it had been convened; repealed the government's obligation to repay bond debts in gold bullion; and set up the Tennessee Valley Authority (TVA), the Civilian Conservation Corps (CCC), the Federal Deposit Insurance Corporation (FDIC), the Public Works Administration (PWA), and the Federal Emergency Relief Administration (FERA).

Throughout the special session the emphasis was on "national recovery" rather than reform of the economic system. The legislation of the first one hundred days was explicitly experimental and temporary; NIRA, for example, was authorized for only two years, while the Home Owners Loan Act (to assist home owners who could not pay their mortgages or back taxes) was set to expire three years after its creation. With the opening of the second session of the Seventy-third Congress, in January 1934, Roosevelt took a few tentative steps in the direction of more permanent reform. While the special session of 1933 had simply abrogated the gold clause in public and private contracts, the second session passed the more comprehensive Gold Reserve Act, which among other provisions established "a permanent policy, [of] placing all monetary gold in the ownership of the Government as a bullion base for its currency."[6] In place of the Securities Act of 1933, which had merely corrected the most serious problems in stock trading, the second session passed the Securities Exchange Act of 1934, setting up the Securities Exchange Commission (SEC) and giving the government such "definitive powers of supervision over exchanges that it will be able to itself correct abuses which may arise in the future."[7] The accomplishments of the 1934 session were a mixed bag; some of the laws it passed were "directed towards reform, others towards recovery, still others towards both objectives."[8]

With the recovery measures fully in place and a few more permanent measures already enacted, Roosevelt was content to sit back and await the results of the 1934 congressional elections before proceeding further. By the fall of 1934, the New Deal was so firmly established that the election was fought not over what the Administration had done during its first two years, but what it ought to do over the next two. Analyzing the campaign just before the election, Arthur Krock, the political columnist for *The New York Times*, saw the entire struggle boiling down to just one issue: "Shall the President be authorized to go ahead with the New Deal in his own way?"[9] Making the same point, the *Literary Digest* viewed the issue as "not between the New Deal and the Old, but between the New Deal and one newer still."[10]

Roosevelt encouraged such an interpretation by underscoring his intention to make the New Deal a permanent feature of the American system. Early in January 1934, he had defined recovery as meaning "a reform of many old methods, a permanent readjustment of many of our ways of thinking and therefore of many of our social and economic arrangements."[11] In late September, in a fireside chat, he pledged to make the National Industrial Recovery Act "a part of the permanent machinery of government,"[12] a comment that was widely seen as indicating a shift of emphasis from the first year. By keeping his rhetoric somewhat ahead of his programs, Roosevelt made sure that the congressional elections were not a referendum on what he had done but an opportunity for the people to authorize him to take even bolder steps. Thus the 1934 elections became, in Senator Wheeler's words, a " 'For God's Sake do something!' vote."[13]

The electorate gave the president an impressive victory. Roosevelt received his desired mandate in the form of his party's unprecedented midterm gains. Beginning in 1935, the Democrats would command majorities of nearly three-quarters of each house of Congress. Accordingly, the president stepped up his calls for reform in the days and weeks following the election. The "accustomed order of our formerly established lives does not suffice to meet the perils and problems which today we are compelled to face," he said on 16 November. "Mere survival calls for a new pioneering on our part."[14] On 18 November he proclaimed what would become the political ideology of the second New Deal: a commitment to what he called "community rugged individualism." Such individualism, the president explained, "means no longer the kind of rugged individualism that allows an individual to do this, that or the other thing that will hurt his neighbors. He is forbidden to do that from now on. But he is going to be encouraged in every known way . . . to use his individualism in cooperation with his neighbors' individualism so that he and his neighbors may improve their lot in life."[15] In his annual message to Congress in January 1935 the president left no doubt that he had shifted in the progressive direction. He dismissed the hitherto important distinction between reform and recovery as an "effort to substitute the appearance of reality for reality itself." Henceforth, no distinction would be made between relieving the symptoms of the nation's economic malaise and removing the causes of the illness. FDR now claimed "a clear mandate from the people, that Americans must forswear that conception of the acquisition of wealth which, through excessive profits, creates undue private power over private affairs and . . . public affairs as well."

Beginning in 1935, the president declared, there would be a "broad program" designed to guarantee to the American people "security of a livelihood," "security against the major hazards and vicissitudes of life," and "security of decent homes." Moreover, Roosevelt promised a permanent solution to the unemployment problem; renewal and "general clarification of the purposes" of the NIRA; "consolidation of Federal regulatory administration over all types of transportation"; and "improvement in our taxation forms and methods."[16] The second New Deal was about to begin.

II

The New Deal came under fire from conservatives of both parties right from the beginning. Though Republicans were greatly outnumbered in the Seventy-third Congress (1933–34), they were extremely vocal, speaking up against the Roosevelt programs sharply and often. Though conservatives did not oppose the Emergency Banking Act, and though they heartily

116

approved of Roosevelt's efforts to reduce government spending, they began to register their disapproval with the introduction of the Agricultural Adjustment Bill and the National Recovery Bill. Mostly, conservatives were concerned about four things: Roosevelt's apparent nonchalance at spending enormous sums of money for various forms of relief and public works; his tendency to ask for and be granted unprecedented discretionary powers, either for himself or for subordinate executive officials; his almost complete control of Congress, which some saw as threatening the power of the legislature as an independent and coordinate branch; and his willingness to surround himself with and listen to progressive intellectuals known collectively as the "Brains Trust."

That conservatives would oppose the New Deal for what they felt was its lack of fiscal restraint was to be expected. Roosevelt himself had pledged to balance the budget; in 1933, however, he contented himself with balancing the "regular" budget while ignoring relief and public works expenditures in his calculation. Though admitting that "it may seem inconsistent" for the government both to save and to spend at the same time, he insisted that he had made the government "live within its income," and conservatives could make little headway against him. Often Roosevelt confused matters by demanding economy in one area while he was being criticized for profligacy in another.

The other conservative charges were more serious. The main one was that Roosevelt sought and was being granted dictatorial powers for himself and for his department heads. Senator David A. Reed (R.-Pa.) compared the U.S. Congress to the overrun German Reichstag, and, by implication, Roosevelt to Hitler.[17] Others warned, for example, that the AAA "creates another dictatorship, with the Secretary of Agriculture in the title role."[18] In an age when the delegation of legislative power to executive departments was limited and strange, measures that would today appear the very model of proper legislation could be described as "extraordinary and revolutionary." Even the Economy Act and the Emergency Banking Bill were attacked along these lines.[19]

Roosevelt's political mastery of the Seventy-third Congress was likewise viewed by some critics as a step toward tyranny. Conservatives warned of the Administration's attempt to transform the old Constitution into "a new Constitution, not formally framed or ratified, but by executive usurpation."[20] Critics also turned their attention to FDR's coterie of aca-

The Supreme Court and the New Deal

demic advisers, who were charged with having communistic tendencies. Raymond Moley, a close personal friend of the President, was especially singled out as an advocate of "collectivism."[21] Moley, Adolf Berle, and Rexford Tugwell all came under fire for advocating government "control" over the economy.

The charges that Roosevelt was leading the country toward communism or fascism (or, paradoxically, toward both at the same time) came only from the extreme right, though from men of both parties. Nonetheless, while such attacks might seem hysterical today, they set the tone for much of the criticism of the New Deal over the next four years. The president did not ignore his critics; in fact, he showed a certain sensitivity to their concerns. He often appointed decidedly conservative men to preside over progressive programs; it was difficult to accuse the president of radicalism when he appointed such men as Hugh Johnson (National Recovery Administration) or Henry Morgenthau (Farm Credit Administration) to key positions. In speeches and messages, Roosevelt stressed the "well-considered and conservative" nature of his proposals and occasionally even answered the collectivism charges directly. In his second fireside chat, for example, he defended the heart of the New Deal from such attacks: "It is wholly wrong to call the measures that we have taken Government *control* of farming, industry, and transportation. It is rather a *partnership* between Government and farming and industry and transportation . . . a partnership in planning."[22]

Throughout the first one hundred days, many also questioned the constitutionality of Roosevelt's programs. Such opposition centered mainly on the question of delegation of power, on congressional power to regulate economic relationships, and on congressional power to tax and spend. The Constitution clearly authorized Congress to "regulate Commerce . . . among the several States," but how much control could Congress exercise over purely local activity? Opponents of the NIRA pointed with satisfaction to the Supreme Court's fifteen-year-old decision in the *Child Labor Case*, in which the commerce clause was held not to grant Congress the power "to control the States in their exercise of the police power over local trade and manufacture."[23] Conservatives also questioned whether agricultural processing taxes constituted an illegal tax on articles exported from a state, in violation of Article I, section 9 of the Constitution, and whether the taxing and spending provisions of the AAA were indeed intended for the "general Welfare of the United States," as the Constitution requires, or only for the benefit of certain economic groups.

Despite all the criticism, the New Deal was highly popular. In a June 1934 *Literary Digest* poll, 61 percent of the American people backed the president, including more than one-third of those who had voted for Hoover in 1932.[24] The New Deal came under fire from a great many groups in 1934, but each group attacked Roosevelt's policies for its own reasons, and there was no alternative program on which the critics of the New Deal could agree. When Hugh Johnson held a series of meetings in February 1934 designed to allow critics of the National Recovery Administration (NRA) to voice suggestions and complaints, his agency was attacked for various reasons by "large distributors, consumers' groups . . . government purchasing agents . . . small businessmen . . . political leftists . . . [and] labor leaders."[25] Some of the complaints were over minor matters, and some were fundamental objections to the idea of the NRA, but there was no single or common criticism. Conservatives, who had opposed the NRA in 1933, were conspicuously absent from the list of its critics in 1934. Opponents of the New Deal could not deny that economic conditions had improved since 1932–33, and, because the president held off on really progressive legislation until after the 1934 elections, his conservative opponents had little they could grab on to and attack.

Not that they did not try; on 7 July 1934, Republicans kicked off the congressional campaign with their party's eightieth birthday party, a gala anti–New Deal extravaganza. In rousing speeches, party chairman Henry Fletcher and Senator Arthur Vandenberg (R.-Mich.) challenged the president. Vandenberg, sounding what was by then a well-worn theme, charged that Congress had given the president power and authority "comparable only to those possessed by Mussolini and Hitler." Fletcher raised the constitutional questions once again, charging that the administration had taken the "first steps to emasculate" the Constitution.[26] The party leaders' attempt to place the Republican Party on a firm anti–New Deal footing for the ensuing campaign failed completely, however, since most Republican congressional candidates found it too costly to run against so popular a president; many, indeed, had even voted for the president's programs during the congressional session of 1934. Roosevelt's political chief, Postmaster General James Farley, summed up his opponents' problem most

The Supreme Court and the New Deal

clearly: the Republicans, he said, "have no issue . . . so they leap for the constitutional issue, about which they can be as vague as they wish."[27] The president himself joked later that his opponents were so desperate for an issue that they were going to "come out in favor of the Ten Commandments . . . [and] sweep the country."[28] The Republicans were discouraged and demoralized, reportedly reconciled to defeat as early as mid-October.[29]

The campaign itself, as we have seen, centered largely on the more progressive programs which Roosevelt had hinted at but not yet fully articulated. A few who directly challenged the first New Deal were soundly trounced in November. The list of losing Republicans included Pennsylvania's outspoken Senator David Reed, Indiana's Senator Arthur Robinson, and Ohio's Senator Simeon Fess. A few Republicans survived, but the new Congress showed overwhelming Democratic majorities in each house. Some of the newly elected Democrats were moderates or conservatives, but the list of confirmed New Dealers was long and included Harry S Truman of Missouri, Joe Guffey of Pennsylvania, and future Supreme Court justice Sherman Minton of Indiana.

One group of conservative Republicans and Democrats, largely men out of office, joined together in August 1934 to form what became the strongest antiadministration group in the country: the American Liberty League. The league was set up as "a non-partisan organization . . . intended to combat radicalism, preserve property rights, and uphold and preserve the Constitution."[30] Roosevelt declared that these goals "could be subscribed to by every American citizen; that they were what might be called axiomatic, [un]equivocally acceptable to all Americans."[31] Still, the group was by all accounts an anti–New Deal coalition, though it is a measure of the popularity of the New Deal in late 1934 that the founders of the league denied that this was their purpose. No one took this claim seriously, however; Roosevelt even joked at one point that League President Jouett Shouse's failure to invite him to join "must have been an oversight."[32] While the group attracted former Democratic presidential nominees Alfred E. Smith and John W. Davis, conservative Democratic senators moved hastily to distance themselves from the organization.[33]

After the 1934 elections, Roosevelt had his mandate, the Republican Party lay in ruins, and the new Liberty League was hardly being taken seriously. When the Seventy-fourth Congress convened in January 1935

Roosevelt was set to consummate the task he had begun two years before; and no one was left to stop him, except the Supreme Court of the United States.

III

The Supreme Court had the power to strike down the New Deal on constitutional grounds, but as of early January 1935 it had given no sign of doing so. The Court had been deeply divided for several decades on questions of federal and state power to regulate private economic relationships, reflecting divisions in the legal profession and in the nation at large. In a few areas, the Court did indeed strike down state and federal laws aimed at economic regulation; for example, it did not permit minimum wage laws or laws which prohibited "yellow dog" contracts. These conservative decisions were counterbalanced by a great many decisions permitting state and federal regulation in other areas. Over the course of the late nineteenth and early twentieth century, as Robert McCloskey argues, the Court developed a set of judicial techniques by which it could nullify state and federal economic regulations as unconstitutional. The key question is not whether such techniques existed, however, but how the Court used those techniques. As McCloskey explains, "The court could use them to govern marginally, to moderate the pace of social reform, to force the nation to take a second look at extreme programs. It could, in short, operate as one influential factor among others in the process of social decision-making. Or it could alternatively seek to decide all the great political-economic questions that faced America, to halt the trend toward government intervention, to use its veto absolutely rather than suspensively." "The majority of the cases of the twentieth century through 1934," McCloskey concluded, "reflect . . . the former, modest approach."[34] Indeed, McCloskey's survey of the early-twentieth-century Court record revealed a curious dialectic at work: "Sometimes the judges talked in this period as if they were determined to halt the regulatory movement in its tracks and as if they had the will and the power to veto any political impulse they disapproved. Yet at other times, and often even concurrently, they ratified many inroads on the free enterprise system and sought only to moderate, not to stop, the growth of government intervention."[35]

The Supreme Court and the New Deal

The key question for the New Dealers was whether the Court would follow its liberal precedents or its conservative precedents. Four of the justices—James C. McReynolds, Pierce Butler, George Sutherland, and Willis Van Devanter—were confirmed conservatives. Three others—Louis D. Brandeis, Harlan F. Stone, and Benjamin Cardozo—were committed liberals. Chief Justice Charles Evans Hughes was considered a middle-of-the-roader, and Owen Roberts was as yet largely untested. The Court's October 1932 term (ending mid-1933) provided little evidence to suggest the direction the Court would take, but there were a few hopeful signs for the New Deal. Key economic decisions now seemed to lean in the pro-regulation direction. In one case, the Court sustained a North Dakota statute which required sellers of complicated farm equipment to give prospective buyers a "reasonable time for inspection and testing" of the products with a guaranteed return privilege.[36] In another case, the Court allowed California to reduce gas rates by 7 percent, holding that such action was not a confiscation of property despite the gas company's expectation of payment at the higher rate.[37] Such decisions were by no means predictive of the Court's attitude toward the federal programs of the New Deal, but any time the Court sustained progressive legislation in such areas there was room for hope.

The 1933 term (October 1933 through June 1934) was even more positive. Again the key decisions involved state regulation, but at least two of them had far-reaching implications. The first was *Home Building and Loan Assoc.* v. *Blaisdell*,[38] commonly referred to as the Minnesota mortgage moratorium case, in which the Court upheld a Minnesota statute authorizing state courts to postpone foreclosure actions against homeowners who were unable to pay their mortgages or back taxes. The law was contested primarily on the grounds that it violated the Contract Clause,[39] but Roberts and Hughes joined the three liberals to produce a five-to-four majority rejecting the challenge. Hughes, who wrote the opinion of the Court, began from the rather enigmatic premise that while "emergency does not create power, emergency may furnish the occasion for the exercise of power."[40] In this case, Hughes found that the state's police power did indeed extend to a law "directly preventing the immediate and literal enforcement of contractual obligations, by a temporary and conditional restraint, where vital public interests would suffer."[41] Hughes appeared to be impressed by the careful and cautious nature of the law; by the clear existence of an economic emergency; and by the fact that the law was strictly conditioned and of limited duration.

Although the Minnesota case dealt with a state law and with the Contract Clause, it was widely interpreted as an indicator of the Court's position on the New Deal, especially with regard to those federal measures which were similarly temporary and in direct response to emergency conditions. Language in the Hughes opinion seemed to hint at Court approval of the NIRA or the AAA: "Where, in earlier days, it was thought that only the concerns of individuals or of classes were involved . . . it has later been found that . . . the question is no longer merely that of one party to a contract as against another, but of the use of reasonable means to safeguard the economic structure upon which the good of all depends."[42] Hughes dismissed the contention that the Contract Clause ought to be read "with literal exactness like a mathematical formula," thus apparently endorsing a method of constitutional interpretation that augured well for the New Deal. Indeed, some Court-watchers saw the decision as "a clear indication that the highest court in the land intends to recognize the NRA and the recovery program of the President." Others, more cautious, stressed the Court's emphasis on the temporary nature of the Minnesota law and warned that the decision indicated only that the Court "will sustain the legality of NRA and other governmental enterprises so long as they are of a temporary nature."[43]

The New Deal received a second boost two months later when the Court upheld a New York statute fixing a minimum retail price for milk. Leo Nebbia, a grocer, sold a customer two quarts of milk for eighteen cents— the legal minimum—but then violated the law by throwing in a free loaf of bread. He was fined five dollars and eventually brought his case to the Supreme Court of the United States. As in the Minnesota mortgage moratorium case the Court found in favor of the state, holding by a five-to-four vote that the Constitution permitted a state "upon proper occasion and by appropriate measures" to "regulate a business in any of its aspects including the prices to be charged for the products or commodities it sells."[44] Supporters of the New Deal were elated not only by the result of the case but by the fact that the opinion of the Court was written by the previously untested Roberts. Roberts's attitude seemed as important as his vote, as he showed a very liberal approach to constitutional adjudication: "So far as the requirement of due process is concerned, and in the absence of other constitutional restriction, a state is free to adopt whatever economic policy may reasonably be deemed to promote public welfare, and to enforce that policy by legislation adopted to its purpose."[45] Roberts dismissed the argument that the right to contract was unlimited, or that price regulation was inherently beyond the states' police power: "These . . . rights . . . of a citizen to exercise exclusive dominion over property and freely to contract about his affairs, and that of the state to regulate the use of property and the conduct of business, are always in collision. No exercise of the private right can be imagined which will not in some respect, however slight, affect the public; no exercise of the legislative prerogative to regulate the conduct of the citizen which will not to some extent abridge his liberty or affect his property. But subject to constitutional restraint the private right must yield to the public need."[46] Once more the four conservatives dissented, but again the position of the majority seemed clear. A "new era has dawned," beamed the *New York World Telegram*; "NRA is significantly strengthened," observed the *Cleveland Plain Dealer*. Those who read the decision carefully and with a view toward the legal technicalities involved were less sanguine, however, for the Court was careful to point out that in the American system the states and the federal government were each to be supreme in their respective jurisdictions; the constitutionality of the NRA would thus depend on whether the federal government possessed the same regulatory powers that *Nebbia* granted to the states. One correspondent warned readers of the *Literary Digest* that "one of these days we shall be surprized with a decision from the Supreme Court holding unconstitutional the National Industrial Recovery Act insofar as it transcends the power of the Federal Government and seeks to regulate commerce within a State."[47] For the time being, however, few paid attention to such pessimism.

IV

The New Deal had been so successful in 1934—in Congress, before the courts, and at the polls—that the Supreme Court's first anti–New Deal decision came as something of a shock to the nation. The Court's rebuff came exactly three days after Roosevelt's triumphant and forward-looking 1935 annual message to Congress, just when the New Deal seemed to have overcome all opposition. Limited though this first anti–New Deal decision was, it had a sobering effect on the administration and its supporters, and gave renewed hope and strength to the president's critics.

The decision in *Panama City Refining* v. *Ryan*[48] (commonly referred to as "the Hot Oil case") invalidated one minor section of the National Industrial Recovery Act. By an eight-to-one margin, with only Cardozo dissenting, the Court held that Congress was not authorized to delegate to the president the power to "interdict the transportation in interstate and foreign commerce of petroleum . . . produced or withdrawn from storage in excess of the amounts permitted by state authority." The ruling, while important, was limited to the delegation of power question; put simply, the Court ruled that Congress could not vest in the president the authority to make laws without establishing clear standards under which he must act. In the case of section 9(c) of the NIRA, the Court said, Congress gave to the president "an unlimited authority to determine the policy and to lay down the prohibition [of oil shipments], or not to lay it down, as he may see fit."[49] It was therefore unconstitutional.

What the Court did not do was as important as what it did. Counsel for the oil companies urged the Court to strike down the hot oil provisions of the NIRA on the grounds that the production of oil is by definition not interstate commerce and was therefore beyond the reach of congressional authority.[50] Hughes, however, restricted his opinion to the delegation question only, assuming rather than deciding that Congress possessed the requisite power under the Commerce Clause. Moreover, the chief justice refused to rule the entire NIRA unconstitutional on the basis of the illegality of section 9(c) alone, holding that the statute as a whole could survive the loss of the hot oil provision. Cardozo, in dissent, found in the totality of the NIRA a "reasonably clear" standard for executive action, emphasizing the magnitude of the "national disaster" facing the nation and belittling the importance of the case by declaring, "There is no fear that the nation will drift from its ancient moorings as the result of the narrow delegation of power permitted by this section."[51]

Proponents of the New Deal emphasized the narrowness of the Court's holding, interpreting the decision not "as a blow to the New Deal, but as a guide to it."[52] Roosevelt himself took the decision as simply requiring that the New Deal effect its policies with "the correct language" and looked ahead to "a dozen or one hundred other cases where the language isn't correct yet."[53] Within the Justice Department, the narrowness of this and other decisions provided hope that the Court would seek to "avoid . . . the central issues of Federal power" in future cases as well.[54] Conservatives, however, jumped at the Court's decision to predict nullification of the entire NIRA and of the rest of the New Deal as well. The *New York Herald-Tribune*, for example, acclaimed the Court for tossing "this revolutionary nonsense into the Potomac where it belongs."[55]

In retrospect, it is tempting to view the Hot Oil case as the first volley in the Supreme Court's campaign against the New Deal, but such analysis by hindsight must be avoided. In fact the case pointed in two directions at once, and proponents and opponents of the New Deal analyzed the Court's ambiguity only to reach divergent conclusions. As it turned out, the decision was the precursor of more general attacks on the New Deal, as conservatives had hoped and predicted. It is not entirely clear, however, that Roosevelt was wrong in claiming the difference between the Court and the administration was one of "language" only. Both sides could find hopeful signs: conservatives in the Court's assertion of authority and in the near-unanimity of its position, and liberals in the Court's narrow ruling and in its nonhostile tone.

Over the next four months, however, the Court's attitude shifted to one of utter opposition to the New Deal. Perhaps the key transition point was the Court's series of decisions in the all-important *Gold Clause Cases*.[56] Although the Court upheld the administration on all the important practical questions in these cases, Roosevelt's victory cost him greatly in terms of moderate and conservative support.

The *Gold Clause Cases* were a test of the administration's monetary policy, which had dramatically altered the relationship between gold and the U.S. dollar. First, Congress had made it illegal to hold, sell, buy, or trade gold without a government license; then it abrogated the gold clauses in all private and public contracts (including bonds issued by the U.S. government itself), relieving debtors of their contractual obligations to pay debts in gold; finally, it permitted the president to devalue the U.S. dollar with respect to gold by forty percent, a prerogative which Roosevelt promptly exercised. In arguments before the Supreme Court, the government estimated that the gold policy had knocked some $70 billion off the total public and private debt.

The importance of the case was underscored by the personal appearance of Attorney General Homer S. Cummings to argue the government's case before the high bench.[57] If the Court should strike down the Gold Clause resolution, Cummings argued before the Supreme Court, the result would be "a stupendous catastrophe . . . such as to stagger the imagination." The country would not be brought "back to the Constitution," but "back to chaos."[58] Furthermore, the Court risked making the United States "a cripple among the nations of the earth" if it found against the government.[59]

The weeks following the oral arguments were tense ones for the administration. The anxiety surrounding the case was highlighted by the Court's unprecedented action in announcing, on two consecutive Saturdays, that the *Gold Clause* decisions would *not* be handed down on the following Monday. When the Court failed to make a similar announcement on 17 February, it was clear that the decision would be forthcoming two days later, on 19 February.

The opinions of the Court in the *Gold Clause Cases*, all written by the chief justice, are long and complex. In the first two cases, Hughes found that Congress's power to regulate the currency is so complete that the government can abrogate the gold clauses in every private contract and can refuse to redeem gold certificates in bullion. The more difficult case involved the question of whether Congress could refuse to pay the debts of the United States government in gold, despite an express promise to do so. Hughes held that the government's repudiation of its own gold debts was unconstitutional, finding a "clear difference between the power of Congress to control or interdict the contracts of private parties when they interfere with the exercise of its constitutional authority, and the power of Congress to alter or repudiate the substance of its own engagements when it has borrowed money under the authority which the Constitution confers."[60] "The United States are as much bound by their contracts as are individuals," Hughes concluded. "If they repudiate their obligations, it is as much repudiation, with all the wrong and reproach that the term implies, as it would be if the repudiator had been a State or a municipality or a citizen."[61] The Constitution gives Congress the power to borrow money on the credit of the United States, he explained, but it does not confer authority "to alter or abolish these obligations." Despite the binding nature of the obligation on the "conscience of the sovereign," however, it would be impossible for a creditor to obtain judicial relief, since Congress "is under no duty to provide remedies through the Courts."[62] Hughes in effect

The Supreme Court and the New Deal

accused the government of breaching its moral duty but refused to do anything about it.

The Court's lecture to Congress and the administration was attacked by Justice Stone, who entered a separate concurrence in order to set forth his belief that "it is unnecessary, and I think undesirable, for the Court to undertake to say that the obligation of the gold clause in Government bonds is greater than in the bonds of private individuals." It would have been more appropriate, Stone contended, for the Court to have disposed of the case by stating simply that "there is no damage because Congress, by the exercise of its power to regulate the currency, has made it impossible for the plaintiff to enjoy the benefits of gold payments promised by the government." He concluded: "I therefore do not join in so much of the opinion as may be taken to suggest . . . that although there is and can be no present cause of action upon the repudiated gold clause, its [Congress's] obligation is nevertheless, in some manner and to some extent, not stated, superior to the power to regulate the currency which we now hold to be superior to the obligation of the bonds."[63]

Justice McReynolds filed an extraordinarily passionate dissent, joined by his three conservative colleagues, to all the *Gold Clause Cases*. In perhaps his most famous line from the bench, the aging justice moaned that "the Constitution as many of us have known it, the Instrument that has meant so much to us, has gone." He reminded his brethren that "to let oneself slide down the easy slope offered by the course of events and to dull one's mind against the extent of the danger . . . that is precisely to fail in one's obligation of responsibility." McReynolds believed that Congress's abrogation of the Gold Clauses was not really part of a national monetary policy but was instead "a plan primarily designed to destroy private obligations, repudiate national debts, and drive into the Treasury all gold within the country, in exchange for inconvertible promises to pay, of much less value." In the oral presentation of his opinion, McReynolds fumed at his colleagues and called Roosevelt "Nero in his worst form." "Shame and humiliation are upon us now," he concluded. "Moral and financial chaos may confidently be expected."[64]

From Hughes's stern lecture and McReynolds emotional dissent, it was clear to most observers that the Court was unhappy with its decision and really had had no choice. The *Indianapolis Star* observed that "no power on earth could unscramble the egg the New Dealers handed to the Court"; others noted that the Court deliberately "went very wide of giving approval to the Administration's currency policy" and had clearly refused to give Roosevelt "a clean bill of health with respect to the future."[65] Though Hughes claimed from the bench that the justices were "not concerned with [the] consequences, however serious" of the Court's decision, it seems clear that Hughes went as far as he could in reproaching the Administration without actually striking down its already operative monetary policy. The chief justice's deliberate consideration of what was in fact an academic question—whether the government was morally required to pay its debts in gold—contrasts sharply with his narrow ruling in the Hot Oil case and was a bad omen of things to come.

The administration had been prepared to take drastic measures if it had lost in the *Gold Clause Cases*. Roosevelt had prepared a speech and a message to Congress urging the passage of legislation "withdrawing the right to sue the United States on its bonds, currency, and similar obligations" and making it unlawful for any officer of the United States to pay any amount in excess of the face value of such obligations. "I do not seek to enter into any controversy with the distinguished members of the Supreme Court of the United States," wrote Roosevelt in his never-delivered speech. "They have decided these cases in accord with the letter of the law as they read it." But, after quoting Lincoln on *Dred Scott*, Roosevelt added: "It is the duty of the Congress and the President to protect the people of the United States to the best of their ability. . . . To stand idly by and to permit the decision of the Supreme Court to be carried through to its logical, inescapable conclusion would so imperil the economic and political security of this nation that the legislative and executive officers of the Government must look beyond the narrow letter of contractual obligations, so that they may sustain the substance of the promise originally made."[66] Stanley Reed, who acted as a special assistant to the attorney general during the Gold Clause controversy, was busy meanwhile sifting through other alternatives. Reed received proposals to withdraw the appellate jurisdiction of the Supreme Court in specific cases; to amend the Constitution; and to withdraw the right of citizens to sue the government of the United States. At one point, fully two years before Roosevelt introduced the Court-packing plan, Reed jotted down the observation that "In the long run increasing the court will have the fewest economic and political dangers."[67] Since the Court found in favor of the administration, however, none of these extraordinary measures were necessary.

Through February 1935, then, the Court had shown itself unwilling to interfere with a major New Deal program despite the serious moral and constitutional issues involved. To this extent, at least, there was room for optimism. Still, as Roosevelt noted, "I shudder at the closeness of five to four decisions in these important matters."[68] Whatever hope the optimists had that the Court would stand aside and permit the New Deal to progress unimpeded was quickly dashed, however, when in May the Court announced no fewer than four important anti–New Deal decisions.

First, on 6 May, Roberts held for a five-man majority that the Railroad Retirement Act was unconstitutional.[69] The same judge who had written the liberal *Nebbia* (New York milk-pricing) opinion a year before now found a system of compulsory pensions both a violation of due process of law, in that it took "the property of one and bestowed it upon another," and an exercise of power not authorized under the Commerce Clause. The Court held that compulsory pensions could be upheld only if it could be demonstrated that they promoted "efficiency and safety in interstate transportation." Roberts held that the pension act did not promote safety and efficiency; hence it was "in no proper sense a regulation of the activity of interstate transportation. It is an attempt for social ends to impose . . . upon the relation of employer and employee . . . as a means of assuring a particular class of employees against old age dependency."[70] What the Court seemed to be saying, as the chief justice pointed out in dissent, was that "a pension measure, however sound and reasonable as such, is *per se* outside the pale of regulation of interstate carriers, because such a plan could not possibly have a reasonable relation to the ends which Congress is entitled to serve."[71] Roberts adopted a very narrow standard of congressional power under the Commerce Clause, limiting it to the actual transportation of goods in commerce. Justice Stone, who joined Chief Justice Charles Evans Hughes's vehement dissent, wrote Felix Frankfurter that "The Railroad Retirement Act decision was . . . about the worst performance of the Court since the Bake Shop case [*Lochner* v. *New York* in 1905]."[72]

On 27 May 1935, the Court made its opposition to the New Deal unequivocal, ruling against the Administration in three important cases. By far the most dramatic case was that of *Schechter Bros.* v. *United States*, in which the Court invalidated the entire NIRA.[73] Following the Hot Oil case, Chief Justice Hughes found for a unanimous Court that Congress had illegally delegated power to the president in authorizing him to set up "codes of fair competition." Hughes, however, did not stop here; he also found NIRA to be an illegal regulation of intrastate activities as well. Congress, he wrote, could regulate local activities only if those activities had a "direct effect" on interstate commerce. Even Cardozo concurred in the judgment of the Court; as he put it, "to find directness here is to find it almost everywhere."[74]

On the same day, the Court also unanimously struck down the Frazier-Lemke Farm Mortgage Act.[75] In that law, Congress had provided a mechanism whereby farmers faced with foreclosure could obtain relief from a federal court through bankruptcy proceedings. Justice Brandeis, writing for a unanimous Court, held this to be a deprivation of private property without compensation, in that Congress was impairing "substantive rights of mortgagees." Brandeis carefully distinguished the Minnesota mortgage moratorium case, thus leaving open the door for a more limited statute to achieve the same purpose. Since the Frazier-Lemke Act had not been an administration measure, moreover, Roosevelt was not particularly concerned about its demise.[76]

Finally, the Court chose the same day to decide, in *United States* v. *Humphrey's Executor*, that executive subordinates specifically invested with tenure by Congress could not be fired at the president's pleasure.[77] Humphrey had been a conservative Hoover appointee to the Federal Trade Commission; because his personal views were so at variance with Roosevelt's policies, the president asked him to resign. When Humphrey refused, he was fired. Since Congress had specified that Federal Trade Commissioners were removable only for cause, the Court held it outside Roosevelt's power to remove him without reason. Though Humphrey died before the case was resolved, the Court ruled that his estate was entitled to back pay.

Had *Humphrey's Executor* been decided at another time in American history it would have been hailed as an important step in guaranteeing the independence of the "quasi-legislative" and "quasi-judicial" functions of the federal bureaucracy. Not long after the end of the 1930s, in fact, constitutional scholars and practical politicians recognized the importance and correctness of the decision. At the time, however, it was seen as a personal affront to the president—and a reversal of the precedent that the president was supreme in his power to remove executive subordinates.[78] Court observers viewed *Humphrey's Executor*, along with the other three anti–New Deal decisions of May, as part of a concerted effort by the Court to block the New Deal and frustrate the president.[79] "The significance of this decision," wrote Homer Cummings in his diary, "lies in the disposition of the Court to curb the executive powers of the President."[80]

Between the *Gold Clause Cases* in February 1935 and the *Railroad Retirement Case* in early May, the Supreme Court moved from a position basically supportive of the administration to one of clear opposition. The *Gold Clause Cases* and the *Railroad Retirement Case* were both five-to-four decisions; in each case, Cardozo, Stone, Hughes, and Brandeis supported the administration while McReynolds, Van Devanter, Butler, and Sutherland opposed it. The difference between the results in the two cases was that Owen Roberts was on the liberal side in the *Gold Clause Cases* and on the conservative side in the *Railroad Retirement Case*.

Roberts had voted on the pro–New Deal side in every case prior to the *Railroad Retirement Case* except the Hot Oil case. That decision, in which only Cardozo voted on the pro–New Deal side, was a narrow, careful decision which was not basically unfriendly to the administration. His proadministration vote in the *Gold Clause Cases*, however, was apparently a reluctant one. The majority in the *Gold Clause Cases*, writes William Leuchtenburg, "was vexed at having been coerced into upholding legislation it thought invalid and unjust. Commentators predicted that the Court would seize the first opportunity to right the scales."[81] As the columnist TRB reported,

> Some of the more thoughtful observers here believe that the decision sustaining the government in these [Gold Clause] cases increases the probability of adverse decisions in the pending cases affecting the constitutionality of N.R.A. and A.A.A.
>
> The theory upon which this belief is founded is not one that I should care publicly to espouse, but it is worth repeating. In brief, it asserts that the five Justices who made up the Supreme Court majority are human beings with certain ineradicable human frailties. Since they were forced by circumstances and expediency into a clearly reluctant backing of the New Deal in the gold cases, the natural

tendency of at least one or two of them will be to react in the other direction at the earliest opportunity.[82]

Roberts's switch in the *Railroad Retirement Case*, the Court's very next important decision, fulfilled those prophecies.

Three of the May decisions were unanimous: *Humphrey's Executor*, the Frazier-Lemke farm mortgage case, and the *Schechter* decision. Neither *Humphrey's Executor* nor the farm mortgage case were anti–New Deal decisions: the Court's unanimity was based not on a feeling of hostility toward the administration but on sound legal principles. The unanimity of the *Schechter* decision seems puzzling at first, since suddenly all nine justices—even the liberals—joined in opposition to the administration. The key to explaining the Court's unanimity lies in the behind-the-scenes maneuverings of Louis D. Brandeis.

Brandeis, though a liberal, was a committed opponent of "bigness."[83] The "curb of bigness is indispensable to true Democracy and Liberty," he wrote in 1933, adding that "if the Lord had intended things to be big, he would have made men bigger—in brains and character."[84] Brandeis's opposition to bigness made him a lifelong supporter of vigorous antitrust legislation and an opponent of government centralization and of big business. Throughout 1934 and 1935, Brandeis and his followers made it clear to the president that Roosevelt should, in Frankfurter's words, "dump business" and move in a more progressive direction.[85] Up to the *Schechter* decision, however, Roosevelt hesitated to do so.

Brandeis therefore worked to see that the NIRA was gutted by the Supreme Court. The conservatives opposed the law because it involved too much governmental regulation of the economy; Brandeis opposed it because it was in essence a repeal of the antitrust laws and because it involved too much centralization of power.[86] Though they made strange bedfellows, Brandeis and the four conservatives could agree that the NIRA should go. The other liberals agreed as well, and the Court unanimously struck down the Blue Eagle.

Brandeis could hardly restrain himself after the decision; he summoned Tommy Corcoran to the justices' robing room and gave the young lawyer a message to take back to the White House: "This is the end of this business of centralization, and I want you to go back and tell the President that we're not going to let this government centralize everything. It's come to an end. As for your young men, you call them together and tell them to get out of Washington—tell them to go home, back to the states. That is where they must do their work."[87] If Brandeis wanted above all to push the president in a leftward direction, his strategy worked: after *Schechter*, Roosevelt indeed embraced the progressive second New Deal. Brandeis watched the developments with "delight"; "F.D. is making a gallant fight," he wrote in August 1935, "and seems to fully appreciate the evils of bigness."[88]

Of the series of anti–New Deal decisions in May, the two most important were, of course, *Schechter* and the *Railroad Retirement Case*. The invalidation of the NIRA provoked a mixed response both within the administration and in the nation at large. Symbolically, the act was of the highest importance, representing as it did the entire New Deal. It had many critics, however, including many of the men close to the president; as for the people, one survey showed them to be almost equally divided for and against the NIRA.[89] The critics of the NIRA came from both sides of the political spectrum. On the right, the *Schechter* decision was hailed as "tyranny overthrown"; radicals like Huey Long were equally happy that the Court had "saved . . . [the] nation from fascism." The Brandeisian liberals were pleased that big business and monopoly had been dealt a blow. In general, the reaction of the nation was an "indecipherable mixture of dismay, delight and confusion." Justice Stone, who joined the unanimous *Schechter* opinion, best expressed the liberals' ambivalence about the case. The result in the NIRA case, he wrote in a letter to the Harvard Law School professor Thomas Reed Powell, "is one in which I can take no comfort, for I think I am as aware as anyone that the power to deal with industry, which has now become national, in a national way, should reside somewhere. According to such light as I have been able to get, the only way in which it can be dealt with adequately would require departure from our traditional distinction between the control of national interests which we call interstate commerce, and local interests which we call intrastate commerce, to such an extent as practically to end the local control of business by the states."[90] Only one group was decidedly and unequivocally upset by the decision, and that was organized labor.[91] The *Railroad Retirement Case*, on the other hand, had no direct impact outside the railroad industry; the case was of great importance, however, because the logic of the Court's decision pointed directly to the conclusion that the proposed social security bill and other New Deal legislation was unconstitutional as well.

Whatever their immediate impact, *Schechter* and the *Railroad Retirement Case* did make it clear that the future of the New Deal required a resolution of several constitutional issues. "We cannot afford . . . to give people the idea that the thing [NIRA] can be worked out as the Court dictated," Roosevelt told Tugwell, "because it cannot."[92] "If this decision [*Schechter*] stands and is not met in some way," wrote Cummings, "it is going to be impossible for the Government to devise any system which will effectively deal with the disorganized industries of the country, or root out, by any affirmative action, manifest evils, sweatshop conditions, child labor, or any other unsocial or anti-social aspects of the economic system."[93] For Cummings, the administration's choice was clear: "We can throw up our hands and say we have done our best . . . or we can strive for some alternative and more circumscribed line of action until the thing can work itself out more naturally."[94]

Just what to do and how to do it was not immediately clear, however. Tugwell suggested an immediate push for a constitutional amendment, but soon realized, as he put it, that "the opinion of everyone seems to be against me on this."[95] Frankfurter counseled a less confrontational strategy, suggesting that Roosevelt take a series of steps to deal with the vacuum created by the defeat of the NIRA, including the strengthening of federal contract provisions to require compliance with the old NIRA provisions; continuation of the National Recovery Administration's administrative structure to assist voluntary and state programs; passage of the Wagner Bill (which became the National Labor Relations Act of 1935); and other measures not inconsistent with *Schechter*. "Postponement of the fighting out" of the "issue of the Supreme Court vs. The President," wrote Frankfurter to Roosevelt, "does not rule the issue out as one on which you may later go to the country. I assume that a strategist like you will select time and circumstances most favorable for victory. I suspect that events may give you better conditions for battle than you have even now."[96]

The chain of events set off by the Court's 1935 decisions would indeed lead to an election campaign in 1936 that would finally resolve the issue sidestepped in the 1934 midterm elections: should the New Deal go forward or be scrapped entirely?

V

The Supreme Court's entrance onto the political stage early in 1935 came at a critical point in the first Roosevelt administration. Despite the rousing Democratic victory in the 1934 elections, Roosevelt was in a difficult position as 1935 began. His opponents on the left, led by Huey Long in the Senate and Father Coughlin over the radio, mounted a successful drive to prevent the United States from joining the World Court, inaugurating the new year with an inauspicious defeat for the administration. Then the Senate voted to defy the president and mandate that prevailing wages be paid to public works employees, and the House gave the president unexpected trouble over social security. Roosevelt's leadership wavered; for the first time, as the historian Arthur Schlesinger notes, "Congress was defying him—and getting away with it." The president's legislative program was "thrown into a state of confusion bordering on chaos."[97]

Roosevelt's lack of leadership at this point stemmed from his own indecision. Caught between two warring groups of advisers, he hesitated. On the left, Brandeis, Frankfurter, and Tugwell were urging him to break with big business and move decisively to the side of labor. On the right, Moley and Bernard Baruch urged the president to stop short of long-term reforms and endorse Moley's declaration that "The New Deal is practically complete." "Inside the group of movements we call the New Deal," wrote Norman Hapgood, "are two philosophies, both wishing to curb the power of plutocracy, but one wishing to do it with a few basic changes, the other believing in a mass of new administrative activities from Washington."[98] Before dealing with mounting threats from the radical left in Congress, Roosevelt had to settle this dispute within his own administration. For the moment, however, the president was unwilling to break with his policy of "striving to hold together a coalition of all interests."

The Court's decisions in the Hot Oil case and the *Gold Clause Cases* caused further problems. After the 1934 election, conservative opposition was scattered and weak. The Republican Party, as Moley described it, was too weak even to be "a suitable target for Roosevelt" to attack; the Liberty League, as we have seen, had yet to get off the ground. With the Court's sudden hint of support for the league's fundamental tenet—that the New Deal was unconstitutional—conservative critics perked up. All at once the Supreme Court held out the possibility that the right-wing position was not only plausible but the law of the land. At its annual Lincoln Day meeting in February 1935, the Republican Party came back to life: Colonel Theodore Roosevelt denounced the New Deal, charging that it "flouted the Constitution, emasculated Congress," and threatened to shake "the foundation of our liberty and democratic government." Herbert Hoover declared that "whatever violates, infringes, or abrogates fundamental American liberty violates the life principle of America as a nation."[99] It became instantly clear that the conservative wing of the Republican Party had seized control and had set the party's 1936 campaign strategy: to make a stand on the Constitution itself. From that point on, the Republicans insisted that only two choices were open to the American people. As presented by one particularly vitriolic newspaper, they were: "(1) Abolition of the planned economy of the New Deal and a return to a constitutional government of specifically described Federal powers, and the resumption by the States of powers which have been usurped in Washington under the present Administration; [or] (2) amendments to the Constitution which will destroy our Federal Constitution and substitute therefore a centralized unitary state armed with sufficient powers to set up and carry on a planned economy administered either by a thinly disguised Caesar, or by a centralized and largely self-perpetuating bureaucracy, or both."[100] Roosevelt continued his attempt to hold together the "all-class coalition" until late May, but the events of that month made it more and more difficult. First, business broke with the administration, a split symbolized by the U.S. Chamber of Commerce's official denunciation of the New Deal. Then came the four key Supreme Court decisions, the most important of which was *Schechter*, the NIRA case.

The Court's opposition to the New Deal might have made Roosevelt more circumspect in promoting his programs, as some of his opponents hoped. *Schechter*, Senator Vandenberg (R.-Mich.) predicted in a letter to Stanley Reed, "would stop the President's ultra-radical advisers from insisting on measures such as the Wagner Labor Bill and the Holding Company Bill at this time" and would give the president "an appeal to those interested in social legislation that he had gone as far as anyone could towards their goal."[101] In fact, however, Roosevelt reacted in precisely the opposite way. Seeing that the right was no longer in any mood to compromise with him and recognizing that the administration's best friend was now organized labor, the president dropped the whole strategy of planning and cooperation with business that had given rise to the NIRA in the first place. The *Schechter* decision especially gave Roosevelt the impetus and motivation to adopt unequivocally the recommendations of his most liberal advisers. In June he began to push forward the most progressive legislation of his first term, inaugurating the "second hundred days," a period in which Congress passed social security, the National Labor Relations Act, and a host of other important measures.

By its firm and uncompromising anti–New Deal decisions in May 1935, the Supreme Court itself became a political issue. Roosevelt added the Court to the Liberty League and big business on his list of political opponents and lashed out at its insistence on keeping the country in the "horse and buggy age." It was widely thought that the anti–New Deal decisions would be helpful to Roosevelt's political chances and that any further conservative decisions would help him even more. Only by such judicial reverses, wrote Arthur Krock, could "the people be induced to extend the Federal power sufficiently to make room for the New Deal."[102] Or, as Felix Frankfurter advised Roosevelt, "Decisions in other cases may accumulate popular grievances against the Court on issues so universally popular that the Borahs, the Clarks, the Nyes, and all the currents of opinion they represent will be with you in addition to the support you have today."[103]

VI

If the president wanted further judicial setbacks, the Supreme Court was willing to oblige. In 1936, the Court continued its crusade against the New Deal with another series of controversial and hostile decisions. In January, the first of these, *United States* v. *Butler*, struck down the Agricultural Adjustment Act.[104] By a six-to-three margin, with Justice Roberts again writing for the Court, the majority held that Congress had no power to control agricultural production, which it deemed a "purely local activity"; that it could not use its taxing power as a means to an unconstitutional end; and that without the taxing provisions the AAA could not stand. Roberts held that the constitutional provision granting Congress the power to "lay and collect taxes . . . to . . . provide for the . . . general welfare of the United States" meant only that Congress could tax to achieve a purpose otherwise constitutional, provided that in addition the tax provided for the general welfare. The General Welfare Clause, in others words, did not expand congressional power but limited it.

Roberts's argument in the AAA case recalled the debate among the Founders as to the meaning of the General Welfare Clause, as Cummings noted. Roberts claimed to support the Hamiltonian position, under which the clause gives Congress "a power separate and distinct from those later enumerated . . . to tax and to appropriate, limited only by the requirement that it shall be exercised to provide for the general welfare of the United States."[105] By reserving to the Court the power to decide the boundaries of that power, however, Roberts seemed to move closer to the view, espoused by Madison and Jefferson, that "Congress is not free to lay taxes *ad libitum, for any purpose they please*, but only to *pay the debts; or provide for the welfare, of the Union.*" "In the long run this [Roberts's] position will be untenable," wrote Cummings in his diary. "In a popular Government the power to decide what is for the general welfare is much safer in the hands of the representatives of the people than in the hands of a permanent body having no direct responsibility to the public and serving for life."[106]

Robert's opinion in *Butler* also placed great stress on states' rights. The crux of the argument was that federal regulation of production was an invasion of the states' police power. Nowhere in the Constitution was there a provision giving Congress the power to convert the United States "into a central government exercising uncontrolled police power in every state of the Union, superseding all local control or regulation of the affairs and concerns of the states," Roberts wrote. Interpreting the taxing power as broadly as the administration wanted to interpret it would lead to "obliterating the constituent members of the Union" and would turn Congress into "a parliament of the whole people, subject to no restrictions save such as are self-imposed."[107]

Just what motivated Roberts to take so extreme a position in the AAA case is difficult to say, for the justice's papers no longer exist and the other justices were careful in the record of the incident they left to posterity. There were rumors that Roberts was angling for the Republican presidential nomination, with Hughes's support, but no confirmation of this assertion is possible. A few years later, Felix Frankfurter asked Roberts if he realized "what a door you opened in your . . . *Butler* decision as to the scope of the 'general welfare,' " and Roberts replied "I do realize it, and often wonder why the hell I did it just to please the Chief."[108] The significance of this correspondence remains unclear.

Justice Stone, with Brandeis and Cardozo, entered a bitter dissent. The Constitution gave Congress the power to tax and spend, they argued; surely Congress could do so conditionally. Roberts and the majority, wrote Stone, had produced a "tortured construction of the Constitution" to arrive at a result motivated by judicial "judgment on the wisdom of legislative action." "Courts," he concluded, "are not the only agency of government that must be assumed to have the capacity to govern."[109] Privately, Stone said simply that "I have a sincere faith that history and long time perspective will see the function of our court in a different light from that in which it is viewed at the moment."[110]

United States v. *Butler* had a profound effect on the developing showdown between liberals and conservatives. For one thing, unlike any New Deal program previously invalidated by the Court, the AAA was both popular and important. Unlike the *Schechter* case, which was applauded even by many who were friendly toward the administration, *Butler* was supported only by the anti-Roosevelt right. Farmers gave strong support to the agency, as did their representatives in Washington, for the simple reason that the program worked. A powerful grass-roots force was thus thrown into the anti-Court movement. More important, the Court's reasoning in *Butler* made it very clear that the judiciary's standing claim to be "above politics" was, in this instance at least, a sham. The Court had invented a new rule of law to strike down an act with which it disagreed and which on the surface seemed to be a valid exercise of congressional power. Stone's warning in dissent that judicial power may also be abused rang true; the danger of this case, unlike any of the 1935 cases, was that the Court seemed intent on making "effective government virtually impossible."[111]

Thus it was *Butler* which inaugurated the six-month-long period in which attacks on the Court reached a peak, and in which constitutional amendments and statutory schemes to curb the Court were discussed with the most frequency. Roberts's insistence on casting the decision in terms of states' rights reinforced the Republican Party's tendency to present itself as the states' rights party and underscored the importance of the federalism question in the upcoming presidential campaign. Both before and after *Butler*, the Republican strategy was to combine support for state (as opposed to federal) power with support for the Constitution itself.

One month after *Butler*, the Court approved the Tennessee Valley Authority Act, upholding Congress's right to create power for defense purposes and to sell the excess to local power companies. By an eight-to-one margin, the Court handed the New Deal its first major victory since the *Gold Clause Cases*. The decision did little to mollify critics of the Court, however, since most took the attitude that the Court tried but simply could not find anything wrong with the act. "If Congress ever passed a measure that was Constitutional," said Senator George Norris (Progressive-Neb.), "this was it." Had the decision gone the other way, pressure for immediate Court reform might well have been unstoppable; even before the decision, Senator Joseph P. Monaghan (D.-Mont.), in a grandiose gesture, introduced a bill that would have removed from office any justice who voted against the Tennessee Valley Authority. Republicans and conservative Democrats stressed the narrow basis of the TVA opinion and tried to counter some of the anti-Court pressure. One Republican paper was reassured that "the nearly unanimous decision at least refuted the weird assumption that the Supreme Court is functioning as a reactionary body bent on blocking the New Deal."[112]

The forces opposing Court reform were bolstered soon after the TVA case by a Court decision striking down a Louisiana licensing tax on newspapers.[113] The case, which grew out of Huey Long's attempts to intimidate opposition newspapers in his state, underscored the importance of the independent judiciary and led even the liberal press to stop for a moment and praise the institution of judicial review. This temporary setback was not the real barrier to the Court reformers, however; the real barrier was the president's continued silence on the Court issue.

With the national party conventions fast approaching, the Supreme Court handed down two more anti–New Deal decisions. The first was *Carter* v. *Carter Coal Co.*, which by a five-to-four vote invalidated the Guffey Coal Act.[114] The Guffey Act had reenacted the Coal Code of the NIRA by statute, thus avoiding the delegation of power problems raised in the Hot Oil and *Schechter* cases. In *Carter*, the Court reaffirmed the rigid distinction between production and commerce, classified the coal industry as engaged primarily in the former, and held it therefore outside the regulatory powers of the United States. The decision paralleled the *Schechter* reasoning, but the chief justice and the three liberals were unconvinced. Hughes, in dissent, stated his belief that the Court should have upheld all of the act except those provisions regulating wages and prices. On that issue, however, he was adamant. "If the people desire to give Congress the power to regulate industries within the States . . . they are at liberty to do so," he wrote, "but it is not for the Court to amend the Constitution."[115] Cardozo, speaking for Brandeis and Stone, would have sustained the law in its entirety.

The *Carter* decision, predictably, drew praise from Republicans and conservatives. Democratic politicians and liberal newspapers fully expected the decision, and it had no real impact on their anti-Court attitudes. After the NIRA and AAA decisions, said the *Chattanooga Times*, the Carter decision "was as inevitable as anything in this uncertain present can be." The issue, said the *Baltimore Sun*, "is essentially what it was when the *Schechter* case was decided a year ago."[116]

The final decision of the October 1935 term was also the most dramatic. In *Morehead* v. *New York* ex rel. *Tipaldo*, the Court held by five to four that the states could not mandate a minimum wage for women and children.[117] Technically all the Court decided was that a New York minimum wage law for women was indistinguishable from a Washington, D.C., statute held unconstitutional in 1923.[118] The Court was not asked to reconsider that case and did not do so. The minority, led by Hughes, found the New York law distinguishable from the older law and in any event found "nothing in the Federal Constitution which denies to the State the power to protect women from being exploited by overreaching employers through the refusal of a fair wage." In view of the "conditions to which the exercise of the protective power of the state was addressed" and the state's requirement that the wage be related to the "reasonable value of the service which the employee performs," Hughes would have sustained the New York law.[119]

The public and the politicians did not recognize the legal complexities of the *Morehead* case and saw only the refusal of the Court to allow the states to do what it had already prohibited the federal government from doing in *Schechter* and *Carter*. Even many of those who had previously opposed Roosevelt were upset with the New York minimum wage decision. The *New York Herald-Tribune*, for example, which according to Roosevelt's speechwriter Stanley High had "hailed every one of the Supreme Court's adverse decisions," declined to editorialize on *Morehead*. The *Morehead* decision, wrote High to his boss, "more than any other previous decision—may solidify opinion in favor of an [constitutional] amendment."[120] Roosevelt broke his year-long silence to decry the existence of a "no-man's-land" in which neither the states nor the federal government could legislate.[121] "The Supreme Court issue seems to be coming to a head," he wrote to his personal secretary Marvin H. McIntyre, "and in the long run it has got to be settled in the right way."[122]

The Republican Party, set to meet in convention only days after the decision, was utterly taken aback. The *Morehead* decision, according to Arthur Krock, caused "one of the swiftest changes on a convention agenda that observers can remember."[123] The Republicans' dilemma was that they had campaigned for a year on a platform stressing two positions which until *Morehead* had been mutually reinforcing but which were now suddenly in conflict. The first was a strong defense of states' rights; the second was a strong stand in favor of "any Supreme Court decision" and against any change in the Constitution. "The true nature of the contemporary constitutional issue," the *St. Paul Pioneer Press* had written back in February, was not economic liberalism against conservatism, but "centralization or decentralization of authority."[124] The Supreme Court's decision in *Morehead* had suddenly shown the importance of that distinction. The Republican Party was not so much a party of economic reaction as a party of states' rights.

The Republican Party was now as opposed to the Court as the Democratic Party, or at least so it seemed, and any chance of campaigning as the party of the Court and of the Constitution was shattered. With many Republicans demanding a constitutional amendment, the Republicans' problem was clear: how could they criticize their opponents for seeking to tamper with the fundamental law when they wanted to do so themselves? Days before the convention, former president Hoover proposed that "the Constitution should be amended" so that states could prevent "sweated hours and wages."[125] Candidate Alf Landon, on the eve of the convention, also moved to back such a proposal.[126] Despite these developments, the party denounced "all attempts to impair the authority of the Supreme Court" and pledged its support for "the American system of Constitutional and local self-government."[127] On the minimum wage issue, however, it included in the platform a pledge to "support the adoption of state laws and interstate compacts to abolish sweatshops and child labor, and to protect women and children with respect to maximum hours, minimum wages and working conditions." Sounding much like Roosevelt, the platform added only, "We believe that this can be done within the Constitution as it now stands."[128]

The extent to which the Republican Party had planned to base its campaign on states' rights and on the Constitution—and the extent to which the two issues were related—should not be underestimated. The platform adopted in 1936 was fairly liberal, except that it relied on the states and not the federal government for much of the governmental action needed. The platform supported federal grants-in-aid to support local relief; proposed a minimum income for Americans over sixty-five, paid out of current receipts rather than by insurance; supported organized labor's right to bargain collectively; opposed private monopolies; supported federal regulation of securities trading and of public utilities; favored "equal opportunity for our colored citizens"; and, in general, assumed "the obligations and duties imposed upon Government by modern conditions." The platform was conservative only in its approaches to farm relief, currency laws, and the federal budget, and in its insistence on limited delegation of power to the executive. Where the party differed most from the Democrats was in its emphasis on state (instead of federal) action to achieve these ends.

Landon, soon to be nominated, did not hide his position on the amendment issue. If the convention were wrong and the Constitution as written did not permit state minimum wage laws for women and children, he announced, he would "favor a constitutional amendment permitting the states to adopt such legislation as may be necessary adequately to protect women and children in the matter of maximum hours, minimum wages and working conditions."[129] The candidate thus abandoned his party's strongest position; as *the New York Times* put it a few days before Landon's remarks, "For months [the Republicans'] . . . chief battle cry has been 'stand by the Court'. . . . To advocate . . . [a constitutional amendment] now at Cleveland, merely because public opinion has been disturbed and distressed by a single decision of the Supreme Court, would be inviting Republican orators to swallow their own words."[130]

The Republicans had been pushed into an impossible position, and Roosevelt, with the politician's killer instinct, moved in to press his advantage. In a speech delivered at the Arkansas Constitution Centennial celebration in Little Rock on 10 June, while the Republican Convention was still in session, the president turned the constitutional issue on its head. Whereas Republicans were calling for a constitutional amendment to overturn *Morehead*, Roosevelt expressed his long-held belief that the Constitution "is intended to meet and fit the amazing physical, economic and social requirements that confront us in this modern generation."[131] He put himself squarely behind both progress and the Constitution by equating the "constitutional guarantees of life, liberty and the pursuit of happiness" with the solution of the problems of "prices, wages, hours of labor, fair competition, conditions of employment, [and] social security."[132]

The *Morehead* decision eliminated any possibility that Roosevelt would endorse a constitutional amendment to deal with the Court. Though many Democrats favored amendment, it became clear to FDR and his close advisers that the Republicans' dilemma called for precisely the opposite approach. The "primary difficulty" with the platform plank calling for an amendment, wrote Cummings, "seems to be that if we attempt to deal specifically with this problem we must go further than the Republican Platform, or its candidate, that an entirely new situation is apt to be created which may shift the emphasis of the campaign." In drafting language of a possible amendment, therefore, it was necessary to avoid "too apparent a criticism of the Supreme Court."[133]

Ultimately, the president refused to endorse any constitutional amendment or to attack the Supreme Court directly, thus taking much of the sting out of Republican charges that he was a radical opponent of the Constitution. Likewise, he refused to indicate how he would deal with the Court problem once the campaign was over. Though the majority of delegates on the Democratic Platform Committee supported an amendment, Roosevelt's lieutenants persuaded the committee to support a plank calling only for an amendment "if necessary."[134] Roosevelt's political managers were anxious to avoid making the issue of constitutional change the dominant issue of the campaign, preferring instead to focus on the accomplishments of Roosevelt's first term and on the need for completion of the New Deal.

Roosevelt accepted his party's nomination with a speech in which he declared that the New Deal was a "war for the survival of democracy." As such, it was he and not Landon who was the true friend of the Constitution: "In vain they seek to hide behind the flag and the Constitution. In their blindness they forget what the Flag and the Constitution stand for. Now, as always, they stand for democracy, not tyranny; for freedom, not subjection; and against a dictatorship by mob rule and the overprivileged elites."[135]

The president never changed his basic campaign strategy: the New Deal was necessary and in keeping with American values; the states were not capable of achieving the necessary reforms by themselves; it was he and not the conservatives who truly understood the spirit of the Constitution. He stressed the success of his administration in fighting the economic crisis; cast the campaign as one between the people and the "privileged princes" of the "new economic dynasties," and called for carrying forward "American freedom and American peace by making them living facts in a living present."[136]

The Republicans, led by Landon, were on the defensive. Landon warned against the destruction of "American institutions" and accused the administration of trying "to change the fundamental principles of our American government."[137] He upbraided Roosevelt for centralizing power in the federal government and for doing this "under cover . . . and not with the consent of the people's Constitution."[138] Toward the end of the campaign he stepped up his rhetoric on the Court issue, accusing Roosevelt, for example, of a "deliberate attempt to break down the confidence of our people in the independence of the Supreme Court" and of regarding the Court "as a minor barrier to be circumvented if it can't be hurdled."[139] Since Landon could charge FDR with no specific act of defiance against the Court, and since Roosevelt claimed to support the Constitution fully, these charges appeared to be made more in desperation at the end of a difficult campaign than anything else.

The results in November were overwhelmingly in favor of Roosevelt and the New Deal. FDR's landslide was even greater than in 1932; he won every state except two, Maine and Vermont. Implicitly, the election was also a rejection of the Supreme Court's interpretation of the Constitution. Everyone expected some sort of action by Roosevelt in the wake of his fresh mandate, or some indication that the Court might "follow the election returns." Stanley Reed, for example, noted two days after the election that one argument in favor of delaying a court test of the Social Security Act was that "there may be growing changes in the attitude of the Supreme Court following the election."[140] Cummings had mixed feelings about the future of the Court. On 15 November he reported, "I told the President that the atmosphere of the Court had manifestly changed since the election. Apparently the Supreme Court had read the election returns, to use the old phrase of Mr. Dooley. There is always the bare chance that we may begin to get some more enlightened opinions, though I have not much hope in that direction."[141]

In late November, the Court showed the first signs of a shift toward the administration's position, approving a state unemployment compensation statute despite arguable similarities to the *Railroad Retirement Case* and other previous cases.[142] The vote upholding the law was four to four—but Justice Stone, normally on the liberal side, did not participate due to illness. Thus—possibly—Roberts had moved to the president's side.[143] The tie vote, while upholding the law, did not set a precedent and was decided upon technical grounds. At the time, however, there was considerable speculation that the Court was indeed reading the papers, and that with Stone's return a majority in favor of the New Deal would replace the majority against it. Cummings wired Roosevelt that "the result is encouraging since it indicates increasing liberalism of one justice probably Justice Roberts," but, Cummings cautioned, the case "throws little light on the constitutionality of the federal social security statute."[144]

The insurance case was in fact a precursor of things to come; by the following April, the New Deal was firmly upheld as consistent with the Constitution. In between, of course, came Roosevelt's remedy; but before turning to the "Court-packing" plan, it is necessary to examine the alternatives available to the president. Those alternatives, in turn, were closely related to the criticisms leveled against the Court by the president and others.

VII

Roosevelt's first move after *Schechter* in May 1935 was to act swiftly and surely to comply with the letter of the Supreme Court's law. Within days of the decision he ordered the Justice Department to drop over 400 cases against alleged violators of the NIRA codes. He terminated the operation of fourteen agencies which had been established in whole or in part under the Recovery Act. In order to continue skeleton operations of the National Recovery Administration itself, he specifically asked Congress for new, limited legislation. Still, Roosevelt's compliance by no means signified a willingness to abandon the New Deal: he proposed federal approval of state compacts to regulate oil production; supported legislation to enact a new NRA-style code for the coal industry through the direct provisions of the Guffey Coal Act; and pushed ahead with plans for social security and other new legislation despite serious doubts as to their constitutionality under the decisions in *Schechter* and the *Railroad Retirement Case*.

Like Lincoln eighty years before, Roosevelt did not let the Court's decisions interfere with his support of new programs similar to those just invalidated. Unlike Lincoln, Roosevelt did not simply ignore the Court and insist that Congress and the president had the right to form their own judgments as to constitutional questions. Instead, he argued that the legal questions involved in the New Deal cases were so complicated that minor differences in phraseology between two particular laws could have a critical impact on their constitutionality. In defending his support for the Guffey Act despite similarities to the NIRA, Roosevelt told the Congress that no one could be sure whether the act was or was not constitutional, since "you can get not ten but a thousand differing legal opinions on the subject."[145] In view of the uncertainties involved, Roosevelt suggested that the Congress simply act and allow the Court to rule on the constitutional issue in each particular case. "A decision by the Supreme Court relative to this measure would be helpful as indicating with increasing clarity, the constitutional limits within which this government must operate," he said in a famous letter on the Guffey Act. Thus Congress ought not to "permit doubts as to constitutionality, however reasonable, to block the suggested legislation."[146]

While he made no immediate move to reform the Court or to pressure it into a reversal of its position, the president did voice his objections to the Court's decisions at a press conference immediately after *Schechter*. It was at this point that he accused the Court of being stuck in the "horse-and-buggy age," and he predicted that "we are facing a very, very great national non-partisan issue" which the nation would have to decide "one way or the other."[147] As a result of these relatively mild statements the president was subjected to a barrage of criticism and accusations that he was disrespectful of the Court and the Constitution. Consequently, Roosevelt adopted a strict strategy of silence on the Court issue, deviating only to declare the existence of a "no-man's-land" after the Court invalidated the New York State minimum wage law in 1936. Instead, Roosevelt made only general statements about the desirability and constitutionality of the New Deal, implying but not articulating the same sentiments he had expressed in the post-*Schechter* press conference. Shortly after the AAA decision, in fact, FDR received a memo, apparently from Assistant Press Secretary Stephen T. Early, cautioning him, "Please resist all—say nothing about the case."[148]

Roosevelt revealed his views on the Court issue only after the introduction of the Court-packing plan in February 1937. Other opponents of the Court, both inside and outside the administration, were less concerned with appearances and so spoke out on the Court issue throughout 1935 and 1936. These critics fell roughly into two groups, depending on their views on the Constitution itself, and on their views as to the inherent validity of judicial review.

The first group believed that the Court and the Constitution were inherently antidemocratic and hence illegitimate. Following the intellectual leadership of the historian Charles A. Beard, they argued that the Constitution was designed and adopted by men who represented "the solid, conservative, commercial and financial interests," men whose first priority was to prevent the attack by legislative majorities on private economic rights.[149] In this view, the Court's judicial review function (which Beard called judicial "control") fit precisely into the larger purposes of the Founders. The Court was specifically given the power to review and strike down acts of Congress in order to guard "the established rights of property" from popular assault. Using this historical argument, Beard and his followers discredited both the Court and the Constitution as essentially antidemocratic.

To those like Beard, the Court's power of judicial review was an intolerable encroachment on the power of the people to govern. "It amazes the public that nine men, sitting as a supreme court, are willing to stop the wheels of recovery when it is perfectly apparent that the people of every State of the Union want the machinery of government to go ahead," wrote a former Congressman in 1935.[150] Congressman Fred H. Hildebrandt (D.-S.D.) saw the New Deal as a battle between "democracy and plutocracy" and asked "whether Congress may enact legislation intended to lessen or abolish poverty without having its will thwarted by an oligarchy of 'untouchables' beyond governmental reach and utterly indifferent to human rights."[151] To those to whom the opposite of democracy was aristocracy, the justices were aristocrats; to those to whom the opposite of democracy was despotism, they were supreme despots, "a group of public dictators and tyrants and without responsibility to anyone."[152]

No one called for the abolition of the Constitution, but these more radical progressives did demand changes so fundamental that they would have permanently altered the nature of American government. Hildebrandt, for example, favored a constitutional convention to enact major changes. Others called for a limitation on the term of federal judges, forcing them, like congressmen, to "make an accounting to their constituents."[153] Congressman Robert L. Ramsay (D.-W.Va.) proposed the establishment of a national referendum process, the results of which would be beyond judicial scrutiny. Donald Richberg, formerly general counsel of the NRA and an intimate of Roosevelt, favored an amendment allowing Congress to reenact a law that had been declared unconstitutional.[154] There were proposals to eliminate the Court's power of judicial review entirely, either by amendment or by statute. One popular remedy was to require a supermajority of the Court in order to invalidate a federal statute; usually, the suggested margin was a minimum of seven to two or six to three. Benjamin Cohen suggested that Congress be given the power to override a judicial "veto" by a two-thirds vote.[155] Finally there were proposals that appeared moderate in form but which would have had a profound impact on the American system, whether intentional or not. One congressman introduced a constitutional amendment giving Congress the power to make all laws "which in its judgment shall be necessary for the general welfare of the people."[156]

In numbers, those who supported such comparatively extreme proposals were far outweighed by more moderate critics of the Court; indeed, most influential members of the administration, and most leading Congressmen and Senators, eschewed such proposals in favor of less controversial remedies. To these men, the Constitution as written was not inherently antidemocratic; it was simply in need of updating to cope with modern economic realities. Whatever the merits of the constitutional system when it was adopted in 1787, it was not suitable for the modern age unless given a new interpretation. The greatness of the document, however, lay precisely in the fact that the Founders had foreseen the necessity of updating it and had provided appropriate mechanisms for change. Thus they had provided the amendment process. More importantly, they had phrased constitutional provisions in broad, open-ended language that could grow and be adapted as necessary. "Our Constitution is so simple and practical that it is possible always to meet extraordinary needs by changes in emphasis and arrangement without loss of essential form," Roosevelt had told the nation in 1933.[157] By periodic amendment and reinterpretation, the Constitution could become "the broad highway through which alone true progress may be enjoyed."[158] Instead of viewing the Constitution as a barrier to popular rule, the moderates saw it as "an instrument designed to secure justice through giving full expression to the deliberate and well-thought-out judgment of the people."[159]

To the moderates, the Court problem was not the result of any inherent bias in the Constitution or in the judicial branch but of the particular interpretation of the Constitution adhered to by the majority of present justices. "The real difficulty," wrote Cummings, "is not with the Constitution but with the Judges who interpret it."[160] By miring themselves in the past, the "nine old men" refused to bring themselves or the Constitution into modernity and thus perverted the intent of the Founders.[161] The issue of the justices' advanced years itself became symbolic of their outdated attitude. The justices were accused of standing "in the path of progress," of "beating the living with the bones of the dead," and of being the medium through which the "dead and withered hand of Alexander Hamilton" directed "the policies of every administration."[162]

The main disagreement among the moderates was whether or not the updating of the Constitution required constitutional amendment. To Rexford Tugwell and Raymond Moley, for example, amendment was the only way out. They and many others supported narrow amendments directed specifically at expanding Congress's power to regulate economic affairs. There were innumerable variations on the theme; one amendment, for example, would have given Congress the power to regulate agriculture but no other segment of the economy; another would have simply eliminated all restrictions on congressional regulation of wages, hours, and working conditions.

Many, however, believed and hoped that constitutional change was not necessary, among them Homer Cummings, Robert Jackson, and Stanley Reed at the Justice Department, and Edward S. Corwin, a constitutional scholar then at Princeton University. Instead, they insisted that a new interpretation of the old text was all that was required; the important thing, therefore, was to get the Supreme Court to change its mind. In their view the correct mode of constitutional interpretation involved not a slavish devotion to the particular formulation given to the text by the Founders, but rather a requirement that the justices give due weight to changing economic and social conditions and to the changing views and moral standards of the people. Except when the constitutional text was explicit and incapable of being updated, in which case amendment was called for, judges had to take it upon themselves to seek out the popular will and apply it to the Constitution's broad and vague language. The leaders in the Justice Department best specified the new standards for judicial interpretation. "I cannot but feel," Reed said simply, "that the broad and general powers, which the Constitution has conferred upon the National Government, will prove adequate to meet our national needs."[163] Homer Cummings, in a similar vein, declared that

> The Courts may give, and as a rule do give, less weight to what they feel to be temporary currents of opinion, casual pressures for reform, evanescent aspirations, or momentary ideals, as contrasted with what they may properly regard as the confirmed and enlightened sense of justice developed by the changing life of a vital and growing nation.
>
> If the Courts prove mistaken in their reading of this ultimate will, or if the Constitution itself in some clearly expressed provision no longer conforms thereto, then, by its very terms the people are guaranteed the right to make their desires effective through the solemn process of amendment.[164]

The Court, like the Constitution, had to be flexible. "If our Constitution is to be a living thing, if it is not to be hard and brittle and crack under the strain of actuality," said one New Dealer, then it must be "interpreted in no spirit of formal logic but as a vital, growing framework for a government capable of ministering to the needs of a nation of 150,000,000 people."[165]

VIII

Early in 1936 it appeared that those insisting that a constitutional amendment was necessary to reverse the Supreme Court's series of anti–New Deal decisions were right. There were several problems with the amendments route, however, most of which were practical or logistical. For one thing, the process was both slow and uncertain. After months or years of debate, the ratification process might well end in defeat, since it was possible that "13 states which contain only 5 percent of the voting population can block ratification even though the 35 states with 95 percent of the population are in favor of it."[166] For another, even those who agreed that an amendment was necessary and desirable had yet to agree on any particular phraseology, and there was the chance that they would never agree. Third, once an amendment was passed it would be subject to judicial interpretation just like the rest of the Constitution; as the future Justice Jackson put it, "Judges who resort to a tortured construction of the Constitution may torture an amendment. You cannot amend a state of mind and mental attitude of hostility to exercise of governmental power."[167] Finally, any proposed amendment would be likely to create a strong pro-Constitution backlash, making the amending process a "practical impossibility. . . . The proposer of an amendment would be heralded as a monster. The gentlest proponent imaginable would be greeted by three-fourths of the headlines of the Nation's papers as 'Wants to Smash the Constitution.' "[168] Arthur Krock of *The New York Times* summed up the problems facing potential backers of an amendment: "An amendment is difficult to write, and most dangerous to defend."[169]

Ultimately it was Roosevelt and Cummings who rejected the amendment process, and their reasoning went beyond these practical considerations. The amendment process was unacceptable to these men simply because the Constitution, according to their philosophy, was not at fault. The fault lay instead with the conservative justices who insisted on interpreting the Constitution in an erroneous and dangerous spirit. "We must find a way to take an appeal from the Supreme Court to the Constitution itself," Roosevelt told the nation in March 1937 when at last he broke his silence over the Court issue. "We must have judges who will bring to the courts a present-day sense of the Constitution."[170] In selecting a solution to the Court problem, Roosevelt began with the assumption that it was the current membership of the Court, and not judicial review itself, that had to be altered. "Our difficulty with the Court today rises not from the Court as an institution but from human beings within it," he said.[171] "The permanence of the Court personnel," he told the journalist Arthur Krock, "was the outstanding flaw."[172] Constitutional amendment simply would not reach the heart of the problem, which was to find a way "to restore the

Court to its rightful and historic place in our system of constitutional government and to have it resume its high task of building anew on the Constitution 'a system of living law.' "[173]

IX

Once Roosevelt had decided against a constitutional amendment, there were still several alternatives. One of these was simply to wait until death or resignation provided the president with one or two new Supreme Court appointments. By all odds Roosevelt should have had several opportunities to appoint new justices during his first term; given the advanced age of many of the justices, it was a near certainty that such opportunities would be available during the second term. The sheer obstinacy of men like McReynolds and Van Devanter, who appeared at times determined never to resign but to hang on to their lives as long as was necessary to frustrate Roosevelt, makes it at least understandable that Roosevelt did not choose to wait for nature to take its course.

Various statutory schemes were proposed to solve the Court problem. All were controversial, and some were of dubious constitutionality. The most common proposals were to alter the size of the Court; to eliminate or modify judicial review by congressional declaration; to withdraw the Court's jurisdiction to review all or certain acts of Congress, utilizing the Constitution's provision that Congress can make exceptions to the Court's appellate jurisdiction; and to impeach and remove recalcitrant judges from office. Of these, the elimination of judicial review was rejected as probably unconstitutional, and the impeachment idea, though suggested several times, never caught on, presumably because of the long-standing tradition against such actions except in cases of criminal or other gross misconduct.

That left the expansion of the Court and the modification of its jurisdiction as the only viable alternatives. Both had historical precedents—the size of the Court was left entirely to Congress and had been changed often in the past, once, arguably, to prevent the invalidation of important legislation.[174] In addition, a similar idea had been tried successfully in England against the House of Lords two decades before. The Court's appellate jurisdiction had been modified for similar purposes once before, with mixed success, during the days of Reconstruction.[175]

Cummings and Roosevelt eventually settled on the idea of expanding the size of the Court.[176] As finally presented to the Congress, the idea was to permit the president to appoint a new justice for every justice over seventy who refused to retire. At the time, the law would have given Roosevelt six new appointees (provided that no one retired in the meantime), clearly enough to create a majority to overrule every major case except *Schechter*. The other possibility, of course, was that the Court might feel the pressure of the proposed law and switch of its own accord, much the way the House of Lords did in 1910–12.

Just why the president and Cummings settled on the Court-packing plan instead of trying to limit the Court's appellate jurisdiction is not entirely clear. Joseph Alsop, in his contemporary account of the Court-packing crisis, claims that both men feared "the possibility that the lower courts might prove as recalcitrant as the high bench" and were afraid that the Court would find some way to hear the New Deal cases through its original jurisdiction involving the states.[177] Leuchtenburg asserts that the president was captivated by the English precedent and that Roosevelt "took a mischievous pleasure" in the ironic fact that Justice McReynolds himself, when Wilson's attorney general, had made exactly the same proposal.[178] Roosevelt and Cummings may also have feared the possibility that the Court would strike down a limitation on its appellate jurisdiction as unconstitutional. The most important feature of the Court-packing plan from Roosevelt's point of view, however, was probably the fact that it alone struck at the root of the problem: the five or six old men who had held the New Deal ransom to their interpretation of the Constitution.

Roosevelt sent what was now called the Judicial Reorganization Act to Congress in February 1937, accompanied by a written message and a letter from the attorney general. The White House kept the plan a careful secret. Roosevelt told Frankfurter only, "Very confidentially, I may give you an awful shock in about two weeks," while Ben Cohen and Tommy Corcoran, though intimately connected with the inner circles of the administration, were apparently told nothing.[179] Word that a Court bill was on the way had been circulating in Washington for several weeks, but the specifics of the proposal occasioned a great deal of surprise when finally released. Given the intensity and volume of speculation on whether Roosevelt would indeed "pack" the Court, it is especially surprising that the president would present the plan in a disingenuous manner, but nonetheless he buried the packing provisions deep inside a major judicial reorganization bill, most of which would have been otherwise uncontroversial.[180] In his message, he argued that the aged justices were unwilling to pursue "an examination of complicated and changed conditions" and were unable to keep up with their workload.[181] The bill, he said deviously, had four purposes: "First, to eliminate congestion of calendars and to make the judiciary as a whole less static by the constant and systematic addition of new blood . . . ; second, to make the judiciary more elastic by providing for temporary transfers of circuit and district court judges [to other districts] . . . ; third, to furnish the Supreme Court practical assistance in supervising . . . the lower courts; fourth, to eliminate inequality, uncertainty, and delay now existing in the determination of constitutional questions."[182] Playing the charade to the limit, Roosevelt included a letter from Homer Cummings that decried "delay in the administration of justice" as "the outstanding defect of our Federal judicial system."[183] Chief Justice Hughes later sent a famous letter to Senator Burton K. Wheeler, contesting Roosevelt's charge that the Court was behind in its work. "The Supreme Court is fully abreast of its work," he wrote. "There is no congestion upon our calendar."[184]

Roosevelt's presentation in fact fooled no one. There was a great deal of immediate criticism of the Court-packing plan, from the press, from Congress, and from other prominent voices. The major purpose of the bill, wrote the *Cleveland Plain Dealer*, was to bend the Supreme Court "to the will of a popular executive."[185] "Surely Mr. Roosevelt's mandate was to function as President, not as Der Fuehrer," wrote William Allen White. "How long will the people be fooled?" To Raymond Moley, by now estranged from the administration, the Court-packing plan was "perilously near to a proposal to abandon Constitutional Government."[186]

The bar, for the most part, also responded negatively. Among the prominent lawyers who criticized the plan were Clarence Darrow; Morris L. Ernst; Roosevelt's former mentor, Henry L. Stimson; the president of the American Bar Association and a number of past presidents; and former attorneys general William Mitchell and George H. Farnum. Many congressional Democrats supported the president's idea, at least publicly, but most Republicans and a significant number of Democrats opposed it.[187]

Overall, the Court-packing plan caused a great deal of dissension. "Certainly, the sentiment is rolling up against him," wrote Henry Morgenthau in his diary a few days after the bill was introduced. "I hear it on every side. I have not met anybody who thinks well of it."[188]

In this atmosphere, Roosevelt took to the radio to make a direct appeal to the American people. In his speech, Roosevelt clearly set forth his belief in the propriety of the bill, speaking out against the Court in the harshest language he had used since his post-*Schechter* press conference, and setting out his constitutional philosophy in defense of the Court-packing plan. He reiterated his belief that the Framers intended the Constitution to be adaptable and flexible and chastised the Court for its unwillingness to presume the constitutionality of validly adopted statutes. The Court, he said, had assumed the power "to pass on the wisdom" of the laws rather than on their constitutionality, and had thus set itself up as a "super-legislature."[189] The president defended the plan as the only practical way to regenerate "a Supreme Court which will do justice under the Constitution—not over it." Amendments were out for all the reasons discussed above; the only alternative was to replace the old blood on the Court with younger men "who have had personal experience and contact with modern facts and circumstances." He insisted that "There is nothing new or radical about this idea."

From Roosevelt's perspective, the reorganization plan was the least radical of all the alternatives. He displayed a curious yet consistent unwillingness to amend the Constitution, an unwillingness that seems to have gone beyond the practical difficulties involved in the amendment process. Indeed, the practical difficulties might not have been as big a problem as FDR suggested; as Norman Hapgood put it, "Suppose a movement is set on foot to amend the Constitution. If the amendment is one that has the approval of Justices Brandeis, Stone, and Cardozo the opposition will be archaic and futile."[190] As he saw it, the Court-packing plan would have preserved the Constitution and the Court, eliminating only the justices who by their misunderstanding of the Constitution threatened democracy itself.

Despite all the criticism of the Court-packing plan, Roosevelt's chances of getting the bill through Congress were not overwhelmingly negative. On 15 February, just a few days after the plan was announced, Morgenthau put FDR's chances at around "50-50."[191] An early survey of senatorial opinion by the *Literary Digest* found 31 senators in favor of the proposal, 24 against, and 41 undecided.[192] As late as 17 June a White House headcount predicted 45 senators for the plan, 39 against, and 12 uncommitted, with 49 needed for victory in the Senate.[193]

The Court-packing proposal is commonly regarded as one of Roosevelt's most serious political blunders. According to polls at the time, over half the American people opposed the bill, despite overwhelming support for the New Deal. The plan was rightly regarded as a threat to the "ambiguous and delicately balanced American tradition of government."[194] Lawyers declared forthrightly that "we want an independent judiciary";[195] liberals and conservatives alike now defended the Court as "the sole bulwark of our personal liberties."[196] In the end, the Senate Judiciary Committee killed the bill by recommending to the full Senate that the bill "should be so emphatically rejected that its parallel will never again be presented to the free representatives of a free people."[197]

The president's misreading of the public pulse stemmed not simply from his underestimation of popular sympathy for the Supreme Court as an institution nor from a belief that his mandate was so complete that he could succeed on any course. Instead, as Leuchtenburg points out, the plan "was not a capricious act but the result of a long period of gestation." Alternatives were considered and rejected "on not unreasonable grounds." In the end, packing the Court was the only proposal that fit in with Roosevelt's attitude toward the Constitution, for it alone preserved the integrity of the Constitution from judicial attack. That the American people saw it as a radical and irresponsible proposal should not cloud our judgment as to Roosevelt's viewpoint.

The resolution of the Court-packing crisis comes as a sort of anticlimax. At the height of the controversy, the Court handed down its decision in a case called *West Coast Hotel* v. *Parrish*,[198] reversing *Adkins* (the Washington, D.C., minimum wage case) and allowing state minimum wage laws for women. The key switcher was Roberts, who joined Hughes, Brandeis, Cardozo, and Stone in the majority. The nation had scarcely recovered from this shock when the Court summarily overruled *Schechter* and *Carter Coal* by the same five-to-four vote in *National Labor Relations Board* v. *Jones and Laughlin Steel*.[199] Chief Justice Hughes wrote both opinions, declaring in the latter case that the Court would no longer "shut our eyes to the plainest facts of our national life."[200] The aged and broken Van Devanter announced his retirement in mid-May, and by 1941 only Stone and Roberts would be left from the New Deal Court.

Whether Roberts switched as a result of the election or the Court-packing plan—or even earlier—is impossible to say.[201] Roberts's support of the New York State unemployment compensation law in November

1936 may indicate an early switch, though this is purely speculation, given the technical grounds of that decision. In any event, the results of the 1936 elections made it highly likely that some resolution of the crisis in favor of the New Deal would be worked out; through the appointment process alone, Roosevelt had the opportunity in his second term to name an almost entirely new Court. Roberts's switch simply made the transition quicker and less painful.

X

The Court crisis of the 1930s must be interpreted as one part of the larger crisis that rocked the nation during the New Deal era. The strains and dislocations brought on by the onset of the Great Depression forced a reconsideration of the role of the federal government in economic regulation, and this question dominated national politics for over four years. In the process, the Republican majority at the national level was shattered and replaced by a Democratic coalition centered around the urban working class. The Roosevelt administration reached the conclusion that a satisfactory solution to the economic emergency would require a fundamental restructuring of the American economy, a task that could be accomplished only with greatly expanded federal involvement. Roosevelt believed, moreover, that this revolution in the role of the national government could be accomplished without formal constitutional change. The Court became a factor in the New Deal realignment when it challenged this assumption.

It was by no means inevitable that the Court would oppose the New Deal on constitutional grounds. Though the New Deal legislation expanded federal power beyond anything previously attempted, the Court's precedents by no means clearly indicated that the New Deal was unconstitutional. Those on and off the Court who believed the New Deal to be compatible with the Constitution could do so without doing violence to the Constitution or to the Supreme Court's previous decisions. Over the course of some fifty years, the Court had created a patchwork crazy-quilt of precedents, some expanding and some constricting federal power. For every decision in this period hostile to the expansion of federal power, there is another one friendly to it. The New Deal cases presented new questions of law and required an interpretation and extension of precedents, but the final outcome was by no means determined by those precedents. In some cases, the Court had only to draw on the conservative precedents to invalidate New Deal legislation; examples are *Schechter* and the New York minimum wage case. In others—most notably the *Railroad Retirement Case* and *United States* v. *Butler*—the Court invented wholly new law in order to strike down New Deal programs.

Whether or not the Court was following its own precedents throughout the 1930s is not really the important issue, however. It is far more important to understand just how conservative the Court was in 1935 compared to the other actors in the political system. Both the Democratic and Republican parties were divided at the time into centrist and polar wings; the election of 1934 had been fought between the moderates in both parties over whether to move ahead with the New Deal cautiously or not at all. The Court's actions in 1935—especially its lecture to the administration in the *Gold Clause Cases*—gave legitimacy to the polar wing of the Republican Party, and to groups like the Liberty League which had been outcasts in 1934. The Court's sudden opposition to the New Deal contributed to business's break with the administration and to the resultant countermovement of the Democratic Party to the left. As in the case of *Dred Scott*, the Supreme Court helped to precipitate the polarization of the party system by establishing the platform of the most conservative party as the law of the land. The Republican Party did not polarize around Herbert Hoover's 1932 platform; the 1932 election was fought between two candidates whom many in the electorate could not tell apart. Nor did the party polarize over the 1934 election, which was fought over narrow issues. It was only after the Court had entered on their side that the ultraconservatives were able to wrest control of the Republican Party away from the moderate centrists.

By bringing the constitutional issue to the surface in its 1935 and 1936 decisions, the Supreme Court in effect established the agenda for the 1936 presidential campaign. In 1936 the New Deal was put to the test for the first time; the 1936 election was the only one of the period to involve two polarized positions on a single, dominant issue. The results of the election were definitive in terms of the shape of public policy and were widely regarded as such at the time.

Though the Court could play a critical role in bringing the constitutional implications of the New Deal into the open, it could no more resolve those issues for the nation than it could have resolved the national crises over slavery or Reconstruction. By trying to do so, the Court brought down upon itself the fury of a powerful and popular president, backed by an overwhelmingly supportive Congress. Yet even this was not enough to harm the Court in any serious way. The Court-packing plan failed, its defeat helped by the Court's better-late-than-never realization that it could never win the battle it had sought for itself. The Court emerged from the crisis to play an even greater role in the formation of public policy in the years after the New Deal than it had before. Much of the Court's rapid recovery can be attributed to the extremely negative response to the Court-packing plan, which by threatening the Court actually highlighted its strength. To a great extent, however, the Court survived the New Deal crisis because virtually no one—including Roosevelt—sought to harm it. Once again the nation had no real complaint with judicial power but only a disagreement with the Court over critical issues of national policy. Once those issues were resolved, the Court was quickly and unmistakably put back on its pedestal.

V

The Modern Supreme Court:
Crisis as Usual?

"IN THE FIELD of public education," declared Chief Justice Earl Warren on 17 May 1954, "the doctrine of 'separate but equal' has no place." With those words Warren—and the unanimous Supreme Court for which he spoke—forever changed American society. Warren's decision in the landmark case of *Brown* v. *Board of Education* also transformed the Supreme Court; with *Brown*, the Court reasserted itself as an independent force in American politics and ended nearly two decades of relative docility in the wake of the New Deal crisis.[1]

Like the Supreme Court's earlier excursions into the world of politics, the *Brown* decision exposed the Court to a considerable amount of criticism and controversy. Unlike the crises of the past, however, the controversy that swirled around the Court in the 1950s was not limited to a single issue, or even to a group of closely related issues. Furthermore, also in contrast to the pattern of past crises, the controversy that began with *Brown* did not subside quickly, but persisted for more than three decades, and continues even today. The Court, apparently thriving on controversy, also moved into the areas of criminal procedure, school prayer, reapportionment, school busing, abortion, and many others. As its decisions provoked more and more criticism and controversy, the Court became even more active and involved in affecting the nature of American politics and society. Furthermore, the Supreme Court's lead emboldened the lower federal courts to extend their supervision of state action beyond anything previously imagined—leading to judicial oversight and even direct judicial management of prisons, mental hospitals, and state election systems.

The scope and impact of the Court's many controversial decisions over the past thirty years, and the remarkably persistent and intense criticism they have produced, requires a new evaluation of the nature of and the limits to the Court's power. The historical arguments of the last three chapters provide a baseline of comparison against which the controversies of the past three decades can be measured. With the crises of *Dred Scott*, Reconstruction, and the New Deal as yardsticks, it is possible to address the critical questions raised by the Court's performance in the modern era: Just how serious is the modern controversy for the Court? How has the Court managed to survive and thrive in the modern era, and what are its prospects for the future? Is the Supreme Court truly the head of an "imperial judiciary"? These questions, in turn, require an examination of the turbulent and unprecedented history of the modern Supreme Court.

I

The story of the modern Supreme Court begins with *Brown* v. *Board of Education* in 1954. In *Brown*, the Court reversed its own long-standing decision permitting "separate but equal" schools and other facilities for blacks and whites.[2] The first *Brown* case (which is commonly referred to as *Brown I*), decided on 17 May 1954, held only that "separate" schools were "inherently unequal," thus condemning a practice followed in seventeen states and the District of Columbia.[3] Precisely what should be done to bring about the desegregation of the Southern schools the Court did not say; instead, it ordered new arguments to be heard the following December. Only in May 1955 did the Court rule that Southern schools were to be desegregated "with all deliberate speed," and that the decree would be carried out under the equity powers of the federal district courts. The 1955 enforcement decision is commonly referred to as *Brown II*.[4]

The importance of *Brown I* was clear from the start. Said *Time* magazine: "In its 164 years the court has erected many a landmark of U.S. history: Marbury v. Madison, the Bank of the United States case, Dred Scott, the Slaughterhouse cases, the "Sick Chicken" case that killed the NRA, 1952's steel seizure. None of them, except the Dred Scott case . . . was more important than the school segregation issue. None of them directly and intimately affected so many American families. The lives and values of some 12 million schoolchildren . . . will be altered, and with them eventually the whole social pattern of the South. . . . The international effect may be scarcely less important."[5] If *Time*'s prediction was wrong, it was only in understating the importance of the *Brown* case.

Brown led not only to the transformation of Southern society but to major changes in Northern society as well. Moreover, *Brown* forever changed the role of the United States Supreme Court in American politics and society. Never before, as Arthur Krock wrote in *The New York Times*, had the Court exercised it power of judicial review "more sweepingly."[6]

Reaction to *Brown I* was predictably mixed. Northern public opinion overwhelmingly supported the Court; a Gallup poll taken a few days after the decision showed 72 percent of Easterners, 57 percent of Midwesterners, and 65 percent of Westerners supporting the decision.[7] Southern opinion ran the gamut from support from a few progressives to grudging acceptance to outright defiance. Overall, Southern whites objected to sending their children to desegregated schools by a margin of better than five to one.[8] *The New Republic's* assessment of the political repercussions was accurate: "Northern Democrats will applaud the decision. Southern Democrats, however, will disavow it as the evil work of Earl Warren, a Republican."[9]

In general, the Southern reaction to *Brown I* was muffled and disorganized, due in large part to the Court's brilliant political strategy of separating the announcement of the antisegregation principle from the actual enforcement decree. The "time lag allowed for carrying out the decree," wrote a reporter for the *Times*, "seemed to be the major factor" in tempering the Southern response.[10] The Court's critics also found themselves facing an unexpectedly unanimous Court and thus without the benefit of a dissenting opinion around which to rally their forces. "For a long succession of jittery Monday mornings the South had braced itself for an ultimatum" from the Court, wrote Harold C. Fleming, a leading Southern advocate of civil rights. "Many Southerners expected the Court to demand an end to legally separate schools, and they never doubted that the terms of surrender would be dictated in galling detail. No one was prepared for the disarming affirmation of principle that Chief Justice Warren read for a unanimous Court."[11]

Many leading Southerners responded to *Brown I* with caution. Virginia's Governor Thomas Stanley, for example, though later a critic of *Brown*, at first promised "a plan which will be acceptable to our citizens and in keeping with the edict of the Court."[12] Such moderation was especially prevalent in the border and non-Southern states: Maryland's governor Theodore R. McKelden declared that his state "would accept readily the Supreme Court's interpretation of the law," while in Arkansas, according to one reporter, "the general feeling . . . was gratitude for the time granted by the Court" for the implementation of the decree.[13]

A few Southern leaders—most notably Governor Herman Talmadge of Georgia—expressed outright defiance. "The United States Supreme Court," Talmadge declared, "has blatantly ignored all law and precedent . . . and lowered itself to the level of common politics. . . . The people of Georgia . . . will fight for the right to manage their own affairs. . . . [We will] map a program to insure continued and permanent segregation of the races."[14] Talmadge's views would eventually be echoed by politicians across the South; in the immediate aftermath of the first *Brown* decision, however, his "rebel yells of defiance" were atypical, if not "a jarring and isolated note."[15]

As the impact of *Brown I* settled in, however, Deep South opposition to the decision began to mount. For one thing, summer was primary season in most Southern states, and 1954 was an election year. Politicians quickly sensed that moderation toward or support for the desegregation ruling was not a strategy inclined to garner votes, especially in rural constituencies. Many state legislators, who in those pre-reapportionment days overwhelmingly represented such areas, began to make their opposition to *Brown* known. As a result, no Deep South state moved ahead with plans to comply voluntarily with *Brown I* by the opening of the new school year. Instead, the antidesegregation position hardened in state after state. Georgia's General Assembly passed and sent to the voters a constitutional amendment that would have abolished the public schools if necessary to avoid integration, as did Mississippi's; Louisiana's governor declared that his state would maintain "segregation in fact" regardless of the Court's decree; and Virginia's Governor Stanley, under intense pressure from leading segregationists, now pledged to use "every legal means at my command to continue segregated schools."[16]

In the border and non-Southern states that had practiced de jure segregation, the process of integration went more smoothly. Schools in Baltimore, Maryland, and Washington, D.C., and in parts of Missouri, Arkansas, New Mexico, West Virginia, Delaware, and Kansas, were voluntarily desegregated in September 1954, well in advance of the Supreme Court's enforcement ruling. These were areas in which "Negro populations are low and racial tolerance is generally good."[17]

The Modern Supreme Court

Deep South pressure to avert the implementation of *Brown I* grew steadily in the months preceding the *Brown II* implementation decision of May 1955. In April, Mississippi passed a law making it illegal for whites to attend schools with blacks, under penalty of fine or perhaps imprisonment.[18] The Georgia Senate unanimously approved a bill cutting off funds from mixed state schools; the North Carolina House passed a resolution opposing integration; the new governor of South Carolina urged Congress to take away the Supreme Court's power to ban segregation; and Marvin Griffin, the new governor of Georgia, pledged in his inaugural address that "as long as Marvin Griffin is your governor there will be no mixing of the races in classrooms of our schools and colleges in Georgia."[19]

The Supreme Court's strategy of separating the announcement of principle from the enforcement decree helped minimize the reaction to *Brown*, at least in 1954. The enforcement decree in *Brown II* also seemed deliberately crafted to ease the decision's reception in the Deep South. Chief Justice Warren's approach, wrote Justice Reed's law clerk, "was to send the cases back to the trial court for the entry of appropriate decrees. Such action would have the dual advantage of allowing more time for compliance and also would better allow for local variations in the mode of compliance depending upon the intensity of the problem in the area."[20] In his opinion for the again unanimous Court, Warren accepted the argument of the Eisenhower Justice Department (and of several of the Southern states) that desegregation be implemented gradually and that the process be supervised by the federal district courts acting under their equity jurisdiction. "The courts will require that the defendants make a prompt and reasonable start toward full compliance with our May 17, 1954, ruling," Warren wrote. "Once such a start has been made, the courts may find that additional time is necessary to carry out the ruling in an effective manner. The burden rests upon the defendants to establish that such time is necessary in the public interest and is consistent with good faith compliance at the earliest possible date." Warren remanded the various cases to the appropriate district courts with instructions to take such actions as were "necessary and proper to admit to public schools on a racially nondiscriminatory basis with all deliberate speed the parties to these cases."[21]

The Court's carefully formulated enforcement decree again delayed the actual desegregation of schools in the Deep South. Critics differ on whether the Court's acquiescence in the Southern request for gradualism was "a great mistake" or an unavoidable concession to necessity, but either way the result of the decision was to delay for years the actual desegregation of Southern school systems.[22] As in the year before the implementation decision was handed down, school districts in the non-South and in the border states continued to make progress, while those in the deep South did not.[23]

In the year after *Brown II*, opposition to desegregation crystallized throughout the Deep South. By the end of 1956, perhaps 250,000 white Southerners had joined anti-*Brown* "Citizens' Councils" organized to resist the imposition of integration.[24] By the winter of 1955–56 the prosegregationists had developed a series of well-worn arguments against *Brown* and a workable strategy for resisting desegregation of the schools. Despite this outpouring of energy and activity, the resistance movement of the Deep South never provoked a direct confrontation with the Supreme Court or the federal authorities. The reason is simple: with only gentle pressure coming from Washington, Deep South leaders were able to stave off any desegregation efforts, especially in areas of highest black population (and hence of highest white resistance). The crisis between state and federal power did not come in the Deep South at all, but in Little Rock, Arkansas, in the fall of 1957.

II

Meanwhile, events in Washington were slowly changing the political climate surrounding the Court. As late as the beginning of 1956, Southern opposition to *Brown* had not translated into general opposition to Warren or the Supreme Court, and efforts to reverse *Brown* or curb the Court got nowhere in either house of Congress. Before President Eisenhower announced in February 1956 that he would seek reelection, Warren was widely regarded as the Republican Party's best hope for the 1956 presidential election, and his name was prominently mentioned despite his consistent statements that he would not be a candidate. "He is undoubtedly the [Republican] party's best vote-getter, outside of Ike himself," wrote Roscoe Drummond in the *New York Herald-Tribune*.[25] Eisenhower, though privately upset by the *Brown* decision and resentful of being "trapped" by the Supreme Court "into taking a politically risky public stance on Southern segregation," nonetheless was circumspect in his official statements. There is evidence that Eisenhower openly lobbied against the decision on at least one occasion, at a state dinner in the White House, and it is certain that the president was far less energetic in opposing segregation than many within his own administration. Nevertheless, Eisenhower stated officially only that he opposed the idea of nominating a sitting chief justice for president, and, whatever his private views, had nothing but praise for Warren in public. In December 1955, for example, he told James Hagerty that Warren "wants to go down in history as a great Chief Justice, and he certainly is becoming one. He . . . is getting the Court back on its feet and back in respectable standing again."[26]

So high was Warren's political standing that in February 1956, shortly before Eisenhower's reelection announcement, Vice President Richard Nixon sought to make political capital out of the chief justice and his decision in *Brown*. "Speaking for a unanimous Supreme Court," Nixon declared in a political speech, "a great Republican Chief Justice, Earl Warren, has ordered an end to racial segregation in the nation's schools."[27] Nixon was attacked directly by Adlai Stevenson and *The New York Times*, and indirectly by President Eisenhower, for his "blunder" of trying to gain partisan advantage at the expense of the Court's integrity.[28] What is most striking about this incident is that Nixon would want to invoke the chief justice's name and his decision in *Brown* in support of the Republican Party. Nixon's support of Warren and *Brown* is surprising only in retrospect, however; at the time, neither Warren nor *Brown* was in disrepute except among extremist Southern Democrats. In fact, Court-watchers would have had a hard time assessing the new chief justice's judicial philosophy in early 1956. In both *Brown* cases, he spoke for a unanimous Court that included such conservatives as Frankfurter and Reed; in *Brown II*, moreover, his approach was the model of judicial prudence and caution.

Four cases decided in 1956 changed that perception fully and forever. In *Slochower* v. *Board of Education of New York City*[29] the Court held that a public university could not dismiss a professor simply because he invoked the Fifth Amendment before a congressional committee. In *Communist Party of the United States* v. *Subversive Activities Control Board*[30] the Court refused to validate the finding of the Board that the American Communist Party was a "Communist action organization" under the Internal Security Act of 1950. In making that determination, the Court held, the Subversive Activities Control Board had been influenced by perjured testimony. In *Cole* v. *Young*,[31] the Court struck down summary dismissals of federal employees in "non-sensitive" positions, holding that, under its interpretation of the relevant statute, such employees could be dismissed for reasons of loyalty or security only after ordinary civil service processes had been followed. Finally, in *Pennsylvania* v. *Nelson*,[32] the Court held that states could not punish sedition against the United States because the federal government had preempted such authority under the Smith Act, a major federal antisedition law.

Of the four 1956 antisubversion cases, *Pennsylvania* v. *Nelson* caused the greatest outcry. On the surface it is difficult to see why. Though the Court struck down a state law purporting to punish sedition against the United States as a whole, it left the federal law intact; indeed, it struck down the state statute precisely *because* of the existence of the federal law. Moreover, the Court's decision turned not on constitutional issues but on statutory construction and could have been remedied by a simple statute.

Nelson provoked a strong response from three quarters: Northern anti-Communist hawks; Southern segregationists who were inclined to oppose the Court because of *Brown* and were generally sympathetic to anti-Communist legislation; and a few states'-rights legislators, notably Senator Harry Byrd (Ind.-Va.) and Representative Howard Smith (D.-Va.), who for years had been fighting what they saw as the Court's growing tendency to misinterpret federal statutes by reading into them congressional intent to preempt state laws. The Southerners gave the anti-*Nelson* movement energy; the Northerners gave it legitimacy; and Byrd and Smith gave it direction and leadership.

A handful of Northern and Southern congressmen accused Chief Justice Warren and his fellow justices of taking the "Communist line" in their decisions. "The Slochower and Nelson decisions are only the latest in a recent series of judicial rulings that aid the Communist party," said Senator Joseph R. McCarthy (R.-Wisc.). "The Federal judiciary is making a full-scale assault on efforts by various Government authorities to protect American institutions."[33] "I'm not accusing . . . [Chief Justice] Warren of being a [Communist] Party member," said Senator James O. Eastland (D.-Miss.), "but he takes the same position they do when he says the Communist Party is just another political party."[34]

More common were attacks by Southern segregationists, who linked *Nelson* to *Brown* and then attacked both decisions and the Court as well. *Nelson*, according to the Southerners, was akin to *Brown* in that it invaded states' rights, usurped legislative power, and revealed a Communist influence on the justices. Former justice James R. Byrnes of South Carolina, for example, responded to *Nelson* by charging that "the Supreme Court must be curbed." He continued: "Tragic as may be the consequences in destroying the public school system in the South, more frightening are the consequences of the trend to destroy the powers of the 48 states." "The record of the Supreme Court in the past two years," echoed Representative James C. Davis (D.-Ga.), "is replete with factual evidence that demonstrates the Court's intention to change the Constitution whenever it desires. . . . In a step-by-step process, the Supreme Court has usurped the functions of the legislative branch of government." The Court's action in *Nelson*, Davis concluded, was "a brazen and irresponsible attack on the sovereignty of all the States."[35]

A few Southern critics of the Court tried to link the "pro-Communist" 1956 decisions to *Brown* by alleging a Communist influence on the desegregation decision. "I think its [the Court's] members have been brain washed," said Henderson Lanham (D.-Ga.). "The brain washing has been done by the alleged sociologist and psychologist, Dr. Karl Gunnar Myrdal and his associates." Myrdal, whose research had been cited by Warren as an authority in *Brown*, was denounced with others as "wild Communist inspired pseudo-scientists," while his associates were "shocking pink, if not Red."[36]

The real movers behind the attempt to overturn *Nelson* were Senator Harry Byrd and Representative Howard Smith. Both had been concerned for some time about a variety of Court decisions reading congressional intent to preempt state laws into federal statutes. Both Byrd and Smith introduced legislation not only to reverse *Nelson*, but also to counteract the Court's general tendency in the preemption area. Identical bills introduced in the House and Senate stated that "no act of Congress shall be construed as indicating an intent on the part of Congress to occupy the field in which such act operates, to the exclusion of all State laws, . . . unless such act contains an express provision to that effect."[37] Similar bills had been introduced long before the *Nelson* case reached the Supreme Court; *Nelson* was the catalyst Byrd and Smith needed to get their proposals on the congressional agenda. Byrd, in fact, declared himself opposed to "other bills which . . . would only correct the decision in the Steve Nelson case." "To correct only one case at a time," Byrd argued, "would be a sham and subterfuge."[38]

Hearings on the Smith Bill (H.R. 3) and various Senate versions were held shortly after the *Nelson* case. Spurred by the outcry over *Nelson*, conservatives forced a committee vote in July 1956, but House and Senate leaders arranged matters so that the vote was on a narrow bill that would have overturned preemption only in cases of state sedition laws. This bill passed the House judiciary committee on 3 July, but with Smith and others holding out for a more general bill, and with the House leadership opposing everything but the narrow bill, the legislation was effectively stalemated.

III

Hostility toward the Court's decision in *Nelson* quickly died down, and attempts to reverse the Court by legislation got nowhere. Nevertheless, the congressional response to *Nelson* is instructive, for it foreshadows what would in time become a pattern of opposition to the decisions of the Burger and Warren Courts. After *Nelson*, Southern conservatives—whose main concern was still the segregation issue—joined forces with others who opposed the Court's decision on substantive grounds. While ostensibly attacking the *Nelson* decision, the Southerners made continual references to *Brown* and attacked the Court in general terms. The campaign against *Nelson*, like later opposition to the school prayer, reapportionment, criminal law, and other decisions, was fueled at least in part by a persistent attempt to discredit the Court and hence delegitimate the *Brown* decision and its progeny.

The reasons behind this Southern strategy are obvious. For one thing, there was very little support among non-Southern congressmen for action against *Brown*; any such proposal was doomed to failure. Furthermore, such action was actually unnecessary, since the primary strategy used by Southerners to block the impact of *Brown* was resistance at the local level. If Congress simply stayed out of the picture, local resistance would continue to work its way. What the Southerners needed, then, was to delegitimate the Court and the *Brown* decision in order to maintain local popular support for the resistance movement. The anti-Court campaigns of 1956 and after were thus part of a larger campaign to bring "southern opinion into an embattled, unified state of feeling which will brook no compromise."[39]

Opposition to the Court, which had been building since *Brown*, peaked during and after the 1956–57 term. The proximate cause of the excitement was a series of decisions involving criminal defendant rights; antisubversion laws and investigations; free speech; and, of course, race relations.

In *Mallory* v. *United States*, the Court overturned the conviction of a confessed rapist who had been held for seven and one-half hours before being arraigned before a federal magistrate.[40] The case broke no new ground, except that it signaled the Warren Court's strict insistence that police officers, at least at the federal level, obey established rules and procedures. *Mallory*, like many later Warren Court cases, drew fire from those already convinced that the Court was "soft" on crime.

A number of the controversial 1956–57 decisions involved subversion cases, and, as in the previous term, the Court seemed consistently on the side of alleged or confessed Communists. The most controversial decision of the term was *Jencks* v. *United States*.[41] In *Jencks*, the Court overturned the conviction of a labor union officer charged with violating federal law by falsely swearing that he was not a member of the Communist Party. The government's case against Jencks rested on the testimony of two witnesses, who gave crucial testimony linking him to the activities of the Communist Party. Because of the importance of these witnesses, Jencks asked the trial court to order the government to provide reports submitted by the witnesses to the F.B.I. The trial judge refused to do so.

The Supreme Court reversed. Even if "vital national interests" were at stake, wrote Justice Brennan for a five-to-four majority, "the criminal action must be dismissed when the Government, on the ground of privilege, elects not to comply with an order to produce, for the accused's inspection or for admission in evidence, relevant statements or reports in its possession of government witnesses touching the subject of their testimony at the trial." If the government wanted to keep the witness reports confidential, Brennan held, its only choice was to drop the case against Jencks.[42]

In a concurring opinion, Justice Harold H. Burton laid out an alternative approach. It was up to the trial judge, Burton wrote, to inspect the records in camera and to decide whether the evidence is relevant, whether it is privileged, and whether the privileged material can be "excised from the reports without destroying their value to the defendant." By vesting discretion in the trial judge, Burton concluded, "the conflicting interests are balanced, and a just decision is reached in the individual case without needless sacrifice of important interests."[43]

In two other important cases decided in 1957, the Court protected the constitutional rights of alleged Communists. In *Watkins* v. *United States*,[44] the Court upheld the right of a witness before a congressional subcommittee to refuse to answer questions dealing with alleged Communist activities. When the Congress seeks to compel testimony before one of its committees, the Court held, it had to spell out the committee's "direction and focus"; it could not delegate authority in such vague terms so as to permit the committee to "radiate outward infinitely to any topic thought to be related in some way to armed insurrection."[45] In *Yates* v. *United States*,[46] the Court reversed the conviction of fourteen leaders of the California Communist Party charged with violation of the Smith Act, which makes it a federal crime to "organize . . . or attempt . . . to organize any society, group, or assembly of persons who teach, advocate, or encourage the overthrow or destruction" of any government in the United States by force. In instructing the jury, wrote Justice John Marshall Harlan for the Court, the trial judge "regarded as immaterial . . . any issue as to the character of the advocacy in terms of its capacity to stir listeners to forcible action." In failing to stress the difference between "advocacy of abstract doctrine" and "advocacy directed at promoting unlawful action," Harlan concluded, the trial judge failed to protect the defendant's First Amendment right to free speech.[47] Moreover, in five of the fourteen cases, the Supreme Court ordered the lower court to order an outright acquittal on the grounds that the evidence presented could not support a guilty verdict.

These cases—and especially *Jencks*—touched off a fierce congressional reaction. In dealing with *Jencks*, at least, Congress's task was made easier because those who opposed the decision assumed that the basis of Justice William Brennan's opinion in that case was statutory and not constitutional. Actually, Brennan never made the basis of his opinion clear; he failed, wrote Walter Murphy, "ever to say whether the decision was based on constitutional or statutory grounds, or to spell out in unmistakable terms what portions of the FBI reports should be given to the defense, by whom such a determination should be made, or at what point in the litigation the information could be obtained." Perhaps the very weakness of Brennan's argument, and its "deficiency in judicial craftsmanship," as Murphy calls it, contributed to Congress's willingness to step in and curb the Court.[48]

The immediate result of all this was the passage of the so-called Jencks Act on 29 August 1957.[49] Although the act began life as an attempt to reverse the Jencks decision, by the time it was enacted it was little more than a codification of Justice Burton's moderate concurrence, which provided that the trial judge, and not the defense attorneys, would decide what material was relevant to the defense and what was not. Only a few of its supporters regarded the Jencks Act as an anti-Court bill, and even they considered the act only a mild rebuke. Furthermore, as Murphy pointed out, most of the law's supporters took "great care to point out that they were not attacking the Warren Court."[50]

The Court's critics were hardly satisfied to stop with passage of the mild Jencks Act, however. Over the next year or so the House and Senate considered a series of bills designed to reverse particular decisions of the Court or to strike more generally at the Court's prestige and authority. The most serious of these was the so-called Jenner Bill, named for and introduced by Senator William E. Jenner (R.-Ind.). As introduced, the Jenner Bill would have stripped the Supreme Court of its appellate jurisdiction in five areas, all related to the various security cases decided the previous term. Other bills considered in the second session of the Eighty-fifth Congress included H.R. 3, the old Howard Smith bill designed to reverse *Pennsylvania* v. *Nelson*; H.R. 11477, a bill that would have restricted the impact of *Mallory* (the police detention case); H.R. 13272, which would have overturned the *Yates* decision on the intent of the Smith Act with respect to the meaning of the word "organize"; and S. 1411, which, reversing *Cole* v. *Young*, would have authorized the summary dismissal of federal employees in nonsensitive positions.[51]

Between March and August 1958, the House approved all the anti-Court bills except the Jenner Bill. The latter, now called the Jenner-Butler Bill (after its Senate sponsor, John Marshall Butler (R.-Md.), cleared the Senate Judiciary Committee in greatly attenuated form in April. As modified by the Judiciary Committee, the Jenner-Butler Bill would have stripped the Court of its jurisdiction only in the area of bar admission cases; in other areas, the appellate jurisdiction strategy was abandoned in favor of statutes directly reversing or modifying the Court's nonconstitutional decisions in several security cases. The bill would also have reversed *Watkins*, declaring that "any question" before a congressional committee "shall be deemed pertinent . . . if such question is ruled pertinent by the body conducting the hearing."[52]

All of the anti-Court bills came up in the Senate at the end of the session. First the Senate approved the *Mallory* bill, though only after adding the word "reasonable" so that the bill read "Evidence . . . otherwise admissible, shall not be inadmissible solely because of a reasonable delay in taking an arrested person before a commissioner."[53] Next, the Jenner-Butler Bill was defeated by a vote of 49 to 41, clearly short of a majority but, as Murphy wrote, "an impressive demonstration of anti-Court strength, considering that [Senator] Joseph Robinson, with the full weight of FDR's political magic behind him, had never been sure of more than thirty Senate votes for the 1937 Court-packing plan."[54] Finally, H.R. 3 was defeated, after intense legislative wrangling, by the dramatic vote of 41 to 40. When it was all over in the Senate, only the *Mallory* bill had passed; every other anti-Court bill on the congressional agenda had gone down to defeat.

In the end, even the *Mallory* bill was scrapped. The House and Senate versions of the bill differed by the inclusion of the word "reasonable" in the Senate version. Eventually, House and Senate conferees were able to agree on compromise language. When the time came for a Senate vote on approving the compromise, the bill was killed on a point of order—namely, that the conference committee had added "new material" to the bill in violation of Senate rules. Had the point-of-order motion failed, the bill probably would have been killed by filibuster.

The struggle of 1957–58 was over, with little damage done. In the next term the Court made one or two decisions that mollified its critics, and in the term following it again gave evidence of moving slowly and cautiously in the areas of national security and criminal law. Though there were still decisions which upset the security-conscious conservatives, there were no cases remotely resembling the 1957 cases in impact or importance. Analysis of the Court's more cautious decisions in the 1957–58 and 1958–59 terms reveals, at most, a loss of momentum in the Warren Court's liberalism. Though the Court seemed tentative in those years, it by no means repealed its controversial decisions, nor did it demonstrably retreat under congressional pressure.

I V

The most dramatic decision of 1958 grew out of the confrontation between state and federal authorities in Little Rock, Arkansas. Little Rock, as the historian Numan V. Bartley noted, "was among the least likely scenes for a dramatic confrontation between state and federal power."[55] The city had a relatively small black population, was outside the Deep South, and had no history of segregationist extremism. Almost immediately after *Brown*, in fact, the Little Rock school board had begun to make plans to desegregate the public schools. By 1957, however, what should have been a quick and uneventful process of desegregation became the most direct threat to the Court's authority anywhere in the South.

What turned Little Rock into a debacle was the unfortunate combination of a weak city government and school board; a strong and well-organized segregationist faction which, though at first a minority, grew steadily more powerful; and the political ambition of Governor Orval Faubus, who in time became the leading symbol of Southern resistance. With desegregation of the schools scheduled for September 1957, the segregationists began an intensive campaign for resistance early in the year, a campaign which they pressed throughout the summer. They found an ally in Governor Faubus, who had used the segregation issue to advantage in the 1956 gubernatorial primary, pledging repeatedly that "there will be NO forced integration of public schools so long as I am governor."[56] As the crisis in Little Rock mounted, Faubus was pressed continually to make good on his promise. At the same time, city and school board officials pressured Faubus to enforce the law of the land.

Faubus was caught between his pledge not to force integration on any community and his professed intention of refusing to subvert federal law. In the end, he sided with the segregationists and ordered the national guard into Little Rock with explicit orders to prevent desegregation. Though Faubus insisted that the Guard was there only "to maintain or restore order and to protect the lives and property of citizens," Faubus became, in Bartley's words, "increasingly demagogic and irresponsible." The troops he sent to "maintain order" were a catastrophe waiting to happen; before the crisis at Little Rock was over, they would become a national focal point of racial unrest and violence.

On the morning of 4 September 1957, nine black school children arrived at Central High School in Little Rock to find a mob of antiintegrationists surrounding the school and Faubus's national guardsmen blocking the entrance. They were refused admittance and returned home. Soon afterward the various parties to the dispute returned to the federal court, which, after a brief hearing, ordered desegregation to proceed and told the National Guard to stay out of the way. The students entered the school on 23 September but were removed later the same day for fear of impending violence. The following evening, at long last, President Eisenhower ordered the 101st Airborne Division to Little Rock to enforce the federal desegregation decree.

The crisis at Little Rock was far from over, however. Under the protection of the federal troops, black children were able to attend classes throughout the 1957–58 school year. But in 1958, Faubus became even more outspoken in his opposition to desegregation, openly declaring in January that he would prevent desegregation from continuing in the fall of 1958 and proclaiming, for the first time, that "the Supreme Court's decision [in *Brown*] is not the law of the land."[57] On the basis of such pronouncements, Faubus was reelected to a third term in July, just in time to face the second round of school desegregation in Little Rock.

The crisis came to a head in the late summer of 1958. The Arkansas state legislature, acting at Faubus's behest, passed a series of measures designed to forestall integration; at the same time, school officials petitioned the courts to permit a two-and-one-half-year delay in the implementation of integration, arguing that "because of extreme public hostility . . . the maintenance of a sound educational program at Central High School, with the Negro students in attendance, would be impossible."[58] The federal district court agreed to this request in June 1958, but the Eighth Circuit Court of Appeals reversed on 18 August. When the Circuit Court stayed its mandate until the Supreme Court could review the case, the Supreme Court convened in special session to consider the case, known as *Cooper* v. *Aaron*. Arguments were heard on 28 August and 11 September 1958; on 12 September, the High Court handed down a brief decision unanimously upholding the Court of Appeals (and thus ordering desegregation to proceed). Two weeks later the Court released a full opinion in the case.

The opinion of the Court, in no uncertain terms, made it clear that the resistance of Governor Faubus and the state legislature was unacceptable in the American federal system. (To underscore the vehemence and unanimity of the Court's position, the opinion was signed by all nine justices.) The essence of the opinion was as follows: "The constitutional rights of children not to be discriminated against in school admission on grounds of race or color declared by this Court in the *Brown* case can neither be nullified openly and directly by state legislators or state executive or judicial officers, nor nullified indirectly by them through evasive schemes for segregation whether attempted 'ingeniously or ingenuously.' "[59] Moreover, said the Court in dicta that is as controversial as it is famous, "*Marbury* v. *Madison* . . . declared the basic principle that the federal judiciary is supreme in the exposition of the law of the Constitution, and that principle has ever since been respected by this Court and the Country as a permanent and indispensible feature of our constitutional system. It follows that the interpretation of the Fourteenth Amendment enunciated by this Court in the *Brown* case is the supreme law of the land, and Art. VI of the Constitution makes it of binding effect on the States 'any Thing in the Constitution or Laws of any State to the Contrary notwithstanding.' "[60] Faubus responded by closing every high school in the city, and the schools remained closed until the 1959 school year, when, after moderates gained control of the school board, the schools were reopened "on a basis acceptable to the federal courts."[61]

Despite the Supreme Court's strong statements in *Cooper*, the Little Rock resistance succeeded in slowing the pace of desegregation in the South. Right after the decision in *Cooper*, the Court signaled its approval of an Alabama pupil placement act in a one-sentence per curiam opinion.[62] Massive resistance, combined with the pressures on the Court growing out of the security cases, forced a strategic retreat by the Court. Desegregation would not really get underway in the Deep South in a major way until nearly a decade later.

V

To those who studied the 1954–58 Court controversy without the benefit of the hindsight provided by the passing of several decades, the period ranked with *Dred Scott*, the New Deal, and a handful of other crises as a major confrontation between the Court and the political branches. This "important conflict . . . between Congress and the Warren Court cannot be seen in proper perspective," wrote Walter Murphy in 1962, "without some understanding that this was only one of many similar conflicts in American history."[63] C. Herman Pritchett, in a 1961 study of the same period, described the conflict as one of the "occasional crises" that the Court must endure; between 1954 and 1958, he wrote, Congress engaged in "a determined effort . . . not only to reverse certain decisions, but also fundamentally to limit the Court's powers of judicial review."[64]

Twenty-five years later, however, the 1954–58 conflict between Congress and the Court seems relatively minor. Murphy, Pritchett, and other Court-watchers were not wrong in their assessment of this period; viewed against the background of the Court's history, the controversy over *Brown* and the various security cases was unusually serious. Criticism of the Court was frequent and vitriolic; there was massive resistance to *Brown* across the South; and, as Murphy pointed out, the Court's critics were able to muster an impressive forty-one votes in the Senate in support of their effort to curb Warren and his brethren.

What Court-watchers could not know in 1961 and 1962 was that the "crisis" of 1954–58 was only the opening skirmish in what would become a long and unending war. This opening battle ended with the Court's apparent retreat in 1959, and for a few years the Court held back or advanced only slowly in areas such as race and civil liberties.[65] Beginning as early as 1961, however, the Court returned to and even surpassed its 1950s record of activism and liberalism. By the late 1960s, the kind of "crisis" that had seemed so significant in the mid-1950s had become routine.

An early sign of the Court's revival came on 26 March 1962. On that date, the Supreme Court suddenly and unexpectedly reversed a long-standing precedent and decided that the federal courts could consider whether the malapportionment of a state legislature constituted a violation of the underrepresented voters' constitutional rights. The case of *Baker* v.

Carr grew out of the grotesquely malapportioned Tennessee legislature. Despite a state constitutional provision calling for the apportionment of both houses of the legislature "according to the number of qualified electors" in each county, urban voters were tremendously underrepresented relative to rural voters; and eastern Tennessee (strongly pro-Union during the Civil War and still staunchly Republican) was underrepresented relative to the western part of the state. The legislature had last been reapportioned in 1901, and what had been an inequitable scheme then had become an outrageous one by 1962. According to the record in *Baker* v. *Carr*, counties having only 37 percent of the population elected 61 percent of the state Senate, while 40 percent of the voters elected 64 percent of the state House of Representatives.[66]

For years the Supreme Court had stayed out of what Justice Frankfurter had called the "political thicket" of legislative apportionment. The apportionment issue was one of a handful that the justices had classified as "political questions," a broad label encompassing a series of questions that, for one reason or another, are deemed inappropriate for judicial resolution. In the 1946 case of *Colegrove* v. *Green*, Justice Frankfurter, speaking for the Court, dismissed a challenge to the geographical distribution of congressional seats in Illinois. Questions like legislative reapportionment are of a "peculiarly political nature and therefore not meet for judicial determination," Frankfurter wrote. "Courts," he concluded, "ought not to enter this political thicket."[67] As late as 1959 the Court had affirmed a lower court decision dismissing a challenge to a state income tax on the grounds that it had been passed by a malapportioned legislature.[68] Moreover, in November 1960 the Supreme Court, while striking down a racially discriminatory gerrymandering scheme, had carefully avoided the political problem by basing its decisions not on the Fourteenth Amendment's Equal Protection Clause, but on the Fifteenth Amendment's more specific prohibition against racial discrimination in voting.[69]

Those following the Court closely were not surprised by the *Baker* decision, for, as one of the lawyers for the plaintiffs observed after oral argument, only Justices Frankfurter and Clark indicated "die-hard opposition to our side of the case. Justices Black, Douglas, Harlan, Stewart, and Brennan seemed plainly to favor our side."[70] Nevertheless, the Court's decision, as Alexander Bickel put it, "came like a thunder clap from the Supreme Court."[71] While the actual decision in *Baker* was wholly procedural and created no new substantive law, the very fact that the Court had gone out of its way to reverse *Colegrove* was a signal that the days of at least Tennessee-style malapportionment were numbered.

Two years later, the Court finally considered the merits of the claim that disproportionate legislative districts violated the Equal Protection Clause. In *Reynolds* v. *Sims*, Chief Justice Warren, for an eight-to-one majority, held that the Constitution required that legislative districts be apportioned as nearly as possible on the basis of population.[72] Although "mathematical exactness or precision" was not required by the Constitution, and although "some deviations from the equal-population principle are constitutionally permissible," significant deviations could be justified neither by "history alone, nor economic or other sorts of group interests." "Citizens," Warren concluded, "not history or economic interests, cast votes."[73]

At precisely the same time as the Court was dropping its reapportionment bombshells, it entered into what would become an even more controversial political thicket. Barely three months after *Baker*, in *Engel* v. *Vitale* [*The Regents' Prayer Case*], the Court threw another lightning bolt, this one striking down a regulation of the New York State Board of Regents authorizing the public recitation of a short prayer in the public schools. The prayer, written by the Board of Regents, was as follows: "Almighty God we acknowledge our dependence upon Thee, and beg Thy blessings upon us, our teachers, and our Country." Although no student was required to recite the Regents' prayer, and no school board was required to adopt it, the case posed for the first time the thorny question of whether such an entanglement of Church and State represented a violation of the religious provisions of the First Amendment.

The justices had no trouble striking down the New York Regents' prayer; the six-man majority, led by Justice Black, saw the case as a clear example of an illegal establishment of religion. "Neither the fact that the prayer may be denominationally neutral nor the fact that its observance on the part of the students is voluntary can serve to free it from the limitations of the Establishment Clause," Black wrote.[74] Indeed, as *The New Republic* commented shortly after the decision was handed down, "Once having decided to hear *Engel* v. *Vitale* it is difficult to see how the Court could have reached a substantially different decision."[75] The key decision for the Court may well have been its decision to hear the case in the first place.

Reaction to *Engel* was caustic. "Few recent Supreme Court decisions have provoked so immediately critical a reaction as has the ruling that reading the Regents' prayer aloud in New York public schools violates the Constitution," observed *The New York Times*.[76] Many of the critics were disgruntled Southern politicians, whose views were succinctly summed up by Representative George Andrews (D.-Ala.): "They put the Negroes in the schools," he declared, "and now they're driving God out."[77] This time, however, Northern critics joined the fray. "Under similar misinterpretations of the intent of the first amendment's establishment clause," warned Representative Edwin B. Dooley (R.-N.Y.), "I fear for the very survival of the spiritual and moral values which set our and other nations so far apart from the sterile materialism of our Communist enemies."[78] Even the theologian Reinhold Niebuhr denounced the Court. "This decision," he commented, "practically suppresses religion, especially in the public schools."[79]

The *Regents' Prayer Case* touched off a series of proposals to amend the Constitution or otherwise reverse the Court. Several observers, however, tried to minimize the impact of the decision, by arguing, for example, that "the decision holds only that no branch of government can 'order' the recital of any official prayer without violating the first amendment."[80] Said Senator Wayne Morse (R.-Ore.):

> The decision in the New York case is a much more limited one than most of the news stories have pointed out to the public. The decision does not ban all prayers in public schools. What the Court ruled on was the constitutionality of a requirement that a prayer written by a State agency of the government of New York should be read in the local public schools. . . . It is my guess that what will undoubtedly happen is that many parent groups, student groups, and school boards throughout the country will work out a voluntary procedure for offering a non-denominational prayer at various schools and school programs that will not be in conflict with the Supreme Court decision.[81]

The New Republic observed that the decision in *Engel* "does not preclude public school prayers which are in use as the result of custom or conventional practice by the consent of all groups in a community—a prayer drafted, let us say, by an inter-faith committee."[82]

Just what the Court did mean in the *Regents' Prayer Case* was clarified a year later, when the Court handed down decisions prohibiting state-sponsored readings of the Lord's Prayer and of Bible passages.[83] In an eight-to-one decision that produced a total of five opinions, the Court held that such state-sponsored activities violated the principle of governmental neutrality in matters of religion. Justice Potter Stewart filed a lone dissent, arguing that in the absence of coercion, "a reading from the Bible unaccompanied by comments" did not "represent the type of support of religion barred by the Establishment Clause."[84]

The reapportionment and school prayer cases drew a great deal of fire from the Court's critics, and the criticisms of the Court again followed the 1950s pattern. Once again Southern and Northern conservatives joined forces and attacked the Court for usurping the rights of the states and for making decisions that, they claimed, were based neither on logic, history, or precedent. The reapportionment decisions "mark a new and shocking interference by the federal judiciary with the right of the sovereign states to conduct their domestic affairs," declared Representative William M. Tuck (D.-Va.).[85] The *Wall Street Journal*, commenting on *Schempp*, declared it "wholly ridiculous" to argue that the practice of Bible reading, "followed by generation after generation without injury to our institutions, is now suddenly become a thing to undermine the Republic." Furthermore, said the *Journal*, "It does not augur well for the future to see our highest judges torture history and turn metaphysical handsprings to justify that which they wish to decide. In the real Constitutional issues which face the Nation today we should not have to fear that small minds will be brought to great questions."[86] Such decisions, wrote Arthur Krock of *The New York Times*, were "basic Supreme Court amendments of the Constitution."[87]

It did not take long for Congress to attempt to reverse the decisions in both the reapportionment and school prayer cases. In 1964 a major effort to overturn *Reynolds* was undertaken by Senator Everett Dirksen (R.-Ill.), the Senate minority leader, and Senator Mike Mansfield (D.-Mont.), the majority leader. A similar effort was made by the House leadership on its side of the Capitol.

The House action was nothing short of extraordinary. In July and August 1964, the House Judiciary Committee held hearings on more than one hundred proposals to overturn, restrict, or modify the Court's reapportionment decisions. As the committee's actions dragged on—largely due to the efforts of its chairman, Representative Emanuel Celler (D.-N.Y.), who opposed all such measures—the House leadership became impatient. On 13 August, therefore, the Rules Committee voted to take away from the Judiciary Committee a bill that would have removed the federal courts' jurisdiction to hear any case involving state legislative apportionment. This cleared the way for a floor debate on the measure, despite its having never been acted on by the Judiciary Committee. The last time the Rules Committee had taken such action, apparently, was in 1953. The Court-curbing bill passed the House on 19 August by a vote of 218 to 175; the final version, as amended on the floor, was even tougher than the original, for it prohibited even the enforcement of already existing federal court orders with respect to reapportionment.

In the Senate, meanwhile, Dirksen and Mansfield agreed to cosponsor an antireapportionment rider to a pending foreign aid bill. The Dirksen-Mansfield rider contained compromise language that would have simply delayed the implementation of reapportionment orders until 1 January 1966, thus giving reapportionment opponents the time necessary to push through a constitutional amendment reversing *Reynolds* and its progeny. The Dirksen amendment, as it came to be called, became the victim of a rare liberal filibuster, a marathon that lasted off and on for some six weeks. By mid-September, the Senate had reached a stalemate: opponents of *Reynolds* were unable to cut off the filibuster and were unwilling to back down and withdraw their proposal.

In the end, Senators Eugene McCarthy (D.-Minn.), Hubert Humphrey (D.-Minn.), and Jacob Javits (R.-N.Y.) proposed a mild substitute for the Dirksen-Mansfield language; their bill would have simply expressed the nonbinding sense of the Senate that courts should give states "adequate time" to implement reapportionment decrees. Even this was ultimately rejected by the narrow vote of 42 to 40, with the Republicans and Southern Democrats voting against the measure as too mild. A last-ditch effort to convince the Senate to pass the strong language of the original bill was defeated by 56 to 21. Finally, Senator Mansfield convinced his colleagues to adopt an amendment to the foreign aid bill "urging" the federal courts to give the states six months to comply with reapportionment orders, but the House, objecting to the mildness of this proposal, urged the Senate to drop it altogether. Thus after two months of heated debate and legislative wrangling, the result was no legislation on reapportionment at all.

Congress's 1964 session also saw attempts to reverse the Supreme Court's decisions on prayer and Bible reading in the public schools. Between January 1963 and September 1964 there were a total of 151 measures introduced in the House proposing a constitutional amendment to reverse the religion decisions, along with 9 such measures in the Senate. A total of 115 representatives and 14 senators went on record as sponsoring or cosponsoring these proposals.[88] A year before, 167 representatives had signed a discharge petition that would have forced floor consideration of a school prayer amendment.[89]

Constituent pressure calling for a constitutional amendment on school prayer was intense throughout the session; the letter-writing campaign on behalf of such an amendment "was reportedly one of the largest mail campaigns in history."[90] Representative Celler, who opposed the school prayer proposals just as he opposed the reapportionment bills, again tried to keep the proposed amendment bottled up in his Judiciary Committee. The Judiciary Committee held hearings which stretched out through April and May and into June. By then, the movement for the prayer amendment was lost among Congress's other concerns (including the reapportionment debate) and the impending presidential election, and no further action was taken.

A second attempt to secure passage of some antireapportionment legislation was made by Dirksen in 1965, this time in the form of a proposed constitutional amendment to allow the states to apportion one house of the legislature on the basis of factors other than population. The Dirksen amendment started out with impressive support—thirty-seven senators cosponsored the original proposal—and received the support of the Senate Subcommittee on Constitutional Amendments by a six-to-two margin. This particular amendment was blocked by the full Judiciary Committee, but Dirksen managed to get his resolution to the floor anyway by cleverly substituting it for an innocuous resolution—approved by Dirksen's own Judiciary Subcommittee on Federal Charters, Holidays, and Celebrations —providing for the establishment of "National American Legion Baseball Week." Once the baseball bill was brought to the floor, Dirksen immediately moved to substitute the antireapportionment language. This the Senate agreed to do by 59 to 39, but the amended resolution then failed by a vote of 57 to 39 (seven votes short of two-thirds). With action in the House effectively stalled by Representative Celler's Judiciary Committee, efforts to pass a reapportionment amendment were doomed again. A final effort by Dirksen failed in September, and the minority leader was forced to content himself with passing the baseball week proposal in its original form.[91]

One last attempt to overturn *Baker* and *Reynolds* was made by Dirksen in 1966. Despite an active legislative effort led by the American Farm Bureau Federation and other groups representing business and conservative interests, Dirksen's proposed amendment did no better in 1966 than it had the year before. The Senate Judiciary Committee considered an anti-reapportionment amendment and sent it to the full Senate without a pro or con recommendation. After a comparatively brief floor debate the amendment was defeated by almost exactly the same margin as the year before: 55 to 38 (seven votes short of two-thirds).

By the end of 1966, moreover, it was clear that any attempt to amend the Constitution by calling a constitutional convention would also be defeated. The Constitution provides that Congress "shall" call a constitutional convention upon the application of the legislatures of two-thirds of the states (i.e., 34 of 50). In 1964 and 1965, twenty-eight state legislatures called for a convention to reverse the apportionment decision; no additional states did so in 1966, and the convention idea was as good as dead.[92]

The opposition to reapportionment was also dying down because, despite the efforts of Dirksen and others, the reapportionment decisions were enjoying widespread support and had achieved tremendous results in a short time. A Gallup poll taken in 1964 revealed that Americans supported the *Reynolds* decision by a margin of 47 to 30 percent.[93] Momentum for reapportionment picked up even before the Court's one person–one vote decision of 1964, as lower courts began to hear cases under the *Baker* v. *Carr* precedent, and as the state legislatures themselves began to move toward reapportionment as a way of preempting legal action. By the end of 1963, twenty-six states had acted to equalize representation at least in one house, and state and federal courts were besieged by lawsuits seeking reapportionment decrees. By the time the Dirksen amendment was defeated for the third time, in 1966, it was clear that further efforts to reverse the Supreme Court decisions would have been useless. The controversy over reapportionment, unlike those over desegregation and school prayer, came to an end and never resurfaced.

The 1966 session also saw one additional attempt to overturn the school prayer cases. Again a prime mover was Everett Dirksen, who early in the session introduced a constitutional amendment to allow "voluntary participation by students or others in prayer."[94] The Senate Subcommittee on Constitutional Amendments held hearings in August on the Dirksen amendment but took no action, in part because of subcommittee chairman Birch Bayh's (D.-Ind.) refusal to push the matter enthusiastically. Dirksen, therefore, chose to bring the matter directly to the Senate floor in much the same way as he had maneuvered his reapportionment amendment to the floor in 1965. When a resolution authorizing the president to declare a "National UNICEF Day" reached the Senate floor, Dirksen moved to strike the text of that amendment and replace it with the school prayer bill. After a few days' debate, the Senate rejected Dirksen's amendment by 49 to 37. One of those opposing Dirksen was Senator Sam Ervin (D.-N.C.), who, despite his criticism of *Brown* and other decisions, decried the Dirksen proposal as an "annihilation of the principles of the 1st Amendment."[95]

Further efforts to overturn the school prayer cases were made in 1971 and 1976. In 1971, the House considered a constitutional amendment declaring that "nothing contained in this Constitution shall abridge the right of persons lawfully assembled, in any public building which is supported in whole or in part through the expenditure of public funds, to participate in voluntary prayer or meditation."[96] Again the amendment had been referred to Emanuel Celler's House Judiciary Committee, and again Celler held the amendment without taking action. This time, however, a majority of the House voted to endorse a discharge petition, a procedure whereby a measure can be taken back from a committee and considered by the whole House. When brought to the floor, the amendment received a majority of the vote, but not the necessary two-thirds, and was therefore defeated. Several members who had signed the discharge petition (presumably under pressure from various interest groups) abstained from or voted against the amendment on the House floor.[97] Since the mid-1970s, the school prayer issue has surfaced periodically, a favorite issue of the "moral majority" and the religious right. In 1979, the Senate adopted a bill to withdraw the federal courts' jurisdiction over all cases involving voluntary school prayer. The bill died in the House, however, at the hands of House Judiciary Committee Chairman Peter Rodino (D.-N.J.).

The 1979 debate over school prayer reveals a great deal about the dynamics of anti-Court legislation in the contemporary Congress. First, Senator Jesse Helms (R.-N.C.) attached the school prayer rider to a pending measure to create the Department of Education. The Department of Education Bill had the strong support of the Carter White House but was stalled as long as it contained the Helms amendment. After intense parliamentary maneuvering, Senate leaders decided to take the school prayer rider off the Education Bill and attach it to an uncontroversial bill that would have given the Supreme Court complete control over its docket by eliminating cases of mandatory jurisdiction. The Education Bill was then passed, and the bill to end mandatory jurisdiction was killed by Rodino and the House of Representatives. The transfer of the school prayer rider, wrote *Congressional Quarterly*, "reflected the view that the Supreme Court bill was less important politically than the Education Department bill and could more easily be scuttled by the House than the other measure." Senators who wanted to demonstrate their pro–school-prayer position, but who did not want to tamper with the Court's independence, were the obvious winners. Helms warned his fellow senators that if they voted to remove the school prayer language from the Education Department Bill, they would have to "go back home and explain it." Senator Robert Byrd (D.-W.Va.) replied: "I can go back home and tell my constituents I voted to support the school prayer amendment, as the Senator from North Carolina [Helms] can do."[98]

The doomed bill to eliminate the mandatory jurisdiction of the Court (and with it to reestablish school prayer) passed the Senate by a vote of 61 to 30. Among those voting for the bill were Senator Byrd and Senator Howard Baker (R.-Tenn.), both key principals in the maneuvering to kill the measure. In all, thirteen senators who voted for the Helms language on both the Department of Education Bill and the Mandatory Jurisdiction Bill voted later to remove the school prayer language from the Department of Education Bill—thus ensuring that the new department would be created and killing the school prayer rider for the time being.[99]

After 1979, efforts to reverse the Supreme Court's decisions on school prayer became a staple of the congressional agenda. In 1981 the House overwhelmingly adopted a rider to the Justice Department Appropriations Bill prohibiting the Justice Department from using any funds "to prevent the implementation of programs of voluntary prayer and meditation in the public schools.[100] The Justice Department was never really involved in the school prayer cases to begin with, so the House action was largely, if not entirely, symbolic. Nonetheless, after an emotional debate the Senate voted indirectly to kill the school prayer rider by a vote of 70 to 12.[101]

Prospects for some sort of action on the school prayer issue brightened somewhat when a constitutional amendment restoring voluntary school prayer was endorsed by President Ronald Reagan in 1982.[102] Reagan also announced that he would not oppose Senator Helms's attempts to reverse the school prayer decisions by statute, but he made no strong effort in that direction. In 1982, Helms tried to attach another rider to withdraw the jurisdiction of the Supreme Court in cases dealing with voluntary school prayer to needed legislation to increase the national debt limit; this time, liberals filibustered and the Senate ultimately defeated the measure.[103]

Despite two decades of effort, no school prayer bill has yet passed Congress. The Court, meanwhile, has refused to back down from the original decisions. Nevertheless, organized prayer in the public schools has not disappeared; surveys indicate that, in some parts of the country, the Court's decisions have been evaded or ignored in many school districts. A survey taken in North Carolina in 1984 revealed that schools in thirty-nine out of one hundred counties had regular, organized prayer; a survey taken in South Carolina the following year found that organized prayers or devotionals occur in over half the state's school districts.[104]

Pressure for reversal of the school prayer decisions may have eased recently as a result of the Supreme Court's apparent acceptance of "moments of silence" in at least some circumstances. In 1986, in a technical decision, the Court let stand a lower court decision permitting self-organized student religious groups to meet in school facilities.[105] Whether these decisions will mollify the most outspoken critics of the school prayer decisions is doubtful, but the Court's recent actions may decrease likelihood of congressional action on school prayer in the future.

VI

The early 1960s also saw dramatic developments in the area of criminal law. For some time the Court had been overturning individual criminal convictions based on confessions or evidence obtained through coercion or force. In 1952, for example, the Court reversed the conviction of a man charged with drug possession because the evidence used against him—two capsules of morphine—had been obtained by pumping the suspect's stomach against his will; in 1959, it threw out a confession obtained after an allnight interrogation during which one police officer—a "friend" of the suspect—entreated the accused to confess lest the officer lose his job and hence his livelihood.[106] The Court's decisions in these egregious cases were narrow exceptions to its general practice of refusing to interfere with state and local police practices.

In 1961, however, the Warren Court handed down the first of several sweeping opinions upholding the constitutional rights of criminal suspects. In *Mapp* v. *Ohio*, a six-to-three majority overturned a 1949 precedent and held that evidence seized illegally could not be introduced in a state criminal proceeding (the so-called "exclusionary rule" had been applied to federal proceedings since 1914).[107] Rejecting the logic of the Court's twelve-year-old decision in *Wolf* v. *Colorado*,[108] Justice Clark now committed the Court to closing "the only courtroom door remaining open to evidence secured by official lawlessness in flagrant abuse" of the basic "right to privacy free from unreasonable state intrusion." Clark concluded, "We hold that all evidence obtained by searches and seizures in violation of the Constitution is, by that same authority, inadmissible in a state court."[109]

Mapp was just the beginning of a five-year period during which the Court virtually restructured American criminal procedure. In 1963, the Court unanimously ruled that a state must provide an indigent defendant with an attorney at no charge.[110] Then, in 1964 and 1965, the Court returned to the thorny problem of balancing the right of police to interrogate suspects against the Fifth Amendment's privilege against self-incrimination and the Fourth Amendment's guarantee against unreasonable searches and seizures.

In *Massiah* v. *United States*, decided in 1964, the Court overturned the federal conviction of a merchant seaman for cocaine possession because the federal agents who obtained his confession had done so through trickery and in the absence of Massiah's counsel.[111] Massiah was arrested in April 1958 by customs officials after three and one-half pounds of cocaine were found aboard his vessel. (Other evidence, not relevant to the Supreme

Court's decision in the case, tied Massiah to the cocaine.) He was arraigned and indicted, retained a lawyer, pleaded not guilty, and was released on bail.

Shortly afterwards, one of Massiah's codefendants—one Colson—agreed to cooperate with the government in its investigation of this and other narcotics cases. In November 1959, Colson permitted federal agents to eavesdrop electronically on a conversation held in Colson's car between himself and the unsuspecting Massiah. In the course of that conversation, Massiah "made several incriminating statements." The question for the Court was whether these statements were admissible in evidence in Massiah's subsequent trial.

Justice Stewart, for a six-man majority, said they were not. Having formally indicted Massiah for a crime, Stewart held, the government was obligated to interrogate him only in the presence of counsel. "We hold that the petitioner [Massiah] was denied the basic protections of . . . [the Sixth Amendment's] guarantee when there was used against him at his trial evidence of his own incriminating words, which federal agents had deliberately elicited from him after he had been indicted and in the absence of his counsel."[112]

Massiah was the first case decided by the Supreme Court in which a confession was thrown out even though there was no indication that the confession was tainted in any way. In previous cases, there had always been the possibility that, because the confession was in some way coerced, it might not have been truthful. In *Massiah*, however, the confession was excluded from evidence simply because of the way it had been obtained and not because the validity of the confession had been called into question.

During the same term, the Court also decided *Escobedo* v. *Illinois*, in which the constitutional protection against self-incrimination was extended still further.[113] Escobedo was a suspect in a murder case; he was arrested and interrogated but made no statement. That same day he was released on a writ of habeas corpus. About two weeks later, acting on information from another suspect in the case, the police again took Escobedo into custody, this time not formally arresting him but interrogating him at length. From the beginning, Escobedo refused to answer questions from the police, repeatedly requesting to see his attorney. The police refused that request and continued the interrogation, finally obtaining a

The Modern Supreme Court

confession after hours of questioning. The Supreme Court threw out the confession, holding, by a five-to-four vote, that the Sixth Amendment's guarantee of "the Assistance of Counsel" prohibited the police from questioning Escobedo without permitting his lawyer to be present.

The *Escobedo* case was critical in two respects: first, unlike *Massiah* it was a state, not a federal, case; and second, the Court did not simply conclude that Escobedo's confession was invalid based on the totality of the circumstances involved, but rather that the confession was invalid because Escobedo had an absolute right to the assistance of counsel, even before he had been formally charged with a crime. In this sense, *Escobedo* laid down a general rule rather than merely deciding the outcome of a particular case.

In 1966, finally, came *Miranda* v. *Arizona*, certainly the most significant criminal law decision of the Warren era, if not in the entire history of the United States Supreme Court.[114] In *Miranda*, the Court clarified the rule laid down in *Escobedo*, considering in general "the admissibility of statements obtained from an individual who is subjected to custodial police interrogation and the necessity for procedures which assure that the individual is accorded his privilege under the Fifth Amendment to the Constitution not to be compelled to incriminate himself."[115]

The facts in *Miranda* are straightforward. Police officers took the defendant Miranda into custody on suspicion of murder. Chief Justice Warren continues the story: "The police did not effectively advise him of his right to remain silent or of his right to consult with his attorney. Rather, they confronted him with an alleged accomplice who accused him of having perpetrated a murder. When the defendant denied the accusation and said 'I didn't shoot Manuel, you did it,' they handcuffed him and took him to an interrogation room. There, while handcuffed and standing, he was questioned for four hours until he confessed. During this interrogation, the police denied his request to speak to his attorney, and they prevented his retained attorney, who had come to the police station, from consulting with him."[116] The question for the Court, as in previous cases, was whether the confession could be introduced into evidence at trial.

Warren did not dwell on the specific facts of Miranda's case; instead, he treated Miranda's interrogation as typical of existing police practices and handed down a series of general rules designed to protect the rights of all those charged with crime. In essence, Warren held that the Constitution required law enforcement officials to follow specific procedures whenever "a person has been taken into custody or otherwise deprived of his freedom of action in any significant way."[117] These procedures are as follows: "Prior to any questioning, the person must be warned that he has a right to remain silent, that any statement he does make may be used as evidence against him, and that he has a right to the presence of an attorney, either retained or appointed. The defendant may waive effectuation of these rights, provided the waiver is made voluntarily, knowingly and intelligently. If, however, he indicates in any manner and at any stage of the process that he wishes to consult with an attorney before speaking there can be no questioning."[118]

Criticism of *Miranda* came immediately and was widespread. It did not help Warren that only four of his fellow justices fully supported his opinion[119] or that the dissenters expressed their views in sharp tones. Justice White was particularly strong in dissent. "The proposition that the privilege against self-incrimination forbids in-custody interrogation without the warnings specified in the majority opinion and without a clear waiver of counsel," he wrote, "has no significant support in the history of the privilege or in the language of the Fifth Amendment." Nor, in White's view, could the opinion of the Court be defended by reference to precedent: "Only a tiny minority of our judges who have dealt with the question," he noted, "have considered in-custody interrogation, without more, to be a violation of the Fifth Amendment." White went on to criticize the Court on the grounds that it "has not discovered or found the law in making today's decision, nor has it derived it from some irrefutable sources; what it has done is to make new law and new public policy in much the same way that it has in the course of interpreting other great clauses of the Constitution." Finally, White wrote, application of the Court's decision would "in some unknown number of cases return a killer, a rapist or other criminal to the streets and to the environment which produced him, to repeat his crime whenever it pleases him"; and would have a "corrosive effect on the criminal law as an effective device to prevent crime."[120] In short, White's dissent foreshadowed hundreds of other critics of *Miranda* in arguing that the Court was legislating rather than interpreting the law; that the decision had little support in history, in the constitutional text, or in judicial precedent; and that the decision, when considered purely as public policy, was a disaster.

Reaction to *Miranda* was unusually strong on both sides. "Monday's Supreme Court ruling did not create new pretrial rights for accused persons," commented the *Milwaukee Journal*, "the Court merely spelled out the full meaning that has always been implied in long acknowledged rights." "Though perhaps an unpopular and controversial decision, the Court's opinion may well result in long-range strengthening of law enforcement throughout the country while protecting the basic rights of every citizen," wrote the *Nashville Tennessean*. Southern papers especially were not so sanguine; the conservative *Richmond Times-Dispatch* called the Court "an ally of the criminal element in America," while *The State* (Columbia, S.C.) deplored the decision as allowing "the criminal . . . to thumb his nose at the police until he has a lawyer by his side." A number of papers sought to find a middle position: the *Chicago Daily News*, for example, declared that "safeguarding the suspect's rights is certainly a prime concern of the Court under the Constitution's mandate. If the police can with impunity badger or bully or beat a suspect into confessing a crime, then no citizen is safe. But an era of drastically rising crime has also proved to be an era in which the Supreme Court has piled decision on decision to make convicting and punishing the guilty more difficult and less certain."[121]

Congress, too, reacted vehemently to the Court's decision.[122] Over the next two years, the congressional opposition became even more virulent, fueled by the increasing violence in America's cities. That violence took many forms—race riots, antiwar protests and clashes with police, and, of course, crime. Between 1966 and 1968, the number of violent crimes per 100,000 Americans jumped from 1,671 to 1,926, an increase of 15 percent in just two years.[123] In 1967, President Johnson sent to Congress the comprehensive "Safe Streets and Crime Control Act of 1967," which would have both authorized hundreds of millions of dollars in grants to state and local police forces and strictly controlled firearms. The 1967 proposal got so far as to be approved by the full House of Representatives and by the Senate Subcommittee on Criminal Law and Procedure, but not before the committee amended it to make any confession admissible in federal court if it was "voluntarily given" and to prohibit any federal court review of a state court ruling that a confession was voluntarily given, provided that that ruling had been viewed by the highest court of the state. The full Senate took no action on the proposal.

Johnson reintroduced the Omnibus Crime Control and Safe Streets Act, as it was now called, in early 1968. Again the bill ran into the anti-*Miranda* crusade, and, despite Johnson's efforts, the final measure made any voluntary confession admissible, spelled out the factors which federal judges would have to consider in determining whether or not a confession was admissible (specifying that, in any event, the presence or absence of any specific factor "need not be conclusive on the question of voluntariness of the confession"), and modified the *Mallory* decision by providing that no confession would be inadmissible solely because of a delay between arrest and arraignment if the confession were given within six hours of arrest.[124] Johnson, while expressing reservations about these and other revisions to his original proposal, nonetheless signed the measure into law.

The anti-Court provisions of the Crime Control Act were added by the Senate and might have been removed by the more liberal House (especially given the president's opposition) had it not been for the assassination of Senator Robert F. Kennedy (D.-N.Y.) on the evening of his California primary victory on 5 June. Kennedy's assassination came less than two weeks after Senate passage of the crime bill and just as the House was set to begin reconsideration of the measure. In 1967, the House had passed an earlier version of the bill, one containing no anti-Court language, and on 6 June had to vote on whether to send the bill to conference or simply accept the Senate version. In a vote taken merely twelve hours after Kennedy's murder, the House voted to go along with the Senate bill without a conference.

The Kennedy assassination, combined with the murder of Martin Luther King a few weeks before and unprecedented violence at the Democratic National Convention in August in Chicago, set the stage for "law and order" to become a major issue of the 1968 presidential campaign. Candidates Richard Nixon and George Wallace played the law-and-order theme to the hilt. While critics charged that "law and order" were merely code words for racism, there is no doubt that, with American society seemingly crumbling in the streets, law and order, at least partly, meant just that. Inevitably, the issue of *Miranda* and the other defendant's rights cases came up frequently, sometimes in veiled phraseology and sometimes directly. Ronald Reagan, then governor of California and an active Republican campaigner, linked the RFK assassination to the Court's permissiveness. "This nation," said Reagan, "can no longer tolerate the spirit of permissiveness that pervades our courts and other institutions."[125] George Wallace, who led the way on this and other issues, repeatedly blamed the federal judiciary for the breakdown of law and order. As the Wallace (American Independent Party) platform put it, "In the period of the past three decades we have seen the Federal judiciary, primarily the Supreme Court, transgress repeatedly upon the prerogatives of the Congress and exceed its authority by making judicial legislation. . . . We have seen them, in their solicitude for the criminal and lawless element of our society, shackle the police and other law enforcement agencies; as a result, they have made it increasingly difficult to protect the law-abiding citizens from crime and criminals. This is one of the principal reasons for the turmoil and the near revolutionary conditions which prevail in our country today."[126] Blasting the Supreme Court became a frequent campaign theme for Wallace.[127]

Nixon too began the campaign by repeatedly denouncing the Court. In March, for example, Nixon pledged to sponsor legislation to modify specific criminal law decisions, and the candidate frequently mentioned the Court in his campaign speeches and statements.[128] Responding to pressure from within his own party, however, Nixon softened his anti-Court stance as the campaign wore on. On 11 September 1968, the *Times*, reporting on a Nixon campaign speech, commented that "for the first time in eight months" Nixon "failed to mention the Supreme Court or to accuse it of strengthening the criminal forces at the expense of the peace forces."[129] Nixon refused to comment on the pending nomination of Abe Fortas to be chief justice, and began to speak not just of "law and order," but of "law and order with justice."[130] Spiro Agnew, the Republican vice presidential nominee, continued to sound a strong law-and-order theme, and at the very end of the campaign Nixon again returned to the fray, pledging to nominate to the Supreme Court judges with "experience or great knowledge in the field of criminal justice, and some understanding of the role some of the decisions of the high Court have played in weakening the peace forces in our society."[131] Democratic candidate Hubert Humphrey, on the defensive because of his position in the Johnson administration, could do nothing but protest that Nixon's statements on the Supreme Court "lend themselves to a breakdown of law and order" and enlist the support of senior administration officials—including Attorney General Ramsay Clark, one of Nixon and Wallace's favorite targets—in his campaign to discredit Nixon for exploiting the crime issue.

Still, it would be a mistake to treat the law-and-order issue in 1968 as primarily a Supreme Court issue. Law and order was an issue not because of *Mallory* and *Miranda* but because of the race riots that had plagued the country for three years before the election; the particularly violent and uncontrollable riots, looting, and torchings that followed the King assassination; the murders of King and Kennedy; endemic student riots in protest of the Vietnam War; the "Black Power" movement; and the awful and bloody scenes of demonstrators clashing with police in Chicago during the Democratic convention. It was not "old fashioned crimes like rape, mugging, murder, and assault" that captured the attention of the politicians and the people in 1968, wrote the journalist Theodore White, but political violence. The Court was brought into the picture only because of its high visibility as a national symbol and because, for candidates like Wallace, being against the Court on crime, like being against the Court on racial issues, was good politics.[132]

VII

Just as the controversy over *Miranda* was building to a peak, the Court was again haunted by the old issue of school desegregation. In the early to mid-1960s, the Court had dealt with the issue only occasionally. Quite clearly the Court put the issue on the back burner throughout this period, though clear signs of mounting judicial impatience could be seen. In 1964, the Court struck down a scheme devised by Prince Edward County, Virginia, which involved closing the public schools and subsidizing private school tuition with direct grants to parents.[133] The private schools, Virginia argued, were immune from the influence of the Fourteenth Amendment and hence could remain segregated. But the Supreme Court, speaking through an exasperated Justice Black, held the Virginia plan unconstitutional. Ordinarily, Black ruled, states had wide discretion in deciding the scope and operation of laws and programs; in the Prince Edward County case, however, "the record . . . could not be clearer that Prince Edward's public schools were closed and private schools operated in their place with state and county assistance, for one reason, and one reason only: to ensure . . .

that white and colored children in Prince Edward County would not, under any circumstances, go to the same schools."[134] "The time for mere 'deliberate speed,'" Black concluded, "has run out."[135]

School desegregation again became a major issue before the Court in 1968, fully fourteen years after the original decision in *Brown*. In all that time the South had made but little progress toward the goal of integrated schools; as late as 1966, for example, only 12.5 percent of Southern blacks ended desegregated schools, and more Southern blacks attended segregated schools in 1968 (2.5 million) than in 1954 (2.2 million).[136] Finally, facing another Virginia school district which had virtually escaped integration, the Court took action. The case, *Green v. New Kent County School Board*,[137] presented a textbook example of how determined Southern officials could avoid the clear mandate of the *Brown* decision. New Kent County was a small, rural county which comprised a single school district and a total of two schools. Before *Brown*, one of the schools was white, the other black. There was no residential segregation, and the district was about evenly divided between whites and blacks. If any county ought to have been desegregated, New Kent County was it.

And yet, by 1968, the "white" school was still 85 percent white and the "black" school was still 100 percent black. County officials had achieved this nonresult by implementing a so-called "freedom of choice" plan, under which parents could choose to send their children to whichever school they wanted. For obvious reasons none of the white parents chose to send their children to the "black" school, and, because of inertia combined with various forms of pressure and intimidation, very few black parents had dared to choose the "white" school for their children.

When the case finally reached the Supreme Court, the justices decided they had had enough. The mandate of *Brown* was clear, said Justice Brennan: Southern districts were obligated to make "the transition to a unitary, nonracial system of public education." School boards such as New Kent County's, Brennan continued, were

clearly charged with the affirmative duty to take whatever steps might be necessary to convert to a unitary system in which racial discrimination would be eliminated root and branch. . . . In determining whether the respondent School Board met that command by adoption of a "freedom of choice" plan, it is relevant that this first step did not come until some 11 years after *Brown I* and 10 years after *Brown II* directed the making of a "prompt and reasonable start." This deliberate perpetuation of the unconstitutional dual system can only have compounded the harm of such a system. Such delays are no longer tolerable. . . . The burden on a school board today is to come forward with a plan that promises realistically to work, and promises realistically to work *now*.[138]

The New Kent County School Board's obstinacy in implementing *Brown* had led the Court quite naturally into insisting not simply upon the dismantling of overt segregatory schemes but upon the achievement of results—on the achievement, that is, not simply of desegregation but of integration.

A 1969 case greatly expanded the powers of the federal district judges in overseeing the desegregation process. In *United States* v. *Montgomery Board of Education*, the Court considered district judge Frank Johnson's action in modifying—and then mandating—a desegregation plan proposed by the school board.[139] It was clear that the judge could reject a desegregation plan that he considered unacceptable, but could he take the affirmative steps of changing the plan and then imposing it on the school board?

The Supreme Court unanimously said yes. The Montgomery Board of Education had "attempted in every way possible to continue the dual system of racially segregated schools in defiance of our repeated unanimous holdings that such a system violated the United States Constitution," said Justice Black, and had operated "as though our *Brown* cases had never been decided." Therefore, the situation called for "the coercive assistance of courts." Judge Johnson's order, wrote Black, "was adopted in the spirit of this Court's opinion in *Green*," and later modifications by the Court of Appeals were fully consistent with the court's "capacity to expedite, by means of specific commands, the day when a completely unified, unitary, nondiscriminatory school system becomes a reality instead of a hope."[140]

The combination of *Green*, with its emphasis on results, and *U.S.* v. *Montgomery*, with its emphasis on affirmatively imposed remedies, provides the background to the busing cases of the 1970s. Busing had long been a staple of Southern pupil assignment plans; an early purpose had been to transport students to racially segregated schools that might be far from their homes or neighborhoods. When in the late 1960s and early

1970s district courts began to order busing as part of their desegregation decrees, the stage was set for a major confrontation before the Supreme Court.

The leading case was *Swann* v. *Charlotte-Mecklenburg Board of Education*.[141] The city of Charlotte, North Carolina, unlike the rural school district involved in *Green*, was marked by substantial residential segregation. Like many Northern cities, therefore, the reliance on facially neutral criteria (such as residence zones) resulted in the continuance of substantial segregation. Despite the operation of a court-approved desegregation plan, many of Charlotte's schools remained virtually all black.

Acting in the spirit of *Green* and *U.S.* v. *Montgomery*, Judge James B. McMillan ordered a new desegregation plan, one devised not by the school board but by a court-appointed expert. The plan called for busing elementary school pupils between the white and black schools, in both directions, in an attempt to achieve a more nearly integrated school system. The Supreme Court, in 1971, whole-heartedly endorsed Judge McMillan's plan. Again the Court was unanimous; this time Warren E. Burger, the new chief justice, was the Court's spokesman. When school authorities "default" on their "obligation to proffer acceptable remedies," Burger declared, "a district court has broad power to fashion a remedy that will assure a unitary school system." Thus the central question was whether Judge McMillan's student assignment plan exceeded his discretionary authority under the *Brown-Green-Montgomery* line of precedents.

Judge McMillan's order did assign students to particular schools on the basis of race; under normal circumstances, wrote Burger—in the absence, that is, of a previous constitutional violation—"there would be no basis for judicially ordering assignment of students on a racial basis." All things being equal, Burger admitted, "it might well be desirable to assign pupils to schools nearest their homes. But all things are not equal in a system that has been deliberately constructed and maintained to enforce racial segregation. The remedy for such segregation may be administratively awkward, inconvenient, and even bizarre in some situations and may impose burdens on some; but all awkwardness and inconvenience cannot be avoided in the interim period when remedial adjustments are being made to eliminate the dual school systems." As for the busing remedy itself, such transportation "has been an integral part of the public education system for years," and, unless the "time or distance involved is so great as to risk either the health of the children or significantly impinge on the educational process," busing presented no constitutional problems.[142]

Busing had been controversial even before *Swann*, with President Richard M. Nixon making opposition to busing a major campaign issue in 1968 and a major policy goal of his administration.[143] Thus the reaction to *Swann* was predictable: liberals hailed the ruling as a "reasonable forward step in the long campaign against discrimination in U.S. education"; "a landmark in our country's continuing and often agonizing efforts to eliminate racial discrimination in public schools"; and "the most significant decision on school desegregation since the original Brown ruling in 1954."[144] Liberals were also reassured that the replacement on the Court of Earl Warren by Warren Burger did not foreshadow a retreat from the Supreme Court's commitment to racial equality.[145]

Southerners also reacted as expected. A handful of liberal newspapers supported the decision, but there was considerable opposition. The Supreme Court "performed a truly dazzling rewrite job on the Fourteenth Amendment to the Constitution" in the *Swann* decision, said the *Dallas Times-Herald*; the *Richmond Times-Dispatch* found the decision "appalling for its approval of busing." The *Richmond News Leader* echoed its competitor: "The appalling school desegregation decision handed down yesterday by a unanimous Supreme Court can generate only profound sorrow and shock among those who value the American ethic of freedom of choice."[146]

Politically, the unknown variable in the impact of the decision was its application to Northern school districts which, while not segregated by law, were nonetheless as segregated as their Southern counterparts. Many assumed at first that the *Swann* decision, with its emphasis on the existence of officially sponsored past discrimination, exempted Northern school districts from the integration requirement. The *Richmond Times-Dispatch* objected to the "exclusion of most Northern communities from its effect," while newspapers such as the *Detroit News* expressed relief that the decision, though far-reaching, "does not signal a mandatory, widespread and massive program of bussing [*sic*] of American school children in the name of desegregation." While Southern school districts will be "profoundly affected" by the decision, said the *News*, "we judge from the court's

The Modern Supreme Court

language that the effect upon de facto segregation in Northern states will be considerably less."[147]

The true meaning and impact of *Swann*, both in the South and in the North, would depend on how the Supreme Court's decision was interpreted by lower court judges. In the months after *Swann*, judges began to require busing in cities across the South. The trend toward busing continued despite Chief Justice Burger's attempt to convince lower court judges that his *Swann* opinion did not require drastic measures. In an in-chambers opinion overturning a district court order requiring busing in Winston-Salem, North Carolina, Burger noted "the possibility that there may be some misreading of the opinion of the Court in the *Swann* case." If a lower court "read this Court's opinion as requiring a fixed racial balance or quota," Burger wrote, "it would appear to have overlooked specific language in the opinion in the *Swann* case to the contrary." Burger then cited his own opinion in *Swann*: "If we were to read the holding of the District Court to require, as a matter of substantive constitutional right, any particular degree of racial balance or mixing, *that approach would be disapproved and we would be obliged to reverse*. The constitutional command to desegregate schools does not mean that every school in every community must always reflect the racial composition of the school system as a whole."[148] So concerned was Burger that his *Swann* opinion be correctly interpreted that he sent copies of his memorandum in the Winston-Salem case to lower court judges across the country.

The possible implications of *Swann* really hit home in both the North and the South in January 1972 when federal district court judge Robert R. Merhige, Jr., ordered a merger of the city and suburban schools of Richmond, Virginia, for the purpose of achieving racial integration. Richmond presented a clear example of a phenomenon that was occurring in cities across the country: whites, fearing integration, were moving to virtually all-white suburbs, leaving behind an increasingly black inner city. Thus attempts at integration that stopped at the city line were doomed to at most limited success. In Richmond, for example, "white flight" had left the city schools about 70 percent black, while schools in suburban Chesterfield County were over 90 percent white.[149]

Judge Merhige's first busing plan, which was limited to the Richmond city schools, was a failure, as white flight more than made up for the gains brought by busing. So Merhige, acting in what he thought was the tradition of *Green* and *Swann*, ordered the consolidation of the city and county schools into one huge school district consisting of some 100,000 students, about two-thirds of whom were white. With a massive busing program, Merhige proposed to create a school system in which every school had a black enrollment of between 20 and 40 percent.

Merhige's decision sparked another national debate over the whole issue of busing, and for a while busing dominated the 1972 presidential primaries, especially in the Democratic Party. George Wallace, playing the antibusing theme for all it was worth, rode to victories in Florida (where 41.5 percent of the voters backed Wallace and 74 percent opposed "compulsory busing" in a nonbinding referendum), North Carolina, and Michigan. For a while, as one newspaper observed, it appeared that the busing issue "could transcend all others in this year's political campaigns—not only in the presidential race but in congressional contests as well."[150]

Despite the intensity of the busing issue during the presidential primaries, the issue was of relatively little importance during the general election campaign between George McGovern and Richard Nixon. For one thing, the absence of George Wallace in the general election (Wallace had been shot and nearly killed just before the Maryland primary, forcing him out of the race for the Democratic nomination and ending any possibility of another third-party candidacy) deprived the busing issue of its most vehement critic. For another, the candidacy of George McGovern inevitably focused attention on the Vietnam War as the general election campaign progressed. Most importantly, the busing issue was put on hold during the summer by Congress and by the courts themselves.

In early June, Congress passed a compromise measure that thwarted a drive for stronger antibusing legislation and that had the effect of throwing the issue back to the Supreme Court. Numerous antibusing proposals were introduced in Congress in the wake of Judge Merhige's Richmond busing decision; one, developed by the White House, would have imposed a moratorium on forced busing until 1 July 1973 and would have forced the federal courts to use busing only as a last resort, after all other options had failed. After a heated debate, however, Congress decided in June to pass a compromise measure, attached to a higher education bill, that prevented the imposition of busing until all appeals had been exhausted; denied the use of federal funds for busing except on the "express written voluntary request" of appropriate local school officials and denied federal funds even then if students were being bused to schools offering "substantially inferior" educational opportunities or if the "time or distance of travel is so great as to risk the health of the children or significantly impinge on the educational process"; and barred any federal "official, agent, or employee" from urging, requiring, or compelling any local agency to use state or local funds for busing unless—and this was a key ingredient of the congressional compromise—such busing was "constitutionally required."[151] In effect, Congress's action delayed the debate over busing until after the election and made it highly likely that a Supreme Court decision in the meantime would clarify the issue.

Also in June, the Fourth Circuit Court of Appeals reversed Judge Merhige's plan for the Richmond schools, and a district court in Atlanta refused to order busing, saying that such an order "would only spur the exodus of whites from the city and speed up the transition to an all-black school system."[152] None of this satisfied conservative critics of the Court, and, in fact, these developments might have neutralized a powerful Republican campaign issue.

The busing issue did not go away in the general election campaign, but it figured far less prominently than in the primaries. With George Wallace now out of the picture, only Nixon was left to sound the antibusing theme, which he did repeatedly.[153] Democratic vice presidential candidate Sargent Shriver, under pressure from moderates within his own party, announced that he and McGovern favored busing only when quality education was not compromised.[154] As the campaign wore on, busing became less and less central to the candidates and the voters: a *New York Times*/Yankelovich survey revealed that whereas 29 percent of the American electorate had put busing among the top campaign issues in late July and early August, only 13 percent did so in early October. By then, busing had been eclipsed as an election issue by the war in Vietnam, the economy, crime, and taxes.[155]

After the 1972 election, the Supreme Court quickly applied the logic of *Green* and *Swann* to non-Southern school districts, and the result was massive busing in the North and West. The first such city to come before the Court was Denver, Colorado, in *Keyes* v. *School District No. 1, Denver*.[156] The question in *Keyes* was a difficult one: the schools of Denver were clearly segregated, there was evidence that some of the schools (in the "Park Hill" section of the city) had been deliberately kept all white, but most of the segregation in Denver was the result of residential patterns and not the work of school board officials. Was such a school district subject to the same standards as applied to Southern cities like Charlotte, North Carolina?

The narrow legal question for the Supreme Court was whether proof that the school board had engaged in a deliberate strategy of segregation in some of the schools in a district meant that the *entire* school district could be subjected to court-ordered desegregation. The political question was much broader, for at stake in *Keyes* was whether or not the Court would tackle the extremely difficult and controversial task of desegregating the North. At last the Court had a chance to demonstrate whether it held the North and the South to the same standard; for years, after all, Southerners had been contending that discrimination in the North differed from discrimination in the South only in being more subtle. Senator John Stennis (D.-Miss.) was correct in warning Northerners that, once the North began the process of integration, "you will see what it means to us."[157]

Justice Brennan wrote the opinion in *Keyes* for a divided Court (Rehnquist dissented; Powell filed a separate concurrence; and Burger joined only in the result). Whether segregation existed by law or because of the deliberate but subtle policies of a school board was unimportant; in both cases, the segregation was "de jure"—the result, that is, of the intentional action of state officials—and therefore unconstitutional. That, after all, had been the lesson of *Green*, in which the Court struck down a superficially neutral school assignment plan on the ground that it was a thinly disguised program to segregate. The critical difference between "de jure" segregation and "de facto" segregation was whether or not "*purpose* or *intent* to segregate" could be demonstrated.[158]

Thus it was clear that the deliberate preservation of white schools in the Park Hill area of Denver amounted to a constitutional violation, and that court-ordered remedies were appropriate to desegregate those schools. Moreover, Brennan held, the existence of proven deliberate segregation in one part of the school district called into question all the racially imbalanced schools in the district; as a result of the finding of intent to segregate in one part of the district, the burden of proof shifted to the school board to demonstrate that other segregated schools were *not* the result of deliberate discriminatory policies. The standard of proof to be met by the school board was stringent: the board had to prove not simply that the observed segregation was the result of "some allegedly logical, racially neutral explanation for their actions. Their burden is to adduce proof sufficient to support a finding that segregative intent was not among the factors that motivated their actions." Alternatively, the school board could avoid systemwide desegregation only by "showing that its past segregative acts did not create or contribute to the current segregated condition of the core city schools." Needless to say, the Denver school board failed to meet either of these strict tests.[159]

The Court's endorsement of integration in Denver greatly accelerated the pace at which lawsuits were brought against segregated schools across the country. By the mid-1970s, federal courts were hearing cases against Baltimore, Detroit, Indianapolis, Louisville, Milwaukee, Omaha, St. Louis, Wilmington, Akron, Cincinnati, Cleveland, Columbus, Dayton, Youngstown, Boston, Pasadena, and Kansas City, Kansas. Antibusing pressure arose from Congress and the White House, and there was violence in several Northern cities.

Only a year later, the Court came face to face with an even more controversial issue than had confronted them in *Keyes*: whether the federal courts could impose busing as a remedy across school district lines, and in particular between black inner city schools and white suburban schools. The question, first raised in the Richmond controversy, was presented in stark form in *Milliken* v. *Bradley*, a case arising out of the Detroit school system.[160]

The Detroit case presented an extreme version of a pattern found in many Northern cities. By the early 1970s, the city was becoming overwhelmingly black, as whites fled the inner city for the bigger homes, safer neighborhoods, and better schools of the suburbs. The impending imposition of busing within the city limits gave whites an additional incentive to leave for the suburbs. By the time the Detroit case came to the Supreme Court, nearly 70 percent of the school-age population in the city was black.[161]

There was no question that Detroit's school district and the state of Michigan had engaged in discriminatory practices and that the remedy of busing to achieve integration was called for. The only difficulty involved the scope of the remedy. Busing wholly within the city limits would do very little to desegregate the schools. The district court, therefore, decided to integrate Detroit's schools by busing students between the city and the suburbs, in both directions.

This the Supreme Court refused to endorse. In the first school desegregation case lost by the plaintiff in the Warren and Burger era, the Court held the interdistrict remedy inappropriate. "The constitutional right of the Negro respondents residing in Detroit is to attend a unitary school system in that district," wrote the chief justice for himself and Justices Powell, Rehnquist, and Blackmun.[162] "The controlling principle consistently expounded in our holdings is that the scope of the remedy is determined by the nature and extent of the constitutional violation." Before the boundaries of "separate and autonomous school districts may be set aside," Burger wrote, "it must first be shown that there has been a constitutional violation within one district that produces a significant segregative effect in another district. Specifically it must be shown that racially discriminatory acts of the state or local school districts . . . have been a substantial cause of inter-district segregation."[163] Whatever the effect (or noneffect) of busing wholly within the city limits, suburban school districts could not be asked to pay the price of discrimination within the city.

The four dissenters—Marshall, White, Brennan, and Douglas—were beside themselves with outrage at the Court's apparent retreat in the face of mounting pressure. "Today's holding," wrote Marshall, "is more a reflection of a perceived public mood that we have gone far enough in enforcing the Constitution's guarantee of equal justice than it is the product of neutral principles of law."[164] For Marshall, it was the duty of the *state* to remedy the segregation that it had contributed to by the very creation of the independent school districts and by the vesting in those districts of autonomous power. Moreover, arbitrarily to stop the segregation remedy at the district line meant that, while constitutional violations were proven, effective remedies were unavailable. The Court's decision, wrote Justice White, meant that the state, "the entity at which the Fourteenth Amendment is directed, has successfully insulated itself from its duty to provide effective desegregation remedies by vesting sufficient power over its public schools in local school districts."[165]

The *Milliken* decision was the Court's last landmark busing case; subsequent cases merely clarified or modified principles expounded in *Swann*, *Keyes*, and *Milliken*.[166] The volatility of busing as a political issue did not

The Modern Supreme Court

decrease after *Milliken*, however. *Milliken* only set an outer boundary for busing; for most Northern cities, the real integration process was yet to come. Particularly difficult and even violent busing programs, such as in Boston, kept busing a hot political issue and kept alive congressional attempts to eliminate or curb the courts' use of busing as a remedy for segregation.[167] Throughout the 1970s and 1980s, Congress repeatedly expressed its opposition to busing by banning the use of federal funds for busing and by prohibiting the Department of Health, Education, and Welfare (and, later, the Department of Education) from ordering busing.[168] Stronger measures designed one way or another to eliminate busing altogether as a remedy for segregation have been frequently debated. At times these bills have advanced through congressional committees or even through one house of Congress, but none has become law. In 1977 the Senate Judiciary Committee passed a bill that would have prohibited a federal court from ordering busing unless the court first determined that "a discriminatory purpose in education was a principal motivating factor" in the constitutional violation the busing was designed to correct and unless several other restrictive conditions were satisfied. That bill was tabled by the Senate in 1978 by two votes.[169] Also in 1978, a House provision that would have banned the Justice Department from bringing any legal action designed to promote busing was dropped by a House-Senate conference committee.[170] In 1979, the Senate defeated by only three votes an amendment to the Civil Rights Commission Authorization Act introduced by Senator Jesse Helms (R.-N.C.) that would have banned busing altogether during any "energy emergency."[171] In 1982, the Senate passed the "toughest anti-busing rider ever approved by either chamber"—a bill that would have prohibited the Justice Department from bringing or participating in any lawsuit that could lead to busing, and that prohibited the federal courts from ordering students bused more than five miles or fifteen minutes from their homes—but the bill died in the House.[172] A constitutional amendment to prohibit busing was defeated by the full House in 1979 by a vote of 216 to 209.[173]

VIII

Conservative critics of the Warren Court looked to Richard Nixon's appointments to put the Court back on what was to them a more traditional and acceptable track. Nixon himself, while campaigning for president, had made his views on the role of the Court clear. "I believe in a strict interpretation of the Supreme Court's functions," Nixon said in July 1968. "In essence this means I believe we need a Court which looks upon its function as being that of interpretation rather than of breaking through into new areas that are really the prerogative of the Congress of the United States."[174] In his first term, Nixon was able to appoint four new justices—Warren E. Burger, Harry A. Blackmun, Lewis F. Powell, and William H. Rehnquist—to replace Chief Justice Warren, Abe Fortas, Hugo Black, and John Marshall Harlan. Two of the justices replaced by Nixon (Warren and Fortas) were liberals, and one (Black) was frequently found on the liberal side of controversial issues.

The four Nixon justices immediately showed themselves to be independent and, frequently, even innovative in matters of constitutional interpretation. At first there were signs that the Nixon justices would rule the way Nixon would have wanted; in the Pentagon Papers case, for example, the two Nixon appointees then on the bench (Burger and Blackmun) dissented from the Court's refusal to grant the Nixon administration's request for an injunction against the publication of the papers by *The New York Times*.[175] Burger also dissented from the Court's 1970 holding (by statutory interpretation) that permitted draftees to claim conscientious objector status on the basis of moral or ethical beliefs rather than strictly religious principles. And while only Rehnquist dissented from the Court's holding in the Denver busing case in 1973, all four Nixon appointees were in the majority when the Court retreated in the Detroit case a year later. In the 1973 case of *Miller* v. *California*, all three of the Nixon appointees then on the Court sided with the majority in narrowing the legal definition of obscenity and thus making it easier for states to obtain convictions in obscenity cases.[176] The Nixon appointees were frequently found on the conservative side in freedom of speech cases, and all three Nixon appointees then on the Court voted to reject a "wealth discrimination" case brought against the Texas system of local variation in education taxation and expenditures.[177]

In other areas, one or more of the Nixon justices could be found siding with the liberal wing of the Court. *Swann* is one example. In *Gertz* v. *Robert Welch*, an important libel case, Burger dissented, along with Brennan, White, and Douglas.[178] Blackmun concurred in the Court's 1974 reversal of a conviction of a man who displayed an American flag covered with a peace symbol in violation of a state statute making it a crime to place "any word, figure, mark, picture, design, drawing, or advertisement of any kind" upon the U.S. flag.[179] In a 1971 case, Burger wrote and Blackmun joined a landmark decision calling for heightened scrutiny of laws that discriminate against women.[180] Finally, of course, all three of the Nixon appointees who participated in the case ruled against the president in his attempt to withhold the Watergate tapes from Special Prosecutor Leon Jaworski.[181]

All of these cases, however, pale next to the most controversial opinion of the Burger Court—its 1973 decision upholding a woman's right to obtain an abortion throughout the first two trimesters of her pregnancy. The Court's seven-to-two opinion in *Roe* v. *Wade*[182] was written by Blackmun, joined by Powell, and concurred in by the chief justice. Of the Nixon appointees, only Rehnquist dissented.

The abortion issue had been a politically volatile one for a long time before *Roe*. Prior to the late eighteenth and early nineteenth centuries, there was simply no legislation regulating abortion in any American jurisdiction; under the English common law, abortion was not a crime at least before quickening (when the pregnant woman could feel movement, at about sixteen to eighteen weeks). Beginning in the early nineteenth century, various states passed laws regulating abortion; the first laws simply attempted to proscribe unsafe practices of abortions by unqualified individuals. Beginning around 1840, however, and certainly after 1860, the states began passing far more restrictive antiabortion statutes, usually under the purview of the criminal code. By 1860, twenty-three states had abortion statutes; by 1880, it was illegal in every state, with exceptions typically permitted only in order to save the woman's life or in other extreme circumstances.[183]

Pressure for liberalization of abortion laws grew throughout the 1960s, a function of the women's rights movement (which in turn was influenced by the civil rights movement), the sexual revolution, concerns about overpopulation, and increasing awareness of and distress over the problem of birth defects and deformities. In 1962, the abortion question came suddenly to prominence with the case of Sherri Finkbine, an Arizona woman who had taken thalidomide, a tranquilizing drug that can cause severe birth abnormalities. Fearful of giving birth to a deformed child, Finkbine sought to terminate the pregnancy, but under Arizona law abortions were available only to save the woman's life. Nevertheless, the hospital agreed to perform the abortion, but subsequent publicity caused them to cancel out of fear of prosecution. After the Finkbine case became a national sensation, the hospital sought judicial permission to proceed, but the courts refused. Finkbine eventually went to Sweden and obtained an abortion there.

Over the next ten years, groups favoring reform or repeal of abortion laws—in the beginning, mainly the legal and medical professions—waged a battle in the legislatures of a number of states, with increasing success. By the end of 1970 a total of fourteen states had passed laws relaxing restrictions on abortion, and four more had legalized abortion outright, at least before the fetus was viable.[184] Most of the reform statutes permitted abortion to save the mother's life; to protect her physical and/or mental health; to prevent the birth of a deformed child; and in cases of rape, statutory rape, or incest.

The very success of the abortion reform movement spurred further controversy. As abortion laws were relaxed, of course, antiabortion groups gathered strength and fought harder to prevent reform in states that had not yet acted and to repeal the liberalized laws in states that had. The women's rights movement, by 1970 an active presence in American politics, gave rise to several spinoff groups demanding outright repeal of abortion laws. The freedom to choose to terminate a pregnancy was now cast in terms of women's *rights*. "Without the full capacity to limit her own reproduction," said one activist, "a woman's other 'freedoms' are tantalizing mockeries that cannot be exercised." Therefore, "repeal is based on the quaint idea of *justice*: that abortion is a woman's right and that no one can veto her decision and compel her to bear a child against her will."[185]

The characterization of abortion as a "right" inexorably led repeal advocates to the courts. "Pro-choice" advocates (as they would later be known) relied heavily on the Supreme Court's 1965 decision in *Griswold* v. *Connecticut*,[186] in which the High Court struck down a state statute prohibiting the use or distribution of contraceptives. *Griswold* relied primarily on the "right to privacy," a right that, according to the Court, was inherent in the sexual relationship of a married couple and that derived from the "emanations" and "penumbras" of various provisions of the Bill of Rights. A few years later, the Court extended the right to use contraceptives to unmarried as well as married persons.[187] This newly discovered right to privacy, some legal scholars argued, could be extended to include a woman's right to obtain a legal abortion.[188]

Beginning in 1969, various state and lower federal courts began to recognize the right to an abortion as protected by state or federal constitutional law. In that year, the Supreme Court of California overturned the conviction of a doctor who had performed an abortion on a young girl who had threatened to go to Mexico for an illegal abortion if he did not agree to do so. Fearing for the girl's health and safety if she went to Mexico, the doctor agreed to perform the abortion. He was later convicted under California's old abortion statute, which permitted abortions only when necessary to preserve the life of the mother. In reversing, the California Supreme Court held that the statute was vague and that, furthermore, "the fundamental right of a woman to choose whether to bear children follows from the Supreme Court's and this court's repeated acknowledgment of a 'right to privacy' or 'liberty' in matters relating to marriage, the family, and sex."[189] In the four years between this decision and the Supreme Court's decision in *Roe*, a number of other courts were asked to consider whether the right to obtain an abortion was constitutionally recognized, or asked to invalidate state abortion statutes on more technical grounds. Here and there the lower courts accepted these arguments.[190]

Roe and its companion cases evolved out of challenges to the anti-abortion statutes of Texas and Georgia; the first was a traditional statute which made all abortions illegal except when performed to save the pregnant woman's life.[191] The second was a more modern statute that permitted abortion by a licensed physician when

an abortion is necessary because:

1. A continuation of the pregnancy would endanger the life of the pregnant woman or would seriously and permanently injure her health; or

2. The fetus would very likely be born with a grave, permanent, and irremediable mental or physical defect; or

3. The pregnancy resulted from forcible or statutory rape.[192]

The challenge to both of these abortion statutes drew on the handful of precedents recognizing a constitutional right to "privacy," including the two contraception cases of the 1960s. These in turn were based on earlier cases in which the Court had held that certain private rights, though not explicitly spelled out in the Constitution, were nonetheless protected because they involved fundamental interests such as marriage, procreation, and family life.[193]

Justice Blackmun—formerly resident counsel to the Mayo Clinic—wrote the opinion of the Court in *Roe*. He began by explicitly acknowledging the difficulty of his position: "One's philosophy, one's experiences, one's exposure to the raw edges of human existence, one's religious training, one's attitudes toward life and family and their values, and the moral standards one establishes and seeks to observe, are all likely to influence and to color one's thinking and conclusions about abortion. . . . Our task, of course, is to resolve the issue by constitutional measurement, free of emotion and of predilection."[194] After a long review of the history of human attitudes toward and laws governing abortion—intended primarily to show the diversity of opinion on the subject throughout history—Blackmun briefly recited the constitutional precedents that touched on the privacy issue. He concluded: "This right of privacy, whether it be founded in the Fourteenth Amendment's concept of personal liberty and restrictions upon state action, as we feel it is, or, as the District Court determined, in the Ninth Amendment's reservation of rights to the people, is broad enough to encompass a woman's decision whether or not to terminate her pregnancy."[195]

The pregnant woman, however, "cannot be isolated in her privacy." There are competing interests of a compelling nature which the state is entitled to protect: specifically, the state has "an important and legitimate interest in preserving and protecting the health of the pregnant woman" and "still *another* important and legitimate interest in protecting the potentiality of human life." These interests, Blackmun argued, "are separate and distinct. Each grows in substantiality as the woman approaches term and, at a point during pregnancy, each becomes 'compelling.'" When these state interests become compelling, the state may step in and regulate or even prohibit abortion.[196]

At what point do these state interests become compelling? The state's interest in protecting the health of the mother becomes compelling, according to the Court, when the risk to the mother of having an abortion begins to outweigh the risk of carrying the fetus to term. "In the light of present medical knowledge," Blackmun ruled, the "compelling" point "is at approximately the end of the first trimester." From this point on, "a State may regulate the abortion procedure to the extent that the regulation reasonably relates to the preservation and protection of maternal health."[197]

The state's interest in protecting potential human life, similarly, becomes compelling at the point of viability, that is, at the point at which the fetus "presumably has the capability of meaningful life outside the mother's womb." If a state wishes, it may "go so far as to proscribe abortion" after the point of viability, "except when it is necessary to preserve the life or health of the mother." Viability, according to the Court, occurs at approximately the end of the second trimester, at about 24 to 28 weeks.[198]

Two other points about the Court's decision in *Roe* are worth noting. First, the Court rejected outright the claim that the word "person" in the Fourteenth Amendment (which, in stating that no "person" shall be deprived of life, liberty, or property without due process of law, forms the basis of the pregnant woman's case) includes the unborn. Without this determination, as Blackmun admitted, Jane Roe's case would have collapsed, since the fetus would then be entitled to the same level of constitutional protection as the pregnant woman.[199]

Second, the Court ruled that the state's claim that human life begins at conception could carry no weight, and indeed that the state could not "override the rights of the pregnant woman" by "adopting one theory of life." The Court, however, found it unnecessary to decide when human life begins: "When those trained in the respective disciplines of medicine, philosophy, and theology are unable to arrive at any consensus, the judiciary, at this point in the development of man's knowledge, is not in a position to speculate as to the answer."[200] The Court's phraseology at this point was perhaps unfortunate, since taken out of context it seems to disqualify only the judiciary from deciding when life begins. The Court made it clear that a state could not make that judgment either, however, and by implication seems to suggest that Congress would not be permitted to override the rights of the pregnant woman by adopting "one theory of life."[201]

The Court's lack of clarity on this point has been the basis of congressional attempts to overturn *Roe* by passing a statute defining the point at which life begins.[202] Such attempts are premised on a misinterpretation of Blackmun's position, however. A congressional statute defining the point at which human life begins could have two legal effects: first, it could presume to force the judiciary to conclude that a fetus was a "person" under the Fourteenth Amendment, entitled to the protection of "life, liberty, and property." Second, it could, like Texas's statute, attempt to override the constitutional rights of the pregnant woman by adopting "one theory of life." The latter action would have no legal effect, for Congress's action by statute would not be able to override the constitutionally protected right of the pregnant woman. The former interpretation would seem to infringe on the judiciary's power to "say what the law is"; having already determined that the fetus is not a "person" under the Fourteenth Amendment, would the Court concede Congress's power simply to overturn that decision?[203]

Despite the controversial nature of the decision, only Justices White and Rehnquist dissented.[204] Justice Rehnquist suggested that the right to "privacy" was not involved in *Roe* at all: "Texas, by the statute here challenged bars the performance of a medical abortion by a licensed physician. . . . A transaction resulting in an operation such as this is not 'private' in the ordinary sense of the word. Nor is the 'privacy' which the Court finds here even a distant relative of the freedom from searches and seizures protected by the Fourth Amendment to the Constitution which the Court has referred to as embodying a right to privacy." Moreover, even if it is conceded that the Texas statute deprives a woman of "liberty" under the Fourteenth Amendment, Rehnquist argued, such deprivation is justified because the statute bears "a rational relation to a valid state objective."[205]

Both Rehnquist and White criticized the Court for the way in which it reached its decision in *Roe*. Rehnquist called the decision "judicial legislation" and complained that the Court found within the scope of the Fourteenth Amendment "a right that was apparently completely unknown to the drafters of the Amendment."[206] White's language was even stronger: "I find nothing in the language or history of the Constitution to support the Court's judgment. The Court simply fashions and announces a new constitutional right for pregnant mothers and, with scarcely any reason or authority for its action, invests that right with sufficient substance to override most existing state abortion statutes. . . . As an exercise of raw judicial power, the Court perhaps has the authority to do what it does today; but in my view its judgment is an improvident and extravagant exercise of the power of judicial review which the Constitution extends to this Court."[207]

Moreover, White wrote, the Court's decision in *Roe* was based on its conclusion that "the convenience of the pregnant mother" was to be valued more highly than "the continued existence and development of the life or potential life which she carries." "Whether or not I might agree with that marshaling of values," he concluded, "I find no constitutional warrant for imposing such an order of priorities on the people and legislatures of the States."[208]

The fallout from *Roe* was immediate, with the strongest criticism coming at first from the Catholic church. On the very day the decision was announced, Terence Cardinal Cooke (of New York) called *Roe* "shocking and horrifying," while John Cardinal Krol of Philadelphia called it an "unspeakable tragedy for this nation."[209] Within a month, the Catholic bishops had made the Church's opposition to *Roe* official: in a pastoral letter, the bishops denounced the decision as "erroneous, unjust and immoral"; condoned civil disobedience of laws that may "require" abortion; and warned that any Catholic who obtained or performed an abortion was subject to automatic excommunication.[210] A few members of Congress offered sharp words of criticism in the immediate aftermath of *Roe*, but most were silent; congressional opposition to *Roe* did not crystallize until much later.[211] While the abortion reform and repeal forces welcomed the decision with open arms, some were still not satisfied; Representative Bella Abzug (D.-N.Y.), a leader in the women's rights movement, pledged a few days after the decision to work for the passage of a congressional statute that would go beyond *Roe* and wipe out "any state laws of any nature concerning regulation of abortion."[212]

The antiabortion forces were already in place at the time of the *Roe* decision; groups opposing abortion had formed in states where abortion was an issue, either because of attempts to repeal or modify abortion laws or (as in New York) because of counterattempts to reinstate laws that had already been repealed. In the wake of *Roe*, however, abortion became a fully national issue for the first time. Since the Supreme Court had based its decision on federal constitutional law, any successful effort to reverse *Roe* would have to come at the federal level. The obvious method of reversing the decision was to pass a constitutional amendment; statutory schemes for evading *Roe* had not yet been devised, and any hope that the Court could be persuaded to reverse itself were dim, given the seven-to-two margin on the Court and the fact that only one of the Nixon appointees had dissented. Curiously, the idea of taking away the jurisdiction of the federal courts in abortion cases—an idea applied often enough to school prayer and busing—seems never to have been considered seriously.

Antiabortion groups wasted no time in proposing a constitutional amendment to overturn *Roe*; a number of such proposals were introduced in Congress within a few months of the decision. The most highly publicized proposal was one endorsed by seven prominent U.S. senators, led by Senator James Buckley (Conservative-N.Y.), which would have prohibited abortion except to save the life of the mother.[213] The amendment approach was endorsed by the National Right to Life Committee (NRLC), a group that began within the Catholic Church but became independent soon after the Court's decision in *Roe*. On the first anniversary of the *Roe* decision, some 6,000 antiabortion demonstrators marched on the U.S. Capitol to demand quick congressional action on the Buckley amendment, and in March 1974, Senator Birch Bayh (D.-Ind.), chairman of the Senate Subcommittee on Constitutional Amendments, called for hearings on the Buckley Bill. Bayh, who was not a supporter of the amendment, nonetheless could not resist the pressure to take some action on the measure. Despite this flurry of activity, Congress did not seriously take up an abortion amendment until the early 1980s.

Meanwhile, the antiabortion forces attacked on several other fronts. First, they pressed their campaign to discredit *Roe* as bad law and bad policy. In this they were assisted by several leading legal scholars who, whatever their views on abortion policy, were disturbed about the constitutional aspects of the case. The first conference of the independent National Right to Life Committee adopted a resolution denouncing the decision as an "irresponsible exercise of raw judicial powers."[214] A parade of witnesses before the Bayh subcommittee denounced abortion, *Roe* v. *Wade*, and the United States Supreme Court.[215]

Second, the "Right to Life" movement pressed its efforts to make abortions difficult to obtain, even in the wake of the Supreme Court's decision. One technique was to persuade public and private hospitals to refuse to perform abortions; another was to bring public pressure to bear in an attempt to prevent abortion clinics from opening in areas where the movement had significant support; a third was to get the state legislatures to pass various restrictions making abortions harder to obtain and, in some cases, making the woman's decision to obtain an abortion more difficult emotionally. A number of such restrictions have been struck down by the Supreme Court in the years since *Roe* v. *Wade*.[216]

Finally, the Right to Life movement sought to maximize its power and influence through single-issue electoral politics. The idea of using the abortion issue to influence elections—and, equally important, to influence the actions of elected officials—arose early in the fight against *Roe*. In the New Jersey gubernatorial election of 1973, for example, an antiabortion group distributed a brochure in the last days of the election charging that Democratic candidate Brendan Byrne was an advocate of abortion. Byrne denied the charge but was forced to announce publicly his personal opposition to abortion and his support for public hearings on an antiabortion constitutional amendment.[217] Byrne won the election, but abortion opponents had achieved two important goals: they obtained a great deal of publicity, and they exacted a significant concession from the new governor. Whether Byrne would have supported antiabortion laws in any event is not clear, but the following October he did sign into law a bill permitting hospitals and health care professionals to refuse to perform abortions if they were morally or religiously opposed to the practice.

The full power of the abortion issue in electoral politics was not discovered until a few years later, when a group of conservative activists seized upon the issue. Men such as Richard Viguerie, Terry Dolan, Howard Phillips, and Paul Weyrich—who had contemplated the creation of a new political party or a conservative takeover of the Republican Party since the unsuccessful Goldwater campaign of 1964—recognized abortion as an issue that would unite disparate conservative elements and that would put liberals on the defensive. As a chronicler of the Right to Life movement writes, "Abortion suddenly became the right issue, and what an issue it was. As the bottom-line demand of the women's movement, it was a quick and easy symbol for sexual permissiveness and feminism, and opposition to it signaled an uneasiness about the whole feminist agenda. It was a Catholic issue, theoretically mobilizing those millions of voters. It was a moral issue, giving conservatives that human dimension they so often seemed to lack. It had a fanatic following who had already demonstrated their capacity to work tirelessly. It was definitely the kind of issue that people could rally around."[218] The New Right, as Viguerie explained, discovered "that abortion was only one front in a bigger war against family, religions and many traditions that they hold valuable and dear."[219]

By 1980, the Right to Life movement had joined forces not only with the Catholic church but also with Protestant fundamentalists, such as the Reverend Jerry Falwell's "Moral Majority." In that year, a coalition of New Right conservatives, religious conservatives, and Right to Lifers decided to fight an all-out war against a number of prominent liberal Democrats. Funded by groups such as the National Conservative Political Action Committee, the Moral Government Fund (affiliated with Christian Voice), and Senator Jesse Helms's Congressional Club, the conservatives went after half a dozen liberal Senators, including Frank Church (D.-Idaho), George McGovern (D.-S.D.), Birch Bayh, and John Culver (D.-Iowa). When useful, the abortion issue was played for all it was worth.[220]

Meanwhile, efforts in Congress to overturn *Roe* or at least restrict the availability of abortions continued. As early as 1974, the U.S. Senate approved by a vote of 50 to 34 a rider to the Labor, Health, Education, Welfare Appropriations Bill that would have prohibited the use of federal funds to promote abortions; the House, however, refused to go along, and the rider was dropped in conference.[221] The next year, the Senate reversed itself and voted down a similar measure by a vote of 54 to 36.[222]

In 1976, the antiabortion forces won the first of many victories on the question of abortion funding. This time it was the House that voted to ban the use of federal funds to promote abortions for any reason. The Senate dropped this so-called "Hyde amendment," named for its sponsor, Representative Henry J. Hyde (R.-Ill.), from the Labor-HEW Appropriations Bill, sending the measure to conference. After weeks of debate, the conferees eventually reached a compromise, banning the use of federal funds to promote abortions except when the mother's life would be endangered by carrying the fetus to term. President Gerald Ford, though approving of the abortion ban, vetoed the bill on fiscal grounds, but the House and Senate were able to override the veto.[223]

The following year, the Supreme Court upheld *state* restrictions on the use of federal funds to pay for abortions, rejecting the contention that by doing so the states were in effect discriminating against poor women by preventing them from exercising a constitutionally guaranteed right. By a six-to-three vote (with Blackmun, Brennan, and Marshall dissenting) the Court held that its 1973 decision in *Roe* implied "no limitation on the authority of a state to make a value judgment favoring childbirth over abortion, and to implement that judgment by allocation of public funds."[224] The Court's decision in the state cases made it clear that a pending decision on analogous federal legislation would also be approved, thus making it difficult for opponents of the funding ban to argue that such a measure was unconstitutional. Despite the Court's decision, the Senate again held out against the House for fewer restrictions on the use of federal funds for Medicaid abortions, approving a ban on abortion except when "medically necessary" or in cases of rape, incest, or where the mother's life was endangered. The exception for "medically necessary" abortions was strongly opposed by antiabortion forces in the House, who viewed the language as a large loophole, and the House instead approved a ban on funding in all cases. After two conferences and five months of argument and debate, the House and Senate agreed to a compromise, less restrictive than the 1976 language, which permitted federal funding of abortions when the mother's life was in danger, in cases of rape and incest, or when two or more doctors certified that continuation of the pregnancy would result in "severe and long-lasting physical health damage."[225] Similar restrictions have been enacted ever since. In 1980, the Supreme Court upheld federal restrictions on Medicaid abortions by a vote of five to four.[226]

Meanwhile, efforts to overturn *Roe* outright picked up steam in the early 1980s, the result of gains by antiabortion forces in the Congress (especially the Republican takeover of the Senate in 1980), the defeat of several key liberal proponents of free choice, and the election to the presidency of Ronald Reagan, a confirmed opponent of abortion. During the 1980 campaign, Reagan explicitly endorsed a constitutional amendment banning abortions, and the Republican platform both endorsed a constitutional amendment and pledged the party to appoint antiabortion judges at all levels of the federal judiciary.[227] When he took office in 1981, however, Reagan pressed for action on economic issues and persuaded antiabortion forces to put their measures on hold for the time being.

Though full consideration on the antiabortion measures was thus held up until 1982, preliminary action was taken by two Senate subcommittees in 1981. The Senate Subcommittee on the Separation of Powers, chaired by Senator John P. East (R.-N.C.), approved the so-called "Human Life" Bill, which simply declared that human life begins at conception and allowed states to regulate abortions if they chose. Attached to the Human Life Bill was a provision that would prevent lower courts from considering the constitutionality of state bans on abortion. At the same time, the Senate Subcommittee on the Constitution, chaired by Senator Orrin Hatch (R.-Utah), approved a constitutional amendment (dubbed the "Hatch Amendment") declaring that the right to obtain an abortion was not secured by the Constitution and permitting both the states and the federal government to regulate abortions.

The Human Life Bill grew out of Justice Blackmun's confession of judicial inability to answer the question of when life begins. "When those trained in the respective disciplines of medicine, philosophy, and theology are unable to arrive at any consensus," he wrote, "the judiciary, at this point in the development of man's knowledge, is not in a position to speculate as to the answer." Advocates of the Human Life Bill have read this statement as an invitation to Congress to decide when life begins by legislation. Writes Representative Henry J. Hyde: "The Court pronounced itself incapable of providing a definition [of human life] and thereby signed a death warrant for over one and a half million unborn children annually. In the face of this inaction by the Court, in response to this massive epidemic of destruction, Congress has the responsibility to provide a definition securing the right to life guaranteed by the Fourteenth Amendment to every human, even if it is just a tiny island of humanity known as the fetus."[228] As to whether Congress could reverse the Court's finding in *Roe* that the fetus is not a person under the Fourteenth Amendment, wrote Hyde, "the Court . . . asserted its own incompetency to determine when human life begins."

These arguments leave advocates of the Human Life Bill on shaky legal ground. Their attempt to reconcile *Roe* v. *Wade* with the bill is flawed in at least two respects. First, they confuse the issue of whether the fetus is a person under the Fourteenth Amendment with the question of whether the fetus is a meaningful human life. To the layman, these two questions may seem identical, but in reality they are wholly different. The first question is a matter of constitutional interpretation which the Court had to deal with and which the Court answered unequivocally: the fetus is not a "person" under the technical meaning of that term as used in the Fourteenth Amendment (that the term is used in a technical sense is clear when one considers that corporations, though not human, are "persons" for many purposes under the Fourteenth Amendment). The second question—whether the fetus is a meaningful human life—is ultimately a religious or moral question, and was deemed by Justice Blackmun not to be essential to the resolution of the competing claims in *Roe*. It was not essential because the Court admitted that a state had a legitimate (and ultimately compelling) interest in protecting the *potential* life of the fetus, an interest that outweighs the woman's privacy interest after the end of the second trimester. One point the Court did make clear: no state (nor, by implication, the federal government) could adopt "one theory of life" and so override a woman's constitutional rights.

The antiabortion forces were divided over whether to pursue a constitutional amendment or the more practical (but potentially empty) route of the Human Life Bill. Moreover, Congress spent most of its 1981 session dealing with President Reagan's economic program, shifting abortion and other issues to the back burner. Thus it was not until 1982 that the various antiabortion measures moved forward. In that year, the Hatch amendment was approved by the full Senate Judiciary Committee (controlled, since 1981, by conservative Republicans) but did not reach the Senate floor. Frustrated by the slow pace at which the antiabortion legislation was moving forward, Senator Jesse Helms provoked a debate on abortion and school prayer by proposing riders to much-needed legislation to raise the national debt ceiling. Helms's bill would have declared *Roe* v. *Wade* a mistake for not "recognizing the humanity of the unborn"—language with little if any real effect. After a lengthy filibuster—during which President Reagan came forward to support the antiabortion forces—the Senate finally tabled the Helms proposal by a margin of one vote.[229]

The closest Congress came to endorsing an antiabortion amendment to the Constitution was in 1983, when the Senate took up a revised version of the Hatch amendment. The new amendment, designed as a compromise measure, declared, in its entirety, that "a right to abortion is not secured by this Constitution." The intent of the amendment, its sponsors explained, was to go back to the situation before *Roe*, leaving the regulation of abortion entirely up to the states. The revised Hatch amendment drew fire from both sides: proponents of freedom of choice were of course opposed, and the most radical opponents of abortion were upset that the amendment did not outlaw abortions outright. Senator Jesse Helms bemoaned the "unfortunate fact" that the revised amendment did not "advance the principle that human life is inviolable." Instead, said Helms, "it surrenders forever this principle in exchange for the illusory hope that some lives may be saved."[230] With the antiabortion forces divided, the Hatch amendment was easily defeated.

At the same time, the Human Life Bill stalled as well. The drive to amend the Constitution took some of the steam out of the Human Life Bill campaign; abortion opponents were reluctant to spread their fire too thinly and moved away from the statutory approach. The Human Life Bill, moreover, might well have been struck down by the Supreme Court or simply ignored.

After more than fifteen years, *Roe* v. *Wade* remains the law of the land. The most serious threat to the decision comes not from Congress but from within the Court itself. The decision originally had the support of seven justices, with only Justices White and Rehnquist dissenting. In 1983, in a case in which the Reagan administration urged the Court to reject *Roe*, Sandra Day O'Connor expressed her dissatisfaction with the decision, narrowing the apparent margin in favor of *Roe* to six to three.[231] In 1986, Chief Justice Burger made a tentative statement indicating that he too may have switched to the minority side.[232] If any one decision of the Warren and Burger Courts is in jeopardy of being repudiated by the Court, it is *Roe* v. *Wade*.

IX

The modern conflict between the Court and its critics was greatly exacerbated by the election of Ronald Reagan to the presidency in 1980. Reagan's election, combined with the Republican Party's capture of the U.S. Senate, placed critics of the Supreme Court in a number of important positions within both the legislative and executive branches. During his two terms in office, moreover, Reagan has had the opportunity to appoint three new justices to the Supreme Court, and to promote William Rehnquist to chief justice; and he has appointed a number of outspoken critics of the modern Supreme Court to key lower court positions. The new judicial appointees have not only sharpened the focus of the debate over the Court but have also become active participants.

There is no single "Reagan administration" critique of the modern Court; criticisms of the Court differ quite sharply even within the higher levels of the administration itself. Moreover, the arguments of the administration personnel differ sharply from those of the more outspoken congressmen and senators on the subject, and from the arguments of spokesmen for private interest groups. And, as in the New Deal, the criticisms of the Court leveled by political actors are not the same as those offered by academics or by academics-turned-judges.

The most prominent of the administration critics of the Supreme Court is Attorney General Edwin Meese. Meese's comments on the Court have attracted considerable attention, not only because of his position, but also because of the sweeping and arguably radical nature of at least a handful of his remarks. Beneath the bluster of these statements, however, Meese has attempted to articulate a general critique of the modern Court, going beyond the mere expression of displeasure with the Court's decisions on school prayer, affirmative action, abortion, or criminal defendant rights. Put simply, Meese's criticism of the modern Court is that the justices are in the habit of deciding cases based upon what they think "constitutes sound public policy," rather than on "a deference to what the Constitution—its text and intention—may demand."[233] Instead, Meese advocates a "Jurisprudence of Original Intention" which seeks "to judge policies in light of principle, rather than remold principles in light of policies."[234]

In deciding constitutional cases, then, the key element in the Meese calculus is the intent of the framers of the original document and of its amendments. Needless to say, Meese and the Department of Justice argue that the original intention of the framers is not consistent with the modern Court's decisions on school prayer, abortion, or a range of other issues. "To have argued . . . that the [First] amendment demands a strict neutrality between religion and irreligion," Meese argues, "would have struck the founding generation as bizarre."[235] Meese also claims that the Court's support of affirmative action ignores the intentions of the framers of the Thirteenth, Fourteenth, and Fifteenth Amendments, who, according to Meese, sought to make the Constitution "officially colorblind."[236] Terry Eastland, the director of public affairs in the Justice Department, has made similar attacks on the Court's gender discrimination decisions, claiming that "the Framers of . . . [the Fourteenth] amendment did not contemplate sexual equality."[237] These examples may suggest that Meese's criticisms of the Court are confined to liberal decisions, and indeed for the most part this is true. At least in theory, however, Meese's arguments apply to conservative as well as liberal decisions that distort or ignore the original intent of the framers, and Meese has, in fact, criticized the Court's 1896 separate-but-equal decision (reversed in *Brown*) as based on a disregard of the "clear intent" of the framers of the Fourteenth Amendment.[238]

Meese's advocacy of the original intention approach seems to arise from a broader concern: that the justices of the modern Court have failed to articulate and live by a "coherent jurisprudential stance" that holds together across the range of issues with which they deal, and instead have operated by a "jurisprudence of idiosyncracy."[239] The Court's failure to adopt and stick by a principled jurisprudential theory, in Meese's view, is itself destructive, for it permits the Court to "roam at large in a veritable constitutional forest" unrestrained by anything but their own policy preferences. The Court's lack of jurisprudential mooring, in Meese's view, weakens both democracy and the Constitution: "To allow the court to govern simply by what it views at the time as fair and decent, is a scheme of government no longer popular; the idea of democracy has suffered. The permanence of the Constitution has been weakened. A Constitution that is viewed as only what the judges say it is, is no longer a Constitution in the true sense."[240]

Meese's constitutional theories have sparked a great deal of debate, particularly with Justices William Brennan, Thurgood Marshall, and John Paul Stevens. Meese's critics have responded that it is extraordinarily difficult to determine, after 200 years, just what the framers did intend, or even which of the many men active in 1789 to consult on any given issues; that many of the issues currently facing the Court were nonexistent or, at a minimum, set in a very different context at the time of the founding; that Meese's critique of the Court, far from being a neutral or disinterested expression of constitutional theory, is motivated by a clear political purpose and agenda; and that Meese's history is "facile" and his attitude one of "arrogance cloaked as humility." Justice Brennan has denounced Meese for expressing "antipathy to claims of the minority to rights against the majority," and concludes, "those who would restrict claims of right to the values of 1789 specifically articulated in the Constitution turn a blind eye to social progress and eschew adaptation of overarching principles to changes of social circumstances."[241] Meese's arguments have also been critized by a number of leading constitutional scholars.[242]

Another leading critic of modern judicial activism is Judge Robert Bork, formerly of the U.S. Court of Appeals, whose nomination as an associate justice of the Supreme Court was rejected by the Senate in 1987. For Bork, the decisions of the modern Court—and the legal theory or theories on which those decisions are based—reveal a "fundamental antipathy to democracy."[243] The constitutional ideologies growing in the law schools, Bork argues, "display three worrisome characteristics. They are increasingly abstract and philosophical; they are sometimes nihilistic; [and] they always lack what law requires, democratic legitimacy."[244] When courts usurp the power of the people, moreover, they do worse than merely exercise power illegitimately; they threaten the very liberties they claim to protect. According to Bork, "Our constitutional liberties arose out of historical experience and out of political, moral, and religious sentiment. They do not rest upon any general theory. Attempts to frame a theory that removes from democratic control areas of life the framers intended to leave there can only succeed if abstractions are regarded as overriding the constitutional text and structure, judicial precedent, and the history that gives our rights life, rootedness, and meaning. It is no small matter to discredit the foundations upon which our constitutional freedoms have always been sustained and substitute as a bulwark only abstractions of moral theory."[245] Judge Bork's argument for judicial restraint from deference to democracy is, in turn, consistent with the argument for restraint based on deference to the framers. For, in Bork's view, the framers included among the basic freedoms they intended to guarantee to Americans "the liberty to make laws," or, in other words, the "freedom to choose to have a public morality." The original Constitution, Bork argues, "was devoted primarily to the mechanisms of democratic choice," while "constitutional scholarship today is dominated by the creation of arguments that will encourage judges to thwart democratic choice."[246]

Instead of seeking to justify their decisions with reference to abstract legal or moral theories, Bork suggests that judges should recognize that "in a constitutional democracy the moral content of law must be given by the morality of the framer or legislator, never by the morality of the judge. The sole task of the latter . . . is to translate the framer's or the legislator's morality into a rule to govern unforeseen circumstances." Judges, therefore, should govern "according to the historical Constitution."[247]

Bork has suggested that his argument for judicial restraint is no mere restatement of Meese's call for a jurisprudence of original intention. He admits that phrases like "strict construction" and "judicial restraint" are "slogans" which, by themselves, do not provide enough guidance to the judge as to how to decide constitutional cases. Instead, Bork calls for a "theory that will establish the proposition that the framers' intentions with respect to freedoms are the sole legitimate premise from which constitutional analysis may proceed." Bork himself, however, has elaborated no such theory.

The themes sounded by Meese and Bork are reflected in, and were in many cases developed by, a number of leading academic critics of modern judicial activism. The arguments and orientations of these critics differ substantially, but most focus on the same key issues: first, that judicial activism represents a threat to democracy; second, that judicial power, like legislative and executive power, is political in nature and needs to be kept in check if liberty is to be protected; and third, that judicial activism has become a threat to the Constitution itself, by making its provisions meaningless and easily manipulated. Critics like the political scientist Walter Berns are quick to point out that the Constitution—and not just the Bill of Rights—was meant to be a "Bill of Rights," and that the document was intended to protect liberty through the separation of powers as well as through the courts. When the judges seek to impose their "private judgment" on moral issues for that of the people, they violate the role set out for them by the framers. As Berns concludes, judges cannot "enjoy a jurisdiction over an 'unwritten Constitution,'" for "there can be only private opinions of what is unwritten." The only alternative is for the judges to enforce the Constitution as written; a judge should not "ignore whatever instruction he might receive from the men who ordained and established the Constitution."[248]

At the same time, however, one should not lose sight of the limited nature of the modern critique of judicial activism. It is, in fact, just that —a critique of judicial activism, rather than a fundamental critique of the concept of judicial power. As Gary McDowell has written, "The function of the Court was to patrol the constitutional boundaries of the other branches (the legislature especially) and of the states and keep them within

The Modern Supreme Court

their prescribed limits. The purpose of an independent judiciary was to insure that the limited and supreme Constitution remained so." The problem is not whether there should be a judicial power, but, as Berns puts it, "the scope of this power or the manner in which it is now being exercised."[249]

Nevertheless, it is quite clear from these various arguments against judicial activism that the Court's (or perhaps one should say courts') critics would place more power in the hands of the elected branches and less in the judiciary's. The democratic critique of the judicial power is at the forefront of modern arguments against the Supreme Court's decision making. This argument (which the constitutional scholar Alexander Bickel characterized as the "countermajoritarian difficulty") involves a two-pronged approach: a positive argument that the legislature is the appropriate branch of government to resolve essentially political (or policy) questions; and a negative argument that judges in particular are ill-suited to that role.

Some of the Court's critics have taken rather strong positions in defense of legislative power, especially in relation to the judicial branch. The late Senator John East (R.-N.C.), for example, once told a congressional hearing that Congress "can emasculate the executive branch overnight if we choose to; we can emasculate the judiciary. I am not saying that we should but I am saying that we have the power. I would say the Constitution gave Congress the power because, again, the legislature is the basic, fundamental institution in representative democratic society—which is the fundamental premise of the American experience."[250] Or, as David N. O'Steen, the director of the Committee for a Pro-Life Congress testified, "By denying the people the right to act through their 2 elected representatives in order to decide the fundamental question of protection of human life, a very real and damaging blow was struck at the American system."[251] Even the most careful academic critics of the Court make essentially the same point; McDowell, for example, argues that

Despite the dangers of legislative power, it was still considered by the Framers to be the cardinal principle of popular government. Basic to this principle is the belief that it is legitimate for the people through the instrumentality of law to adjust, check, or enhance certain institutions of government whenever it is deemed necessary and proper. This includes the power of the legislature to exert some control over the structure and administration of the executive and legislative branches.

The qualified power of the legislature to tamper with the judiciary is not as grave a danger to the balance of the Constitution as the friends of judicial activism in every age attempt to make it. . . . Experience indicates that any backlash at all is likely to be weak and ineffectual. But if the negative response is not merely transient but is widely and deeply felt, then the Constitution wisely provides well-defined mechanisms for a *deliberate* political reaction to what the people hold to be intolerable judicial excesses.[252]

Others, instead, focus on what they see as an inherent tension between the courts and the idea of democratic government. Over and over again the Court's critics argue that the judges are apart from, and hence in opposition to, the body of the people. "Plainly it was not the intention of the Framers to make future generations of Americans dependent upon the unfettered and inevitably arbitrary wills of an elite few," wrote Terry Eastland. Antonin Scalia, in the same vein, railed against decision making on policy matters by "a hermetically sealed committee of nine lawyers."[253]

For many of the Court's critics, this devotion to democracy expresses itself in the form of opposition to national power and support of state and local autonomy. The belief that democratic decision making should take place at the state and local level rather than the national level is not surprising, since otherwise it is possible for national majorities to usurp the freedom of choice of local communities. Indeed, many of the Court's critics reveal a deep-seated commitment to states' rights (or, as Meese puts it, "states' responsibilities"). The power of the Supreme Court and the power of the federal government as a whole are closely linked; historically, the Court has strengthened the national government and, at the same time, has used the strong central government as the base of its own power. Past critics of the Supreme Court, including Lincoln, the Reconstruction Republicans, and the New Deal Democrats, were strong supporters of the national government; they opposed the Court specifically when it sought to restrain the federal government's exercise of power. Their criticism of the Court, in turn, was tempered by their recognition that the Court was, in the long run, an important ally in the struggle for federal supremacy, and by the lack of a tradition of opposition to the instruments of federal power.

The Modern Supreme Court

The arguments of modern critics, by contrast, are sharpened rather than blunted by their attitudes on the nation-state relationship and are reinforced by decades of opposition to Washington in general.

This federalism-based critique of the Court cuts across and is reflected in all of the other arguments used by Court critics in the modern era. The Bill of Rights argument, for example, reflects the desire to return to an older, even a pre–Civil War, model of nation-state relations. The argument that the Court is undemocratic is made stronger by the claim that when the national government seeks to impose its will on the people of the fifty states, it in general undermines democratic government. On particular constitutional issues ranging from abortion to school prayer to capital punishment, the arguments of Court critics emphasize the importance of a return to state and local control of political decision making.

Criticism of particular Court decisions, therefore, is frequently expressed in the context of states' rights. When a Senate subcommittee was debating a constitutional amendment designed to overturn the school prayer decisions, Senator Jesse Helms objected on the grounds that the proposed amendment "may actually confer on the Federal government certain authority in church-state relations which, but for erroneous Court rulings, the Federal government never had." Helms encouraged the judiciary committee to modify the proposed amendment "so as to assure that the states retain their traditional plenary authority in church-state relations."[254] The director of an organization called "Project Prayer," on the other hand, saw the same proposed amendment as necessary to "restore to the states and local authorities . . . [the] decision making power taken from them by the courts."[255] Opponents of school busing and abortion have also frequently expressed their criticisms in terms of the question of federalism.[256]

Conservative critics of the Court are not always consistent in their assertions of state sovereignty; some, especially on the abortion issue, have advocated using federal power to impose policy on the states. One antiabortion leader, for example, endorsed a "mandatory human life amendment, not a permissive one, not a States [sic] rights, not one that gives discretion to either a Federal legislature or a State legislature over the issue of who lives or dies."[257] Moreover, there are many critics of judicial activism who support a strong and active federal government, and who argue that the judiciary has usurped congressional as well as state power.

And, since few are opposed to judicial review per se, most concede that the federal courts are justified in protecting at least certain specific rights against state encroachment.

The arguments of the Reagan-era critics of the Court echo long-standing, traditional arguments used throughout history against the Court. As the critics themselves are quick to point out, their arguments follow in the tradition of Jefferson, Lincoln, Roosevelt, and others. Like earlier critics of the Court, the Reagan-era critics have not called for the abolition of the Supreme Court or attempted to undermine the rule of law; at most, they dispute a mode of judicial activity that has never been wholly without critics in any era.

At the same time, the arguments of Meese, Bork, and others seem to be fueled by a deeper, more fundamental critique of the courts than that suggested by Lincoln or Roosevelt. Most importantly, the modern critics, unlike Lincoln or Roosevelt, disagree with the Court on a wide range of issues and cases, most of which have very little to do with one another except for the fact that the Court is connected with them. Because of the wide scope of the modern criticism, and also because of the extraordinary persistence of the modern critics, the arguments against the Court in the modern era have taken on a broad, sweeping character that suggests a critique of judicial power far deeper than mere disagreement with individual cases. When Lincoln or Roosevelt suggested that the Court's decisions need not be accepted as a binding "political rule" for the nation at large, their criticisms, though theoretically applicable to any and all cases, were limited by context to extremely unusual cases like *Dred Scott* or the New Deal cases. By contrast, the comments of modern critics are increasingly directed against the Court in general rather than against a particular case; Attorney General Meese, for example, recently declared that Supreme Court decisions are not "binding on all persons and parts of the government, henceforth and forevermore." The case Meese chose particularly to critique on that occasion was *Cooper* v. *Aaron*, a case that, in Meese's view, is objectionable precisely because it stands for the theoretical principle that the Supreme Court's decisions—like the Constitution itself—are the "law of the land."[258]

The distinction between narrow criticisms of particular decisions and a more generalized critique of the Court and of judicial power is blurred in other ways as well. Consider, for example, Edwin Meese's argument that the Court's long line of decisions applying the Bill of Rights to the states is historically and jurisprudentially flawed. Formally, at least, Meese's argument amounts to nothing more than the assertion that a particular set of Court decisions has been decided incorrectly—an assertion identical to those made by Lincoln or Roosevelt. Moreover, Meese's argument rests on a disagreement over the Court's interpretation of a single clause of the Constitution—the Due Process Clause of the Fourteenth Amendment. The implications of this argument are so sweeping, however, that the distinction between attacking the Court only for particular decisions and attacking the Court as an institution becomes almost meaningless.

Similarly, the modern argument against the Court stresses deference to legislative decisions, an argument parallel to that made by the New Deal critics of the Court. In the hands of the New Dealers, such an argument was a narrow statement about economic regulation by the states and the federal government. When the same argument is applied across a range of issue areas it becomes, at least potentially, a more fundamental critique of the judiciary's role in American politics.

Far more is at stake in the debate between the Court and its critics than the national policy on abortion, school prayer, or any of the other issues that have sparked controversy over the past thirty years. To the Court's critics, at least, "We are dealing with a question of power: who is to govern in our democracy, who is to make policy choices for the nation—a group of unelected and virtually unaccountable Justices or the elected representatives of the people, indeed, the people themselves?"[259] The intensity of the modern Court controversy stems from the underlying importance of these basic questions. The modern conflict is as much a question of who decides as it is a question of what is to be decided. Because that is so, the controversy is unlikely to dissipate quickly, regardless of what the Court does in the future.

X

The arguments of the Reagan-era critics of the Supreme Court reveal a deep distrust of the judicial power, and, if taken to their logical extreme, could constitute a truly fundamental attack on the traditional role of the Supreme Court in American government. For the most part, however, the Reagan-era critics have not attempted to push these arguments very far and have in fact couched their criticisms of the Court in terms of a traditional commitment to the Constitution and to the rule of law. Modern critics of the Court repeatedly assert their belief in the importance of an independent judiciary interpreting the Constitution of the United States and stress that, like Lincoln and Roosevelt, they ask only that judges properly play their appropriate role of constitutional interpretation. There have been calls for judicial restraint, to be sure, but no serious critic of the Court has called for the abolition of the Supreme Court or for the elimination of the power of judicial review. Even when they have walked to the brink of an elemental clash with the independent judiciary, modern critics have been careful to halt at the edge.

Moreover, modern critics have shown no signs of attempting to implement remedies to the Court problem that would seriously jeopardize the independence of the judiciary or undermine the Court's traditional function. Though their rhetoric has often been sharp, the remedies they have proposed have, for the most part, been well within the tradition exemplified by Lincoln and Roosevelt. When they have flirted with more radical remedies, they have exercised caution and recognized the inherent dangers. While a few have called for the adoption of such remedies, others have advised against them or done nothing to promote them.

Reagan-era critics of the Supreme Court have endorsed a number of remedies designed to modify, reverse, or circumvent the many controversial decisions of the Warren and Burger Courts. The two most common proposals, and the two most vigorously pursued by the Reagan administration, are also the most traditional remedies of all and the least objectionable. These are first, to use the presidential power of appointment to replace objectionable justices with friendly ones; and second, to attempt to persuade the Court to reverse itself even without changes in personnel.

President Reagan's opportunities to appoint new justices to the Supreme Court have been limited. The choice of Sandra Day O'Connor drew fire from right-wing opponents of abortion. They saw the moderate-to-conservative O'Connor as a repudiation of the Republican platform plank pledging the appointment of judges with "compassion for human life." At her confirmation hearings, O'Connor stated her personal opposition to abortion but refused to comment specifically on how she would act as a justice.[260] "It does seem inappropriate to me," she said, "to either endorse or criticize a specific case or a specific opinion in a case handed down by those judges now sitting and in a matter which may well be revisited in the Court in the not too distant future."[261]

Once on the Court, O'Connor allied herself firmly with conservatives Burger and Rehnquist. She is generally in line with the Reagan administration's philosophy on federalism, judicial restraint, abortion, religion, and criminal law. In 1983, to the delight of her former critics on the abortion issue, the first woman justice dissented in *Akron* v. *Akron Center for Reproductive Health*, calling into doubt the Court's reasoning and conclusion in *Roe* v. *Wade*.[262]

O'Connor's conservative vote has tipped the scales of justice toward the conservative side in a number of five-to-four decisions. O'Connor sided with the majority in five-to-four decisions permitting the display of city-sponsored nativity scenes; upholding presidential restrictions on travel abroad; upholding the use of "choke holds" by police officers; and limiting the application of the First Amendment in libel cases.[263] But O'Connor has by no means been consistently on the conservative side; in several important cases she has agreed with the Court's liberals. For example, she dissented from the Court's 1984 decision creating a "public safety" exception to the requirement that suspects be read their Miranda rights and wrote the opinion of the Court in a 1982 case striking down the exclusion of men from a state university's nursing program.[264]

Moreover, O'Connor's influence has been diluted because the man she replaced, Potter Stewart, was himself a conservative on many issues. Stewart's views on religion and criminal law, for example, were just as conservative as O'Connor's. The difference between Stewart and O'Connor is most clearly felt in their different approaches to free speech and privacy cases. Stewart was a staunch defender of free speech and voted with the liberal majority in *Roe* v. *Wade* in 1973.

The appointment of O'Connor, then, did not by itself create a counterrevolution on the Court. Many of the modern Court's decisions are so well settled, in fact, that even the replacement of Chief Justice Burger by William Rehnquist and the appointment of Judge Antonin Scalia to the Court had only a partial and marginal impact on the Court's decisions. When the opportunity to replace Lewis F. Powell arose, therefore, the Reagan administration jumped at the opportunity to shift the balance on the Court. Powell, unlike Stewart and Burger, was a centrist on the Court, one who held the balance of power in a number of important cases.

Attempting to take full advantage of the Powell opportunity, the Reagan administration nominated Judge Robert H. Bork, a leading critic of the modern Court and an outspoken advocate of judicial restraint. Once again the administration learned first hand about the uncertainties and difficulties of using the power of appointment to remake the Court: after a fierce confirmation battle, the Bork nomination was finally defeated on the floor of the Senate by a wide margin. The Bork nomination fight clearly demonstrates just how difficult it is to remake the Court without clear, unequivocal support across the polity, and the Reagan administration ultimately retreated, nominating the apparently more moderate Anthony Kennedy. Just what impact the Kennedy appointment will have on the Court remains to be seen, but in all likelihood the appointment will have a marginal rather than dramatic impact on the Court's decision making.[265]

Since the Republicans in control of the White House and the Senate have been unable to accomplish their objective quickly by capturing control of a majority of the Court, they have sought to persuade the Supreme Court to change its own mind and reverse one or more of its controversial decisions. Such a strategy was deliberately and openly adopted by Solicitors General Rex Lee and Charles Fried on behalf of the Reagan Justice Department. Among the decisions or doctrines which the Reagan adminstration has asked the Supreme Court to modify or abandon are *Roe* v. *Wade*, *Miranda* v. *Arizona*, the exclusionary rule, the school prayer decisions, and affirmative action. On several of these issues, the administration has won major or partial victories.[266]

Another remedy supported by critics of the Court is amending the Constitution to overturn objectionable decisions directly. The amendment process presents no theoretical difficulties; it is regarded by all as an appropriate method of overturning Supreme Court decisions, and by some as the only appropriate method. The *Washington Post*, for example, criticizing congressional attempts to reverse the abortion decision by statute, commented that "the Constitution should be changed only by the process the framers designed (on purpose) to be solemn and cumbersome—by two-thirds vote in each house of Congress followed by ratification by 38 state legislatures."[267] "The accepted way to alter Supreme Court decisions, however unpopular," said the *Los Angeles Times*, "has been through constitutional amendment."[268]

While amending the Constitution presents no theoretical problems, it does present enormous practical problems. Aside from the Civil War amendments, the amendment process has been invoked to override a Supreme Court decision only three or four times in 200 years, and one need not look far for the reason. An amendment requires the support of not only two-thirds of each house of Congress, but also three-fourths of the states. Thus thirteen states voting together can block a constitutional amendment. Moreover, such an antiamendment coalition is made even more likely because, historically, amendment politics has been heavily bound up with sectional politics. Thus one region of the country, if united, can keep an amendment from passing. The Equal Rights Amendment, for example, was passed by 35 states and rejected by 15; of the 15 states voting no, 5 were in the west and 10 in the south.

In the past, there was one additional factor working against using the amendment process to upset decisions of the Supreme Court: a general reluctance on the part of key political leaders to tamper with the Constitution. This was clearly evident after *Dred Scott* and during the New Deal. In the modern era, however, constitutional amendment has emerged as one of the two leading strategies pursued by opponents of the Supreme Court. For the most part, the proposed amendments have been narrow and specific, each designed to reverse (or at least modify) a particular court decision. The leading examples are proposed amendments to overturn the Supreme Court's decisions on busing, school prayer, and abortion. Though there have been several amendments introduced that would alter the nature of the judicial system itself, none has ever been seriously considered even by a congressional committee. The leading examples of the latter are proposals to eliminate life tenure for federal judges.[269]

Despite a great deal of debate on these proposals and the vigorous support of President Reagan over the last few years, no constitutional amendment designed to reverse a Supreme Court decision has come close to passage since the relatively uncontroversial reversal of the Court's 1970 decision holding that Congress could not unilaterally extend to 18-year-olds the right to vote in state elections.[270] Even while the Senate was controlled by the Republican Party, there was no chance for passage of any amendment in the Democratic House; the chairman of the House Judiciary Committee, Peter Rodino (D.-N.J.), effectively blocked passage of any amendment in his committee, and it is doubtful that proamendment representatives could gather enough votes on the House side. Even if an amendment somehow passed the Congress, gaining the support of three-fourths of the states would be no easy task, as advocates of the Equal Rights Amendment discovered.

Despite the practical difficulties, the amendment process remains an attractive route for the Court's opponents. Constitutional amendments are dramatic, and they are sure. They focus attention directly on the issues involved. They can be justified as involving no affront to the Court, being merely an expression of the popular will. Amending the Constitution is, in this sense, a conservative gesture, since it recognizes the primacy of the Constitution and tacitly acknowledges the legitimacy of judicial interpretation. Ultimately, however, the amendment process is not useful to critics of the Court except in the most unusual circumstances and thus remains more of a political or rhetorical device than a serious mechanism for checking the Court.

Of the many remedies proposed by the Court's critics to counteract objectionable decisions, the most untraditional—and and the most radical in terms of its implications for the judiciary's role—utilizes Congress's power to control the Court's appellate jurisdiction. This authority derives from Article III of the Constitution, which divides the Court's jurisdiction into two parts—the original jurisdiction, which permits the Supreme Court to hear cases that have not been heard previously in any lower court, and the appellate jurisdiction, which allows the Court to hear cases on appeal from the lower federal courts or from the state courts: "In all cases affecting Ambassadors, other public Ministers and Consuls, and those in which a State shall be a party, the Supreme Court shall have original jurisdiction. In all the other Cases before mentioned, the Supreme Court shall have appellate Jurisdiction, both as to Law and Fact, *with such Exceptions, and under such Regulations, as the Congress shall make.*"[271] Exactly what the framers of the Constitution meant by this clause remains uncertain, despite a great deal of scholarly enquiry and debate. There are at least three possibilities. First, the clause might mean that Congress has complete and unlimited authority to grant or withdraw the Court's appellate jurisdiction at its discretion. Second, it might mean merely that Congress has the power to shift cases between the original and appellate jurisdiction as it sees fit. Finally, it might mean that Congress indeed has the power to take away the

Court's appellate jurisdiction but that this power must be exercised within certain limitations. Some scholars, for example, argue that Congress's power to make exceptions to the appellate jurisdiction cannot be used to deny litigants substantive review of their constitutional rights.[272]

The argument that Article III merely gives Congress the power to shift cases back and forth between the original and appellate jurisdictions, while plausible, was rejected by the Supreme Court in *Marbury v. Madison* in 1803. *Marbury* established the Supreme Court's right to invalidate acts of Congress on constitutional grounds, and it is for that reason that the case is best remembered. The particular law struck down in *Marbury*, however, was (in the Court's view) an act attempting to enlarge the Court's original jurisdiction. Marshall read the Exceptions Clause as giving Congress power only over the Court's appellate jurisdiction, and his interpretation has not been seriously challenged by any Court since.

Congress's power to make exceptions to the appellate jurisdiction has frequently been used as part of its general "housekeeping" function necessary for the efficient operation of the federal court system. But only rarely has Congress attempted to use the exceptions power in order to overturn or prevent a particular constitutional decision. The Reconstruction incident over the *McCardle* case is the leading example, though there are others.[273]

The legal validity of congressional attempts to withdraw the Supreme Court's jurisiction in order to avoid constitutional scrutiny of specific legislation is thus historically suspect. Even those who used the exceptions power during Reconstruction seemed to admit by the stealthy way in which the legislation was introduced that their actions were at least questionable. Several leading constitutional scholars and several Supreme Court justices and lower court judges have held that there are at least some limitations on Congress's power; Justice Douglas, at one point, speculated that "there is a serious question whether the *McCardle* case could command a majority view today," at least insofar as *McCardle* permits Congress to withdraw jurisdiction in a case already briefed and argued.[274]

The reason why the unlimited view of Congress's power is considered suspect relies on a reductio ad absurdum argument. If Congress can remove the Court's jurisdiction in a particular case in order to shield a certain law from constitutional scrutiny, the Supreme Court's power to enforce the Constitution becomes, in effect, a nullity. The power to review acts of Congress for possible conflicts with the Constitution would then fall to the state courts or to the lower federal courts (the jurisdiction of the lower federal courts, however, is also subject to congressional regulation). The result, at best, would be that the Constitution would apply with unequal force and meaning in different states. At worst, states could violate the federal Constitution with impunity. Either way, it is argued, such an arrangement would "violate the Constitution's spirit" by running against "the purpose of the Framers to create an independent judiciary."[275]

Many of those who believe that the appellate jurisdiction approach is constitutionally permissible see Congress's power to withdraw the Court's jurisdiction in particular cases as a means of last resort, to be used only in exceptional circumstances. Others argue that it should not be used at all. Professor Martin H. Redish, for example, has argued that use of the exceptions power "will undoubtedly lead to conflicting constitutional decisions and destruction of the nationally pervasive force that constitutional rights should possess. I therefore do not understand exactly why the Constitution's Framers chose to potentially undermine the unifying power of the Supreme Court by the adoption of the 'Exceptions' clause. I certainly would not have done so in their position. But while the Framers may have made this unfortunate mistake in establishing a constitutional system of checks and balances, I only hope that today Congress does not make an even greater mistake, by exercising this troubling constitutional authority given it by the Framers."[276] When Congress was considering legislation in 1982 to strip the Court of its jurisdiction to hear cases involving school prayer and other issues, Attorney General William French Smith expressed his opposition.[277] Under Edwin Meese, the Justice Department seems more willing to support such an idea, but Congress has shown no signs of seriously considering such a proposal.

There are critics of the Court who claim that Congress's power to eliminate the Court's appellate jurisdiction over particular issues is an essential and intentional part of the federal system of checks and balances. Thomas R. Ascik, of the Heritage Foundation, told a Senate subcommittee that the legislative and executive branches possess several means of checking "judicial encroachment": "Congress appropriates money for the judicial branch; the President appoints the judges; the Senate confirms them; the House can impeach judges; the Senate would try the impeached judges; the Congress creates the inferior Federal courts; and, finally, *and most importantly*, by means of the exceptions clause the Congress has nearly complete authority over the appellate jurisdiction of the Supreme Court."[278] Senator Orrin Hatch, similarly, sees the exceptions power as a way for Congress to defend the Constitution against judicial assault. "The Supreme Court is the body charged with policing the bounds drawn by the Constitution," he wrote in 1981. "When the policeman violates the law, a higher authority must undertake to protect freedoms." That higher authority is the Constitution, as enforced by Congress through the exceptions power.[279]

In the end, the most extreme defenders of the exceptions power rely on an argument that amounts to nothing less than an endorsement of legislative supremacy, an argument not heard seriously since Reconstruction. Senator East, for example, defended congressional power to withdraw the Court's jurisdiction over particular subjects as a way "to check or balance an assertive judiciary." Congress has such checks and balances, East argued, because "the legislature is the fundamental institution in representative democratic society—which is the fundamental premise of the American experience."[280] Senator Sam Ervin (D.-N.C.) also saw the jurisdiction power as part of the system of checks and balances: "The Constitution confers upon the federal judiciary authority to restrain unconstitutional exercise of power by Congress, and upon Congress authority to restrain the unconstitutional exercise of power by the federal judiciary."[281]

Most critics of the Court are willing to concede that judicial review of congressional legislation is a legitimate part of the system of checks and balances, provided Congress has the last word. A few of the most radical critics, however, deny the legitimacy of judicial review altogether or would severely limit its application. Hermine Herta Meyer, for example, resurrects Abraham Lincoln's argument, made in response to *Dred Scott*, that a Supreme Court decision is binding only on the parties to the particular lawsuit involved and does not immediately become the policy of the government, an argument later endorsed by Attorney General Meese. But Meyer goes further than Lincoln (and, for that matter, Meese); whereas Lincoln asserted that the Supreme Court itself might eventually overturn an obnoxious decision, and that it would therefore "never become a precedent for other cases," Meyer calls upon state judges to practice nullification: "To attribute to a decision of the Supreme Court the character of the supreme law of the land as described in the supremacy clause, would be absolutely incompatible with the character of the Constitution and with the constitutional plan. There is nothing in the Constitution which obliges the State courts to follow a decision of the U.S. Supreme Court. On the contrary, their oath of office to support this Constitution, obliges them to follow their own conviction of the meaning of the laws and constitution of the United States."[282] Notre Dame law professor Charles E. Rice, though conceding the Court's right to interpret the Constitution, nonetheless sees congressional regulation of the Court's jurisdiction as a "healthy corrective" to the Supreme Court's "excursions . . . beyond its proper bounds." If Congress withdrew the Court's jurisdiction over cases involving voluntary school prayer, Rice argues, "It may be expected . . . that some state courts would openly disregard the Supreme Court precedents and would decide in favor of school prayer once the prospect of reversal by the Supreme Court had been removed. But that result would not be such a terrible thing. It must be remembered that we are talking about Supreme Court decisions which, in the judgment of the elected representatives of the people and the President . . . would appear so erroneous as to be virtually usurpations."[283]

In addition to stripping the Court of its power to hear cases involving controversial social issues, critics of the Court have also resorted to a series of other statutory measures designed to reverse or modify controversial decisions. These include bills that would restrict the federal courts in the range of remedies they could apply in particular cases; bills prohibiting the Justice Department from using federal funds to enforce or seek court-ordered remedies; and bills endorsing or implementing policies at variance with the Supreme Court's interpretation of the Constitution. Statutory remedies have gathered a good deal of support over the past few years, but no bill directly reversing a Supreme Court decision has gained enough support to be enacted into law.

Stripping the Court of its jurisdiction, like other statutory remedies, has seen only limited support in the modern era. Despite a great deal of hoopla, such proposals have not been supported in the clutch by even a significant minority of federal policymakers. While such remedies follow from some of the more extreme assertions of legislative sovereignty expressed by modern critics of the Court, in the end they do not command enough support to be implemented.

XI

The Supreme Court has not been oblivious to the outcries of its critics. At several points over the past thirty years it has shown its sensitivity to public opinion by retreating from or avoiding particularly controversial decisions. The security cases of the 1950s present one example; the Detroit busing case in 1973 presents another. These strategic retreats did not stop the Court from pursuing its agenda throughout the 1960s and 1970s, but they did slow down the pace and scope of the Court's embrace of liberalism.

By the early 1980s, the Court had begun a measured but clear shift in the other direction. With the appointment of Sandra Day O'Connor, the Court's conservative bloc was strong enough to modify the *Miranda* rule when necessary for public safety considerations, relax the exclusionary rule when and if the police officers involved acted with "good faith," soften the Court's hard line on the separation of church and state, and restrict the application of the First Amendment's free speech clause in a variety of contexts.

The Court's recent conservatism, while significant, should not be exaggerated. All of the core decisions of the Warren and early Burger Courts remain essentially intact, despite modifications at the margins. While *Miranda* and the exclusionary rule decisions have been weakened, they remain in force. The Court's decisions on school prayer, obscenity, and busing remain unchanged. While support for abortion and affirmative action has declined over the past few terms, *Roe* v. *Wade* remains the law of the land and the affirmative action decisions have been weakened only slightly. Still, there is no question that the Court has stopped expanding its liberal doctrines and has begun to contract several. Unlike the temporary retreats of the Warren and early Burger Courts, the current trend seems to reflect a more permanent adjustment in the Court's approach to civil liberties cases.

The Court's shift to the right has not been the result of direct pressure from either the White House or Congress. Though there has been much talk about influencing the Court through constitutional or statutory remedies, none of these proposals has gathered sufficient strength to pose a realistic threat to the Court's independence or autonomy. There has been no equivalent of the New Deal Court-packing plan or the Reconstruction Congress's withdrawal of the Court's jurisdiction.

THE LIMITS OF JUDICIAL POWER

The Court's shift to the right is, instead, the result of a number of more subtle factors and reveals the intimate connection between the Court's decision making and the vicissitudes of American politics. Most important, of course, are the justices appointed by the Reagan administration. The votes of these justices, as discussed earlier, have been crucial in tipping the balance in several key cases. But the appointment process has proved slow and uncertain and is surely not a foolproof or efficient method for influencing the Court. While the Reagan justices have had an effect in modifying many of the decisions of the Warren and Burger Courts, they have not done so in a wholesale manner, or quickly. Moreover, as the Bork nomination fight showed, the appointment process remains subject to the whims of presidential and senatorial politics.

The Reagan Administration has also influenced the Court in less direct ways. The Justice Department has taken a major role in encouraging the justices to break away from their previous decisions, particularly in the areas of criminal law and religion (where they have been reasonably successful) and abortion (where they have not). The administration has also appointed a large number of conservative judges to the lower federal bench, a practice which, over time, has affected the type of cases brought to the Supreme Court and the way issues are framed and presented.

There have also been critical shifts in the ideological positions of sitting justices. As in prior periods of political stress and transition, the justices have shown that they are subject to the same forces that affect other political actors and have behaved accordingly. As the nation has become more conservative under Reagan, the justices have also. Probably the most dramatic example of such a shift is the case of Justice Byron White. Though a moderate through most of his career, White became significantly more conservative in his outlook during the 1980s, in cases ranging from First Amendment law to civil rights.[284]

Finally, the justices appear to have moved to the right because of the nature of the issues now being presented to the Court. The issues of the 1960s and 1970s were major questions of basic doctrine: whether school prayer should be permitted; whether malapportionment could be corrected by the courts; whether the Constitution requires, in general, that illegally seized evidence be excluded from a criminal trial. As these doctrines gained acceptance among even the conservative justices, more narrow questions of clarification and explication came to the fore. In the 1980s, the issues presented to the Court are narrower and more specific: Should the exclusionary rule be applied when the police act in good faith? Should silent prayer be permitted in the public schools? Can there be exceptions to *Miranda* under extraordinary circumstances? When the questions are so framed, it is possible for the justices to make what appear to be "conservative" decisions without rejecting the letter or spirit of the underlying precedents.

The measured conservatism of the recent Court has done little to mollify its critics, who continue to speak out against the Court's decisions on abortion, school prayer, and other issues. In fact, the Court's shift to the right has provoked a counterreaction from the other side, so that vociferous critics of the Court can now be found on both sides of the political spectrum. Frequently, the Court finds itself under fire from liberals and conservatives simultaneously, often on the same issue.

For the modern Supreme Court, a sort of low-level, permanent crisis has become routine. The kind of controversy that shocked commentators in the 1960s—that produced ominous comparisons with *Dred Scott* and the New Deal—is now an unremarkable part of the American political landscape. The controversy surrounding the modern Court presents a paradox: the Court's decisions seem invariably to lead to intense criticism, but, unlike in the past, this criticism has not become so pervasive or so overwhelming as to produce some sort of resolution or settlement. What the Court faces, to borrow a phrase from the literature on British politics, is a perpetual state of "crisis as usual."[285]

Crisis as usual, however, does not seem to have hurt the Court's standing among the American people. The ongoing criticism of the Court's decisions has had remarkably little effect on the Court's prestige in the long run, at least as measured by public opinion surveys and analyses. According to the Gallup polls, public support for the Supreme Court seems quite sensitive to short-term factors, whether positive or negative. The Court's approval ratings dropped in the 1960s on account of the criminal law and busing cases; rose slightly, despite *Roe* v. *Wade*, when the busing controversy died down and when the Court helped to resolve the Watergate scandal; and dropped again during the Reagan administration's all-out anti-Court campaign of 1981–83. Since then, however, the Court's approval rating has risen substantially, probably due to the positive publicity generated by the appointment of Sandra Day O'Connor and to the Court's well-publicized moves toward the right in several key cases. By 1985, public confidence in the Court was significantly higher than at any time in the past twenty years, despite continuing anti-Court rhetoric, and the Court rates near the top when compared with other public and private institutions.[286] Thus the Court's popular support in the long term has been remarkably stable.

Some studies of the sources of the Court's continued popularity suggest that popular support for the Court seems to be based less on specific decisions and more on what is called "diffuse support," defined as "the degree to which the Supreme Court is thought to carry out its overall responsibilities in an impartial and competent fashion." A 1966 study by Walter F. Murphy and Joseph Tannenhaus showed that only one in five Americans has a negative feeling about the Court's overall performance, compared to almost one in three who show negative feelings toward specific decisions. Clearly, as Murphy and Tanenhaus conclude, "many people who are critical of the Court's specific decisions nonetheless support the institution itself."[287] Moreover, many Americans who pay little attention to what the Court does nevertheless register positive feelings toward the institution. The controversy that has surrounded the Court on particular issues seems to have had little effect on public attitudes. As one study concludes after surveying popular attitudes toward the Court in 1972, 1974, and 1976, "among the issue questions, only abortion appears to have had a moderate and continuing relationship to attitudes toward the Court. *Supporters* of the Court are disproportionately drawn from the ranks of abortion advocates even before the rulings on the topic in 1973. The busing issue did not maintain its position as a significant determinant of attitudes toward the Court, reflecting the localized and episodic nature of the issue."[288]

The "diffuse support" hypothesis has been challenged in subsequent studies, which dispute the argument that "the Supreme Court's policies were consistent with diffuse or inchoate values widespread among Americans," and which tie support for the Court more directly to support for specific values.[289] David Adamany and Joel B. Grossman, for example, explain the Supreme Court's success instead by focusing on the level of support among "liberal activists and liberal position-takers." Such a conclusion is not inconsistent with the "diffuse support" hypothesis, which does not depend on a showing of support among the general public of the

Court's values or policies in general. In fact, the level of support for the Court among the general public has remained fairly high despite opposition to specific decisions. In Adamany and Grossman's 1976 survey, for example, only 14.1 percent of nonactivists surveyed were classified as giving the Court a positive rating for specific decisions, while 47.3 percent gave the Court a positive overall performance rating.[290] Given that a majority of the public gave the Court an unfavorable overall rating in 1976 (though the Court's approval rating has exceeded 50 percent in more recent surveys), it seems clear that diffuse support alone cannot explain the Court's success in avoiding attempts to overturn its decisions. At the same time, however, three decades of controversy involving the Court do not seem to have hurt its standing among the general public, and even after all of the controversy of the past thirty years the Court appears to enjoy considerable support even from those opposed to its policy decisions.

Whatever happens to the liberal decisions of the Warren and early Burger Courts, the Supreme Court can count on two constants: it cannot avoid the intense controversy and criticism that has been the hallmark of the modern era unless it drastically changes its political role, and, whatever happens, it can rest assured of continuing popular support. Crisis as usual will continue and will probably not get worse. An end to the pattern of the past three decades would come about only with the contraction of the scope of the Court's activities or the diminution of the federal government's role with respect to the states. Neither seems likely.

VI

Conclusion

THE OUTER LIMITS of the Supreme Court's power, wrote Robert G. McCloskey in 1960, are shaped by the constraints of democratic politics. "The nation expects the judges to aid in deciding policy questions," McCloskey concluded in his landmark study, "but the nation is prone, with sublime inconsistency, to grow fiercely resentful if the aid becomes repression, if the judges bypass certain ill-marked but nevertheless quite real boundaries."[1] Throughout the Court's history, McCloskey wrote, the judges have been constantly aware of this intangible but very real limitation on their power; the Supreme Court, he wrote, "has seldom, if ever, resisted a really unmistakable wave of public sentiment. It has worked with the premise that constitutional law, like politics itself, is a science of the possible."[2]

For McCloskey, the Supreme Court's habit of deference to democracy was not merely a question of preference or constitutional philosophy. It was, quite literally, a matter of survival. Decisions like *Dred Scott* and the New Deal cases were "self-inflicted wounds" (to use Charles Evans Hughes's phrase) that threatened the Court's precarious and painstakingly cultivated role as guardian of the nation's fundamental law. While none of these wounds had been fatal, several had been serious, and McCloskey wondered just how many more such traumas the Court could sustain.[3]

McCloskey was not alone in arguing that the Court was ultimately powerless in the face of a strong expression of popular will. Nor was he the only constitutional scholar to conclude that the Court's failure to heed the demands of the people could, at times, pose dangers to the Court's legitimacy or effectiveness, or even to its very survival. In fact, the theme of judicial weakness and vulnerability became a constant refrain among legal scholars and political scientists, and even among the justices themselves.

Conclusion

Alexander Bickel, for example, argued that "the Supreme Court's law. . . could not in our system prevail . . . if it ran counter to deeply felt popular needs or convictions, or even if it was opposed by a determined and substantial minority and received by indifference by the rest of the country. This, in the end, is how and why judicial review is consistent with the theory and practice of political democracy."[4] Lest the Court forget Alexander Hamilton's admonition that the judiciary "is beyond comparison the weakest of the three departments of power," the political scientist Walter F. Murphy reminded the Court of the overwhelming restraints on judicial action: "Congress can increase the number of Justices, enlarge or restrict the Court's appellate jurisdiction, impeach or remove its members, or propose constitutional amendments either to reverse specific decisions or drastically alter the traditional judicial role in American government."[5] Concern for the Court's safety in the wake of such powerful political controls has been expressed by a number of Supreme Court justices, including Felix Frankfurter, John Marshall Harlan, and, most recently, Lewis Powell. As Powell declared in a 1974 case involving taxpayer standing,

> We risk a progressive impairment of the effectiveness of the federal courts if their limited resources are diverted increasingly from their historic role to the resolution of public-interest suits brought by litigants who cannot distinguish themselves from all taxpayers or all citizens. The irreplaceable value of . . . [judicial review] lies in the protection it has afforded citizens and minority groups against oppressive or discriminatory government action. It is this role, not some amorphous general supervision of the operations of government, that has maintained public esteem for the federal courts and permitted the peaceful coexistence of the countermajoritarian implications of judicial review and the democratic principles upon which our Federal Government in the final analysis rests.[6]

Among political scientists, the idea that the Court was actually weak and under the control of the political branches became a way of justifying the Court's apparently tremendous power. Robert A. Dahl, for example, asserted in a famous article that the Court's primary function throughout its history was not to check the policy decisions of the majority but to legitimate them. As Dahl put it, "First, if the Court did in fact uphold minorities against national majorities, as both its supporters and critics often seem to believe, it would be an extremely anomalous institution from a democratic point of view. Second, the elaborate 'democratic' rationalizations of the Court's defenders and the hostility of its 'democratic' critics are largely irrelevant, for law-making majorities generally have had their way. Third, although the Court seems never to have succeeded in holding out indefinitely, in a very small number of important cases it has delayed the application of policy up to as much as twenty-five years." The "main task of the Court," Dahl concluded, "is to confer legitimacy on the fundamental policies" of the dominant law-making majority at the national level. When the dominant coalition is unstable with respect to a particular issue the Court could perhaps intervene, Dahl admitted, but only "at very great risk to its legitimacy powers."[7]

An institution apparently so weak and so dependent on conformity to the popular will had to move with great care and circumspection, at least in extreme cases. If the justices tried to impose their will on an unwilling public, they were doomed to failure or worse. "Surely the record teaches that no useful purpose is served when the justices seek the hottest political cauldrons of the moment and dive into the middle of them," McCloskey counseled. "Nor is there much to be said for the idea that a judicial policy of fiat and uncompromising negation will halt a truly dominant political impulse." Instead, the justices had to learn history's compelling lesson: "The Court's greatest successes have been achieved when it has operated near the margins rather than at the center of political controversy, when it has nudged and gently tugged the nation, instead of trying to rule it." After two hundred years of struggling to establish itself as a vital force in American politics, McCloskey concluded, "it would be a pity if the judges . . . should now once more forget the limits that its own history so compellingly prescribes."[8]

Obviously, the modern Supreme Court has not taken McCloskey's advice. Instead of pulling back, operating at the margins, nagging and coaxing the people and their representatives, the modern Court has become more involved—and more directly involved—in political controversies than ever before in its history. The school desegregation cases, which so concerned McCloskey and other friends of the Court, were followed by even more controversial decisions on school prayer, busing, defendant rights, reapportionment, and abortion. The modern judiciary has taken an active role in supervising state prisons, mental hospitals, and school districts, and plays a highly visible role in the resolution of countless public policy disputes.

And yet, despite McCloskey's warnings, the modern Court is not in mortal peril. To the contrary, its decisions stand largely unaltered and are generally obeyed, and it has achieved more in terms of governance in the three decades since *Brown* than in all the years of nudging and coaxing that came before. Certainly the past thirty years have been filled with loud and angry attacks on the Court, criticism of its conduct, and threats against its independence and autonomy. But through it all the Court has survived, and is hardly less powerful—or less active—than in the heyday of the Warren era.

The history of the past thirty years—indeed, the entire record of the Court through two centuries of American history—suggests the need for a reassessment of McCloskey's conclusions. Are there, in the modern era, effective political limits on the power of the Supreme Court? Were there ever such limits? Just how dangerous is it for the Court to act as if its power were unlimited?

I

History makes it clear that, in general, the Supreme Court has broad discretion and is relatively free of overt political constraints. Only a handful of the decisions made by the Court in any given year are of any political interest whatsoever, and even those decisions that have political importance rarely cause more than minimal controversy and discussion. Even when a decision of the Court touches an important political issue, the public response rarely goes beyond lively and spirited criticism. Outright defiance or rejection of Supreme Court decisions is rare.

The Supreme Court's extraordinary power to interpret and enforce the Constitution reflects the long-standing American commitment to the ideas of limited government and the rule of law. From the beginning of the Republic Americans desired "a government of laws and not of men," as John Adams put it, and a strong judiciary with the power to nullify acts of Congress on constitutional grounds was a logical, if not inevitable, development. Americans naturally accepted Alexander Hamilton's claim, endorsed by John Marshall, that "Constitutional limitations can be preserved in practice no other way than through the medium of Courts of justice, whose duty it must be to declare all acts contrary to the manifest tenor of the Constitution void."⁹

The American commitment to fundamental law, however, conflicts with another deeply held principle of American politics: the idea of democracy, or popular sovereignty. In the end, as McCloskey observed, these two ideas are clearly incompatible: "Popular sovereignty suggests *will*; fundamental law suggests *limit*. The one idea conjures up the idea of an active, positive state; the other idea emphasizes the negative restrictive side of the political problem." It may be possible to reconcile these two concepts, McCloskey suggested, "but it seems unlikely that Americans in general ever achieved such synthesis and far more probable . . . that most of them retained the ideas side by side."¹⁰ As Bickel observed, "democratic government under law" is a slogan that pulls in two directions at the same time.¹¹

Fortunately for the Court, the tension between popular sovereignty and fundamental law has rarely risen to the boiling point. Exactly why this tension has remained submerged is a matter of considerable dispute, but it seems clear that fundamental conflict over the basic principles of American politics is rare, or, at least, that fundamental conflict rarely surfaces within the context of ordinary political discourse. The political scientist Louis Hartz attributed this decisive feature of American politics to the existence of a broad consensus on fundamental issues, which he described as "liberal" or "Lockian." It is the absence of fundamental conflict, Hartz argued, that makes judicial review possible; as he put it, "judicial review as it has worked in America would be inconceivable without the national acceptance of the Lockian creed, ultimately enshrined in the Constitution." Without agreement on fundamentals, in other words, it would have been impossible to leave substantive political judgments to an unelected Court. "The removal of high policy to the realm of adjudication," Hartz concluded, "implies a prior recognition of the principles to be legally interpreted."¹² Justice Jackson once observed that "struggles over power that in Europe call out regiments of troops, in America call out battalions of lawyers"; but, as Hartz pointed out, "lawyers instead of troops appeared in America because its struggles were not quite the same as those of Europe."¹³ Indeed, as Hartz argued, "the distinctive thing about the battle between majority and minority within the liberal system was precisely the fact that it was not a matter of life and death: that it was forever dissolving into common agreements."[14]

One need not accept Hartz's idea of consensus to recognize that, in general, American politics has been marked by long periods of relative stability in the making of public policy. As Dahl argued, "National politics in the United States, as in other stable democracies, is dominated by relatively cohesive alliances that endure for long periods of time. One recalls the Jeffersonian alliance, the Jacksonian alliance, the extraordinarily long-lived Republican dominance of the post–Civil War years, and the New Deal alliance shaped by Franklin Roosevelt. Each is marked by a break with past policies, a period of intensive struggle, followed by consolidation, and finally decay and disintegration of the alliance."[15]

At key moments in American history—in between such periods of stability—the United States has engaged in fundamental political struggle; once in a while a great political issue emerges that provokes fundamental disagreement and leads to a period of considerable tension and struggle. Normally, the issue that provokes such a division is an old issue that suddenly explodes to the forefront of American politics after one or more "triggering events"—like the passage of the Kansas-Nebraska Act or the onset of the Great Depression. If the nascent political crisis caused by the emergence of such an issue is not quickly dissipated, the nation may be plunged into a brief but intense period of political conflict while it seeks a "redefinition" of the American political formula "in terms which gain overwhelming support from the current generation."[16] Such periods of crisis are known as periods of "critical realignment," because they involve dramatic shifts in voter affiliation and identification between and among the political parties, major shifts or innovations in the course of public policy, clear shifts in the distribution of political or economic power, and fundamental changes in the consensual interpretation of the American constitutional settlement.

The price Americans pay for the submergence of fundamental conflict over most of American history and for the great stability of our political institutions is the periodic disruption of the political system as it seeks to readjust to emerging demands and tensions. The inability of the American political system to respond incrementally to emerging demands for change, in fact, may itself be an underlying cause of these periodic outbursts. As Walter Dean Burnham suggests,

> The periodic rhythm of American electoral politics, the cycle of oscillation between the normal and the disruptive, corresponds precisely to the existence of largely unfettered developmental change in the socioeconomic system and its absence in the country's political institutions. . . . The socioeconomic system develops but the institutions of electoral politics and policy formation remain essentially unchanged. Moreover, they do not have much capacity to adjust incrementally to demand arising from socioeconomic dislocations. Dysfunctions centrally related to this process become more and more visible, until finally entire classes, regions, or other major sectors of the population are directly injured or come to see themselves as threatened by imminent danger. Then the triggering event occurs, critical realignments follow, and the universe of policy formation and of electoral conditions is broadly redefined.[17]

Thus the world of American politics is a world "shot through with escalating tensions, periodic electoral upheavals, and repeated definitions of the rules and outcomes-in-general of the political game, as well as redefinitions—by no means always broadening—of those who are in fact allowed to play it."[18]

It comes as no surprise, then, that the major crises for the U.S. Supreme Court coincide with the great crises of the political system as a whole. The issues which led to and grew out of the Civil War and the New Deal were of a different order than the issues that normally mark the divisions in American political life. They raised essential and fundamental questions about the very nature of the American system—questions with serious implications for the ebbs and flows of political life and for the course of public policy in the long term. Because of their fundamental nature, these issues naturally raised important questions of constitutional law; eventually, these constitutional questions were brought before the Supreme Court of the United States for resolution.

Unfortunately for the Court, it is precisely during these extraordinary episodes of national political crisis—when the pressures on the Court are most acute and when the stakes are at their highest—that the Court is least capable of playing an effective role in American politics. During periods of fundamental crisis, when the overarching principles of American politics are called into question, political debate takes place not within the agreed-upon confines of the fundamental law, but over the very nature of the fundamental law itself. If Hartz is correct that judicial review owes its existence to prior agreement on the principles to be adjudicated, then judicial review is impossible when the nation is plunged into a debate over fundamental principles.

Any attempt by the Supreme Court to resolve so fundamental a dispute brings to the surface the inherent tension between judicial review and popular sovereignty and is likely to end in futility. As the *Dred Scott* and the New Deal cases effectively demonstrate, the Court's attempts to impose its will on the nation under such circumstances provoked a popular reaction so intense and so sustained that the Court, in the end, was unable to stay the course. In the face of what McCloskey called "a really clear wave of public demand," the Court was forced to give ground; the Hughes Court reversed itself outright and the Taney Court was effectively outflanked.

Surely a better strategy for the Court in both instances would have been a measured retreat, a lesson Chief Justice Chase drew from the *Dred Scott* experience when he deferred to Congress in the *McCardle* case. Chase's refusal to "run a race" with Congress or the people was an act of great vision and statesmanship, for the pressures on the Court to attempt to resolve these constitutional crises are enormous indeed. Chase's Court, like those of Taney and Hughes, was polarized and divided; it faced pressures to intervene from all directions, including the press, the public, and even the White House. The issues before the Court were of such magnitude, and the stakes so high, that such an act of judicial self-restraint becomes an act of near heroic proportions.

Episodes like *Dred Scott*, Reconstruction, and the New Deal cases provide the evidence to support Bickel and McCloskey's conclusion that, in extreme cases, the people and not the Court must have the last word. Americans may never have resolved the conflict between popular sovereignty and fundamental law, but in practice they have never given up their right of self-government to the Courts. Wrote Bickel: "Having been checked, should the people persist; having been educated, should the people insist, must they not win over every fundamental principle save one—which is the principle that they must win? Are we sufficiently certain of the permanent validity of any other principle to be ready to impose it against a consistent and determined majority, and could we do so for long? Have not the people the right of peaceable revolution, as assuredly, over time, they possess the capacity for a bloody one?"[19] Whatever the theoretical merits of Bickel's thesis, as a practical matter it has been accepted by the American people. In extraordinary cases, when fundamental disputes rise to the surface of the American political system, the Court lacks the power to oppose a really clear expression of the public will.

The successful reversal of an important Supreme Court decision or line of decisions is no easy task. It requires, at a minimum, overwhelming opposition to the decision in both houses of Congress along with the active opposition of the president. Alternatively, as Reconstruction shows, a very powerful majority in Congress can override presidential opposition. The creation of such a supermajority against the Court requires, in addition, the clear expression of opposition to the Court by the American people, typically in an especially contentious and impassioned presidential campaign. Such clear expressions of public demand, to use McCloskey's phrase, are exceedingly rare in American history.

The ultimate weakness of the Supreme Court in episodes like the *Dred Scott* case, Reconstruction, and the New Deal is hardly convincing evidence that the Court is a fundamentally weak institution, however. These extraordinary cases centered around the most divisive and fundamental issues in American political history and occurred in the context of America's greatest political crises. These episodes placed such stress on the American political system that the party system, Congress, the presidency, and even the nation itself were all profoundly affected. That the Whig Party of the 1850s or the Republican Party of the 1930s was unable to cope with the stresses involved does not prove that American political parties are unable to cope with the ordinary demands of politics; nor 'does Congress's inability to resolve the slavery crisis or the weakness of Presidents Buchanan, Andrew Johnson, or Herbert Hoover signify the institutional weakness of Congress or the presidency. It is hardly reasonable to cite *Dred Scott*, Reconstruction, or the New Deal as evidence of the Court's inability to function independently or effectively.

Dred Scott, Reconstruction, and the New Deal cases clearly reveal the limits of the Supreme Court's power. By their extraordinary character, they also highlight just how powerful the Court has been throughout the rest of its history.

II

McCloskey was correct in suggesting that the Supreme Court would be unable to block the popular will on an issue of extreme importance and urgency, but he was surely wrong to conclude that it was dangerous for the Court to try. Time and again the Court has placed constitutional barriers in the path of a determined majority, and time and again it has survived and prospered. *Dred Scott*, Reconstruction, and the New Deal may reveal the ultimate strength of popular sovereignty in the United States, but they also show the strength and resiliency of the Supreme Court.

McCloskey was by no means alone in emphasizing the ultimate weakness of the Supreme Court. Others too saw the great conflicts between the Court and the people, and especially the New Deal crisis, as dramatic proof that the Court was, as Alexander Hamilton warned, "in continual jeopardy of being overpowered, awed, or influenced by its co-ordinate branches."[20] Justice Robert Jackson, for example, wrote in 1941 that "the Supreme Court can maintain itself and succeed in its tasks only if the counsels of self-restraint urged most earnestly by members of the Court itself are humbly and faithfully heeded." In making this point, Jackson wrote, "I do not join those who seek to deflate the whole judicial process. It is precisely because I value the role that the judiciary performs in the peaceful ordering of our society that I deprecate the ill-starred adventures of the judiciary that have recurringly jeopardized its essential usefulness."[21] Indeed the theme of the Court's weakness and vulnerability became a sort of refrain among post–New Deal Court-watchers; Edward S. Corwin titled his 1934 book "The Twilight of the Supreme Court,"[22] and several years later the constitutional scholar Charles Black bemoaned the possibility that the idea of judicial review—along with the U.S. Supreme Court—might be rejected by the American people: "Every day in our history puts this idea [of judicial review], and its institution, in mortal peril. Behind all other perils lies the one that really matters—the people may change their minds, and decide after all to abandon the idea of self-restraint through law."[23]

Certainly the New Deal crisis, like *Dred Scott* before it, thrust the Court into the midst of political controversy and damaged the Supreme Court's prestige in the short run. In the long term, however, the great crises faced by the Supreme Court have had the paradoxical effect of strengthening the institution and of solidifying its position as the ultimate arbiter of the Constitution. What Charles Evans Hughes concluded in 1928 was even more true after the New Deal crisis: though the Court has suffered from several "self-inflicted wounds," he wrote, it has in every case "come out of its conflicts with its wounds healed, with its integrity universally recognized, [and] with its ability giving it a rank second to none among the judicial tribunals of the world." Despite its historical conflicts with the American people, Hughes declared, "No institution of our government stands higher in public confidence."[24]

That the Court survived the traumas associated with *Dred Scott*, Reconstruction, and the New Deal was no accident. In none of these cases was the Court in any serious danger of suffering lasting damage. In each case the Court's critics and opponents lacked the will, the desire, and the ability to crush the Court. They showed remarkably little inclination to strip the Court of its power of judicial review or to compromise its independence or autonomy, and, through it all, were supportive of the rule of law and of the role of judges. Only rarely did the Court's critics engage in a fundamental critique of the legitimacy of judicial review in general.

Instead, the conflict between the Court and its critics centered each time on a single policy dispute, albeit one of extraordinary interest, divisiveness, and importance. Conflict over the policy in question raged throughout the polity for a brief period, engulfing not only the Court but the political parties, the presidency, and the Congress. Once the policy dispute was settled by the political process (or, in the case of the issues in *Dred Scott*, once the issues were taken away from the political realm altogether) the Court and its critics were quickly reconciled. The crisis over *Dred Scott* lasted four years; the crises over Reconstruction and the New Deal barely two.

The narrowness of the dispute between the Court and its critics is clearly revealed in the nature of the arguments used against the Court. Though there were scattered examples of truly extremist rhetoric in all three periods, for the most part the Court's critics argued that the Court's interpretation in a particular case or group of cases was wrong; that the Court had overstepped its legitimate bounds and had decided an issue not properly before it; or, at most, that the judges' approach to constitutional interpretation was unacceptably narrow. Thus the Court's critics implicitly accepted the legitimacy of judicial review, even as they criticized the way the Supreme Court was exercising that power. Arguments over the proper scope and extent of judicial review, especially under conditions of urgency and crisis, are not trivial. But the importance of the concession that the Court does after all have an important role to play in constitutional interpretation—indeed, that the Court has the most important role to play in constitutional interpretation—should not be underestimated. Given that concession, the Court was assured of regaining its accustomed role as interpreter of the Constitution once the crisis ended.

Thus the criticisms directed at the Court in the wake of *Dred Scott*, the Reconstruction cases, and the New Deal cases were with rare exceptions narrowly focused on the decisions themselves or on the justices who made them and did not extend to a general critique of judicial power. The critics of *Dred Scott* excoriated Taney as an incompetent and denounced him as a tool of the slave power, argued the merits of the constitutional questions involved in the case, and challenged the propriety of the Court's having decided the case in the first place. The Reconstruction Court was criticized for the substance of the *Milligan* case, among others, and particular justices (especially David Davis) were attacked in vicious terms. The critics of Van Devanter, Butler, Sutherland, and McReynolds, similarly, challenged the approach taken by the Nine Old Men to constitutional interpretation, attempted to show that the Court's decisions were bad public policy and bad law, and (most famously) derided the judges as too old to continue to function adequately in their judicial roles. All of these charges, however damaging to the Court in the short run, were rendered moot as soon as the particular decisions involved were resolved and as soon as new judges were appointed to replace the old, discredited ones.

The danger to the Court in each of its past crises was minimized, in addition, because its critics never lost their respect for the Constitution or for the concept of the rule of law. Both Abraham Lincoln and Franklin D. Roosevelt remained staunch supporters of the Constitution; Lincoln insisted that the Constitution fully supported his position on slavery extension, and Roosevelt claimed repeatedly that the Constitution, properly interpreted in the light of modern social facts, was a fully appropriate vehicle for progress. Even the radical Republicans of Reconstruction, who presided over the most intense period of substantive constitutional amendment since the Bill of Rights was adopted in 1791, showed little inclination to change the basic structure or philosophy of the document; the Fourteenth Amendment, after all, merely confirmed Congress's power to do what the radicals had already done (within the Constitution, as they saw it) in the Civil Rights Act of 1866 and the Freedmen's Bureau extension of the same year.

In theory, of course, veneration and respect for the Constitution could be independent of support for the Supreme Court of the United States. In practice, however, the Court had long before indelibly associated itself with the fundamental law of the land as its protector and interpreter. Since the time of Marshall the Court had realized correctly that the Constitution was the ultimate source of its power and had worked long and hard at maintaining its identification with the Constitution.[25] A nation that was unprepared to reject the Constitution or the idea of constitutionalism found it difficult and unseemly to turn its back on the institution most closely associated with it.

In all three crisis periods, moreover, the Court's critics remained staunch supporters of the power of the national government over the states. In this sense, despite their temporary differences with the Supreme Court, they remained essentially friendly to the idea of a strong federal judiciary exercising power on behalf of a powerful national government. For the Court, as a part of the national government, is naturally an ally of that government and has generally been so for most of its history—with the *Dred Scott* and New Deal cases among the few notable exceptions. The policies advocated by Lincoln, the radical Republicans, and Roosevelt required a strong national government and depended on a broad interpretation of the federal government's powers under the Constitution; a strong Supreme Court, as the Court's critics seemed to recognize, could provide such an interpretation and thus legitimate the national government's newly exercised powers. It was therefore essential to Lincoln, Roosevelt, and the radical Republicans that the Court become their ally in the long run, and therefore they set out not to destroy the Court but only to capture it. Nowhere is this ambivalence toward the Court and its powers clearer than during Reconstruction, when Congress expanded and restricted the power of the federal courts almost simultaneously. During Reconstruction, in

Conclusion

fact, Congress had the additional incentive of keeping the Court on its side—or at least off the president's side—in Congress's battle with Andrew Johnson. The support of the other two branches was, in this as in every other case, fundamental in ensuring that, no matter how severe the crisis, the Supreme Court would not be seriously damaged in the long run.

All of this criticism of the Court had the paradoxical effect each time of strengthening the Court as an institution. When critics of the Court call into question the wisdom, competence, or honesty of particular judges, or challenge their approach to constitutional interpretation or their handling of specific issues in the context of a particular case, they suggest, at least implicitly, that the cases in question would have been decided differently, and correctly, by other judges. But that suggestion itself concedes that there is a mode of constitutional interpretation which, if practiced by competent and honest judges with a proper understanding of the meaning of the Constitution, is entirely legitimate and appropriate. Once the particular issues in controversy were resolved and the old justices left the Court, the new justices undertook their duties with the implicit blessing of the Court's most recent critics. Certainly Roger Taney and the Four Horsemen of the Hughes Court were discredited and rejected along with their decisions. But their successors—appointed by Lincoln and Roosevelt—were stamped with an immediate, if implicit, seal of approval. The legitimacy of the post–*Dred Scott* and post–New Deal Courts was guaranteed once they directly or indirectly rejected the old decisions and cast aside the old forms of constitutional adjudication.

The remedies proposed and adopted by the Court's critics also helped to insulate the Court from serious damage and to protect its long-range interests. The Court's critics did not use or even seriously consider many of the more extreme remedies open to them. Impeachment, for example, was virtually never mentioned as a way of speeding up the turnover on the Court or of intimidating the justices; through all the controversy, Congress respected the constitutional provision limiting impeachment to those accused of "High Crimes and Misdemeanors."[26] Quite possibly the Reconstruction Congress might have considered impeaching Chase if he had gone through with a decision striking down the Reconstruction Acts, as they tried to impeach Andrew Johnson, but even that remains speculative, and in any event the Senate could not muster the votes to impeach Andrew Johnson.

THE LIMITS OF JUDICIAL POWER

Nor did Congress choose to use its power of the purse or any of its other powers to coerce, intimidate, or harass uncooperative judges. In theory, as several political scientists have pointed out, Congress could refuse to appropriate the money for the judges' salaries (ignoring the constitutional requirement to the contrary), require the Court to bear an intolerable caseload, or deny the judges the operating expenses necessary to run the Court. Yet despite all the criticism of the Court during the *Dred Scott*, Reconstruction, and New Deal crises, Congress routinely approved judicial appropriations year in and year out, without even a hint of debate over the possibility of not doing so. Ironically, during both the *Dred Scott* and New Deal crises the Court moved, with Congress's blessing, to new and improved quarters; in 1860, the justices moved into the old Senate chamber, and in 1935 they moved across First Street to their present building. In neither case did Congress consider reducing the appropriations for the Court or seek to deny the Court the funds necessary for moving expenses. In fact, the only recorded instance of congressional stinginess toward the Court found in the research for this study was Congress's refusal, for nine years after the death of Roger B. Taney, to appropriate the money to purchase a bust of the late chief justice for display in the Supreme Court room.[27]

Nor, except during Reconstruction, did Congress try to reverse Court decisions by constitutional amendment. For one thing, it knew that controversial amendments are extremely difficult to enact, given the supermajority necessary for approval both in Congress and among the states. More to the point, amending the Constitution would have worked against both Lincoln and Roosevelt's assertion that the problem lay not with the Constitution but with the Court; to have suggested a constitutional amendment in either case would have amounted to a tacit admission that the Supreme Court had been correct in its decisions in *Dred Scott* and the New Deal cases. Worse, endorsing a constitutional amendment would have lent credence to charges that Lincoln and Roosevelt were radicals out to transform the American constitutional system, a charge both presidents sought assiduously to avoid. For the radical Republicans, constitutional amendment was a more attractive alternative. The absence of the Southern states from Congress and the requirement that they approve the proposed amendments before readmission to the Union greatly reduced the practical problems involved, and the Republicans were hardly concerned about the

Conclusion

potential charge of radicalism. Given the fact that none of the Civil War amendments directly overturned any existing Supreme Court decision except the completely discredited *Dred Scott* case, however, the amendments must be viewed more as a preemptive strike against a possible Court decision against the Reconstruction acts than as retaliation for actions already taken by the Court.

What Lincoln and Roosevelt did choose, instead, were remedies that recognized the sanctity of the Constitution and the legitimacy of judicial review. Lincoln's solution was a simple one: to get control of the presidency and the Senate, and appoint new justices who would be sympathetic to the antislavery cause. In the meantime, Lincoln would engage in a verbal assault on the legitimacy of the *Dred Scott* decision, while being careful to avoid broadside attacks on the Court as an institution or on the idea of judicial review, and he would deny that *Dred Scott*, which he admitted was binding on the litigants in the case, created a "political rule" that had to be accepted unquestioningly by the American people. Lincoln's remedy was not a practical one for Roosevelt, though, because he already had control of the appointment process; Roosevelt's problem was that fate had denied him the opportunity to appoint a single justice through four full years of his first term. More drastic measures were necessary, and Roosevelt chose, as Stanley Reed put it, to "increase the Court." The "Court-packing" remedy appears radical (and was so viewed at the time) in that it so boldly attempted to control the Court's decision-making process by political means, and in the end the idea backfired. From Roosevelt's point of view, however, other proposals (especially constitutional amendments) were even more radical; the Court-packing plan, for all its drawbacks, did not tamper with the essential structure of the Court or the Constitution. From Roosevelt's perspective, the Court-packing plan appeared to be a reasonable way to guarantee the constitutionality of the New Deal without upsetting the Constitution or the framework of American government. Above all, the Court-packing plan would have reversed the New Deal decisions while leaving the judges free to decide other cases as they saw fit.

The radical Republicans' approach to the Court problem was also more conservative than is apparent on the surface. Their solution, developed at a critical juncture in the course of Reconstruction politics, was to strip the Supreme Court of its power to hear the *McCardle* case—even though the

THE LIMITS OF JUDICIAL POWER

Court had already heard the case and was preparing to deliver its decision. Though the radicals were clearly determined to get their way, there is no evidence that they wanted to do anything more than delay the *McCardle* decision until after the adoption of the Fourteenth Amendment, when the case would become moot. In taking the radical course of withdrawing the Court's jurisdiction over a particular issue, moreover, the Republicans made no attempt to justify their action, at least before the fact, and indeed took that action surreptitiously. In any event, the Republicans' actions with respect to *McCardle* can in no way be seen as part of a systematic effort to reduce or limit the Supreme Court's power in the long run. It was a desparate act taken in the midst of the impeachment crisis.

The Supreme Court lived through each of its crises not by luck, nor by statesmanship, nor by coincidence. It survived because no one was really attempting to kill it. It survived because, when it suffered its "self-inflicted wounds," its opponents had neither the incentive nor the desire to take advantage of its apparently weakened condition, even when they had the power to do so. Scholars have marveled at the Court's ability to survive the fiercest of battles. What they have failed to realize is that the Court's enemies, for the most part, were shooting blanks.

III

The Supreme Court has always been largely invulnerable to political assault. In the modern era, it seems practically omnipotent as well. Its decisions reach further and sweep more broadly than ever before; its influence on public policy and on American society has never been greater. The Supreme Court, once thought to be the "least dangerous branch," has apparently become the imperial judiciary.

That the modern Court has survived the attacks against it without serious damage to its power or prestige is not surprising. The Court's critics in the modern era, like those of the past, have never made a serious effort to destroy the Court or undermine its power to interpret and enforce the Constitution. For the most part, the critics of the Court accept the idea of judicial review and respect the necessity for judicial independence. Their criticisms of the Court, following Lincoln and Roosevelt, have been largely confined to criticism of particular decisions or justices, or to a particular approach to judicial review. The remedies they have supported

Conclusion

have generally been the traditional ones: they have sought to replace unfriendly justices with new ones, they have tried to convince the Court to modify its own decisions, and they have supported various constitutional amendments designed to reverse specific decisions. More sweeping remedies—such as removing cases from the Court's appellate docket—have gained relatively little support.

What is surprising is that, despite thirty years of effort, the modern Court's critics have been unable to overturn a single one of the Court's many controversial decisions. Although the Court itself has modified a few of these decisions, most from the Warren and Burger Courts remain intact. Moreover, the modern Court has continued to expand its reach and influence, undeterred by criticism or opposition. On the surface, at least, the modern Supreme Court seems both more powerful and less subject to political restraints than ever before.

The modern Court's power and independence, however, is in part deceptive. The Court's success in pursuing its agenda makes it appear all-powerful, but in reality the modern Court has achieved its power and influence by distancing itself from precisely those issues capable of creating full-scale crises and thereby revealing the limits of its political strength. The Court's success in enforcing its decisions, to paraphrase Hartz, obscures the fact that its decisions are not the same as those of the past. Like the nation itself, the Supreme Court's role has been transformed since the end of the New Deal crisis.

The resolution of the slavery issue after the Civil War meant that from that point forward the fundamental divisions in American politics at the national level would revolve around questions of economic policy.[28] Economic questions did not eclipse other issues altogether; the race issue never disappeared, and various social movements surfaced from time to time demanding attention at the federal level. But from the Civil War forward, American politics has centered on the appropriate level of governmental intervention in the private economy and on the distribution of economic power between the state and national governments. The complex constitutional questions raised by these issues preoccupied the Court from the end of Reconstruction until 1937.

The Court's "switch in time" in 1937 settled these questions once and for all. With its approval of the New Deal, the Court removed virtually all the constitutional barriers to federal economic regulation. State regulation of the economy was also permissible unless it conflicted with valid federal law or discriminated against interstate commerce; but, in the end, the resolution of conflicts between the states and the federal government would be left to Congress. As a result of the New Deal settlement, Congress's power to regulate the national economy became all but plenary.

The Court's abandonment of its supervision of federal economic policy, combined with its traditional deference to the president and Congress in the formulation and execution of foreign policy, meant that the post–New Deal Court has permitted the political branches to act with almost complete freedom on the most critical issues on the national agenda. Moreover, the Court permitted Congress to regulate broad areas of social policy, including civil rights, under its power to regulate interstate commerce. As a result, the Court's role in policing the broad contours of federal policy has decreased almost to the vanishing point.

At the state and local levels, however, the revolution of 1937 meant more rather than less judicial intervention. Since 1937 the Court has greatly expanded the applicability of the Bill of Rights to the states and breathed new life into the Equal Protection and Due Process Clauses of the Fourteenth Amendment. It has assumed direct supervision of a wide range of state and local activities including race relations, education, and law enforcement. The Court's expanded involvement in areas traditionally left to the states has greatly increased its influence over public affairs and has practically guaranteed a steady stream of serious controversy.

The modern Supreme Court's expanded role in American politics, therefore, has come almost entirely at the expense of state rather than federal power. For all its activism, the modern Court has never tried to block a major federal policy initiative supported by both Congress and the president. Certainly the Court has invalidated specific federal laws or actions as violating the Bill of Rights, and it has occasionally struck down the means chosen by Congress to implement its policies. But such decisions have never made it impossible for Congress to achieve the objectives it has clearly wanted to pursue.

Certainly the Court's decisions in areas like reapportionment, school desegregation, school prayer, and abortion have created a response at the national level, transforming these issues into national issues. As David Adamany and Joel Grossman have argued, the Court's decisions in such areas led organized interest groups to move into the national political

Conclusion

arena, making the issues in question " 'state' policies only in a technical and legal sense."[29] Moreover, in many cases the Court's nullification of state practices was based on reasoning that would make similar federal policies equally unconstitutional—the best example, perhaps, being abortion. The critical point is not whether these issues are technically state or national issues, however, but whether they have been, in practice, central to the concerns of policymakers at the national level. Here the evidence is clear: despite the obvious importance of these issues to various interest groups, none has ever been important enough in Congress to rise to the top of the agenda. In fact, Congress has consistently sought to avoid direct attempts to block or reverse Supreme Court decisions. And, while many of these issues have played a part in one or more presidential elections, none has become the central focus of a campaign the way slavery extension was central to the 1856 election or the New Deal was to the 1936 election.

Obviously the importance of decisions like *Brown* v. *Board of Education* or *Roe* v. *Wade* should not be minimized; their significance is self-evident. Nor should the controversy engendered by these decisions be underestimated; both supporters and critics of the modern Court have been every bit as committed to their views as the critics and supporters of *Dred Scott* or the New Deal cases. And, by necessity, they have been even more persistent.

The salient fact, however, is that none of the modern Court's decisions has created a "really clear wave of public demand" within the electorate or the Congress in favor of reversal; and only Congress or the electorate can supply sufficient pressure to the Court to make a difference. When the issues decided by the Court have been sufficiently important to provoke a serious crisis—as on the race question in the 1950s and early 1960s—the Court's decisions have been supported by a majority of the American people and by a majority of Congress; or, at a minimum, the country has been so hopelessly divided that a clear expression of public will has been impossible. When a substantial majority of the people have opposed specific Supreme Court decisions—as on school prayer or criminal law questions—the issues have not produced sufficient concern among enough of the electorate or their representatives to create an unmistakable and irresistible public demand for change. And even on those rare occasions when it appeared, however briefly, that a really clear wave of public demand would be forthcoming—as in the case of school busing in 1972 or the national security cases in the late 1950s—other more critical issues quickly appeared to capture the public's attention and eclipse the Court.

Only at the height of the civil rights movement, for example, have any of the Court issues been listed as the "most important problem" facing the country in national opinion polls—in 1957 and 1964–65, when "race relations" was listed.[30] Even then, the broad category of "race relations" certainly encompassed much more than just the Court's decisions in *Brown* and other desegregation cases. No issue decided by the modern Court has ever dominated a presidential election the way such issues dominated in 1856 or 1936; even when such issues have surfaced in presidential elections, they have been largely tangential to the main concerns of the candidates and the voters. In 1964, for example, concerns over war and peace competed with race as the most important issue in the campaign. In 1968, when the "law and order" theme was a major part of the Nixon and Wallace campaigns, it was a far less important issue than the Vietnam war.[31] Nor did the Court issues dominate the presidential campaigns of 1972, 1980, or 1984.[32]

Nor has any issue decided by the modern Court come to dominate the congressional agenda in the manner of the New Deal or Reconstruction issues. Again the race question is a possible exception, particularly in 1964 and 1965, but here again the majority of Congress was actively supporting the Court rather than opposing it. The campaign against the Court's decisions on abortion, school prayer, and busing has always been tangential to Congress's main agenda, and anti-Court bills have been repeatedly crowded out by more pressing issues.

Without a clear majority in Congress united behind the effort to curb the Court, the Court's critics have been unable to surmount the institutional and structural barriers standing in their way. Several times opponents of one or more of the Court's decisions have managed to marshall a majority in one house of Congress, only to find their proposals blocked in the other house. The highly decentralized power structure in Congress has made it possible for influential committee and subcommittee chairmen to push the anti-Court campaign forward through highly publicized hearings, and several times anti-Court measures have been approved in committee; but the same decentralized structure has also given supporters of the Court the power to block such efforts elsewhere in Congress. In other cases, legislators have been content to express their opposition to the Court by making

Conclusion

some symbolic gesture, thus dooming more substantive measures designed to overturn or modify decisions of the Court. On one or two occasions, legislation has made its way through Congress only to be vetoed by the president.

If Congress has been unable to summon the will to curb the Court, presidents have been no more effective. Even those presidents who have had the opportunity to lead an anti-Court campaign have declined to put the full force of their prestige and authority behind the effort. Despite his opposition to busing and his support for "law and order," Nixon, for example, did little more than promise to appoint "strict constructionists" to the Court. Even Ronald Reagan, though extremely outspoken at times in his rhetoric against the Court, placed the Court issues at the bottom of the agenda for his entire first term and well into his second, a policy well noted by some of his more conservative critics. In its early years, in fact, his administration actively opposed some of the most extreme anti-Court measures considered by Congress, and even Attorney General Meese—whose rhetoric has made him the de facto leader of the anti-Court battle—lent only sporadic support to specific efforts to curb the Court.

It was only with the nomination of Judge Robert H. Bork to replace Justice Lewis Powell that the Reagan administration finally committed itself to the task of curbing the Court; the Bork nomination became, in a way, both symbol and substance of the Reagan administration's policy to reverse the decisions of the Warren and Burger Courts. The resignation of Justice Powell provided the president with a clear opportunity to alter the ideological makeup of the Court, and the nomination of the controversial Judge Bork seemed to underscore the administration's commitment to make the most of that opportunity. President Reagan's refusal to withdraw the Bork nomination in the face of stiff opposition only strengthened that impression.

The Bork nomination fight, however, only served to demonstrate the remarkable strength of the modern Court and its decisions. Given the opportunity to cast a decisive vote against the Court's policies, the Senate refused to do so, instead rejecting Bork by a 58-to-42 margin. The Bork fight showed that the Court's controversial decisions on equal protection, religion, and even privacy enjoy considerable public and congressional support; that the Court's supporters are capable of exercising considerable influence; and that opposition to the Court is not nearly so clear in practice as it might appear from the rhetoric of the Court's opponents. In the end, after the ill-fated nomination of Judge Douglas Ginsberg to replace Powell, Reagan backed away from his confrontational strategy and nominated Judge Anthony Kennedy, widely regarded as a moderate conservative, and the Senate readily consented. However Kennedy votes on specific issues in the future, it is clear that his nomination was successful precisely because he appeared to present no threat to the basic doctrines or jurisprudential methods of the modern Court.

Here the contrast between the modern era and the past is particularly striking. The battles over slavery extension, Reconstruction, and the New Deal resulted in clear victories for Lincoln, the radical Republicans, and Franklin D. Roosevelt; in each case, the victors in the political struggle were able to transform their success into success against the Court. The election of Ronald Reagan in 1980 and 1984, however, did not translate into a legislative or executive commitment to defeat the Court. Reagan's rhetoric has tended to play up the anti-Court nature of his election victories, but in practice the Court issues were not the central issues of his campaign, and votes for Reagan did not translate into overwhelming support for his policy of opposition to the Court's liberal decisions.

The modern era of "crisis as usual," then, is far different from the crises of *Dred Scott*, Reconstruction, and the New Deal. Because the nature of the issues decided by the Court are different, the nature of the crisis is different as well. The modern Court has greatly expanded the scope and range of its activities, and in doing so has given rise to a great deal of controversy and criticism. But its decisions have never provoked what McCloskey called "a really clear wave of public demand for reversal" and have therefore never produced the kind of response necessary to bring about a wholesale reversal in the Court's decision making.

At the same time, however, it is a gross exaggeration to conclude that the modern Supreme Court acts as the head of an "imperial judiciary," able to impose its will on the nation without regard to the attitudes of the other branches of government or of the people. The Supreme Court is a political institution and does not operate in a political vacuum. Its decisions are necessarily affected by the actions of Congress, the executive branch, state and local government, the legal community, the press, and public opinion.

The Court's decision making is affected, above all, by the appointment process, at least in the long term. It is difficult to use the appointment process to bring about changes in specific Court decisions, as several presidents have learned; when the president and the Senate disagree on those decisions, as in the Bork nomination fight, it becomes even more difficult to use the appointment process for such a purpose. Nevertheless, personnel changes on the Court do have an effect over time. The appointment of three justices by the Reagan administration has had and will have a significant effect on the Court's decision making in several areas.

The Court's decisions are also influenced by a range of other factors. Like its predecessors, the modern Court has shown itself to be sensitive to the opinions and actions of Congress, the executive, the legal community, and the public. In the modern era, as always, the Court has engaged in what the political scientist Louis Fisher calls a "dialogue" with the other branches, rarely if ever operating alone. This is surely not to say that the Court is a slavish follower of the other branches; far from it. But time and again the Court has shown itself to be aware of and to take into account the exigencies and vicissitudes of American politics.

In many areas of decision making, for example, the Court has worked with Congress and the executive branch in the development of constitutional doctrine. This is especially true in the area of civil rights. In other areas, the Court has been careful not to push ahead too quickly in the face of opposition, as for example in the criminal law cases of the late 1950s. Several times the Court has permitted Congress to modify the scope or impact of its decisions by statute, as in the abortion funding cases of the 1970s.

Three decades after *Brown v. Board of Education*, then, it seems clear that the modern Supreme Court continues to act in the tradition of its predecessors. It has tremendous power and authority and is largely invulnerable to political attack. Yet the Court remains a politically sensitive institution, hardly unaware of the actions and opinions of other actors on the American political scene. If McCloskey, Bickel, and others greatly underestimated the Court's political strength, modern commentators who pronounce the existence of an imperial judiciary surely overestimate the Court's willingness or capacity to govern alone.

Nevertheless, the political constraints on the Supreme Court are indirect, inefficient, and uncertain. In the absence of a clear shift in the

Supreme Court's approach to constitutional jurisprudence, it seems unlikely that the storms that swirl around the Court will become severe enough to force it to alter course.

IV

"While unconstitutional exercise of power by the executive and legislative branches of the government is subject to judicial restraint," wrote Justice Harlan F. Stone at the height of the New Deal crisis, "the only check upon our own exercise of power is our own sense of self-restraint."[33] Because the political checks on the Supreme Court are largely clumsy and ineffectual, the delicate task of finding the appropriate balance between popular sovereignty and fundamental law falls, in the end, to the justices themselves.

The question of when and how much the Supreme Court should intervene to overturn acts of the democratically elected political branches is, needless to say, a difficult one, and there has been no shortage of commentary on the subject. In fact, the country has pondered the question of judicial activism versus judicial restraint for a long time, and the controversy has intensified in the wake of the modern Court's long and continuing record of activism. After two centuries of debate, we appear hardly closer to an answer today than we were in 1789.

The question of when judicial intervention is appropriate is far beyond the scope of this study, but the realization that the Supreme Court is neither weak nor vulnerable bears directly on the debate over the proper role of the Supreme Court in the American political system. The assumption that the Court was in fact weak and vulnerable has formed the basis for arguments on both sides of the question of judicial activism. Advocates of restraint have argued that the Court's weakness is, by itself, an argument for judicial restraint. Advocates of judicial activism have, in turn, used the Court's alleged weakness as a sort of insurance policy, by arguing that the risks involved in judicial activism are reduced by the Court's ultimate lack of power. Both activism and restraint can be and have been defended in theoretical terms. To the extent that either argument is based on the assumption of judicial weakness and vulnerability, however, it is unconvincing.

The argument for self-restraint from weakness was perhaps best ex-

Conclusion

pressed by McCloskey, in words that have formed the basis for this analysis of judicial power. For McCloskey (though, again, not for him alone), the Court's power was a precious but limited reserve that had to be expended carefully and cautiously. A Court which allowed itself to become too involved in the political fray was setting itself up for political disaster, according to this viewpoint. In the end, McCloskey concluded, "It would be a pity if the judges, having done so much, should now once more forget the limits that their own history so compellingly prescribes."[34]

The argument for restraint from weakness echoes throughout the legal and political science literature. It is an argument that has been adopted, at one time or another, by Alexander Bickel, Walter F. Murphy, Jesse H. Choper, John Marshall Harlan, Lewis Powell, and countless others. It is, typically, an argument that springs from sympathy for the Court rather than hostility, an argument that seeks to protect the Court in order to preserve it. Bickel, for example, argued strenuously that the Court could achieve its role "as defender of the faith, proclaimer and protector of goals" not by direct attempts at governance but only indirectly. Since the Court could not impose principled government on the nation, it had to content itself with refusing to legitimate unprincipled government, educating and leading the nation so that the nation could, in the end, choose principled government for itself. The Court, Bickel concluded, "must lead opinion, not merely impose its own."[35]

Supporters of judicial activism have also relied on the assumption that the Court is inherently weak and vulnerable in order to defend their position. In an argument that traces its roots back to Hamilton's *Federalist No. 78*, these advocates of judicial power argue that the power of the judiciary, while apparently overwhelming, is in fact far more limited. Because the Court is ultimately subject to control by the political branches, judicial activism is less dangerous and less worrisome. As Hamilton put it,

the judiciary, from the nature of its function, will always be the least dangerous to the political rights of the constitution; because it will always be least in a capacity to annoy or injure them. The executive not only dispenses the honors, but holds the sword of the community. The legislature not only commands the purse, but prescribes the rules by which the duties and rights of every citizen are to be regulated. *The judiciary on the contrary has no influence over either the sword or the purse, no direction either of the strengths or of the wealth of society, and can take no active resolution whatever. It may truly be said to have neither Force, nor Will, but merely judgment; and must ultimately depend upon the aid of the executive arm even for the efficacy of its judgments.*[36]

Though Hamilton's argument has been revised and extended over the centuries, it remains the basis for one major defense of the exercise of judicial power. Since the Court's major role in American politics is to legitimate the decisions of Congress and the president, and since it can do so little on its own, in this view, judicial power can be safely exercised in a democracy.

Paradoxically, it was Bickel—the great advocate of judicial restraint— who best captured the essence of this argument for judicial power. Bickel, though advocating far more restraint than many of his contemporaries, nonetheless spent his scholarly career seeking some justification for even the limited exercise of judicial power in a democracy. In his final book, Bickel at last concluded that judicial review, however undemocratic, was compatible with American democracy precisely because it was not and could never be final. As he put it, "Because we hope that in the direst need the Court perhaps *can* save us—or to put it more realistically, may show us that we are not as riven as we feared—we allow it continually to try to save us when it cannot, and when authoritarian salvation is not what we need. *We can afford the Court, but only because we are free to, and do, reject salvation from it nearly as often as it is tendered, and we can still afford it, even though it has seldom pushed its patent medicines so far so fast, in a society itself going too fast.*"[37]

In the end, neither the argument for judicial restraint nor the argument for judicial activism can progress from the assumption that the Supreme Court is a weak and vulnerable institution. Judicial restraint is necessary not because the Court is weak but because it is strong. And judicial activism must be defended despite the clear fact that the Court has the capacity to carry out its judgments and impose them on the political branches. The Court's great strength, and not its apparent historical weakness, makes judicial review possible. And it is because of that very strength that the responsible exercise of judicial power is so vitally necessary.

Notes

CHAPTER I

1. McCloskey, *The American Supreme Court* (Chicago: University of Chicago Press, 1960), pp. 229–31.

2. *Federalist* No. 78.

3. Alexander Bickel, *The Least Dangerous Branch: The Supreme Court at the Bar of Politics* (Indianapolis: Bobbs-Merrill, 1962), p. 23.

4. Walter F. Murphy, *Congress and the Court* (Chicago: University of Chicago Press, 1962), pp. 2–3.

5. Jesse H. Choper, *Judicial Review and the National Political Process: A Functional Reconsideration of the Role of the Supreme Court* (Chicago: University of Chicago Press, 1980), p. 156.

6. United States v. Richardson, 418 U.S. 166 (1974), at 191 (Powell, concurring).

7. Flast v. Cohen, 392 U.S. 83 (1968), at 131 (Harlan, dissenting); Baker v. Carr, 369 U.S. 186 (1962), at 267 (Frankfurter, dissenting).

8. Hand, in an oft-quoted remark, said "a society so riven that the spirit of moderation is gone, no court *can* save; . . . a society where that spirit flourishes, no court *need* save." (Quoted in Bickel, *Least Dangerous Branch*, p. 23.)

9. "Law and the Court," *Speeches of Oliver Wendell Holmes* (Boston: Little, Brown, 1918), p. 98.

10. On the early Marshall years, see Richard E. Ellis, *The Jeffersonian Crisis: Courts and Politics in the Young Republic* (New York: W. W. Norton and Co., 1971).

11. New York Trust Co. v. Eisner, 256 U.S. 345 (1921), at 349.

CHAPTER II

1. Roy P. Basler, ed., *The Collected Works of Abraham Lincoln* (New Brunswick, N.J.: Rutgers University Press, 1953), 2:495; Charles Evans Hughes, *The Supreme Court of the United States, Its Foundations, Methods and Achievements: An Interpretation* (New York: Columbia University Press, 1928), pp. 50–51. The classic statement of the thesis that the Court was virtually powerless for years after *Dred Scott* is found in Edward S. Corwin, "The Dred Scott Decision in the Light of Contemporary Legal

Doctrines," *American Historical Review* 17 (1911): 52–69. Robert G. McCloskey echoes these views in *The American Supreme Court* (Chicago: University of Chicago Press, 1960), pp. 91–100. An effective if at times overstated refutation of the Corwin thesis is found in Stanley J. Kutler, *Judicial Power and Reconstruction Politics* (Chicago: University of Chicago Press, 1968), chaps. 1–2.

2. 19 Howard (60 U.S.) 393 (1857). The defendant's name was actually spelled "Sanford"; the Court record (followed here only in citations of the case) was in error.

3. James Buchanan, inaugural address of 4 March 1857, in John Bassett Moore, ed., *The Works of James Buchanan* (Philadelphia: J. B. Lippincott Co., 1910), 10:106. Buchanan knew at the time of his inaugural address that the Court's decision in the case would be favorable to the South; see the discussion below.

4. See Allan Nevins, *The Ordeal of the Union* (New York: Charles Scribner's Sons, 1947), 2:489, and David M. Potter, *The Impending Crisis: 1848–1861* (New York: Harper and Row, 1976), p. 262.

5. Potter, *Impending Crisis*, p. 49.

6. Indeed, the policy of maintaining a balance between slave and free states had been followed throughout the first half of the nineteenth century. After the Missouri Compromise, there were twelve free states and twelve slave states; prior to the admission of California as a free state in 1850, there were fifteen free states and fifteen slave states.

7. The three-way division of the Northern forces opposing slavery is taken from Harold M. Hyman and William M. Wiecek, *Equal Justice under Law: Constitutional Development 1835–1875* (New York: Harper and Row, 1982), pp. 92–93. Calling the Free-Soil movement "moderate abolitionism" is a bit misleading, however, since the Free-Soilers were abolitionists only in an abstract and indefinite sense. See the discussion of the Free-Soilers' views on the ultimate effect of abolition in the territories, below.

8. Joseph G. Raybeck, *Free Soil: The Election of 1848* (Lexington: University Press of Kentucky, 1970), p. 106.

9. Eric Foner, *Free Soil, Free Labor, Free Men: The Ideology of the Republican Party before the Civil War* (New York: Oxford University Press, 1970), p. 77.

10. William Henry Seward, *The Works of William Henry Seward* (Boston: Houghton, Mifflin and Co., 1884), 4:237.

11. Quoted in Robert W. Johannsen, *Stephen A. Douglas* (New York: Oxford University Press, 1973), p. 277.

12. Basler, *Works of Lincoln*, 3:404.

13. See, for example, Foner, *Free Soil*, pp. 115–17.

14. Ibid., pp. 261ff.

15. Quoted in Don E. Fehrenbacher, *The Dred Scott Case: Its Significance in American Law and Politics* (New York: Oxford University Press, 1978), p. 184.

16. Nevins, *Ordeal*, 2:319.

17. Foner, *Free Soil*, pp. 97, 40–43, 56.

18. Ibid., p. 88.

19. Quoted in Johannsen, *Stephen A. Douglas*, p. 418.

20. Nevins, *Ordeal*, 1:28.

21. Kirk H. Porter and Donald Bruce, comps. *National Party Platforms: 1840–1968* (Urbana: University of Illinois Press, 1970), p. 27.

22. Nevins, *Ordeal*, 2:461.

23. Quoted in Robert W. Johannsen, ed., *The Lincoln-Douglas Debates* (New York: Oxford University Press, 1965), p. 67. The comment is attributed to "an Hibernian [Irishman]."

24. Fehrenbacher, *Dred Scott Case*, p. 290.

25. The Constitution gives the federal courts jurisdiction in "Cases . . . between Citizens of different States." (Art. III, sec. 2).

26. 20 Howell State Trials 1. The legal issues involved in Somerset's Case are discussed in Fehrenbacher, *Dred Scott Case*, pp. 53–56. Fehrenbacher also deals with the way American courts interpreted Lord Mansfield's opinion.

27. The facts of the case, along with the full litigation record, are most fully discussed in Walter Erlich, *They Have No Rights* (Westport, Conn.: Greenwood Press, 1979).

28. Ibid., p. 84.

29. 19 Howard (60 U.S.) 393 (1857), at 403; emphasis added.

30. Ibid., at 406; emphasis added.

31. Ibid.

32. See, for example, Art. I, sec. 2; Art. I, sec. 3; Art. II, sec. 1; and Art. III, sec. 2. For later developments, see the Fourteenth Amendment, sec. 1, adopted in 1868.

33. See the discussion of this issue in Corwin, "Dred Scott Decision."

34. 10 Howard (51 U.S.) 83 (1851). See the discussion of Strader below.

35. A full discussion of this portion of Taney's opinion can be found in Fehrenbacher, *Dred Scott Case*, pp. 385–86.

36. 19 Howard (60 U.S.) 393, at 431–32.

37. American Insurance Co. v. Canter, 1 Peters (26 U.S.) 511 (1828), at 546. The American Insurance case dealt with Congress's power to establish a territorial judicial system. For a full discussion of Taney's treatment of the Marshall precedent, see Fehrenbacher, *Dred Scott Case*, pp. 372–73.

38. 19 Howard (60 U.S.) 393 (1857), at 448–51. See also p. 407. Taney's use of the Due Process Clause, interestingly, is the first use by the Supreme Court of the concept that later became known as "substantive due process."

39. See the discussion below.

40. 19 Howard (60 U.S.) 393 (1857), at 451.

41. Johannsen, *Lincoln-Douglas Debates*, p. 55; emphasis in original.

42. 15 Peters (40 U.S.) 449 (1841).

43. 15 Peters (40 U.S.) 518 (1841).

44. 16 Peters (41 U.S.) 539 (1842); 5 Howard (46 U.S.) 215 (1847).

45. Strader v. Graham, 10 Howard (51 U.S.) 83 (1851).

46. 15 Peters (40 U.S.) 449 (1841), at 501.

47. Ibid., at 499–503.

48. Justice Catron did not participate in the case due to illness; Justice Barbour died before the case was decided.

49. 15 Peters (40 U.S.) 449 (1841), at 508.

50. Ibid., at 507.

51. Ibid., at 517, 515.

52. The discussion of this case borrows heavily from Hyman and Wiecek, *Equal Justice*, pp. 107–9. Henry Baldwin concurred with Story's opinion of the Court in a brief note.

53. 5 Howard (46 U.S.) 215 (1847), at 226.

54. Ibid., at 230.

55. 10 Howard (51 U.S.) 83 (1851), at 96–97.

56. Ibid., at 97. Justice Catron (of Tennessee) wrote a separate concurrence but did not disagree on any of the major issues.

57. Benjamin R. Curtis, Jr., ed., *A Memoir of Benjamin Robbins Curtis, LL.D, with some of his Professional and Miscellaneous Writings* (Boston: Little, Brown and Co., 1879; reprint, New York: Da Capo Press, 1970), 1:151. Curtis's steadfast commitment to the enforcement of the fugitive slave law earned him the epithet "the slave catcher judge." It is incorrect to assume from this that he was necessarily proslavery.

58. Leon Friedman and Fred L. Israel, eds., *The Justices of the United States Supreme Court 1789–1969: Their Lives and Major Opinions* (New York: Chelsea House Publishers, 1969), 2:934.

59. Campbell's views on the territorial question were expressed in a letter to John C. Calhoun in 1848. He wrote: "I think congress has the power to organize the inhabitants of a territory of the United States into a body politic. . . . As incident to this power I think that Congress may decide what shall be held and . . . not be held as property." He added: "When you admit that Congress may form a *government* you concede the right to it to define what shall be property and how it may be enjoyed transferred or inherited [*sic*]. It may decide that persons shall or shall not be property." E. I. McCormac, "Justice Campbell and the Dred Scott Decision," *Mississippi Valley Historical Review* 19 (1933): 568–69.

60. Fehrenbacher, *Dred Scott Case*, p. 290.

61. Friedman and Israel, *Justices of the Supreme Court*, 2:823.

62. Fehrenbacher, *Dred Scott Case*, p. 289.

63. Curtis, *Memoir of Benjamin Curtis*, 1:180

64. Friedman and Israel, *Justices of the Supreme Court*, 2:934.

65. One exception, often quoted but actually atypical of the tone of Campbell's opinion, is the following: "The complaint here, in my opinion, amounts to this: that the

judicial tribunals of Missouri have not denounced as odious the Constitution and laws under which they are organized, and have not superseded them on their own private authority, for the purpose of applying the laws of Illinois, or those passed by Congress for Minnesota, in their stead." 19 Howard 393 (1857), at 500.

66. Taney, whose home state (Maryland) remained in the Union, stayed on the Court until his death in 1865; Daniel died in 1861 before Virginia seceded but would have surely voted for secession and resigned his seat on the Court (see Friedman and Israel, *Justices of the Supreme Court*, 1:804); Campbell resigned his seat in 1861; Wayne, like Catron, remained on the bench.

67. Philip Auchampaugh, "James Buchanan, the Court, and the Dred Scott Case," *Tennessee Historical Magazine* 9 (1926): 235. The "two dissentients" turned out to be Curtis and McLean.

68. See, generally, Fehrenbacher, *Dred Scott Case*, pp. 305–14.

69. Auchampaugh, "Buchanan and the Dred Scott Case," p. 237 (emphasis in original).

70. Ibid.

71. Charles Warren, *The Supreme Court in United States History, 1836–1918* (Boston: Little, Brown and Co., 1926), 2:289. Many of the quotes reprinted below are taken from Warren's excellent and balanced summary of press reaction to the Dred Scott decision.

72. Ibid., 2:291. A "doughface," according to 1850s usage, was a "northern man with southern principles."

73. Ibid., 2:292–93.

74. *The New York Times*, 9 March 1857, p. 4.

75. 19 Howard (60 U.S.) 393 (1857), at 407; emphasis added.

76. Warren, *Supreme Court*, 2:303 (emphasis added).

77. Ibid., p. 306.

78. Ibid., p. 310.

79. Ibid., p. 311.

80. Ibid., pp. 292–93.

81. Whether or not Taney was justified in considering the case on the merits even after he refused jurisdiction has been the subject of considerable debate. Edward S. Corwin argued that the decision "cannot be, with accuracy, written down as a usurpation," though it "can and must be written down as a gross abuse of trust by the body that rendered it." (Corwin, "Dred Scott Decision," p. 68). To any non-lawyer, however, the Republican charges seem justified, and the obiter dicta argument had great appeal.

82. Warren, *Supreme Court*, 2:305.

83. *Congressional Globe*, 8 February 1858, p. 620.

84. Ibid., 22 March 1858, p. 1250.

85. Fehrenbacher, *Dred Scott Case*, p. 439.

86. *Congressional Globe*, 18 February 1858, p. 774.

87. Quoted in Johannsen, *Lincoln-Douglas Debates*, p. 14. "Stephen" is Stephen Douglas; "Franklin" is Franklin Pierce; "Roger" is Roger Taney; "James" is James Buchanan.

88. Quoted in ibid., pp. 14, 18.

89. *Congressional Globe*, 3 March 1858, p. 941. Seward's story, historians are now aware, contains some elements of truth, but is wildly distorted and sensationalized. See the discussion above of Buchanan's involvement in the decision.

90. Carl Brent Swisher, *Roger B. Taney* (Hamden, Conn.: Archon Books, 1961), pp. 520–21.

91. *Congressional Globe*, 17 February 1858, p. 753.

92. Warren, *Supreme Court*, 2:319.

93. Remarks of Senator Philemon Bliss (R.-Ohio), *Congressional Globe*, 6 January 1858, p. 209; remarks of Senator Fessenden, ibid., 8 February 1858, p. 617.

94. Remarks of Senator Bliss, *Congressional Globe*, 6 January 1858, p. 209; 5 May 1858, p. 1964; remarks of Senator Fessenden, ibid., 8 February 1858, p. 617.

95. Fehrenbacher, *Dred Scott Case*, p. 424.

96. Data found in Kutler, *Judicial Power*, p. 17.

97. *Congressional Globe*, 15 February 1858, p. 698.

98. Remarks of Senator Robert Hunter (D.-Va.), *Congressional Globe*, 12 March 1858, p. 1097.

99. *New York Courier*, quoted in Warren, *Supreme Court*, 2:308.

100. Warren, *Supreme Court*, 2:306.

101. *Congressional Globe*, 27 January 1858, p. 445.

102. Warren, *Supreme Court*, 2:308. For typical Republican remarks in this vein, see *Congressional Globe*, 17 March 1858, p. 1161; 15 March 1858, appendix p. 89; 31 March 1858, appendix p. 332.

103. See the discussion above.

104. Basler, *Works of Lincoln*, 2:401.

105. Ibid., p. 495.

106. Ibid., p. 496.

107. Ibid., 3:255.

108. Ibid., 4:268.

109. See, for example, remarks quoted in Warren, *Supreme Court*, 2:307; see also *Congressional Globe*, 6 January 1858, p. 209.

110. Basler, *Works of Lincoln*, 3:255; remarks of Seward quoted in Fehrenbacher, *Dred Scott Case*, p. 454.

111. The tenth Court seat was abolished in 1866.

112. Before the restructured Court could address the slavery question, the Thirteenth Amendment (1865) eliminated slavery altogether. The last vestiges of the *Dred Scott* decision were eliminated by the Fourteenth Amendment, which guaranteed citizenship to the new freedmen.

113. The remarks quoted are Fehrenbacher's summary of the traditional viewpoint. See Fehrenbacher, *Dred Scott Case*, p. 455.

114. Warren, *Supreme Court*, 2:357.

115. See Allan Nevins, *The Emergence of Lincoln* (New York: Charles Scribner's Sons, 1950), 1:82–84. Note that Toombs's argument that popular sovereignty was relevant only upon application for statehood was something on which all Republicans could have agreed as well.

116. Ibid., 2:83.

117. Fehrenbacher, *Dred Scott Case*, pp. 455–56.

118. Johannsen, *Stephen A. Douglas*, p. 613.

119. Ibid., p. 641.

120. Quoted in Fehrenbacher, *Dred Scott Case*, p. 483.

121. Johannsen, *Stephen A. Douglas*, p. 569.

122. Fehrenbacher, *Dred Scott Case*, p. 486.

123. A nice summary and analysis of the historical debate can be found in Harry V. Jaffa, *Crisis of the House Divided: An Interpretation of the Issues in the Lincoln-Douglas Debates* (Chicago: University of Chicago Press, 1982), pp. 20–37.

124. Johannsen, *Lincoln-Douglas Debates*, p. 27.

125. At this time, of course, senators were still elected by the state legislatures.

126. Potter, *Impending Crisis*, pp. 329–30.

127. Johannsen, *Lincoln-Douglas Debates*, p. 19. Douglas, of course, meant only that he did not care how individual territories resolved that question for themselves; he was fiercely opposed even to the suggestion that slavery might be imposed upon the free states, and he frequently indicated his personal opposition to slavery.

128. Johannsen, *Stephen A. Douglas*, p. 677.

129. Potter, *Impending Crisis*, p. 395.

130. *Louisville Daily Courier*, 22 February 1860, quoted in Dwight L. Dumond, ed., *Southern Editorials on Secession* (New York: Century Co., 1931), p. 39.

131. See, for example, *Congressional Globe*, 10 December 1859, p. 94.

132. Stephen A. Douglas, "The Dividing Line between Federal and Local Authority: Popular Sovereignty in the Territories," *Harper's Magazine* 19 (1859): 519–37. See also Robert W. Johannsen, "Stephen A. Douglas, 'Harper's Magazine,' and Popular Sovereignty," *Mississippi Valley Historical Review* 45 (1959): 606–31.

133. Johannsen, *Stephen A. Douglas*, p. 707.

134. *Congressional Globe*, 12 January 1860, pp. 420–21.

135. Ibid., 19 January 1860, p. 523; 15 January 1860, p. 458; 12 December 1859, p. 109.

136. Swisher, *Taney*, pp. 526–33 contains a complete discussion of the Booth episode.

137. *Congressional Globe*, 6 December 1859, p. 8.

138. Ibid., 5 January 1860, p. 343.

139. Ibid., 16 January 1860, p. 462.

140. Ibid., 16 December 1859, p. 168; 3 January 1860, p. 300.

141. Ibid., 29 February 1860, pp. 910–14.

142. Porter and Johnson, *National Party Platforms*, pp. 31–33.

143. Potter, *Impending Crisis*, p. 550.

144. *Augusta* [Ga.] *Daily Chronicle and Sentinel*, 13 November 1860, quoted in Dumond, *Editorials*, p. 231.

145. See, for example, remarks of the *New Orleans Daily Crescent*, 13 November 1860, quoted in Dumond, *Editorials*, pp. 235–38.

146. Basler, *Works of Lincoln*, 4:268–69.

147. Porter and Johnson, *National Party Platforms*, p. 25. In the original, this sentence was written completely in capital letters.

148. Potter, *Impending Crisis*, p. 259.

149. It has been reported at the astonishing figure of 0.97, with states as the units of analysis. Jerome M. Clubb, William H. Flanigan, and Nancy H. Zingale, *Partisan Realignment: Voters, Parties, and Government in American History* (Beverly Hills, Calif.: Sage Publications, 1980), p. 58.

150. Clubb, Flanigan, and Zingale report the Democratic correlation coefficient to be 0.67 as compared to the Republican correlation coefficient of 0.97; when the vote for Douglas alone is correlated with percentage Democratic in 1856, the result is −0.49, indicating a low correlation in the wrong direction (ibid.).

151. Another factor in at least some of these states was the decline in nativist voting between 1856 and 1860. See Foner, *Free Soil*, pp. 257–60.

152. Kutler, *Judicial Power*, p. 11 (emphasis in original). On Hale, see ibid., p. 14 and Richard H. Sewell, *John P. Hale and the Politics of Abolition* (Cambridge: Harvard University Press, 1965), p. 195.

153. Quoted in Swisher, *Taney*, p. 573.

CHAPTER III

1. The Prize Cases, 2 Black (67 U.S.) 635 (1863).

2. *Ex Parte* Vallandingham, 1 Wallace (68 U.S.) 243 (1864).

3. Harold M. Hyman and William M. Wiecek, *Equal Justice Under Law: Constitutional Development, 1835–1875* (New York: Harper and Row, 1982), p. 273.

4. Herman Belz, *Reconstructing the Union: Theory and Policy during the Civil War* (Ithaca, N.Y.: Cornell University Press for the American Historical Association, 1969), pp. 232, 235.

5. Art. II, sec. 2.

6. Wade-Davis Manifesto, quoted in Belz, *Reconstructing the Union*, p. 242.

7. See Belz, *Reconstructing the Union*, pp. 239–43.

8. Ibid, p. 241.

9. H.R. 244, 38th Cong., 1st sess.; reprinted in James D. Richardson, ed., *A Compilation of the Messages and Papers of the Presidents, 1789–1897*, vol. 6, *1861–1869* (Washington, D.C.: Government Printing Office, 1897), pp. 223–26.

10. Edward McPherson, *The Political History of the United States of America during the Great Rebellion, 1860–1865* (1865; reprint, New York: Da Capo Press, 1972), pp. 318–19.

11. Wade-Davis Manifesto, in McPherson, *Political History during the Great Rebellion*, p. 332.

12. See Belz, *Reconstructing the Union*, pp. 230–31.

13. Roy P. Basler, ed., *The Collected Works of Abraham Lincoln* (New Brunswick, N.J.: Rutgers University Press, 1953), 8:333.

14. A third possibility was Montgomery Blair, who desperately wanted the office. Blair was so unpopular both with the legal profession and the radicals that his appointment would have been a political disaster. Blair, according to Allan Nevins, "was distrusted by Moderate Republicans, [and] hated by such Radicals as Schuyler Colfax and Thaddeus Stevens." Perhaps with a touch of irony, Lincoln informed Blair's father that the opposition of the legal profession made the nomination of Blair impossible: "Although I may be stronger as an authority," Lincoln wrote in mid-November 1864, "yet if all the rest oppose I must give way." See Allan Nevins, *The War for the Union* (New York: Charles Scribner's Sons, 1971) 4:105, 118–19; Charles M. Segal, ed., *Conversations with Lincoln* (New York: Putnam, 1961), pp. 361.

15. David Donald, *Charles Sumner and the Rights of Man* (New York: Alfred A. Knopf, 1970), p. 190.

16. Donald, *Sumner*, p. 190; David Donald, ed., *Inside Lincoln's Cabinet: The Civil War Diaries of Salmon Portland Chase* (New York: Longmans, Green and Co., 1954), p. 239.

17. Willard L. King, *Lincoln's Manager: David Davis* (Cambridge: Harvard University Press, 1960), p. 224.

18. The precedent against appointing a sitting justice to the top spot on the Court was broken only by President William Howard Taft, who promoted Justice Edward D. White to chief justice in 1910. Justice Davis, in answer to Lincoln's concern over precedent, pointed out that the last treasury secretary to be appointed chief justice was none other than Taney. Taney's appointment, Davis concluded, was a compelling argument against appointing a chief justice for partisan political reasons and, by implication, an argument against appointing former treasury secretary Chase and in favor of appointing Swayne. See the letters of Davis to Lincoln, 22 October and 29 November 1864, Abraham Lincoln Papers, Library of Congress.

19. Donald, *Inside Lincoln's Cabinet*, p. 211.

20. Ibid., diary entry of 30 June 1864, pp. 224–25.

21. King, *Davis*, p. 223.

22. Ibid.

23. Nevins, *War for the Union*, 4:118.

24. Carl Brent Swisher, *The Taney Period, 1836–64*, vol. 5 of the *History of the Supreme Court of the United States* (New York: Macmillan Co., 1974), p. 961.

25. David M. Silver, *Lincoln's Supreme Court* (Urbana: University of Illinois Press, 1957), p. 57.

26. Ibid., p. 90.

27. David Donald, *The Politics of Reconstruction, 1863–67* (Baton Rouge: Louisiana State University Press, 1965), pp. 29–31, 83–90. Schuyler Colfax of Indiana, as speaker, typically did not vote.

28. Ibid., pp. 30–31.

29. Quoted in Nevins, *War for the Union*, 4:129; 1:198.

30. 4 Wallace (71 U.S.) 2 (1866).

31. The issue arose most directly in *Ex Parte* Vallandingham, 1 Wallace (68 U.S.) 243 (1864), but the Court avoided a decision by declaring that it did not have jurisdiction over appeals from the military courts.

32. McPherson, *Political History during the Great Rebellion*, p. 209.

33. Quoted in King, *Davis*, p. 245; on Justice Davis's views, see pp. 204, 254.

34. *The New York Times*, 6 March 1866, p. 1.

35. See, for example, the *National Intelligencer*, 7 March 1866, p. 3; 8 March 1866, p. 3.

36. 4 Wallace (71 U.S.) 2 (1866), at 107.

37. Justice Grier told Orville H. Browning (soon to be Johnson's secretary of the interior) that the Court "had unanimously decided in favor of the Habeas Corpus, and against the Commissions—the only difference being that some of the Judges desired to confine the decision to the legality of the Commission which tried the case in question, but that the majority extended it to all military commissions for the trial of persons not in the Military or Naval service." (Diary of Orville Browning, quoted in Charles Fairman, *Mr. Justice Miller and the Supreme Court, 1862–1890* [New York: Russell and Russell, 1939], p. 94.) However, Justice Davis, who would write the opinion of the Court, "afterwards complained that the majority did not know, when the Court adjourned, what position the dissenters would take." (King, *Davis*, pp. 253–54.) Davis's confusion becomes clear when it is recognized that Grier's prediction was not entirely correct.

38. *New York World*, 9 April 1866, p. 4.

39. Charles Warren, for example, though reporting extensively on Republican criticism of the opinion, cites no examples from before December 1866; *The Supreme Court in United States History, 1836–1918* (Boston: Little, Brown and Co., 1926), 2:426–47.

40. King, *Davis*, p. 255.

41. See for example Hyman and Wiecek, *Equal Justice*, pp. 381–85. Silver reports, incorrectly, that "Chase's announcement [on April 3] created a sensation!" (Silver, *Lincoln's Supreme Court*, p. 232). Several works erroneously report that the *opinion* of the Court in *Milligan* was handed down on 3 April 1866; see, for example, J. G. Randall and David Donald, *The Civil War and Reconstruction*, 2d ed. (Lexington, Mass.: D. C. Heath and Co., 1969), p. 304; and Avery Craven, *Reconstruction: The Ending of the Civil War* (New York: Holt, Rinehart and Winston, 1969), p. 208.

42. Warren, *Supreme Court*, 2:423–24.

43. King, *Davis*, pp. 255–56.

44. Stanley I. Kutler, *Judicial Review and Reconstruction Politics* (Chicago: University of Chicago Press, 1968), pp. 91–92.

45. Eric L. McKitrick, *Andrew Johnson and Reconstruction* (Chicago: University of Chicago Press, 1960), p. 274. McKitrick is referring to the Senate's repassage of the Civil Rights Act; similar action in the House was a foregone conclusion. Final House action on the bill came on April 9.

46. Quoted in ibid., pp. 258–59.

47. Ibid., p. 259. Its chairman was William Pitt Fessenden, a moderate senior statesman of the Republican party. Kenneth Stampp, *The Era of Reconstruction, 1865–1877* (New York: Alfred A. Knopf, 1966) describes Fessenden as a "moderate radical" (p. 84). McKitrick writes that Fessenden functioned "as a kind of balance wheel" in the government (*Johnson and Reconstruction*, p. 270).

48. On the Black Codes, see generally Theodore B. Wilson, *The Black Codes of the South* (University: University of Alabama Press, 1965).

49. A summary of the original act can be found in McPherson, *Political History during the Great Rebellion*, pp. 594–95.

50. On the Freedmen's Bureau, see generally Donald G. Nieman, *To Set the Law in Motion: The Freedmen's Bureau and the Legal Rights of Blacks, 1865–1868* (Millwood, N.Y.: KTO Press, 1979) and George R. Bentley, *A History of the Freedmen's Bureau* (New York: Octagon Books, 1970).

51. William H. Barnes, *History of the Thirty-Ninth Congress of the United States* (New York: Harper and Brothers, 1868; reprint, New York: Negro University Press, 1969), pp. 106–7.

52. *New York Tribune*, 9 January 1866, quoted in McKitrick, *Johnson and Reconstruction*, p. 280.

53. The veto message appears in Richardson, *Messages and Papers*, pp. 398–405.

54. Quoted in Barnes, *History of the Thirty-Ninth Congress*, p. 88.

55. Ibid., pp. 121–22.

56. 14 *Statutes at Large* 27 (9 April 1866).

57. The complete act can be found in 14 *Statutes at Large* 27–30 (9 April 1866).

58. *Congressional Globe*, 26 February 1866, p. 130A.

59. McKitrick, *Johnson and Reconstruction*, p. 305.

60. John Sherman, *Recollections of Forty Years in the House, Senate, and Cabinet: An Autobiography* (Chicago: Werner, 1895), 2:368–69.

61. Richardson, *Messages and Papers*, p. 413; the complete message appears at pp. 405–13.

62. Ibid., pp. 431–32; the complete messages appears at pp. 429–32.

63. McKitrick, *Johnson and Reconstruction*, pp. 339–40. The amendment, as finally adopted, contained these provisions in section one.

64. Edward McPherson, *The Political History of the United States of America during the Period of Reconstruction*, (N.p.: Solomons and Chapman, 1875; reprint, New York: Negro University Press, 1969), p. 79. The act also allowed the president to use the army and navy as necessary "to prevent the violation and enforce the due execution of the act," though it seems clear that Johnson had no intention of actually doing so.

65. Quoted in James E. Sefton, *The United States Army and Reconstruction 1865–77* (Baton Rouge: Louisiana State University Press, 1967), p. 78.

66. Ibid., p. 79.

67. Quoted in ibid.

68. *New York World*, 13 April 1866, p. 4.

69. Donald, *Politics of Reconstruction*, pp. 56–57.

70. McKitrick, *Johnson and Reconstruction*, pp. 455–56.

71. Ibid., p. 456.

72. Warren, *Supreme Court*, 2:427.

73. 4 Wallace (71 U.S.) 2 (1866), at 120–21.

74. Ibid., at 121–22.

75. Ibid., at 127.

76. Ibid., at 136.

77. Ibid., at 140.

78. Ibid., at 109.

79. Davis to Julius Rockwell, 24 February 1867, quoted in King, *Davis*, p. 258.

80. 14 *Statutes at Large* 173–77 (16 July 1866).

81. Bentley, *Freedmen's Bureau*, pp. 152–68.

82. Quoted in Warren, *Supreme Court*, 2:443.

83. McKitrick, *Johnson and Reconstruction*, pp. 474–75; see also Donald, *Politics of Reconstruction*, pp. 26–52.

84. Warren, *Supreme Court*, 2:429.

85. Ibid.

86. Martin E. Mantell, *Johnson, Grant, and the Politics of Reconstruction* (New York: Columbia University Press, 1973), pp. 78–85.

87. In general, historians have tended to overestimate both the intensity and the duration of the Republican response. "The Radical press and politicians," writes Wil-

lard King, "savagely assailed Davis's opinion in the Milligan case, classing it with the Dred Scott decision and Taney's opinion in Merryman's case." "In 1866, and for two years following," he adds, "the Supreme Court, as well as the President, was the target for furious Radical attack" (King, *Davis*, pp. 256, 260). The Republicans' attacks on the Court after *Milligan* did not last long; they were all but exhausted after the passage of the Reconstruction Act in March 1867. Warren's citations in his rather full discussion of press reaction to *Milligan* are instructive. His quotations from various Republican newspapers are drawn from the following dates: Jan. 3; Jan. 3, 4, 5, 7; Jan. 10; Jan 3, 4, 5; Dec. 19, 20, 23; Jan. 2, 8; Jan. 4; Jan. 19; Jan. 3; Dec. 19, 22, 29, "and *passim* through January, 1867." His quotations from Democratic papers are from similar dates. (See pages 428–54.) In Charles Fairman's summary of press opinions, there is only one reference to an article or document dated after January. See Charles Fairman, *Reconstruction and Reunion, 1864–88*, vol. 6 of the *History of the Supreme Court of the United States* (New York: Macmillan, 1971), pp. 214–22. The Republican newspapers made scattered references to *Milligan* after January 1867 but nothing resembling a concerted attack on the Court.

88. *Congressional Globe*, 22 February 1867, p. 1484.

89. Ibid., 2 March 1867, p. 1962.

90. Ibid., 22 February 1867, p. 1487.

91. Henry J. Raymond (R.-N.Y.), ibid., 24 January 1867, p. 717; see also the remarks of James H. D. Henderson (U.R.-Ore.), 20 February 1867, pp. 1642–43.

92. Warren, *Supreme Court*, 2:437–38.

93. *National Intelligencer*, 3 January 1867, p. 2.

94. Comments of the *Richmond Enquirer*, quoted in Warren, *Supreme Court*, 2:439.

95. *Congressional Globe*, 21 January 1867, p. 624.

96. Ibid., 7 February 1867, p. 1078.

97. Ibid., p. 1079. For similar comments, see the remarks of Aaron Harding (D.-Ky.), 12 February 1867, p. 1167; Elijah Hise (U.D.-Ky.), 23 February 1867, p. 1533; and of Senators Willard Saulsbury (D.-Del.) and Reverdy Johnson (D.-Md.), 2 March 1867, pp. 1959–60.

98. 4 Wallace (71 U.S.) 2 (1866), at 127.

99. Ibid.

100. Quoted in Kutler, *Judicial Power*, p. 67.

101. *Congressional Globe*, 14 January 1867, p. 439. See also the remarks of Samuel L. Warner (R.-Conn.), 18 January 1867, p. 567.

102. All quotes in this paragraph from Warren, *Supreme Court*, 2:431–33.

103. *Ex parte* Garland, 4 Wallace (71 U.S.) 333 (1867); Cummings v. Missouri, 4 Wallace (71 U.S.) 277 (1867).

104. Fairman, *Reconstruction and Reunion*, pp. 244–48.

105. *Congressional Globe*, 16 January 1867, p. 502.

106. Ibid.

107. See, for example, the remarks of Frederick A. Pike (R.-Me.), ibid., 3 January 1867, p. 255.

108. Kutler, *Judicial Power*, pp. 16–20.

109. Quoted in ibid., p. 48.

110. Congress increased the Court back to nine (where it has stood ever since) in 1869. Here again the political motives behind the increase have been overstated. Although the new justices appointed by President Grant played a critical role in the favorable decision in the Legal Tender Cases, 8 Wallace (75 U.S.) 603 (1870), attributing the increase to a deliberate attempt to influence the Court's resolution of this or other cases is without much foundation. See Kutler, *Judicial Power*, pp. 57–59, 120–27; Sidney Ratner, "Was the Supreme Court Packed by President Grant?" *Political Science Quarterly* 50 (1935): 343–58; and Charles Fairman, "Mr. Justice Bradley's Appointment to the Supreme Court and the Legal Tender Cases," *Harvard Law Review* 54 (1941): 977–1034, 1128–55.

111. 14 *Statutes at Large* 558–59 (2 March 1867).

112. 14 *Statutes at Large* 385–86 (5 February 1867).

113. Fairman, *Reconstruction and Reunion*, p. 448.

114. *Congressional Globe*, 18 February 1867, pp. 1498–99.

115. The first Reconstruction Act can be found at 14 *Statutes at Large* 428 (2 March 1867). Later acts are found at 15 *Statutes at Large* 2 (23 March 1867); 15 *Statutes at Large* 14 (19 July 1867); 15 *Statutes at Large* 41 (11 March 1868).

116. See Randall and Donald, *Civil War and Reconstruction*, p. 593.

117. Mantell, *Johnson, Grant*, p. 24.

118. Years later, the Supreme Court of the United States agreed with Johnson, at least with respect to purely executive officials, holding that the Senate's power to confirm appointments did not extend to dismissals. Myers v. United States, 272 U.S. 52 (1926). For further judicial consideration of the removal power, see also United States v. Humphrey's Executor, 295 U.S. 602 (1935) and Wiener v. United States, 357 U.S. 349 (1958).

119. Richardson, *Messages and Papers*, p. 472.

120. See Mantell, *Johnson, Grant*, pp. 28–30.

121. See McKitrick, *Andrew Johnson and Reconstruction*, p. 495. Gideon Welles's diary, as McKitrick notes, is "virtually a week-by-week chronicle of the curious relationship between Johnson and Stanton, a relationship in which, behind an elaborate mask of mutual politeness, each was perfectly aware of the other's mistrust of himself."

122. Mantell, *Johnson, Grant*, p. 40.

123. Ibid., p. 32; 12 Opinions of the Attorney General 141 (1867), at 184–85.

124. McPherson, *Political History during Reconstruction*, p. 335.

125. Ibid., p. 36.

126. The vote was 57 to 108.

127. Richardson, *Messages and Papers*, pp. 558–69.

128. Randall and Donald, *Civil War and Reconstruction*, p. 606.

129. *Congressional Globe*, 24 February 1868, p. 1395.

130. Senator Oliver H. P. T. Morton (R.-Ind.), quoted by Senator James R. Doolittle (R.-Wisc.), *Congressional Globe*, 24 February 1868, p. 1375.

131. Gideon Welles to John A. Welles, 1 March 1868, Gideon Welles Papers, Library of Congress.

132. Mississippi v. Johnson, 4 Wallace (71 U.S.) 475 (1867), dismissing a suit against the president seeking an injunction against enforcement of the Reconstruction Act; *Ex Parte* Yerger, 8 Wallace (75 U.S.) 75 (1869), in which the Court confined itself to the narrow question of circuit court jurisdiction to hear habeas corpus petitions; and Georgia v. Grant, 6 Wallace (73 U.S.) 241 (1868), in which the Court did not deal with the merits of the Reconstruction issue at all. In Mississippi v. Stanton (1868, unreported) the Court evenly divided on the question of whether a challenge to the Reconstruction Acts could be based on property rights. Thus the Court never ruled on the constitutionality of the Reconstruction Acts.

133. *Congressional Globe*, 12 March 1868, p. 1860.

134. Ibid., p. 1847.

135. Ibid., 14 March 1868, p. 1882.

136. Ibid., 25 March 1868, p. 2094.

137. Chase to John D. Van Buren, 6[?] April 1868, Chase Papers, Library of Congress.

138. In re McArdle [*sic*], Protest of Mr. Justice Grier. Jeremiah H. Black Papers, Library of Congress.

139. *Ex Parte* McCardle, 7 Wallace (74 U.S.) 506 (1869).

140. In U.S. v. Klein, 13 Wallace (80 U.S.) 128 (1872), at 145, the Court held that while Congress could remove the Court's appellate jurisdiction in "a particular class of cases," it could not do so "as a means to an end," namely, in this case, "to deny to pardons granted by the President the effect which this court had adjudged them to have." See also the discussion in Chapter 5 of modern attempts to control the Supreme Court's appellate jurisdiction.

141. Kutler, *Judicial Power*, pp. 163–64.

142. *Ex Parte* McCardle, 7 Wallace (74 U.S.) 506 (1869), at 514.

143. Ibid.

144. Quoted in Kutler, *Judicial Power*, p. 3; see the essay, pp. 3–6.

145. Warren, *Supreme Court*, 2:418.

146. Kutler, *Judicial Power*, pp. 161, 163.

147. Ibid., p. 161.

148. Robert McCloskey, *The American Supreme Court* (Chicago: University of Chicago Press, 1960), p. 110.

149. See the discussion above of the reduction of the Court.

150. *Congressional Globe*, 4 December 1867, p. 19.

151. Ibid., 13 January 1868, p. 478.

152. Ibid.

153. Ibid., p. 483.

154. Ibid., p. 488.

155. See the remarks of the *Nation*, the *Chicago Republican*, and other papers in Warren, *Supreme Court*, 2:469–70.

156. Kutler, *Judicial Power*, p. 77.

157. *Congressional Globe*, 13 January 1868, p. 478. Wilson never specified what that case was and even doubted its existence; perhaps some were afraid of the Court's pending release of the opinion in the case of Georgia v. Stanton, though the Court had already announced months before that it would dismiss Georgia's suit and refuse, in that case at least, to decide upon the constitutionality of the Reconstruction Acts.

158. Ibid., 14 March 1868, p. 1883.

159. Ibid., 21 March 1868, p. 2062.

160. Ibid., 27 March 1868, p. 2170.

161. Ibid.

162. *Harper's Weekly*, 9 February 1867, p. 82.

CHAPTER IV

1. William E. Leuchtenburg, *Franklin D. Roosevelt and the New Deal, 1932–1940* (New York: Harper and Row, 1963), pp. 10–11.

2. Ibid., pp. 11–12.

3. Ibid., p. 13.

4. Diary Notes, 1935, 1 February 1935, Rexford G. Tugwell Papers, FDR Library.

5. Franklin D. Roosevelt, *The Public Papers and Addresses of Franklin D. Roosevelt*, comp. Samuel I. Rosenman (New York: Random House, 1938–50), 2:11–16 (hereafter cited as *Public Papers of FDR*).

6. Ibid., 3:42.

7. Ibid., p. 170.

8. *Literary Digest*, 23 June 1934, p. 6.

9. *The New York Times*, 28 October 1934, p. 6.

10. *Literary Digest*, 27 October 1934, p. 13.

11. *Public Papers of FDR*, 3:8.

12. Ibid., p. 417.

13. Diary Notes, 1935, 1 February 1935, Tugwell Papers.

14. *Public Papers of FDR*, 3:457.

15. Ibid., pp. 462–63.

16. Ibid., 4:15–25.

17. *Congressional Record*, 13 April 1933, p. 1642.

18. Ibid., 21 March 1933, p. 677.

19. Ibid., 18 April 1933, p. 1884; 13 March 1933, p. 261.

20. Ibid., 25 May 1933, p. 4212.

21. See James E. Sargeant, *Roosevelt and the Hundred Days* (New York: Garland Publishers, 1981), pp. 230–31.

22. *Public Papers of FDR*, 2:164, emphasis added.

23. Hammer v. Dagenhart, 247 U.S. 251 (1918), at 273–74, striking down a law which prohibited the shipment in interstate commerce of goods produced in factories that employed children.

24. *Literary Digest*, 30 June 1934, p. 9. Poll data from the 1930s is not to be taken too seriously, due to the unsophisticated nature of survey techniques. Numbers such as these are roughly indicative of public attitudes, however, and are supported by other nonquantitative data.

25. Ellis W. Hawley, *The New Deal and the Problem of Monopoly: A Study in Economic Ambivalence* (Princeton: Princeton University Press, 1966), p. 92.

26. *The New York Times*, 8 July 1934, pp. 1, 18.

27. Ibid., 10 July 1934, p. 2.

28. FDR to Newton Baker, 26 September 1935, President's Personal File 669, FDR Papers, FDR Library.

29. *Literary Digest*, 13 October 1934, p. 39.

30. Ibid., 1 September 1934, p. 39.

31. *Complete Presidential Press Conferences of Franklin D. Roosevelt* (New York: Da Capo Press, 1972), 4:17 (hereafter cited as *FDR Press Conferences*).

32. Ibid., p. 19.

33. *Literary Digest*, 22 September 1934, p. 13.

34. Robert McCloskey, *The American Supreme Court* (Chicago: University of Chicago Press, 1960), p. 162.

35. Ibid., p. 137.

36. Advance-Rumely Thresher Co. v. Jackson, 287 U.S. 283 (1932).

37. Los Angeles Gas and Electric Corp. v. Railroad Commission, 289 U.S. 287 (1933).

38. 290 U.S. 398 (1933).

39. The Contract Clause stipulates that "No state shall . . . pass any . . . law impairing the obligation of contracts." (U.S. Constitution, Art. I, sec. 10).

40. 290 U.S. 398, at 426.

41. Ibid., at 440.

42. Ibid., at 442.

43. Both comments are newspaper editorials quoted in the *Literary Digest*, 20 January 1934, p. 5.

44. Nebbia v. New York, 291 U.S. 502 (1934), at 537.

45. Ibid., at 537.

46. Ibid., at 524–25.

47. All quotes in this paragraph from *Literary Digest*, 17 March 1934, p. 9.

48. 293 U.S. 388 (1934).

49. Ibid., at 415.

50. Ibid., at 391–98.

51. Ibid., at 443.

52. *Literary Digest*, 19 January 1935, p. 6.

53. *FDR Press Conferences*, 5:42–46.

54. G. Stanleigh Arnold to Homer Cummings, 18 March 1935, Box 8, Solicitor General Series, Stanley Reed Papers, University of Kentucky Libraries, Department of Special Collections.

55. *Literary Digest*, 19 January 1935, p. 6.

56. Norman v. Baltimore and Ohio Railroad Co., 294 U.S. 240 (1934); Nortz v. U.S., 294 U.S. 317 (1934); Perry v. U.S., 294 U.S. 330 (1934). These and other cases were argued together and produced a common dissenting opinion.

57. Cummings was deeply involved in the preparation of the cases as well. "I have spent so much time, day and night, on these briefs and in the preparation of my oral argument," he wrote on the day the arguments began, "that I begin to feel a bit like King Midas." Cummings wore his presidential cufflinks—made of gold—for good luck. Homer Cummings to Marguerite LeHand, 8 January 1935, Box 170, Homer S. Cummings Papers (#9973), Manuscripts Department, University of Virginia Library.

58. 294 U.S. 240 (1934), at 256. The complete oral argument of the attorney general is reproduced at 251–72.

59. Ibid., at 271.

60. Perry v. U.S., 294 U.S. 330 (1934), at 350–51.

61. Ibid., at 351.

62. Ibid., at 354.

63. Ibid., at 360–61.

64. "Revision of Report Concerning 'Justice McReynolds's remarks on the Gold Clause decision,' published by the *Wall Street Journal*, February 23, 1935. . . .'" Box 2, Cummings Papers; 294 U.S. 330 (1934), at 362, 369; Max Freedman, ed., *Roosevelt and Frankfurter: Their Correspondence, 1928–45* (Boston: Little, Brown and Co., 1967), p. 256.

65. *Literary Digest*, 2 March 1935, pp. 37, 36.

66. Elliott Roosevelt, ed., *F.D.R.: His Personal Letters, 1928–45* (New York: Duell, Sloan and Pearce, 1950), 1:459–60; Memorandum and accompanying documents, Donald B. Richberg to FDR, 12 February 1935, President's Personal File, Box 1055, FDR Papers.

67. Box 4, Reconstruction Finance Corporation Counsel series, "Gold Clause Moratorium" file, Reed Papers.

68. FDR to Angus MacLean, 21 February 1935, President's Personal File 1055, FDR Papers.

69. Railroad Retirement Board v. Alton, 295 U.S. 330 (1935).

70. Ibid., at 374.

71. Ibid., at 377.

72. Harlan F. Stone to Felix Frankfurter, Box 171, Folder 14, 9 May 1935, Felix Frankfurter Papers, Harvard Law School Library.

73. 295 U.S. 495 (1935).

74. Ibid., at 554.

75. Louisville Joint Stock Bank v. Radford, 295 U.S. 555 (1935).

76. Nelson Lloyd Dawson, *Louis D. Brandeis, Felix Frankfurter, and the New Deal* (Hamden, Conn.: Archon Books, 1980), p. 127.

77. Humphrey's Executor v. U.S., 295 U.S. 602 (1935).

78. See Myers v. U.S., 272 U.S. 52 (1926), which held that Congress could not interfere with the president's power to remove postmasters.

79. Basil Rauch, *The History of the New Deal, 1933–1938*, 2d ed. (New York: Octagon Books, 1975), p. 197.

80. Cummings diary, vol. 5, p. 64, 27 May 1935, Box 234, Cummings Papers.

81. Leuchtenburg, *Roosevelt and the New Deal*, p. 144.

82. *The New Republic*, 6 March 1935, p. 100. See also *Time*, 25 February 1935, p. 11.

83. For a short summary of Brandeis's attitude toward bigness, see Dawson, *Brandeis, Frankfurter, and the New Deal*, pp. 14–19. See also Phillipa Strum, *Louis D. Brandeis; Justice for the People* (Cambridge: Harvard University Press, 1984), pp. 339–53.

84. Melvin I. Urofsky and David W. Levy, eds., *Letters of Louis D. Brandeis*, vol. 5, *1921–24: Elder Statesman* (Albany: State University of New York Press, 1978), p. 527.

85. H. N. Hirsch, *The Enigma of Felix Frankfurter* (New York: Basic Books, 1981), p. 115.

86. Strum, *Brandeis*, pp. 349–50.

87. Quoted in Arthur M. Schlesinger, Jr., *The Age of Roosevelt* (Boston: Houghton Mifflin, 1957), 3:280.

88. Ibid., p. 389. Whether in the long run the second New Deal was a triumph for the Brandeisian spirit is open to debate. The traditional view is that it was; for a dissent, see Dawson, *Brandeis, Frankfurter, and the New Deal*.

89. Schlesinger, *Age of Roosevelt*, 3:283.

90. Harlan F. Stone to Thomas Reed Powell, 31 May 1935, Box A, Folder A13, Thomas Reed Powell Papers, Harvard Law School Library.

91. Schlesinger, *Age of Roosevelt*, 3:283–84.

92. Tugwell diary, 5 June 1935, Box 17, Tugwell Papers.

93. Cummings diary, vol. 5, p. 65, 27 May 1935, Box 234, Cummings Papers.

94. Ibid., p. 66.

95. Tugwell diary, 31 May 1935, Tugwell Papers, FDR Library.

96. Felix Frankfurter to FDR, 29 May 1935; FDR to Felix Frankfurter, 30 May 1935; Box 170, Cummings Papers.

97. Schlesinger, *Age of Roosevelt*, 3:5. See also Alan Brinkley, *Voices of Protest: Huey Long, Father Coughlin, and the Great Depression* (New York: Alfred A. Knopf, 1982), pp. 79–81.

98. Hapgood to FDR, 20 February 1936, President's Personal File 2278, "Norman Hapgood" File, FDR Papers.

99. George Wolfskill and John A. Hudson, *All But the People: Franklin D. Roosevelt and His Critics, 1933–39* (Toronto: Macmillan Co., 1969), p. 237.

100. *Literary Digest*, 27 July 1935, p. 5.

101. Quoted in Stanley Reed to Homer Cummings, 29 May 1935, Official File 10, Box 3, FDR Papers.

102. *Literary Digest*, 27 July 1935, p. 3.

103. Felix Frankfurter to FDR, 29 May 1935, Box 170, Cummings Papers; see also memorandum, Stanley F. Reed to Homer S. Cummings, 29 May 1935, Official File 10, FDR Papers.

104. 297 U.S. 1 (1936).

105. Ibid., at 65–66.

106. Cummings diary, vol. 6, 10 January 1936, pp. 11–12, Box 235, Cummings Papers.

107. U.S. v. Butler, 297 U.S. 1 (1936), at 177–78.

108. Frankfurter to Owen J. Roberts, and reply, ca. November 1940, Box 171, folder 1 (Frankfurter Papers).

109. 297 U.S. 1 (1936), at 87.

110. Stone to Homer S. Cummings, 9 January 1936, quoted in Cummings's diary, vol. 6, 10 January 1936, p. 12, Box 235, Cummings Papers.

111. *Today*, 18 January 1936, p. 13.

112. *Literary Digest*, 22 February 1936, p. 5; *The New York Times*, 18 February 1936, p. 13.

113. Grosjean v. American Press Co., 297 U.S. 233 (1936).

114. 298 U.S. 238 (1936).

115. Ibid., at 317–18.

116. Both quotes from *The New York Times*, 19 May 1936, p. 17.

117. 298 U.S. 587 (1936).

118. Adkins v. Children's Hospital, 261 U.S. 525 (1923).

119. 298 U.S. 587 (1936), at 619, 625, 623.

120. High to Roosevelt, June 1936, President's Secretary's File Box 185, FDR Papers.

121. *FDR Press Conferences*, 7:280.

122. FDR to McIntyre, 4 June 1936, Official File 355, FDR Papers.

123. *The New York Times*, 5 June 1936, p. 20.

124. Quoted in ibid., 18 February 1936, p. 13.

125. Ibid., 7 June 1936, p. 1.

126. Ibid.

127. *Official Report of the Proceedings of the Twenty-first Republican National Convention, held in Cleveland, Ohio June 9, 10, 11 and 12, 1936* (New York: Tenney Press, 1936), p. 138.

128. Ibid., p. 140.

129. *The New York Times*, 12 June 1936, p. 1.

130. Ibid., 9 June 1936, p. 22.

131. *Public Papers of FDR*, 5:200.

132. Ibid., p. 201.

133. Cummings to FDR, 20 June 1936, President's Secretary's File 76, FDR Papers.

134. *The New York Times*, 27 June 1936, p. 6.

135. *Public Papers of FDR*, 5:234.

136. Ibid., pp. 232, 544.

137. *The New York Times*, 24 October 1936, p. 8.

138. Ibid., 2 October 1936, p. 4.

139. Ibid., 24 October 1936, p. 8; 22 October 1936, p. 21.

140. Reed to McIntyre, 5 November 1936, Official File 1710, FDR Papers.

141. Cummings diary, vol. 6, 15 November 1936, Box 235, Cummings Papers.

142. Assoc. Industries of New York State v. Dept. of Labor of New York et al., 299 U.S. 515 (1936) [per curiam].

143. Hughes, as was pointed out above, had "switched" in *Morehead* and partially in *Carter* as well.

144. Cummings to FDR, 24 November 1936, Official File 10, FDR Papers.

145. *Public Papers of FDR*, 4:297.

146. Ibid. The original of this letter, dated 5 July 1935 and drafted by Cummings, can be found in Official File 274, no. 1, FDR Papers. Politician that he was, Roosevelt was not above using the Court as an excuse to discourage legislation which he did not want to see enacted. One month after *Alton*, he encouraged Congress to drop consideration of a new Railroad Retirement Act, which would have split the law into two, one providing for the payment of pensions and the other taxing railroads and their employees. "In view of the sweeping character of the *Alton* [railroad retirement] decision," wrote Attorney General Cummings, "it was determined that it would be unwise to attempt to secure new legislation at this session of Congress." (*Public Papers of FDR*, 4:234.) Left unsaid, however, was the possibility that the enactment of a new railroad pension plan might get in the way of the more general social security bill being vigorously supported by the administration—which by any interpretation consistent

with the railroad retirement decision was clearly unconstitutional as well.

147. *Public Papers of FDR*, 4:209, 218.

148. Stephen Early [?] to FDR, 9 January 1936, Official File 1K, FDR Papers.

149. Charles A. Beard, *The Supreme Court and the Constitution* (New York: Macmillan Co., 1912; reprint, Englewood Cliffs, N.J.: Prentice-Hall, 1962), pp. 85–88. See also Beard, *An Economic Interpretation of the Constitution* (New York: Macmillan Co., 1913).

150. *Congressional Record*, 5 June 1935, p. 8670.

151. Ibid., 7 January 1936, p. 132.

152. Ibid., 14 May 1935, p. 7536.

153. Ibid., 3 June 1935, p. 8563.

154. Schlesinger, *Age of Roosevelt*, 3:491. Reed noted that there was a "consensus" that such an approach was best, but he himself endorsed the idea only weakly; Reed to Frankfurter, 17 December 1936, General Correspondence, Box 242, Reed Papers.

155. Benjamin V. Cohen to Charles N. Clarke, 26 December 1936, Benjamin V. Cohen Papers, Library of Congress.

156. *Congressional Record*, 7 June 1935, p. 8904; *Today*, 29 February 1936; memorandum from the attorney general, 21 January 1935, President's Personal File 1055; FDR to Charles Burlingham, 19 February 1937, President's Secretary's File 186, FDR Papers.

157. *Public Papers of FDR*, 2:14–15.

158. FDR quoting Chief Justice White, ibid., 3:421.

159. Congressman Lewis quoting Theodore Roosevelt, *Congressional Record*, 7 June 1935, p. 8834. See also Thomas Corcoran to Stanley F. Reed, 9 September 1936, and attached excerpts from a speech by Woodrow Wilson, Box 284 (misc. series), Reed Papers.

160. Cummings to FDR, 29 January 1936, Box 170, Cummings Papers.

161. The epithet "The Nine Old Men" was popularized when it was adopted as the title of a book by Drew Pearson and Robert S. Allen (Garden City, N.Y.: Doubleday, Doran and Co., 1936). The book, a scathing critique of the Court and of the individual justices, was a best-seller in 1936.

162. *Philadelphia Record*, 19 May 1935; *Congressional Record*, 31 May 1935, p. 8470; 22 January 1936, p. 851.

163. Address by Stanley F. Reed to Georgia Bar Association, Savannah, Ga., 29 May 1936, Speech Series, Box 284, Reed Papers; see also "The Constitution—Guide or Gaoler," speech by Stanley F. Reed to the New York State Bar Association, 25 January 1936, in *Vital Speeches of the Day*, 24 February 1936, pp. 318–22.

164. *Vital Speeches*, 13 January 1936, p. 235. Cummings's speech was delivered before the Association of the Bar of New York on December 18, 1935.

165. *Congressional Record*, 20 May 1935, p. 7796.

166. *Public Papers of FDR*, 6:131. See also FDR to W. T. Dickerson (memorandum

dictated by James Roosevelt), 23 February 1937, President's Personal File 4448, and FDR to Charles Burlingham, 23 February 1937, President's Secretary's File 186, FDR Papers.

167. U.S. Congress, Senate, Committee on the Judiciary, *Reorganization of the Federal Judiciary, Hearings before the Committee on the Judiciary on S. 1352.* 75th Cong., 1st sess., 1937, pp. 42–43.

168. *Congressional Record*, 18 January 1936, p. 644.

169. *The New York Times*, 2 June 1936, p. 26.

170. *Public Papers of FDR*, 6:126–27.

171. Ibid., p. 130.

172. Reported by Arthur Krock, confidential memorandum, 13 April 1937, Box 1, p. 82A, Arthur Krock Papers, Princeton University.

173. *Public Papers of FDR*, 6:130.

174. See the discussion of the Legal Tender Cases in Stanley I. Kutler, *Judicial Power and Reconstruction Politics* (Chicago: University of Chicago Press, 1968), chap. 7.

175. See *Ex Parte* McCardle, 7 Wallace (74 U.S.) 506 (1869), which affirmed Congress's power to limit the Court's appellate jurisdiction, and U.S. v. Klein, 13 Wallace (80 U.S.) 128 (1872), which seems to limit that power.

176. A detailed discussion of the development of the Court-packing plan can be found in William E. Leuchtenburg, "The Origins of Franklin D. Roosevelt's 'Court-Packing' Plan," *Supreme Court Review* (1966), 347–400.

177. Joseph Alsop and Turner Catledge, *The 168 Days* (Garden City, N.Y.: Doubleday, Doran and Co., 1938), p. 29.

178. Leuchtenburg, "Origins of Roosevelt's 'Court-Packing' Plan," p. 394.

179. FDR to Felix Frankfurter, 15 January 1937, quoted in Freedman, ed., *Roosevelt and Frankfurter: Correspondence*, p. 377; Benjamin V. Cohen to Louis D. Brandeis, 30 July 1937, Cohen Papers.

180. *Public Papers of FDR*, 6:51–66.

181. Ibid., p. 55.

182. Ibid., p. 59.

183. Ibid., p. 60.

184. U.S. Congress, Senate, Committee on the Judiciary, *Report on the Reorganization of the Federal Judiciary, S. Rept. 711 to Accompany S. 1352*, 75th Cong., 1st sess., 1937, pp. 36–39.

185. Quoted in *The New York Times*, 6 February 1937, p. 10.

186. Quoted in *Literary Digest*, 13 February 1937, pp. 5–8.

187. Ibid.

188. Morgenthau diary, 15 February 1937, p. 95, Henry Morgenthau Papers, FDR Library.

189. All quotes from this speech are taken from *Public Papers of FDR*, 6:122–33.

190. Article written by Hapgood and sent to FDR, ca. 6 November 1936, President's Personal File 2278, Hapgood File, FDR Papers.

191. Morgenthau diary, 15 February 1937, p. 95, Morgenthau Papers.

192. *Literary Digest*, 13 February 1937, p. 6.

193. 17 June 1937, President's Secretary's File 186, FDR Papers.

194. McCloskey, *American Supreme Court*, p. 169.

195. U.S. Congress, Senate, Committee on the Judiciary, *Reorganization of the Federal Judiciary, Hearings* 75th Cong., 1st sess., 1937, p. 1461.

196. Julia E. Johnson, comp., *Reorganization of the Supreme Court* (New York: H. W. Wilson Co., 1937), p. 277.

197. U.S. Congress, Senate, Committee on the Judiciary, *Report on the Reorganization of the Federal Judiciary*, p. 276.

198. 300 U.S. 379 (1937).

199. 301 U.S. 1 (1937).

200. Ibid., at 41.

201. The controversy will likely continue forever, given that the Roberts papers no longer exist.

CHAPTER V

1. The word "relative" should perhaps be underscored here. Between 1937 and 1954 the Court decided many important cases, though rarely did it challenge state or federal power on an issue of critical importance. Among the cases in which the Court did do so were West Virginia v. Barnette, 319 U.S. 624 (1943), holding compulsory flag salutes in the public schools unconstitutional; and Youngstown Sheet & Tube v. Sawyer [The Steel Seizure Case], 343 U.S. 579 (1952), in which the Court struck down President Truman's seizure of U.S. steel mills during the Korean War. The Steel Seizure Case, however, represents less of a bold challenge to the political branches than is sometimes assumed; see the discussion in Maeva Marcus, *Truman and the Steel Seizure Case: The Limits of Presidential Power* (New York: Columbia University Press, 1977), pp. 212–17. During the 1937–54 period, moreover, the Court upheld federal power to intern Japanese-Americans during World War II (Korematsu v. U.S., 323 U.S. 214 [1944]); upheld broad restrictions on the liberties of alleged Communists (for example, in Dennis v. U.S., 341 U.S. 494 [1951]); and virtually abandoned judicial review of federal power to regulate the economy or of state power to do so when not in conflict with federal law. See the discussion in Robert McCloskey, *The American Supreme Court* (Chicago: University of Chicago Press, 1960), pp. 184–87.

2. Brown v. Board of Education [Brown I], 347 U.S. 483 (1954). Argued together with Brown I were cases arising from Kansas, South Carolina, Virginia, Delaware, and Washington, D.C. The last case was decided as Bolling v. Sharpe, 347 U.S. 497

(1954). The "separate but equal" doctrine had been laid down in Plessy v. Ferguson, 163 U.S. 537 (1896); cases before Brown striking down segregation in higher education include Missouri *ex rel.* Gaines v. Canada, 305 U.S. 337 (1938); Sipuel v. Oklahoma, 332 U.S. 631 (1948); Sweatt v. Painter, 339 U.S. 629 (1950); and Mc-Laurin v. Oklahoma State Regents, 339 U.S. 637 (1950).

3. In addition, four other states permitted but did not require segregated schools.

4. 349 U.S. 294 (1955). On Brown, generally, see Richard Kluger, *Simple Justice: The History of Brown v. Board of Education and America's Struggle for Equality*, 2 vols. (New York: Alfred A. Knopf, 1975), and Stephen L. Wasby, Anthony D'Amato, and Rosemary Metrailer, *Desegregation from Brown to Alexander: An Exploration of Supreme Court Strategies* (Carbondale: Southern Illinois University Press, 1977).

5. *Time*, 24 May 1954, p. 21.

6. *The New York Times*, 20 May 1954, p. 30.

7. George H. Gallup, *The Gallup Poll: Public Opinion 1935–71* (New York: Random House, 1972), 1:1249.

8. Ibid., p. 1251.

9. *The New Republic*, 24 May 1954, p. 3.

10. *The New York Times*, 18 May 1954, p. 1.

11. Harold C. Fleming, "The South Will Go Along," *The New Republic*, 31 May 1954, p. 6.

12. *Time*, 24 May 1954, p. 22.

13. *The New York Times*, 18 May 1954, p. 20.

14. Ibid.

15. *The New Republic*, 31 May 1954, p. 6.

16. *The New York Times*, 3 October 1954, p. 74.

17. Ibid., 26 September 1954, 4:6.

18. Ibid., 6 April 1955, p. 20.

19. Ibid.; 25 January 1955, p. 20; 6 April 1955, p. 20; 19 January 1955, p. 13; 12 January 1955, p. 19; *Atlanta Constitution*, 12 January 1955, p. 14.

20. Quoted in Kluger, *Simple Justice*, 2:930.

21. Brown v. Board of Education [Brown II], 349 U.S. 294 (1955), at 300–301.

22. For the former view, see J. Harvie Wilkinson III, *From Brown to Bakke: The Supreme Court and School Integration: 1954–1978* (New York: Oxford University Press, 1979), p. 66, quoting Loren Miller of the National Association for the Advancement of Colored People; for the opposite view, see Numan V. Bartley, *The Rise of Massive Resistance: Race and Politics in the South during the 1950's* (Baton Rouge: Louisiana State University Press, 1969).

23. *The New York Times*, 4 September 1955, p. 1.

24. Bartley, *Massive Resistance*, p. 84.

25. Quoted in Bernard Schwartz, *Super Chief: Earl Warren and His Supreme Court; A Judicial Biography* (New York: New York University Press, 1983), p. 170.

26. Robert F. Burk, *The Eisenhower Administration and Black Civil Rights* (Knoxville: University of Tennessee Press, 1984), pp. 134–50, 172; *The New York Times*, 26 January 1956, p. 12.

27. *The New York Times*, 14 February 1956, p. 18.

28. Ibid., 18 February 1956, p. 10; 16 February 1956, p. 28; 1 March 1956, p. 1.

29. 350 U.S. 551 (1956).

30. 351 U.S. 115 (1956).

31. 351 U.S. 536 (1956).

32. 350 U.S. 497 (1956).

33. *Congressional Record*, 11 April 1956, p. 6064.

34. *The New York Times*, 27 June 1956, p. 18.

35. *Congressional Record*, 16 April 1956, p. 6384.

36. Ibid., 22 May 1956, p. 8758.

37. Ibid., 10 May 1956, p. 7903; *Congressional Quarterly Almanac*, 1956, pp. 586–87.

38. *The New York Times*, 14 May 1956, p. 25; *Congressional Record*, 10 May 1956, p. 7994.

39. Bartley, *Massive Resistance*, p. 190.

40. 354 U.S. 449 (1957).

41. 353 U.S. 657 (1957).

42. Ibid., at 670, 672.

43. Ibid., at 675–77 (Burton, J., concurring).

44. 354 U.S. 178 (1957).

45. Ibid., at 205, 204.

46. 354 U.S. 298 (1957).

47. Ibid., at 315, 318.

48. Walter F. Murphy, *Congress and the Court* (Chicago: University of Chicago Press, 1962), pp. 120–21.

49. 71 *Statutes at Large* 595–96 (1957).

50. Murphy, *Congress and the Court*, p. 153. On the various versions of the Jencks Act prior to passage, and the act itself, see pp. 127–53.

51. S. 1411 as eventually passed by the Senate was an uncontroversial bill that had nothing to do with the Court; the summary given here represents the bill as modified by the House Post Office and Civil Service Committee.

52. U.S. Congress, Senate, *Limitation of Supreme Court Jurisdiction and Strengthening of Antisubversive Laws, S. Report 1586 to Accompany S. 2646*, 85th Cong., 2d sess., 1958, p. 2.

53. Murphy, *Congress and the Court*, p. 195.

54. Ibid., p. 200.

55. Bartley, *Massive Resistance*, p. 251.

56. Ibid., p. 261.

57. Ibid., p. 273.

58. Cooper v. Aaron, 358 U.S. 1 (1958), at 12.

59. Ibid., at 17.

60. Ibid., at 18.

61. Bartley, *Massive Resistance*, p. 331.

62. Shuttlesworth v. Birmingham, 368 U.S. 101 (1958).

63. Murphy, *Congress and the Court*, p. 4.

64. C. Herman Pritchett, *Congress versus the Supreme Court* (Minneapolis: University of Minnesota Press, 1961), pp. viii, vii.

65. See Murphy, *Congress and the Court*, pp. 245–46; Pritchett, *Congress versus the Court*, p. 121.

66. 369 U.S. 186 (1962), at 189, 253. See also Richard C. Cortner, *The Reapportionment Cases in Law and Politics* (Knoxville: University of Tennessee Press, 1970), pp. 28–30; Robert G. Dixon, *Democratic Representation: Reapportionment in Law and Politics* (New York: Oxford University Press, 1968), pp. 119–21; and Nelson W. Polsby, ed., *Reapportionment in the 1970s* (Berkeley and Los Angeles: University of California Press, 1971).

67. Colegrove v. Green, 328 U.S. 549 (1946), at 552, 556.

68. Matthews v. Handley, 361 U.S. 127 (1959).

69. Gomillion v. Lightfoot, 364 U.S. 339 (1960).

70. Quoted in Cortner, *The Reapportionment Cases*, p. 133.

71. *The New Republic*, 9 April 1962, p. 13.

72. Reynolds v. Sims, 377 U.S. 533 (1964) arose out of Alabama. It was decided together with cases arising from Colorado, Maryland, New York, Virginia, and Delaware. These other cases were Lucas v. Forty-Fourth General Assembly (Col.), 377 U.S. 713 (1964); WMCA v. Lomenzo (N.Y.), 377 U.S. 633 (1964); Maryland Commission for Fair Representation v. Tawes, 377 U.S. 656 (1964); Davis v. Mann (Va.), 377 U.S. 678 (1964); and Roman v. Sincock (Del.), 377 U.S. 695 (1964).

73. Reynolds v. Sims, 377 U.S. 533 (1964), at 577, 579–80.

74. Engel v. Vitale, 370 U.S. 421 (1962), at 430.

75. *The New Republic*, 9 July 1962, p. 4.

76. *The New York Times*, 27 June 1962, p. 34.

77. Quoted in *The New Republic*, 9 July 1962, p. 2.

78. *Congressional Record*, 8 August 1962, p. 15991.

79. *The New Republic*, 9 July 1962, p. 4.

80. John Knight, publisher of the Knight newspapers, quoted in *Congressional Record*, 1 August 1962, p. 15228.

81. *Congressional Record*, 27 July 1962, p. 14885.

82. *The New Republic*, 9 July 1962, p. 5.

83. Abington School District v. Schempp, 374 U.S. 203 (1963), together with Murray v. Curlett.

84. Ibid., at 314, 316.
85. *Congressional Record*, 16 June 1964, p. 13949.
86. *The Wall Street Journal*, 19 June 1963, p. 12.
87. *The New York Times*, 16 June 1964, p. 38.
88. *Congressional Quarterly Almanac*, 1964, p. 400.
89. Ibid., p. 401.
90. Ibid.
91. *Congressional Quarterly Almanac*, 1965, pp. 525–32.
92. On the Dirksen Amendment, see generally Dixon, *Democratic Representation*, pp. 385–436.
93. Gallup, *Public Opinion 1935–71*, 3:1897.
94. *Congressional Quarterly Almanac*, 1966, p. 516.
95. Ibid., p. 51.
96. Ibid., 1971, p. 625.
97. Ibid., pp. 624–29.
98. Ibid., 1979, pp. 396–98.
99. Ibid., p. 10-S.
100. *Congressional Record*, 9 September 1981, pp. 19833–34.
101. *Congressional Quarterly Almanac*, 1981, pp. 364–68.
102. *The New York Times*, 18 May 1984, p. 24.
103. *Congressional Quarterly Almanac*, 1982, pp. 403–5.
104. *The New York Times*, 11 March 1984, pp. 1, 32; *Greenville* [S.C.] *News*, 26 May 1985, pp. 1, 7, 8.
105. Wallace v. Jaffrey; Smith v. Jaffrey, 472 U.S. 38 (1985) (prelim. print); Bender v. Williamsport Area School Dist., No. 84-773, 54 L.W. 4307 (1986).
106. Rochin v. California, 342 U.S. 165 (1952); Spano v. New York, 360 U.S. 315 (1959).
107. 367 U.S. 643 (1961). Five justices agreed to apply the exclusionary rule to the states; three did not. One—Stewart—refused to consider the Fourth Amendment issue.
108. 338 U.S. 25 (1949).
109. 367 U.S. 643 (1961), at 654–55.
110. Gideon v. Wainwright, 372 U.S. 335 (1963).
111. 377 U.S. 201 (1964).
112. Ibid., at 206.
113. 378 U.S. 478 (1964).
114. 384 U.S. 436 (1966).
115. Ibid., at 439.
116. Ibid., at 440.
117. Ibid., at 478.
118. Ibid., at 444–45.
119. Justices Harlan, Stewart, and White dissented; Justice Clark dissented in three

of the cases decided with *Miranda* and concurred in the result in one, but in any event did not join in the opinion of the Court.

120. 384 U.S. 436 (1966), at 526, 530, 531, 542, 543.

121. All quotes in this paragraph are from *The New York Times*, 19 June 1966, 4:13.

122. For typical congressional responses, see *Congressional Record*, 20 June 1966, p. H3287a (Dague); 26 June 1966, p. H3298a (Derwinsky); 28 June 1966, p. H3448a (Michael); 19 July 1966, p. H3814a (Quillen); 28 July 1966, p. S17438 (Mundt); 29 July 1966, p. S17626 (Ervin); 8 August 1966, p. H18495 (Whitten); 10 August 1966, pp. S18874–79 (Byrd, W.Va.); 22 August 1966, p. H20127 (Hosmer); 1 September 1966, p. H21687 (Randall).

123. U.S. Bureau of the Census, *Historical Statistics of the United States, Colonial Times to 1970* (Washington, D.C.: Government Printing Office, 1975), p. 413.

124. 82 *Statutes at Large* 210–11 (1968).

125. *The New York Times*, 6 June 1968, p. 29.

126. *Congressional Quarterly Almanac*, 1968, p. 1046.

127. See, for example, *The New York Times*, 22 June 1968, p. 17; 1 August 1968, p. 18; 16 October 1968, p. 30; 3 November 1968, p. 77; 5 November 1968, p. 30.

128. See, for example, ibid., 11 March 1968, p. 1; 31 May 1968, p. 1.

129. Ibid., 11 September 1968, p. 29.

130. Ibid., 8 September 1968, p. 78.

131. Ibid., 3 November 1968, p. 79.

132. Theodore H. White, *The Making of the President, 1968* (New York: Atheneum, 1969), pp. 230–32. It is interesting to note that the Supreme Court is cited only three times in White's book, despite the fact that he devotes an entire chapter to the law-and-order issue.

133. Griffin v. County School Board of Prince Edward County, 377 U.S. 218 (1964).

134. Ibid., at 231.

135. Ibid., at 234.

136. Wilkinson, *From Brown to Bakke*, p. 108; *The New York Times*, 12 January 1968, p. 49.

137. 391 U.S. 430 (1968).

138. Ibid., at 437–39.

139. 395 U.S. 225 (1969). See Tinsley E. Yarbrough, *Judge Frank Johnson and Human Rights in Alabama* (University: University of Alabama Press, 1981), pp. 150–51.

140. 395 U.S. 225 (1969), at 228, 235.

141. 402 U.S. 1 (1971). See generally Bernard Schwartz, *Swann's Way: The School Busing Case and the Supreme Court* (New York: Oxford University Press, 1986).

142. 402 U.S. 1 (1971), at 29–31.

143. *The New York Times*, 7 August 1968, p. 30; 15 August 1968, p. 76; 2 October

Notes to Pages 200–206

1968, p. 27; *Weekly Compilation of Presidential Documents*, 26 October 1970, 6:1424; 9 November 1970, 6:1485.

144. *Detroit News*, 22 April 1971; *Philadelphia Inquirer*, 23 April 1971; *Pittsburgh Post-Gazette*, 22 April 1971.

145. *Chicago Daily News*, 22 April 1971; *The New York Times*, 23 April 1971; *Virginia Pilot*, 22 April 1971.

146. *Dallas Times-Herald*, 22 April 1971; *Richmond Times-Dispatch*, 25 April 1971; *Richmond Leader*, 21 April 1971.

147. *Richmond Times-Dispatch*, 25 April 1971; *Detroit News*, 22 April 1971.

148. Winston-Salem/Forsyth County Board of Education v. Scott, 404 U.S. 1221 (1971), at 1227–28 (emphasis added by Chief Justice Burger).

149. *U.S. News and World Report*, 24 January 1972, p. 30; Wilkinson, *From Brown to Bakke*, p. 151.

150. *The New York Times*, 15 March 1972, p. 1; 5 May 1972, p. 27; 8 May 1972, p. 42; 17 May 1972, pp. 1, 30; *Oklahoma City Daily Oklahoman*, 15 February 1972. Of the six leading candidates for the Democratic presidential nomination, only George McGovern and John Lindsay unequivocally supported busing (*U.S. News and World Report*, 28 February 1972, p. 28).

151. Public Law 92–318, 23 June 1972, 86 *Statutes at Large* 371–72.

152. *The New York Times*, 7 June 1972, p. 1; 9 June 1972, p. 16.

153. See, for example, ibid., 6 October 1972, p. 28; 22 October 1972, p. 52; 29 October 1972, p. 1.

154. Ibid., 4 October 1972, p. 32.

155. Ibid., 27 October 1972, p. 23.

156. 413 U.S. 189 (1973).

157. Wilkinson, *From Brown to Bakke*, p. 193.

158. 413 U.S. 189 (1973), at 208.

159. Ibid., pp. 210–13.

160. 418 U.S. 717 (1974).

161. Wilkinson, *From Brown to Bakke*, p. 219.

162. 418 U.S. 717 (1974), at 746. Justice Stewart filed a concurrence.

163. Ibid., at 744–45.

164. Ibid., at 814.

165. Ibid., at 763.

166. In later cases, the Court affirmed the central message of *Swann*, *Keyes*, and *Milliken*, though some of the justices (including Chief Justice Rehnquist) have argued that these later cases have actually expanded busing beyond the *Keyes-Milliken* boundaries. See Columbus Board of Education v. Penick, 443 U.S. 449 (1979), and Dayton Board of Education v. Brinkman, 443 U.S. 526 (1979), especially the dissenting opinions of Rehnquist. The Court has continued to insist on the distinction between de facto and de jure segregation, holding that the former does not require judicial interven-

tion. See Pasadena City Board of Education v. Spangle, 427 U.S. 424 (1976), rejecting a case based on the "resegregation" of a previously desegregated school system.

167. For an excellent discussion of the Boston case, see J. Anthony Lukas, *Common Ground: A Turbulent Decade in the Lives of Three American Families* (New York: Alfred A. Knopf, 1985).

168. Such prohibitions were passed by Congress in 1975 (*Congressional Quarterly Almanac*, 1975, pp. 894–97); 1976 (ibid., 1976, p. 576); 1977 (ibid., 1977, pp. 301–2, 307); 1978 (ibid., 1978, p. 107); 1979 (ibid., 1979, p. 107); 1980 (ibid., 1980, pp. 219, 223); and 1983 (ibid., 1983, p. 508).

169. *Congressional Quarterly Almanac*, 1977, pp. 510–11; ibid., 1978, p. 566.

170. Ibid., 1978, p. 183.

171. Ibid., 1979, p. 381.

172. *Congressional Quarterly Weekly Report*, 6 March 1982, p. 522.

173. *Congressional Quarterly Almanac*, 1979, p. 482.

174. Ibid., 1969, p. 130.

175. New York Times v. United States, 403 U.S. 713 (1971).

176. 413 U.S. 15 (1973).

177. San Antonio v. Rodriguez, 411 U.S. 1 (1973).

178. 418 U.S. 323 (1974).

179. Spence v. Washington, 418 U.S. 405 (1974).

180. Reed v. Reed, 404 U.S. 71 (1971).

181. U.S. v. Nixon, 418 U.S. 683 (1974). Rehnquist did not participate.

182. 410 U.S. 113 (1973).

183. Eva R. Rubin, *Abortion, Politics, and the Courts: Roe v. Wade and Its Aftermath* (Westport, Conn.: Greenwood Press, 1982); Betty Sarvis and Hyman Rodman, *The Abortion Controversy*, 2d ed. (New York: Columbia University Press, 1974), pp. 30–33. See also *Abortion in Nineteenth Century America*, Sex, Marriage and Society Series (New York: Arno Press, 1974).

184. Sarvis and Rodman, *Abortion Controversy*, pp. 30–33.

185. Rubin, *Abortion*, pp. 22–25.

186. 381 U.S. 471 (1965)

187. Eisenstadt v. Baird, 405 U.S. 440 (1972).

188. The leading article was Roy Lucas, "Federal Constitutional Limitations on the Enforcement and Administration of State Abortion Statutes," *North Carolina Law Review* 46 (1968): 730–38. The classic article on the question of privacy is, of course, Samuel D. Warren and Louis D. Brandeis, "The Right to Privacy," *Harvard Law Review* 4 (1890): 193–220. On privacy law, see generally David M. O'Brien, *Privacy, Law, and Public Policy* (New York: Praeger, 1979).

189. People v. Belous, 71 Cal.2d. 954, 458 P.2d. 194 (1969), quoted in Rubin, *Abortion*, p. 43.

190. Rubin, *Abortion*, pp. 42–55.

191. Roe v. Wade, 410 U.S. 113 (1973).

192. Doe v. Bolton, 410 U.S. 179 (1973), at 183. An interesting account of the events leading up to the decision can be found in Fred W. Friendly and Martha J. H. Elliott, *The Constitution: That Delicate Balance* (New York: Random House, 1984), pp. 188–208.

193. See Meyer v. Nebraska, 262 U.S. 390 (1923), striking down a state law prohibiting the teaching of foreign languages to children; Pierce v. Society of Sisters, 268 U.S. 510 (1925), upholding the right of parents to send their children to private schools; and Skinner v. Oklahoma, 316 U.S. 535 (1942), overturning on the basis of equal protection a state law requiring forced sterilization of thrice-convicted felons, on the grounds that procreation was "one of the basic civil rights of man."

194. 410 U.S. 113 (1973), at 116.

195. Ibid., at 153.

196. Ibid., at 159, 162–63.

197. Ibid., at 163.

198. Ibid., at 163–64.

199. Ibid., at 156–58.

200. Ibid., at 159.

201. Ibid., at 162.

202. See the discussion below of the Human Life Bill.

203. See the discussion of this issue, which pits Congress's power to enforce the Fourteenth Amendment (under section 5) against the Court's power to interpret it, in U.S. Congress, Senate, *The Human Life Bill, Hearings before the Subcommittee on Separation of Powers of the Committee on the Judiciary*, 97th Cong., 1st sess., 1981. On the "ratchet theory," so named because it suggests that Congress can increase but not decrease constitutional protections under the Fourteenth Amendment, see Katzenbach v. Morgan, 384 U.S. 641 (1966). "Congress's power under §5 [wrote Justice Brennan for the Court] is limited to adopting measures to enforce the guarantees of the [Fourteenth] Amendment; §5 grants Congress no power to restrict, abrogate, or dilute these guarantees." Ibid., at 651. See also William Cohen, "Congressional Power to Interpret Due Process and Equal Protection," *Stanford Law Review* 27 (1975): 603–20 and Jesse H. Choper, "Congressional Power to Expand Judicial Definitions of the Substantive Terms of the Civil War Amendments," *Minnesota Law Review* 67 (1982): 299–341.

204. Chief Justice Burger and Justices Douglas and Stewart concurred.

205. 410 U.S. 113 (1973), at 172–73.

206. Ibid., at 174.

207. Ibid., at 221–22.

208. Ibid., at 222.

209. *The New York Times*, 23 January 1973, p. 1.

210. Ibid., 18 February 1973, 4:10.

211. For one of the few direct attacks on *Roe* immediately after the decision, see *Congressional Record*, 23 January 1973, p. 1862 (Senator Allen).

212. *The New York Times*, 27 January 1973, p. 8.

213. Ibid., 1 June 1973, p. 12.

214. Ibid., 12 June 1973, p. 21.

215. U.S. Congress, Senate, *Abortion, Hearings before the Subcommittee on Constitutional Amendments of the Committee on the Judiciary*, 97th Cong., 1st sess. (1974).

216. Restrictions on abortion invalidated by the Supreme Court include: laws requiring spousal consent (Missouri v. Danforth, 428 U.S. 52 [1976]); laws requiring parental consent for minors (Belotti v. Baird, 448 U.S. 622 [1979]); and laws requiring that early abortions be performed in hospitals (Akron v. Akron Center for Reproductive Health (462 U.S. 416 [1983]). Akron also struck down a number of other regulations, including a requirement that *all* minors obtain the consent of one parent or of a court, a requirement that physicians provide information about possible physical and emotional complications resulting from the abortion procedure, and a mandatory twenty-four-hour waiting period prior to the actual abortion procedure.

217. *The New York Times*, 3 November 1973, p. 63; 6 November 1973, p. 77.

218. Connie Page, *The Right to Lifers: Who They Are, How They Operate, Where They Get Their Money* (New York: Summit Books, 1983), p. 151.

219. Ibid., p. 152.

220. *The New York Times*, 6 November 1980, p. 299; 7 November 1980, p. 16.

221. Ibid., 18 September 1974, p. 31; *Congressional Quarterly Almanac*, 1974, pp. 97, 106, 108.

222. *Congressional Quarterly Almanac*, 1975, p. 594.

223. Ibid., 1976, p. 790. Public Law 94–439, sec. 209, 90 *Statutes at Large* 1434 (30 September 1976).

224. Maher v. Roe, 432 U.S. 464 (1977), at 474.

225. *Congressional Quarterly Almanac*, 1977, p. 295.

226. Harris v. McRae, 448 U.S. 297 (1980).

227. *The New York Times*, 18 July 1980, pp. 10, 12; 1980 Republican Platform, printed in *Congressional Quarterly Almanac*, 1980, pp. 58B–84B. The antiabortion planks appear on pp. 62B and 74B.

228. Henry J. Hyde, "The Human Life Bill: Some Issues and Answers," *Human Life Review* 8 (1982): 9.

229. *Congressional Quarterly Almanac*, 1982, pp. 403–4.

230. *Congressional Record*, 27 June 1983, p. S9097. For criticism of the proposed amendment from the pro-choice side, see generally *Congressional Record*, 27–28 June 1983.

231. Akron v. Akron Center for Reproductive Health, 462 U.S. 416 (1983).

232. Thornburgh v. American College of Obstetricians and Gynecologists, 476 U.S. 747 (1986) [prelim. print], 106 S.Ct. 2169 (1986).

233. Elder Witt, *A Different Justice: Reagan and the Supreme Court* (Washington, D.C.: Congressional Quarterly, 1986), p. 176.

234. Ibid., pp. 176–77.

235. Ibid., p. 176.

236. *The New York Times*, 18 September 1985, p. 15.

237. Ibid., 9 January 1986, p. 23.

238. Ibid., 16 November 1985, p. 9; see also the remarks of Terry Eastland, 9 January 1986, p. 23.

239. Witt, *A Different Justice*, p. 173.

240. Ibid., p. 177.

241. Ibid., p. 185. See also the remarks of Thurgood Marshall, *Washington Post*, 7 May 1987, pp. A1, A18.

242. See, for example, Louis Fisher, "Methods of Constitutional Interpretation: The Limits of Original Intent," *Cumberland Law Review* 18 (1987–88): 43–67, and H. Jefferson Powell, "The Original Understanding of Original Intent," *Harvard Law Review* 98 (1985): 885–948.

243. Robert H. Bork, "Tradition and Morality in Constitutional Law," in Mark W. Cannon and David M. O'Brien, eds., *Views from the Bench: The Judiciary and Constitutional Politics* (Chatham, N.J.: Chatham House Publishers, 1985), p. 170.

244. Ibid., pp. 169.

245. Ibid., pp. 169–70.

246. Ibid., p. 170.

247. Ibid., pp. 171–72, 169.

248. This summary is taken largely from Walter Berns, "Judicial Review and the Rights and Laws of Nature," in his *In Defense of Liberal Democracy* (Chicago: Gateway Editions, 1984), pp. 29–62. See in the same volume Berns's "The Constitution as a Bill of Rights," pp. 1–28, and his "Has the Burger Court Gone Too Far?" *Commentary* 78 (1984): 27–33.

249. Gary L. McDowell, "A Modest Remedy for Judicial Activism," *Public Interest* no. 67 (1982): 15–20; Berns, "Constitution as a Bill of Rights," p. 20.

250. U.S. Congress, Senate Committee on the Judiciary, *Court-Ordered School Busing, Hearings before the Subcommittee on the Separation of Powers of the Committee on the Judiciary*, 97th Cong., 1st sess., 1981, p. 267.

251. U.S. Congress, Senate Committee on the Judiciary, *Constitutional Amendments Relating to Abortion, Hearings before the Subcommittee on the Constitution of the Committee on the Judiciary*, 2 vols., 97th Cong., 1st sess., 1981, 1:1243.

252. McDowell, "Modest Remedy," pp. 18–19.

253. Antonin Scalia, "A Note on the Benzene Case," *Regulation* (July/August 1980): 28.

254. U.S. Congress, Senate Committee on the Judiciary, *Proposed Constitutional Amendment to Permit Voluntary Prayer, Hearings before the Committee on the Judiciary on S. J. Res. 199*, 97th Cong., 2d sess., pp. 27–28.

255. Ibid., p. 155.

256. See *Court-Ordered School Busing, Hearings*, p. 442 (Helms); p. 468 (Ervin); *Constitutional Amendments Relating to Abortion, Hearings*, 1:14–20 (Hatch); 1:1216–18 (Professor Robert M. Byrn, Fordham University School of Law).

257. Statement of Nellie Gray, president of the March for Life, *Constitutional Amendments Relating to Abortion, Hearings*, 1:1173.

258. Edwin Meese III, "The Law of the Constitution," speech at Tulane University, New Orleans, La., 21 October 1986, pp. 7, 12–13.

259. Raoul Berger, "The Role of the Supreme Court," *University of Arkansas at Little Rock Law Journal* 3 (1980): 3.

260. "My own view in the area of abortion is that I am opposed to it as a matter of birth control or otherwise," O'Connor said. (U.S. Congress, Senate Committee on the Judiciary, *The Nomination of Judge Sandra Day O'Connor of Arizona to Serve as an Associate Justice of the Supreme Court of the United States, Hearings before the Committee on the Judiciary*, 97th Cong., 1st. sess., 1981, p. 61.) See also p. 98.

261. Ibid., p. 199.

262. 462 U.S. 416 (1983), at 452–75.

263. Lynch v. Donnelly, 465 U.S. 668 (1984); Regan v. Wald, 468 U.S. 222 (1984); City of Los Angeles v. Lyons, 461 U.S. 95 (1983); Dun and Bradstreet v. Greenmoss Builders, 472 U.S. 749 (1985) [prelim. print].

264. Mississippi University for Women v. Hogan, 458 U.S. 718 (1982); New York v. Quarles, 467 U.S. 649 (1984). For an excellent and thorough discussion of O'Connor's record through the 1984–85 term, see Witt, *A Different Justice*, pp. 45–73.

265. The appointment process has been the subject of considerable debate and discussion in recent years; see, for example, Lawrence Tribe, *God Save This Honorable Court: How the Choice of Supreme Court Justices Shapes Our History* (New York: Random House, 1985). For a scholarly study of the appointments process in historical terms, see Henry J. Abraham, *Justices and Presidents: A Political History of Appointments to the Supreme Court* (New York: Oxford University Press, 1974).

266. See Witt, *A Different Justice*, chaps. 6, 7.

267. *Washington Post*, 1 September 1982.

268. *Los Angeles Times*, 9 September 1982.

269. See the following constitutional amendments, all introduced in the 98th and 99th Congresses: S.J.Res. 39 and H.J.Res. 17 (98th Congress), providing for a ten-year term for federal judges; H.J.Res. 264 (98th Congress), requiring reconfirmation of judges by the Senate at designated intervals; H.J.Res. 90, 144, 252, and 374 (98th

Congress), regarding judicial tenure; H.J.Res. 557 (99th Congress), providing for a fifteen-year term for federal judges. Many similar amendments have been introduced in years past.

270. Oregon v. Mitchell, 400 U.S. 112 (1970), overturned by the Twenty-sixth Amendment in 1971.

271. U.S. Constitution, Art. III, sec. 2 (emphasis added).

272. Raoul Berger, for example, argues that Article III gives Congress the power only to shift the Court's cases between the original and appellate jurisdiction (*Congress v. the Supreme Court* [Cambridge: Harvard University Press, 1969], pp. 285–96). Henry M. Hart, Jr., in a classic article, argued that Congress could not use its power over the Court's jurisdiction to strip the Court of its "essential function" in the American political system ("The Power of Congress to Limit the Jurisdiction of the Federal Courts: An Exercise in Dialectic," *Harvard Law Review* 66 [1953]: 1352–1402). After a review of the arguments, Lawrence Gene Sager finds that Congress's power under Article III is "fully bound by the constitutional provisions that ordinarily constrain its behavior" ("Forward: Constitutional Limitations on Congress' Authority to Regulate the Jurisdiction of the Federal Courts," *Harvard Law Review* 95 [1981]: 30). See Sager's article generally, and pp. 37–42 and the sources cited there.

273. Among the most important examples are the Norris–La Guardia Act, 47 *Statutes at Large* 70 (1932); the Emergency Price Control Act of 1942, 56 *Statutes at Large* 23 (1942); and the Portal-to-Portal Act, 29 U.S.C. secs. 251–62 (1976). See generally Sager, "Forward," pp. 68–74.

274. Glidden Co. v. Zdanok, 370 U.S. 530, at 605 n. 11.

275. U.S Congress, Senate Committee on the Judiciary, *Constitutional Restraints upon the Judiciary, Hearings before the Subcommittee on the Constitution of the Committee on the Judiciary*, 97th Cong., 1st. sess., 1981, p. 53 (statement of Paul M. Bator).

276. Ibid., p. 98.

277. *The New York Times*, 9 September 1982, p. 1.

278. *Constitutional Restraints Upon the Judiciary, Hearings*, p. 238.

279. *Washington Post*, 3 May 1981, p. C7.

280. *Court-Ordered School Busing, Hearings*, pp. 266–67.

281. Ibid., p. 503.

282. *Constitutional Restraints Upon the Judiciary, Hearings*, p. 268.

283. Ibid., p. 163. See also Charles E. Rice, "Congress and the Supreme Court's Jurisdiction," *Villanova Law Review* 27 (1981–82): 959–87.

284. For an interesting summary of White's career and of his shift to the right in the 1980s, see Nathan Lewin, "White's Flight," *The New Republic*, 27 August 1984, pp. 17–20. See also Witt, *A Different Justice*, pp. 52–53.

285. T. Nairn, "The Future of Britain's Crisis," *New Left Review*, 113/114 (1979), p. 44.

286. The percentage of Americans rating the Court's record as "excellent" or "good" dropped from 43 percent in 1963 and 45 percent in 1967 to 36 percent in 1968 and only 33 percent in 1969. The percentage of Americans expressing a "great deal" or "quite a lot" of confidence in the Court measured 44 percent in 1973, 49 percent in 1975, 46 percent in 1977, 45 percent in 1979, and 46 percent in 1981. It fell to only 42 percent in 1983, then rose to 51 percent in 1984, and 56 percent in 1985. Sources: 1973–85 data from *Gallup Reports* no. 238 (July 1985), p. 3. Earlier data from George H. Gallup, *The Gallup Poll: Public Opinion 1935–71* (New York: Random House, 1972), 3:1836–37, 2068, 2147, 2200–2201.

287. Walter F. Murphy and Joseph Tanenhaus, "Public Opinion and the United States Supreme Court: A Preliminary Mapping of of Some Prerequisites for Court Legitimation of Regime Changes," in Joel B. Grossman and Joseph Tanenhaus, eds., *Frontiers of Judicial Research* (New York: John Wiley, 1969), pp. 290–91. See also Tanenhaus and Murphy, "Patterns of Public Support for the Supreme Court: A Panel Study," *Journal of Politics* 43 (1981): 24–39.

288. Roger Handberg and William S. Maddox, "Public Support for the Supreme Court in the 1970s," *American Politics Quarterly* 10 (1982): 333–46; citation at 340–41, emphasis added.

289. David Adamany and Joel B. Grossman, "Support for the Supreme Court as a National Policymaker," *Law and Policy Quarterly* 5 (1983): 405–37.

290. Ibid., p. 413.

CHAPTER VI

1. Robert G. McCloskey, *The American Supreme Court* (Chicago: University of Chicago Press, 1960), pp. 18–19.

2. Ibid., p. 23.

3. Ibid., p. 100.

4. Alexander Bickel, *The Least Dangerous Branch: The Supreme Court at the Bar of Politics* (Indianapolis: Bobbs-Merrill, 1962), p. 258.

5. Walter F. Murphy, *Congress and the Court* (Chicago: University of Chicago Press, 1962), p. 2.

6. United States v. Richardson, 418 U.S. 166 (1974), at 192 (Powell, concurring).

7. Robert A. Dahl, "Decision-Making in a Democracy: The Supreme Court as a National Policy-Maker," *Journal of Public Law* 6 (1957): 291, 294. Dahl's conclusion has been echoed down through the years by a generation of public law scholars. See, for example, Richard Funston, "The Supreme Court and Critical Elections," *American Political Science Review* 69 (1975): 795–811; David Adamany, "Legitimacy, Realigning Elections, and the Supreme Court," *Wisconsin Law Review* 1973 (1973), 790–846.

8. McCloskey, *American Supreme Court*, pp. 229–30.

9. *Federalist* No. 78.

10. McCloskey, *American Supreme Court*, pp. 12–13.

11. Bickel, *Least Dangerous Branch*, p. 27.

12. Louis Hartz, *The Liberal Tradition in America: An Interpretation of American Political Thought since the Revolution* (New York: Harcourt, Brace and Co., 1955), p. 9.

13. Ibid., pp. 281–82n.

14. Ibid., p. 281.

15. Dahl, "Decision-Making in a Democracy," p. 293.

16. Walter Dean Burnham, *Critical Elections and the Mainsprings of American Politics* (New York: W. W. Norton and Co., 1970), pp. 181–82.

17. Ibid., p. 181.

18. Ibid., p. 183.

19. Bickel, *Least Dangerous Branch*, p. 28.

20. *Federalist* No. 78.

21. Robert H. Jackson, *The Struggle for Judicial Supremacy: A Study of a Crisis in American Power Politics* (New York: Alfred A. Knopf, 1941), pp. 321–22.

22. Edward S. Corwin, *The Twilight of the Supreme Court: A History of Our Constitutional Theory* (New Haven: Yale University Press, 1934).

23. Charles Black, *The People vs. the Court: Judicial Review in a Democracy* (New York: Macmillan, 1960), p. 224.

24. Charles Evans Hughes, *The Supreme Court of the United States, Its Foundation, Methods and Achievements: An Interpretation* (New York: Columbia University Press, 1928), pp. 50, 55.

25. McCloskey, *American Supreme Court*, p. 51; see also Hartz, *Liberal Tradition*, p. 9.

26. Impeachment of Supreme Court justices for political purposes has not been seriously considered by the Congress, in fact, since the attempt to impeach the first Justice Chase in the early nineteenth century.

27. Carl Brent Swisher, *Roger B. Taney* (New York: Macmillan, 1935), pp. 581–82. Upon the death of Chief Justice Chase in 1873, money for busts of both Chase and Taney was approved by Congress without incident.

28. James L. Sundquist, *Dynamics of the Party System: Alignment and Realignment of Political Parties in the United States*, rev. ed. (Washington, D.C.: Brookings Institution, 1983), p. 442.

29. David Adamany and Joel B. Grossman, "Support for the Supreme Court as a National Policymaker," *Law and Policy Quarterly* 5 (October 1983): 425.

30. The list, from 1954 to 1981, includes keeping peace (1954–63); race relations (1957, 1963–65); Vietnam (1966–72); high cost of living (1967, 1971, 1973–81); Watergate (1972); unemployment (1958, 1975–77, 1980–81); and energy problems

(1978–79). (More than one problem was listed in certain years.) *Gallup Report*, no. 198 (March 1982), p. 27.

31. A Gallup poll taken in the summer of 1968 revealed that 52 percent of the American people regarded the war as the "most important problem facing the country today," compared with only 29 percent who listed "crime and lawlessness." The poll grouped under "crime and lawlessness" the following issues: "riots, looting, juvenile delinquency." *Miranda* was not listed. George H. Gallup, *The Gallup Poll: Public Opinion 1935–71* (New York: Random House, 1972), 3:2107.

32. Busing was a major issue in the 1972 primaries but was overwhelmed by other issues in the general election. In August 1972, 25 percent of those polled listed Vietnam as the most important issue; 23 percent, inflation; and 10 percent, crime and lawlessness; George H. Gallup, *The Gallup Poll: Public Opinion 1972–77* (Wilmington: Scholarly Resources Inc., 1978), 1:48. In 1980 the most important issues were inflation (74 percent) and international problems (17 percent). The only issue even remotely related to the Court was crime, at 2 percent (*The Gallup Poll Index*, April–May 1980, no. 177, p. 25). In 1984, the most important issues were cited as foreign policy/defense (27 percent); unemployment (26 percent); inflation (14 percent); government spending (11 percent); and crime (3 percent), *Gallup Report*, no. 226 (July 1984), p. 17. The abortion issue appeared during the campaign as one issue among several, but was cited by only 8 percent of voters as one of the two most important factors leading to their final vote; even "born again" white Christians put the abortion issue third behind the economy and defense, and only 8 percent of Catholics cited abortion as a key issue compared to 41 percent who cited economic issues (*The New York Times*, 11 November 1984, 1:30; 25 November 1984, 4:2). The issue of Ronald Reagan's potential appointments to the Supreme Court surfaced in the 1984 presidential debates but was ultimately unimportant compared to the economy, the Reagan record, and Reagan's personal appeal. The major effect of the various religion-related issues, writes Gerald Pomper, was to "distract attention" from other issues (*The Election of 1984*, pp. 3, 74).

33. U.S. v. Butler, 297 U.S. 1 (1936), at 78–79.

34. McCloskey, *American Supreme Court*, p. 231.

35. Bickel, *Least Dangerous Branch*, p. 239.

36. *Federalist* No. 78, emphasis added.

37. Alexander M. Bickel, *The Supreme Court and the Idea of Progress* (New Haven: Yale University Press, 1978), p. 179.

Bibliography

GENERAL WORKS

Abraham, Henry J. *The Judicial Process*. 5th ed. New York: Oxford University Press, 1986.

———. *Justices and Presidents: A Political History of Appointments to the Supreme Court*. New York: Oxford University Press, 1974.

Adamany, David. "Law and Society: Realigning Elections and the Supreme Court." *Wisconsin Law Review* 1973 (1973): 790–846.

Ball, Howard. *Courts and Politics: The Federal Judicial System*. 2d ed. Englewood Cliffs, N.J.: Prentice Hall, 1987.

Beard, Charles A. *The Supreme Court and the Constitution*. New York: Macmillan Co., 1912. Reprint, Englewood Cliffs, N.J.: Prentice Hall, 1962.

Beck, Paul Allen. "Critical Elections and the Supreme Court: Putting the Cart after the Horse." *American Political Science Review* 70 (1976): 930–32.

———. "The Electoral Cycle and Patterns of American Politics." *British Journal of Political Science* 9 (April 1979): 129–36.

———. "A Socialization Theory of Partisan Realignment." In *The Politics of Future Citizens: New Dimensions in the Political Socialization of Children*, edited by Richard G. Niemi. San Francisco: Jossey-Bass, 1974.

Bickel, Alexander. "The Decade of School Desegregation: Progress and Prospects." *Columbia Law Review* 64 (1964): 193–229.

———. "Forward: The Passive Virtues." *Harvard Law Review* 75 (1961): 40–79.

———. *The Least Dangerous Branch: The Supreme Court at the Bar of Politics*. Indianapolis: Bobbs-Merrill Co., 1962.

———. *The Morality of Consent*. New Haven: Yale University Press, 1975.

———. *The Supreme Court and the Idea of Progress*. New Haven: Yale University Press, 1978.

Black, Charles. *The People and the Court*. New York: Macmillan Co., 1960.

Blaustein, Albert B., and Mersky, Roy P. *The First One Hundred Justices: Statistical Studies on the Supreme Court of the United States*. Hamden, Conn.: Archon Books, 1978.

Burnham, Walter Dean. *The Crisis of American Politics*. New York: Oxford University Press, 1982.

Bibliography

_____. *Critical Elections and the Mainsprings of American Politics*. New York: W. W. Norton and Co., 1970.

Campbell, Angus; Converse, Philip E.; Miller, Warren E.; and Stokes, Donald E. *The American Voter*. New York: John Wiley, 1960.

Cannon, Mark W., and O'Brien, David M., eds. *Views From the Bench: The Judiciary and Constitutional Politics*. Chatham, N.J.: Chatham House Publishers, 1985.

Canon, Bradley C., and Ulmer, S. Sidney. "The Supreme Court and Critical Elections: A Dissent." *American Political Science Review* 70 (1976): 1215–21.

Carter, Lief. *Contemporary Constitutional Lawmaking: The Supreme Court and the Art of Politics*. New York: Pergamon Press, 1985.

Chambers, William Nisbet, and Burnham, Walter Dean. *The American Party Systems: Stages of Political Development*. New York: Oxford University Press, 1975.

Choper, Jesse H. *Judicial Review and the National Political Process: A Functional Reconsideration of the Role of the Supreme Court*. Chicago: University of Chicago Press, 1980.

Clubb, Jerome M.; Flanigan, William H.; and Zingale, Nancy H. *Partisan Realignment: Voters, Parties, and Government in American History*. Beverly Hills, Calif.: Sage Publications, 1980.

Converse, Philip E.; Miller, Warren E.; and Stokes, Donald E. *Elections and the Political Order*. New York: John Wiley, 1966.

Corwin, Edward S. *The "Higher Law" Background of American Constitutional Law*. Ithaca, N.Y.: Cornell University Press, 1965.

Cox, Archibald. *The Role of the Supreme Court in American Government*. New York: Oxford University Press, 1976.

Culp, Maurice S. "A Survey of the Proposals to Limit or Deny the Power of Judicial Review by the Supreme Court of the United States." *Indiana Law Journal* 4 (1929): 386–98, 474–90.

Dahl, Robert A. "Decision-Making in a Democracy: The Supreme Court as a National Policy-Maker." *Journal of Public Law* 6 (1957): 279–95.

Elazar, Daniel. "The Generational Rhythm of American Politics." *American Politics Quarterly* 6 (January 1978): 55–94.

Elliott, Shelden D. "Court-Curbing Proposals in Congress." *Notre Dame Lawyer* 33 (1958): 597–612.

Ely, John Hart. *Democracy and Distrust: A Theory of Judicial Review*. Cambridge: Harvard University Press, 1980.

Ernst, Morris L. *The Great Reversals*. New York: Weybright and Talley, 1973.

Friedman, Leon, and Israel, Fred L., eds. *The Justices of the United States Supreme Court 1789–1969: Their Lives and Major Opinions*. 5 vols. New York: Chelsea House Publishers, 1969.

Funston, Richard. "The Supreme Court and Critical Elections." *American Political*

Science Review 69 (1975): 795–811.

Gaziano, Cecelie. "Relationship between Public Opinion and Supreme Court Decisions: Was Mr. Dooley Right?" *Communication Research* 5 (1978): 131–49.

Gunther, Gerald. *Cases and Materials on Constitutional Law*. 11th ed. Mineola, N.Y.: Foundation Press, 1985.

Halpern, Stephen C., and Lamb, Charles M. *Supreme Court Activism and Restraint*. Lexington, Mass.: Lexington Books, 1982.

Hartz, Louis. *The Liberal Tradition in America: An Interpretation of American Political Thought since the Revolution*. New York: Harcourt, Brace, 1955.

Hughes, Charles Evans. *The Supreme Court of the United States, Its Foundation, Methods and Achievements: An Interpretation*. New York: Columbia University Press, 1928.

Israel, Fred L., and Schlesinger, Arthur M., eds. *History of American Presidential Elections 1789–1968*. 4 vols. New York: Chelsea House Publishers, 1971.

Jackson, Robert H. *The Struggle for Judicial Supremacy: A Study of a Crisis in American Power Politics*. New York: Alfred A. Knopf, 1941.

_____. *The Supreme Court in the American System of Government*. New York: Harper and Row, 1963.

Key, V. O. *Politics, Parties, and Pressure Groups*. 5th ed. New York: Thomas Y. Crowell Co., 1964.

Kleppner, Paul, et al. *The Evolution of American Electoral Systems*. Westport, Conn.: Greenwood Press, 1981.

Kurland, Philip B. *Politics, the Constitution, and the Warren Court*. Chicago: University of Chicago Press, 1970.

Ladd, Everett Carll, Jr. *American Political Parties: Social Change and Political Response*. New York: W. W. Norton and Co., 1970.

Lasser, William. "Crisis and the Court: Judicial Politics in Periods of Critical Realignment." Ph.D. Diss., Harvard University, 1983.

_____. "The Supreme Court in Periods of Critical Realignment." *Journal of Politics* 47 (1985): 1174–87.

Levy, Leonard W. *Judicial Review, History and Democracy: An Introduction to Judicial Review and the Supreme Court*. New York: Harper and Row, 1967.

_____, ed. *The Supreme Court under Earl Warren*. New York: Harper and Row, 1972.

Lichtman, Allen J. "Critical Election Theory and the Reality of American Presidential Politics, 1916–40." *American Historical Review* 81 (April 1976): 317–48.

McCloskey, Robert G. *The American Supreme Court*. Chicago: University of Chicago Press, 1960.

_____. *The Modern Supreme Court*. Cambridge: Harvard University Press, 1972.

McCormick, Richard L. "The Realignment Synthesis in American History." *Journal of Interdisciplinary History* 13 (Summer 1982): 85–105.

Bibliography

Mayer, George H. *The Republican Party 1854–1964*. New York: Oxford University Press, 1964.

Murphy, Walter F. *Congress and the Court*. Chicago: University of Chicago Press, 1962.

———. *Elements of Judicial Strategy*. Chicago: University of Chicago Press, 1964.

Nagel, Stuart S. "Court-Curbing Periods in American History." *Vanderbilt Law Review* 18 (1965): 925–44.

Nie, Norman H.; Verba, Sidney; and Petrocik, John. *The Changing American Voter*. Cambridge: Harvard University Press, 1976.

O'Brien, David M. *Storm Center: The Supreme Court in American Politics*. New York: W. W. Norton and Co., 1986.

Pomper, Gerald. "Classification of Presidential Elections." *The Journal of Politics* 29 (August 1967): 535–66.

———. *Elections in America*. New York: Dodd, Mead Co., 1968.

Porter, Kirk H., and Johnson, Donald Bruce, comps. *National Party Platforms: 1840–1968*. Urbana: University of Illinois Press, 1970.

Posner, Richard A. *The Federal Courts: Crisis and Reform*. Cambridge: Harvard University Press, 1985.

Pritchett, C. Herman. *Congress versus the Supreme Court*. Minneapolis: Minnesota University Press, 1961.

Samuels, Richard J. *Political Generations and Political Development*. Lexington, Mass.: Lexington Books, 1977.

Scigliano, Robert. *The Supreme Court and the Presidency*. New York: Macmillan Co., 1971.

Steamer, Robert J. *The Supreme Court in Crisis: A History of Conflict*. Amherst: University of Massachusetts Press, 1971.

Strum, Phillipa. *The Supreme Court and Political Questions: A Study in Judicial Evasion*. University: University of Alabama Press, 1974.

Sundquist, James L. *Dynamics of the Party System: Alignment and Realignment of Political Parties in the United States*. Rev. ed. Washington, D.C.: Brookings Institution, 1983.

Swindler, William F. *Court and Constitution in the Twentieth Century*. 3 vols. Indianapolis: Bobbs-Merrill Co., 1969.

Swisher, Carl Brent. *American Constitutional Development*. Westport, Conn.: Greenwood Press, 1978.

———. *The Supreme Court in Modern Role*. New York: New York University Press, 1958.

Tribe, Lawrence H. *American Constitutional Law*. Mineola, N.Y.: Foundation Press, 1978.

U.S. Bureau of the Census. *Historical Statistics of the United States, Colonial Times to 1970*. Washington, D.C.: Government Printing Office, 1975.

Bibliography

Warren, Charles. *The Supreme Court in United States History, 1836–1918.* 2 vols. Boston: Little, Brown and Co., 1926.

THE *DRED SCOTT* CASE

Acheson, Dean G. "Roger Brooke Taney: Notes upon Judicial Self-Restraint." *Illinois Law Review* 31 (1937): 705–17.

Auchampaugh, Philip. "James Buchanan, the Court, and the Dred Scott Case." *Tennessee Historical Magazine* 9 (1926): 231–40.

Baker, George E., ed. *The Works of William Henry Seward.* 5 vols. Boston: Houghton Mifflin, 1884.

Bander, Edward J. "The Dred Scott Case and Judicial Statesmanship." *Villanova Law Review* 6 (1961): 514–24.

Bardolph, Richard. *The Civil Rights Record: Black Americans and the Law, 1849–1970.* New York: Crowell, 1970.

Barney, William. *The Road to Secession: A New Perspective on the Old South.* New York: Praeger, 1972.

Bartlett, Ruhl Jacob. *John C. Fremont and the Republican Party.* Columbus: Ohio State University Press, 1930.

Basler, Roy P., ed. *The Collected Works of Abraham Lincoln.* 9 vols. New Brunswick, N.J.: Rutgers University Press, 1953.

Bell, Derrick A., ed. *Race, Racism, and American Law.* Boston: Little, Brown, 1973.

Belz, Herman. *Emancipation and Equal Rights: Politics and Constitutionalism in the Civil War Era.* New York: W. W. Norton and Co., 1978.

Benton, Thomas Hart. *Historical and Legal Examination of that Part of the Decision of the Supreme Court of the United States in the Dred Scott Case, Which Declares the Unconstitutionality of the Missouri Compromise Act. . . .* New York: Appleton, 1857. Reprint. New York: Kraus Reprint Co., 1969.

――――. *Thirty Years' View . . . 1820 to 1850.* 2 vols. New York: Appleton, 1854–56.

Berlin, Ira. *Slaves without Masters: The Free Negro in the Antebellum South.* New York: Pantheon Books, 1975.

Berwanger, Eugene H. *The Frontier against Slavery: Western Anti-Negro Prejudice and the Slavery Extension Controversy.* Urbana: University of Illinois Press, 1967.

Bestor, Arthur. "The American Civil War as a Constitutional Crisis." *American Historical Review* 69 (1963–64): 327–52.

――――. "State Sovereignty and Slavery: A Reinterpretation of Proslavery Constitutional Doctrine, 1846–1860." *Journal of the Illinois State Historical Society* 54 (1961): 117–80.

Bibliography

Beveridge, Albert J. *Abraham Lincoln, 1809–1858*. 4 vols. Boston: Houghton Mifflin Co., 1928.

Blue, Frederick S. *The Free Soilers: Third Party Politics 1848–54*. Urbana: University of Illinois Press, 1973.

Burnham, Walter Dean. *Presidential Ballots, 1836–1892*. Baltimore: Johns Hopkins University Press, 1955.

Capers, Gerald M. *Stephen A. Douglas, Defender of the Union*. Edited by Oscar Handlin. Boston: Little, Brown, 1959.

Catterall, Helen T. *Judicial Cases Concerning American Slavery and the Negro*. 5 vols. New York: Octagon Books, 1968.

———. "Some Antecedents of the Dred Scott Case." *American Historical Review* 30 (1924): 56–71.

Catton, Bruce. "The Dred Scott Case." In *Quarrels That Have Shaped the Constitution*, edited by John A. Garraty. New York: Harper and Row, 1975.

Chambers, William Nisbet. *Old Bullion Benton, Senator from the New West: Thomas Hart Benton, 1782–1858*. Boston: Little, Brown, 1956.

Congressional Globe, 1854–1861.

Connor, Henry G. *John Archibald Campbell, Associate Justice of the United States Supreme Court*. Boston: Houghton Mifflin, 1920.

Corwin, Edward S. "The Dred Scott Decision in the Light of Contemporary Legal Doctrines." *American Historical Review* 17 (1911): 52–69.

Cover, Robert M. *Justice Accused: Antislavery and the Judicial Process*. New Haven: Yale University Press, 1975.

Crandall, Andrew Wallace. *The Early History of the Republican Party*. Boston: R. G. Badger, 1930.

Craven, Avery O. *The Coming of the Civil War*. 2d ed. Chicago: University of Chicago Press, 1957.

———. *The Growth of Southern Nationalism 1848–1861*. Baton Rouge: Louisiana State University Press, 1953.

Crenshaw, Ollinger. *The Slave States in the Presidential Election of 1860*. Baltimore: Johns Hopkins University Press, 1945.

Curtis, Benjamin R. Jr., ed. *A Memoir of Benjamin Robbins Curtis, LL.D, with some of his Professional and Miscellaneous Writings*. 2 vols. Boston: Little, Brown, 1879. Reprint. New York: Da Capo Press, 1970.

Curtis, George Ticknor. *Constitutional History of the United States: From the Declaration of Independence to the Close of the Civil War*. 2 vols. New York: Harper and Brothers, 1903.

Davis, David Brion. *The Slave Power Conspiracy and the Paranoid Style*. Baton Rouge: Louisiana State University Press, 1970.

Donald, David. *Charles Sumner and the Coming of the Civil War*. New York: Knopf, 1960.

Bibliography

————. *Lincoln Reconsidered: Essays on the Civil War Era*. 2d ed. New York: Knopf, 1966.

Duberman, Martin, ed. *The Antislavery Vanguard: New Essays on the Abolitionists*. Princeton: Princeton University Press, 1965.

Dumond, Dwight L. *Antislavery: The Crusade for Freedom in America*. New York: W. W. Norton and Co., 1966.

————. *The Secession Movement, 1860–1861*. New York: Macmillan Co., 1931.

————. *Southern Editorials on Secession*. New York: Century Co., 1931.

Eaton, Clement. *A History of the Old South*. New York: Macmillan Co., 1949.

Ehrlich, Walter. *They Have No Rights*. Westport, Conn.: Greenwood Press, 1979.

————. "Was the Dred Scott Case Valid?" *Journal of American History* 55 (1968): 256–65.

Ewing, Elbert William R. *Legal and Historical Status of the Dred Scott Decision: A History of the Case and an Examination of the Opinion Delivered by the Supreme Court of the United States, March 6, 1857*. Washington, D.C.: Cobden Publishing Co., 1909.

Fehrenbacher, Don E. *The Dred Scott Case: Its Significance in American Law and Politics*. New York: Oxford University Press, 1978.

————. "The Election of 1860." In *Crucial American Elections*, edited by Arthur S. Link. Philadelphia: American Philosophical Society, 1973.

————. *Prelude to Greatness: Lincoln in the 1850s*. Stanford, Calif.: Stanford University Press, 1962.

Foner, Eric. *Free Soil, Free Labor, Free Men: The Ideology of the Republican Party before the Civil War*. New York: Oxford University Press, 1970.

————. "The Wilmot Proviso Revisited." *Journal of American History* 56 (1969): 262–79.

Frank, John P. *Justice Daniel Dissenting: A Biography of Peter V. Daniel, 1784–1860*. Cambridge: Harvard University Press, 1964.

Frankfurter, Felix. *The Commerce Clause under Marshall, Taney and Waite*. Chapel Hill: University of North Carolina Press, 1937.

Franklin, John Hope. *From Slavery to Freedom: A History of Negro Americans*. 5th ed. New York: Alfred A. Knopf, 1980.

Friedman, Lawrence M. *A History of American Law*. New York: Simon and Schuster, 1973.

Going, Charles Buxton. *David Wilmot, Free-Soiler: A Biography of the Great Advocate of the Wilmot Proviso*. New York: Appleton, 1924.

Graham, Howard Jay. *Everyman's Constitution: Historical Essays on the Fourteenth Amendment, "Conspiracy Theory," and American Constitutionalism*. Madison: State Historical Society of Wisconsin, 1968.

Hagan, Horace H. "Ableman v. Booth, Effect of Fugitive Slave Laws on Opinions as

Bibliography

to Rights of Federal Government and of States in the North and South." *American Bar Association Journal* 17 (1931): 19–24.

———. "The Dred Scott Decision." *Georgetown Law Review* 15 (1947): 95–114.

Haines, Charles Grove, and Sherwood, Foster H. *The Role of the Supreme Court in American Government and Politics, 1835–1864.* Berkeley and Los Angeles: University of California Press, 1957.

Halstead, M. *Caucuses of 1860: A History of the National Political Conventions of the Current Political Campaign.* Columbus, Ohio: Follett, Foster and Co., 1860.

Hamilton, Holman. *Prologue to Conflict: The Crisis and Compromise of 1850.* Lexington: University of Kentucky Press, 1964.

Harris, Robert J. "Chief Justice Taney: Prophet of Reform and Reaction." *Vanderbilt Law Review* 10 (1957): 227–57.

Hay, Logan. "Lincoln's Attitude toward the Supreme Court and the Dredd [*sic*] Scott Decision." In *Annual Report of the Illinois State Bar Association*, 1937. Springfield: Schnepp and Barnes, 1937.

Heckman, Richard Allen. *Lincoln vs. Douglas: The Great Debate Campaign.* Washington, D.C.: Public Affairs Press, 1967.

Hodder, Frank H. "Some Phases of the Dred Scott Case." *Mississippi Valley Historical Review* 16 (1929): 3–22.

Hogan, John Charles. "The Role of Chief Justice Taney in the Decision of the Dred Scott Case." *Case and Comment* 18 (1953): 3–8.

Holt, Michael F. *The Political Crisis of the 1850s.* New York: John Wiley, 1978.

Hopkins, Vincent C. *Dred Scott's Case.* New York: Fordham University Press, 1951.

Hughes, Charles Evans. "Roger Brooke Taney." *American Bar Association Journal* 17 (1931): 785–90.

Hurd, John Codman. *The Law of Freedom and Bondage in the United States.* 2 vols. Boston: Little, Brown, 1858, 1862.

Hyman, Harold M., and Wiecek, William M. *Equal Justice Under Law: Constitutional Development 1835–1875.* New York: Harper and Row, 1982.

Isely, Jeter Allen. *Horace Greeley and the Republican Party, 1853–1861, a Study of the New York Tribune.* New York: Octagon Books, 1965.

Jaffa, Harry V. *Crisis of the House Divided: An Interpretation of the Issues in the Lincoln-Douglas Debates.* Chicago: University of Chicago Press, 1982.

Jaffa, Harry V., and Johannsen, Robert W., eds. *In the Name of the People: Speeches and Writings of Lincoln and Douglas in the Ohio Campaign of 1859.* Columbus: Ohio State University Press, 1959.

Johannsen, Robert W. *Stephen A. Douglas.* New York: Oxford University Press, 1973.

———, ed. *The Letters of Stephen A. Douglas.* Urbana: University of Illinois Press, 1961.

Bibliography

_____, ed. *The Lincoln-Douglas Debates*. New York: Oxford University Press, 1965.

Klein, Philip Shriver. *President James Buchanan: A Biography*. University Park: Pennsylvania State University Press, 1962.

Kutler, Stanley I., ed. *The Dred Scott Decision: Law or Politics?* Boston: Houghton Mifflin, 1967.

_____. *Judicial Power and Reconstruction Politics*. Chicago: University of Chicago Press, 1968.

Lawrence, Alexander L. *James Moore Wayne, Southern Unionist*. Chapel Hill: University of North Carolina Press, 1943.

_____. "Justice Wayne and the Dred Scott Case." In *Report of the Proceedings of the Fifty-Seventh Annual Session of the Georgia Bar Association*, edited by John B. Harris. Macon, Ga.: J. W. Burke and Co., 1940.

Leach, Richard H. "Benjamin Robbins Curtis: Judicial Misfit." *New England Quarterly* 25 (1952): 507–23.

_____. "Justice Curtis and the Dred Scott Case." *Essex Institute Historical Collections* 94 (1958): 37–56.

Lewis, Walker. *Without Fear or Favor: A Biography of Chief Justice Roger Brooke Taney*. Boston: Houghton Mifflin, 1965.

Luthin, Reinhard H. *The First Lincoln Campaign*. Gloucester, Mass.: Peter Smith, 1964.

McCormac, E. I. "Justice Campbell and the Dred Scott Decision." *Mississippi Valley Historical Review* 19 (1933): 565–71.

McCormick, Richard P. *The Second American Party System: Party Formation in the Jacksonian Era*. Chapel Hill: University of North Carolina Press, 1966.

Meerse, David E. "The Northern Democratic Party and the Congressional Elections of 1858." *Civil War History* 19 (1973): 119–37.

Mendelson, Wallace. "The Dred Scott Case Revisited." *Louisiana Law Review* 7 (1947): 398–407.

_____. "Dred Scott's Case Reconsidered." *Minnesota Law Review* 38 (1953): 16–28.

Milton, George Fort. *The Eve of Conflict: Stephen A. Douglas and the Needless War*. New York: Octagon Books, 1963.

Moore, Glover. *The Missouri Controversy, 1819–1821*. Lexington: University of Kentucky Press, 1953.

Moore, John Bassett, ed. *The Works of James Buchanan*. 10 vols. Philadelphia: J. B. Lippincott Co., 1910.

Morrison, Chaplain W. *Democratic Politics and Sectionalism: The Wilmot Proviso Controversy*. Chapel Hill: University of North Carolina Press, 1967.

Nevins, Allan. *The Emergence of Lincoln*. 2 vols. New York: Charles Scribner's Sons, 1950.

Bibliography

————. *Fremont, Pathmarker of the West*. New York: Appleton-Century, 1939.

————. *The Ordeal of the Union*. 2 vols. New York: Charles Scribner's Sons, 1947.

Newmyer, R. Kent. *The Supreme Court under Marshall and Taney*. New York: Crowell, 1968.

The New York Daily Times, 1854–1861.

Nichols, Roy Franklin. *The Disruption of American Democracy*. New York: Macmillan Co., 1948.

Patterson, Isabel. "The Riddle of Chief Justice Taney in the Dred Scott Decision." *Georgia Review* 3 (1949): 192–203.

Potter, David M. *The Impending Crisis, 1848–1861*. New York: Harper and Row, 1976.

————. *Lincoln and His Party in the Secession Crisis*. New Haven: Yale University Press, 1942.

Proceedings of the [Democratic] Conventions at Charleston and Baltimore. Washington, D.C.: n. p., 1860.

Proceedings of the Republican National Convention held at Chicago, May 16, 17, and 18, 1860. Albany, N.Y.: Weed, Parsons and Co., 1860.

Rawley, James A. *Race and Politics: "Bleeding Kansas" and the Coming of the Civil War*. Philadelphia: J. B. Lippincott Co., 1969.

Raybeck, Joseph G. *Free Soil: The Election of 1848*. Lexington: University Press of Kentucky, 1970.

Rhodes, James Ford. *History of the United States from the Compromise of 1850*. 8 vols. New York: Macmillan Co., 1909–19.

Russell, Robert R. "The Issues in the Congressional Struggle over the Kansas-Nebraska Bill, 1854." *Journal of Southern History* 29 (1963): 187–210.

Schmidhauser, John R. "Judicial Behavior and the Sectional Crisis of 1837–1860." *Journal of Politics* 23 (1961): 615–40.

Schwartz, Bernard. *From Confederation to Nation: The American Constitution, 1835–1877*. Baltimore: Johns Hopkins University Press, 1973.

————. *The Reins of Power: A Constitutional History of the United States*. New York: Hill and Wang, 1963.

Schwartz, Harold. "The Controversial Dred Scott Decision." *Missouri Historical Review* 54 (1960): 262–72.

Scrapbook of the Dred Scott Decision etc. N.p., n.d. Widener Library, Harvard University, Cambridge, Mass.

Sewell, Richard H. *Ballots for Freedom: Antislavery Politics in the United States*. New York: Oxford University Press, 1976.

————. *John P. Hale and the Politics of Abolition*. Cambridge: Harvard University Press, 1965.

Smith, Charles W. *Roger B. Taney: Jacksonian Jurist*. Chapel Hill: University of North Carolina Press, 1936.

Bibliography

Smith, Elbert B. *The Death of Slavery: The United States, 1837–1865*. Chicago: University of Chicago Press, 1967.

Spector, Robert M. "Lincoln and Taney: A Study in Constitutional Polarization." *American Journal of Legal History* 15 (1971): 199–214.

Stampp, Kenneth M. *The Peculiar Institution: Slavery in the Ante-Bellum South*. New York: Alfred A. Knopf, 1956.

Stewart, James Brewer. "The Aims and Impact of Garrisonian Abolitionism, 1849–1860." *Civil War History* 15 (1969): 197–209.

―――. *Holy Warriors: The Abolitionists and American Slavery*. New York: Hill and Wang, 1976.

Swierenga, Robert P., ed. *Beyond the Civil War Synthesis: Political Essays of the Civil War Era*. Westport, Conn.: Greenwood Press, 1975.

Swisher, Carl Brent. "Dred Scott One Hundred Years After." *Journal of Politics* 19 (1957): 167–83.

―――. *Equal Under Law*. New York: Collier Books, 1965.

―――. "Mr. Chief Justice Taney." In *Mr. Justice*, edited by Allison Dunham and Philip B. Kurland. Chicago: University of Chicago Press, 1964.

―――. *Roger B. Taney*. New York: Macmillan Co., 1935. Reprint. Hamden, Conn.: Archon Books, 1961.

―――. *The Taney Period, 1836–40*. Vol. 5 of the *History of the Supreme Court of the United States*. Edited by Paul A. Freund. New York: Macmillan Co., 1971.

Tyler, Samuel. *Memoir of Roger Brooke Taney, LL.D.* 2d ed. New York: Da Capo Press, 1970.

Van Deusen, Glyndon C. *William Henry Seward*. New York: Oxford University Press, 1967.

Voegeli, V. Jacque. *Free but Not Equal: The Midwest and the Negro during the Civil War*. Chicago: University of Chicago Press, 1967.

Warren, Charles. *The Supreme Court in United States History*. Rev. ed. 2 vols. Boston: Little, Brown, 1937.

Weisenburger, Francis P. *The Life of John McLean: A Politician on the United States Supreme Court*. New York: Da Capo Press, 1971.

Wells, Damon. *Stephen Douglas, the Last Years, 1857–1861*. Austin: University of Texas Press, 1971.

White, G. Edward. *The American Judicial Tradition*. New York: Oxford University Press, 1976.

Wiecek, William M. "Slavery and Abolition before the United States Supreme Court, 1820–1860." *Journal of American History* (1978): 34–59.

―――. "*Somerset*: Lord Mansfield and the Legitimacy of Slavery in the Anglo-American World." *University of Chicago Law Review* 42 (1974): 86–146.

―――. *The Sources of Antislavery Constitutionalism in America, 1760–1848*. Ithaca, N.Y.: Cornell University Press, 1977.

Wiltse, Charles M. *John C. Calhoun, Sectionalist 1840–1850*. 3 vols. Indianapolis: Bobbs-Merrill, 1951.

RECONSTRUCTION

Manuscript Sources

Jeremiah Black Papers, Library of Congress.
Salmon Portland Chase Papers, Library of Congress.
George William Curtis Papers, Harvard University.
David Davis Papers, Chicago Historical Society.
William Pitt Fessenden Papers, Library of Congress.
Thaddeus Stevens Papers, Library of Congress.
Charles Sumner Papers, Harvard University.
Lyman Trumbull Papers, Library of Congress.
Gideon Welles Papers, Library of Congress.

Published Sources

Adams, Ephraim Douglas. *Great Britain and the American Civil War*. New York: Russell and Russell, 1924.

Andrews, Rena Mazyck. "Johnson's Plan of Restoration in Relation to That of Lincoln." *Tennessee Historical Quarterly*, 2d ser., 1 (1931): 165–81.

Barnes, William H. *History of the Thirty-Ninth Congress of the United States*. New York: Harper Brothers, 1868. Reprint. New York: Negro University Press, 1969.

Beale, Howard K. *The Critical Year: A Study of Andrew Johnson and Reconstruction*. New York: Harcourt, Brace, 1930.

Belz, Herman. *Emancipation and Equal Rights: Politics and Constitutionalism in the Civil War Era*. New York: W. W. Norton and Co., 1978.

Benedict, Michael Les. *A Compromise of Principle: Congressional Republicans and Reconstruction, 1863–1869*. New York: W. W. Norton and Co., 1974.

——. "Preserving the Constitution: The Conservative Basis of Radical Reconstruction." *Journal of American History* 61 (1974): 65–90.

Bentley, George R. *A History of the Freedmen's Bureau*. New York: Octagon Books, 1970.

——. *Reconstructing the Union: Theory and Policy during the Civil War*. Ithaca, N.Y.: Cornell University Press for the American Historical Association, 1969.

Bowers, Claude G. *The Tragic Era: The Revolution after Lincoln*. Cambridge, Mass.: Riverside Press, 1957.

Brock, W. R. *An American Crisis: Congress and Reconstruction, 1865–1867*. New York: St. Martin's Press, 1963.

Bibliography

Burgess, John W. *Reconstruction and the Constitution, 1866–1876.* New York: Charles Scribner's Sons, 1902.

Canby, Courtlandt, ed. *Lincoln and the Civil War: A Profile and a History.* New York: George Braziller, 1960.

Carpenter, John A. *Sword and Olive Branch: Oliver Otis Howard.* Pittsburgh: University of Pittsburgh Press, 1964.

Clemenceau, Georges. *American Reconstruction, 1865–1870, and the Impeachment of President Johnson.* Edited by Fernand Baldensperger and translated by Margaret MacVeagh. New York: Dial Press, 1928.

Coleman, Charles H. *The Election of 1868: The Democratic Effort to Regain Control.* New York: Columbia University Press, 1933.

Congressional Globe, Thirty-ninth and Fortieth Congresses, 1865–1868.

Coulter, E. Merton. *The South during Reconstruction, 1865–1877.* Baton Rouge: Louisiana State University Press, 1947.

Cox, Lawanda, and Cox, John A. *Politics, Principle, and Prejudice, 1865–1866.* New York: Free Press of Glencoe, 1963.

Craven, Avery. *Reconstruction: The Ending of the Civil War.* New York: Holt, Rinehart and Winston, 1969.

Current, Richard N. *Old Thad Stevens: A Story of Ambition.* Madison: University of Wisconsin Press, 1942.

Dewitt, David M. *The Impeachment and Trial of Andrew Johnson, Seventeenth President of the United States.* New York: Macmillan Co., 1903. Reprint. New York: Russell and Russell, 1967.

Dodd, Dorothy. *Henry J. Raymond and the New York Times during Reconstruction.* Chicago: University of Chicago Libraries, 1936.

Donald, David. *Charles Sumner and the Rights of Man.* New York: Alfred A. Knopf, 1970.

―――. *The Politics of Reconstruction, 1863–1867.* Baton Rouge: Louisiana State University Press, 1965.

―――, ed. *Inside Lincoln's Cabinet: The Civil War Diaries of Salmon Portland Chase.* New York: Longmans, Green and Co., 1954.

Dorris, Jonathan T. *Pardon and Amnesty under Lincoln and Johnson: The Restoration of the South to Their Rights and Privileges.* Chapel Hill: University of North Carolina Press, 1953.

Fairman, Charles. "Mr. Justice Bradley's Appointment to the Supreme Court and the Legal Tender Cases." *Harvard Law Review* 54 (1941): 977–1034; 54 (1941): 1128–55.

―――. *Mr. Justice Miller and the Supreme Court, 1862–1890.* New York: Russell and Russell, 1939.

―――. *Reconstruction and Reunion: 1864–88.* Part 1. Vol. 6 of the *History of the*

Bibliography

Supreme Court of the United States. Edited by Paul A. Freund. New York: Macmillan Co., 1971–.

Fessenden, Francis. *The Life and Public Services of William Pitt Fessenden.* 2 vols. Boston: Houghton Mifflin, 1907.

Fleming, Walter L. *Documentary History of Reconstruction: Political, Military, Social, Religious, Educational & Industrial, 1865 to the Present Time.* 2 vols. Cleveland: Arthur H. Clark Co., 1906.

Foner, Eric. *Politics and Ideology in the Age of the Civil War.* New York: Oxford University Press, 1980.

Franklin, John Hope. *Reconstruction: After the Civil War.* Chicago: University of Chicago Press, 1961.

Garfield, James. *Life and Letters of John Abram Garfield.* Edited by J. A. J. Creswell. New York: Harper and Bros., 1867.

Gipson, Lawrence H. "The Statesmanship of President Johnson: A Study in the Presidential Reconstruction Policy." *Mississippi Valley Historical Review* 2 (1915): 363–83.

Graham, Howard Jay. "The 'Conspiracy Theory' of the Fourteenth Amendment." *Yale Law Journal* 47 (1938): 171–94.

Harper's Weekly, various issues, 1864–1870.

Hayes, Rutherford B. *Diary and Letters of Rutherford Birchard Hayes.* Edited by Charles R. Williams. 5 vols. Columbus: Ohio State Archaeological and Historical Society, 1922–26.

Hesseltine, William B. *Lincoln's Plan of Reconstruction.* Tuscaloosa, Ala.: Confederate Publishing Co., 1960.

———. *Ulysses S. Grant, Politician.* New York: Dodd, Mead, 1935.

Hoeveler, J. David. "Reconstruction and the Federal Courts: The Civil Rights Act of 1875." *The Historian* 31 (1969): 604–17.

Hyman, Harold M. *New Frontiers of the American Reconstruction.* Urbana: University of Illinois Press, 1966.

———, ed. *The Radical Republicans and Reconstruction, 1861–1870.* Indianapolis: Bobbs-Merrill, 1967.

James, Joseph B. *The Framing of the Fourteenth Amendment.* Urbana: University of Illinois Press, 1956.

Kaczorowski, Robert J. *The Politics of Judicial Interpretation: The Federal Courts, Department of Justice and Civil Rights, 1866–1876.* New York University School of Law Series in Legal History. New York: Oceana Publications, 1985.

Kendrick, Benjamin B. *The Journal of the Joint Committee of Fifteen on Reconstruction.* New York: Columbia University Press, 1914.

King, Willard L. *Lincoln's Manager: David Davis.* Cambridge: Harvard University Press, 1960.

Bibliography

Krug, Mark M. *Lyman Trumbull: Conservative Radical*. New York: A. S. Barnes, 1965.

Kutler, Stanley I. *Judicial Power and Reconstruction Politics*. Chicago: University of Chicago Press, 1968.

McCulloch, Hugh. *Men and Measures of Half a Century: Sketches and Comments*. New York: Charles Scribner's Sons, 1900.

McDonough, James L., and Alderson, William T. "Republican Politics and the Impeachment of Andrew Johnson." *Tennessee Historical Quarterly* 26 (1967): 177–83.

McFeely, William S. *Yankee Stepfather: General O. O. Howard and the Freedmen*. New York: W. W. Norton and Co., 1970.

McKitrick, Eric L. *Andrew Johnson and Reconstruction*. Chicago: University of Chicago Press, 1960.

McPherson, Edward. *The Political History of the United States of America during the Great Rebellion, 1860–1865*. N.p., 1865. Reprint. New York: Da Capo Press, 1972.

_____. *The Political History of the United States of America during the Period of Reconstruction*. N.p.: Solomons and Chapman, 1875. Reprint. New York: Negro University Press, 1969.

McPherson, James M. *Ordeal by Fire: The Civil War and Reconstruction*. New York: Alfred A. Knopf, 1982.

_____. *The Struggle for Equality: Abolitionism and the Negro in the Civil War and Reconstruction*. Princeton: Princeton University Press, 1964.

Mantell, Martin E. *Johnson, Grant, and the Politics of Reconstruction*. New York: Columbia University Press, 1973.

Milton, George Fort. *The Age of Hate: Andrew Johnson and the Radicals*. New York: Coward-McCann, 1930.

The National Intelligencer, various issues, 1864–1870.

The New York Times, various issues, 1864–1870.

Nevins, Allan. *The War for the Union*. Vol. 4, *The Organized War to Victory, 1864–1865*. New York: Charles Scribner's Sons, 1971.

Nieman, Donald G. *To Set the Law in Motion: The Freedmen's Bureau and the Legal Rights of Blacks, 1865–1868*. Millwood, N.Y.: KTO Press, 1979.

Oakes, James. "Failure of Vision: The Collapse of the Freedmen's Bureau Courts." *Civil War History* 25 (1979): 66–76.

Peirce, Paul Seeks. *The Freedmen's Bureau: A Chapter in the History of Reconstruction*. Iowa City: University of Iowa, 1904. Reprint. St. Claire Shores, Mich.: Scholarly Press, 1970.

Perman, Michael. *Reunion without Compromise: The South and Reconstruction, 1865–1868*. Cambridge: Cambridge University Press, 1973.

Bibliography

Randall, James G. *Constitutional Problems under Lincoln.* New York: Appleton, 1926.
———. *Lincoln the President.* 4 vols. New York: Dodd, Mead, 1945–55.
Randall, James G., and Donald, David. *The Civil War and Reconstruction.* 2d ed. Lexington, Mass.: D. C. Heath and Co., 1969.
Richardson, James D., ed. *A Compilation of the Messages and Papers of the Presidents, 1789–1897.* Vol. 6, *1861–1869.* Washington, D.C.: Government Printing Office, 1897.
Sefton, James E. "Chief Justice Chase as an Advisor on Presidential Reconstruction." *Civil War History* 12 (1967): 247–64.
———. "The Impeachment of Andrew Johnson: A Century of Writing." *Civil War History* 14 (1968): 120–47.
———. *The United States Army and Reconstruction 1865–77.* Baton Rouge: Louisiana State University Press, 1967.
Sherman, John. *Recollections of Forty Years in the House, Senate and Cabinet: An Autobiography.* 2 vols. Chicago: Werner, 1895.
Sherman, William T. *The Sherman Letters: Correspondence between General and Senator Sherman from 1837 to 1891.* Edited by Rachel Sherman Thorndike. New York: Charles Scribner's Sons, 1909.
Silver, David M. *Lincoln's Supreme Court.* Urbana: University of Illinois Press, 1957.
Stampp, Kenneth M. *And the War Came: The North and the Secession Crisis, 1860–61.* Baton Rouge: Louisiana State University Press, 1950.
———. *The Era of Reconstruction, 1865–1877.* New York: Alfred A. Knopf, 1966.
Stryker, Lloyd Paul. *Andrew Johnson, A Study in Courage.* New York: Macmillan Co., 1929.
Sumner, Charles. *The Works of Charles Sumner.* 15 vols. Boston: Lee & Shepard, 1870–83. Reprint. New York: Negro University Press, 1969.
Thomas, Benjamin P., and Hyman, Harold M. *Stanton: The Life and Times of Lincoln's Secretary of War.* New York: Alfred A. Knopf, 1962.
Trefousse, Hans L. "The Acquittal of Andrew Johnson and the Decline of the Radicals." *Civil War History* 14 (1968): 148–61.
Warren, Charles. *The Supreme Court in United States History.* Rev. ed. 2 vols. Boston: Little, Brown, 1937.
Weisberger, Bernard. "The Dark and Bloody Ground of Reconstruction Historiography." *Journal of Southern History* 25 (1959): 427–47.
Welles, Gideon. *Diary of Gideon Welles, Secretary of the Navy under Lincoln and Johnson.* Edited by John T. Morse, Jr. 3 vols. Boston: Houghton Mifflin, 1911.
White, Horace. *The Life of Lyman Trumbull.* Boston: Houghton Mifflin, 1913.
Wiecek, William M. "The Reconstruction of Federal Judicial Power, 1863–1875."

Bibliography

American Journal of Legal History 13 (1969): 333–59.

Wilson, Theodore B. *The Black Codes of the South*. University: University of Alabama Press, 1965.

Winston, Robert W. *Andrew Johnson, Plebeian and Patriot*. New York: Henry Holt, 1928.

Zornow, William F. *Lincoln and the Party Divided*. Norman: University of Oklahoma Press, 1954.

THE NEW DEAL

Manuscript Sources

Benjamin V. Cohen Papers, Library of Congress.

Homer S. Cummings Papers, University of Virginia Library.

Felix Frankfurter Papers, Harvard Law School Library.

Arthur Krock Papers, Princeton University.

Henry Morgenthau Papers, Franklin D. Roosevelt Library.

Thomas Reed Powell Papers, Harvard Law School Library.

Stanley Reed Papers, University of Kentucky Libraries, Department of Special Collections.

Franklin Delano Roosevelt Papers, Franklin D. Roosevelt Library.

Rexford G. Tugwell Papers, Franklin D. Roosevelt Library.

Published Sources

Alsop, Joseph, and Catledge, Turner. *The 168 Days*. Garden City, N.Y.: Doubleday, Doran and Co., 1938.

Baker, Liva. *Felix Frankfurter*. New York: Coward-McCann, 1969.

Brinkley, Alan. *Voices of Protest: Huey Long, Father Coughlin, and the Great Depression*. New York: Alfred A. Knopf, 1982.

Burns, James MacGregor. *Roosevelt: The Lion and the Fox*. New York: Harcourt, Brace and Co., 1956.

Complete Presidential Press Conferences of Franklin D. Roosevelt. 25 vols. New York: Da Capo Press, 1972.

Congressional Record. Vols. 76–81, 1933–1937.

Corwin, Edward S. *Court over Constitution*. Princeton: Princeton University Press, 1938.

———. *The Doctrine of Judicial Review*. Princeton: Princeton University Press, 1914.

Danelski, David J., and Tulchin, Joseph S., eds. *The Autobiographical Notes of Charles Evans Hughes*. Cambridge: Harvard University Press, 1973.

Bibliography

Dawson, Nelson Lloyd. *Louis D. Brandeis, Felix Frankfurter, and the New Deal.* Hamden, Conn.: Archon Books, 1980.

Eriksson, Erik M. *The Supreme Court and the New Deal.* Rosemead, Calif.: Rosemead Review Press, 1940.

Frankfurter, Felix. "Mr. Justice Roberts." *University of Pennsylvania Law Review* 104 (1955): 311–17.

Freedman, Max, ed. *Roosevelt and Frankfurter: Their Correspondence, 1928–45.* Boston: Little, Brown and Co., 1967.

Freidel, Frank. *Franklin D. Roosevelt, The Apprenticeship.* Boston: Little, Brown and Co., 1952.

_____. *Franklin D. Roosevelt, The Ordeal.* Boston: Little, Brown and Co., 1954.

Hawley, Ellis W. *The New Deal and the Problem of Monopoly: A Study in Economic Ambivalence.* Princeton: Princeton University Press, 1966.

Hirsch, H. N. *The Enigma of Felix Frankfurter.* New York: Basic Books, 1981.

Howe, Mark DeWolfe, ed. *The Holmes-Laski Letters.* Cambridge: Harvard University Press, 1953.

Ickes, Harold L. *The Secret Diary of Harold Ickes.* 3 vols. New York: Simon and Schuster, 1953–54.

Irons, Peter H. *The New Deal Lawyers.* Princeton: Princeton University Press, 1982.

Johnson, Julia E., comp. *Reorganization of the Supreme Court.* New York: H. W. Wilson Co., 1937.

Leonard, Charles. *A Search for a Judicial Philosophy: Mr. Justice Roberts and the Constitutional Revolution of 1937.* Port Washington, N.Y.: Kennikat Press, 1971.

Leuchtenburg, William E. *Franklin D. Roosevelt and The New Deal, 1932–1940.* New York: Harper and Row, 1963.

_____. "The Origins of Franklin D. Roosevelt's 'Court-Packing' Plan." *Supreme Court Review* (1966): 347–400.

Literary Digest. Vols. 112–123, 1932–1937.

Mason, Alpheus T. "Harlan Fiske Stone and FDR's Court Plan." *Yale Law Journal* 61 (1952): 791–817.

_____. *Harlan Fiske Stone: Pillar of the Law.* New York: Viking Press, 1956.

_____. *The Supreme Court from Taft to Warren.* Baton Rouge: Louisiana State University Press, 1958.

Murphy, Bruce. *The Brandeis-Frankfurter Connection.* New York: Oxford University Press, 1982.

The New Republic. Vols. 73–92, 1932–1937.

The New York Times. 1932–1937.

Niedziela, Theresa A. "Franklin D. Roosevelt and the Supreme Court." *Presidential Studies Quarterly* 6 (1976): 51–56.

Official Report of the Proceedings of the Democratic National Convention Held at Philadelphia, Pennsylvania, June 23rd to June 27th, inclusive, 1936. Washington,

Bibliography

D.C.: Master Reprint Co., n.d.

Official Report of the Proceedings of the Twenty-first Republican National Convention, held in Cleveland, Ohio June 9, 10, 11 and 12, 1936. New York: Tenney Press, 1936.

Olsen, James S., ed. *Historical Dictionary of the New Deal: From Inauguration to Preparation for War.* Westport, Conn.: Greenwood Press, 1985.

Paschal, Joel Francis. *Mr. Justice Sutherland: A Man against the State.* Princeton: Princeton University Press, 1951.

Pearson, Drew, and Allen, Robert S. *The Nine Old Men.* Garden City, N.Y.: Doubleday, Doran and Co., 1936.

Pritchett, C. Herman. *The Roosevelt Court: A Study in Judicial Politics and Values, 1937–47.* New York: Octagon Books, 1963.

The Public Papers and Addresses of Franklin D. Roosevelt. Compiled by Samuel I. Rosenman. 13 vols. New York: Random House, 1938–50.

Pusey, Merlo J. *Charles Evans Hughes.* New York: Macmillan Co., 1951.

Rauch, Basil. *The History of the New Deal, 1933–1938.* 2d ed. New York: Octagon Books, 1975.

Roberts, Owen J. *The Court and the Constitution.* Cambridge: Harvard University Press, 1951.

Rodell, Fred. *Nine Men: A Political History of the Supreme Court from 1790 to 1955.* New York: Random House, 1955.

Roosevelt, Elliott, ed. *F.D.R.: His Personal Letters, 1928–45.* 4 vols. New York: Duell, Sloan and Pearce, 1950.

Sargeant, James E. *Roosevelt and the Hundred Days.* New York: Garland Publishers, 1981.

Schlesinger, Arthur M., Jr. *The Age of Roosevelt.* 3 vols. Boston: Houghton Mifflin, 1957.

Sirevag, T. "Roosevelt's Ideas and the 1937 Court Fight: A Neglected Factor." *Historian* 33 (1971): 578–95.

Strum, Phillipa. *Louis D. Brandeis: Justice for the People.* Cambridge: Harvard University Press, 1984.

Swisher, Carl Brent. *Selected Papers of Homer Cummings.* New York: Charles Scribner's Sons, 1939.

Time. Vols. 21–30, 1933–1937.

Today. Vols. 1–7, 1933–1937.

U.S. Congress. Senate. Committee on the Judiciary. *Reorganization of the Federal Judiciary, Hearings before the Committee on the Judiciary on S. 1352.* 75th Cong., 1st sess., 1937.

U.S. Congress. Senate. Committee on the Judiciary. *Report on the Reorganization of the Federal Judiciary, Senate Rept. 711 to Accompany S. 1352,* 75th Cong., 1st sess., 1937.

Bibliography

Urofsky, Melvin I. *Louis D. Brandeis and the Progressive Tradition.* Edited by Oscar Handlin. Boston: Little, Brown, 1981.

Urofsky, Melvin I., and Levy, David W., eds. *Letters of Louis D. Brandeis.* Vol. 5, *1921–24: Elder Statesman.* Albany: State University of New York Press, 1978.

Vital Speeches. Vols. 1–3, 1934–1937.

Wolfskill, George, and Hudson, John A. *All But the People: Franklin D. Roosevelt and His Critics, 1933–39.* Toronto: Macmillan Co., 1969.

THE MODERN COURT

Auerbach, Carl A. "The Reapportionment Cases: One Person, One Vote—One Vote, One Value." *Supreme Court Review* (1964): 1–87.

Bartley, Numan V. *The Rise of Massive Resistance: Race and Politics in the South During the 1950's.* Baton Rouge: Louisiana State University Press, 1969.

Berger, Raoul. "Congressional Contraction of Federal Jurisdiction." *Wisconsin Law Review* 1980 (1980): 801–9.

————. *Congress v. The Supreme Court.* Cambridge: Harvard University Press, 1969.

————. *Government by Judiciary: The Transformation of the Fourteenth Amendment.* Cambridge: Harvard University Press, 1977.

————. "The Role of the Supreme Court." *University of Little Rock Law Journal* 3 (1980): 1–12.

Berns, Walter. "Has the Burger Court Gone Too Far?" *Commentary* 78 (1984): 27–33.

Brant, Irving. "Appellate Jurisdiction: Congressional Abuse of the Exceptions Clause." *Oregon Law Review* 53 (1973): 466–91.

Brown, Ernest J. "Quis Custodiet Ipsos Custodies?—The School Prayer Cases." *Supreme Court Review* (1963): 1–33.

Burk, Robert F. *The Eisenhower Administration and Black Civil Rights.* Knoxville: University of Tennessee Press, 1984.

Carter, Robert L. "The Warren Court and Desegregation." *Michigan Law Review* 67 (1968): 237–48.

Congressional Quarterly Almanac, 1954–1987.

Congressional Quarterly Weekly Report, 1956–1987.

Congressional Record, 1954–1987.

Cortner, Richard C. *The Reapportionment Cases in Law and Politics.* Knoxville: University of Tennessee Press, 1970.

Dixon, Robert G. *Democratic Representation: Reapportionment in Law and Politics.* New York: Oxford University Press, 1968.

Editorials on File, 1970–1987.

Bibliography

Friendly, Fred W., and Elliott, Martha J. H. *The Constitution: That Delicate Balance.* New York: Random House, 1984.

George H. Gallup. *The Gallup Poll: Public Opinion 1935–71.* 3 vols. New York: Random House, 1972.

———. *The Gallup Poll: Public Opinion 1972–77.* 2 vols. Wilmington, Del.: Scholarly Resources, 1978.

———. *The Gallup Poll: Public Opinion 1978.* Wilmington, Del.: Scholarly Resources, 1979.

———. *The Gallup Poll: Public Opinion 1979.* Wilmington, Del.: Scholarly Resources, 1980.

Graglia, Lino A. "The Supreme Court's Abuse of Power." *National Review* 30 (1978): 892–96.

Handberg, Roger. "Public Opinion and the United States Supreme Court, 1935–1981." *International Social Science Review* 59 (1984): 3–13.

Handberg, Roger, and Maddox, William S. "Public Support for the Supreme Court in the 1970s." *American Politics Quarterly* 10 (1982): 333–46.

Hart, Henry M., Jr. "The Power of Congress to Limit the Jurisdiction of the Federal Courts: An Exercise in Dialectic." *Harvard Law Review* 66 (1953): 1362–1402.

Horowitz, David. *The Courts and Social Policy.* Washington: Brookings Institution, 1976.

Katz, Ellis. "Patterns of Compliance with the *Schempp* Decision." *Journal of Public Law* 14 (1965): 396–408.

Kelso, Charles D. "Justice O'Connor Replaces Justice Stewart: What Effect on Constitutional Cases?" *Pacific Law Journal* 13 (1982): 259–72.

Kilpatrick, James Jackson. *The Southern Case for School Segregation.* New York: Crowell-Collier, 1963.

———. *The Sovereign States: Notes of a Citizen of Virginia.* Chicago: Regnery, 1957.

Kluger, Richard. *Simple Justice: The History of Brown v. Board of Education and America's Struggle for Equality.* 2 vols. New York: Alfred A. Knopf, 1975.

LaMorte, Michael W., and Dorminy, Fred N. "Compliance with the *Schempp* Decision: A Decade Later." *Journal of Law and Education* 3 (1974): 399–402.

Lucas, Roy. "Federal Constitutional Limitations on the Enforcement and Administration of State Abortion Statutes." *North Carolina Law Review* 46 (1968): 730–38.

Lukas, J. Anthony. *Common Ground: A Turbulent Decade in the Lives of Three American Families.* New York: Alfred A. Knopf, 1985.

McCloskey, Robert G. *The Modern Supreme Court.* Cambridge: Harvard University Press, 1972.

McDowell, Gary L. "A Modest Remedy for Judicial Activism." *Public Interest* 67 (1982): 3–20.

Bibliography

McKay, Robert B. "Reapportionment: Success Story of the Warren Court." *Michigan Law Review* 67 (1968): 223–36.

Marcus, Maeva. *Truman and the Steel Seizure Case: The Limits of Presidential Power.* New York: Columbia University Press, 1977.

Merry, Henry J. "Scope of the Supreme Court's Appellate Jurisdiction: Historical Basis." *Minnesota Law Review* 47 (1962): 53–69.

Mitau, G. Theodore. *Decade of Decisions: The Supreme Court and the Constitutional Revolutions, 1954–1964.* New York: Charles Scribner's Sons, 1967.

Moynihan, Daniel P. "What Do You Do When the Supreme Court is Wrong?" *Public Interest* 57 (1979): 3–24.

Murphy, Walter F. *Congress and the Court.* Chicago: University of Chicago Press, 1962.

The New Republic, various issues, 1954–1987.

Newsweek, various issues, 1954–1987.

The New York Times, various issues, 1954–1987.

Page, Connie. *The Right to Lifers: Who They Are, How They Operate, Where They Get Their Money.* New York: Summit Books, 1983.

Peltason, Jack W. *Fifty-Eight Lonely Men: Southern Federal Judges and School Desegregation.* New York: Harcourt Brace and World, 1961.

Pfeffer, Leo. *Church, State, and Freedom.* Rev. ed. Boston: Beacon Press, 1967.

Polsby, Nelson W., ed. *Reapportionment in the 1970s.* Berkeley and Los Angeles: University of California Press, 1971.

Pritchett, C. Herman. *Congress versus the Supreme Court.* Minneapolis: University of Minnesota Press, 1961.

Roper, Robert, and Jaros, Dean. "The U.S. Supreme Court: Myth, Diffuse Support, Specific Support, and Legitimacy." *American Politics Quarterly* 8 (1980): 85–105.

Rubin, Eva R. *Abortion, Politics, and the Courts: Roe v. Wade and Its Aftermath.* Westport, Conn.: Greenwood Press, 1982.

Sarvis, Betty, and Rodman, Hyman. *The Abortion Controversy.* 2d ed. New York: Columbia University Press, 1974.

Schmidhauser, John R., and Berg, Larry L. *The Supreme Court and Congress: Conflict and Interaction (1945–1968).* New York: Free Press, 1972.

Schwartz, Bernard. *Super Chief: Earl Warren and His Supreme Court; A Judicial Biography.* New York: New York University Press, 1983.

———. *Swann's Way: The School Busing Case and the Supreme Court.* New York: Oxford University Press, 1986.

Tanenhaus, Joseph, and Murphy, Walter F. "Patterns of Public Support for the Supreme Court: A Panel Study." *Journal of Politics* 43 (1981): 24–39.

Time Magazine, various issues, 1954–1987.

Tribe, Lawrence H. *God Save This Honorable Court: How the Choice of Supreme*

Bibliography

Court Justices Shapes Our History. New York: Random House, 1985.

U.S. Congress. House. *Hearings on the Equal Access Act, Hearings before the Subcommittee on Elementary, Secondary, and Vocational Education.* 98th Cong., 1st. sess., 1983.

U.S. Congress. House. Committee on the Judiciary. *Prayer in Public Schools and Buildings—Federal Court Jurisdiction, Hearings before the Subcommittee on Courts, Civil Liberties, and the Administration of Justice.* 96th Cong., 2d. sess., 1980.

U.S. Congress. House. *Religious Speech Protection Act, Hearing before the Subcommittee on Elementary, Secondary, and Vocational Education.* 98th Cong., 2d. sess., 1984.

U.S. Congress. Senate. *Abortion, Hearings before the Subcommittee on Constitutional Amendments of the Committee on the Judiciary.* 4 pts. 97th Cong., 1st. sess., 1974.

U.S. Congress. Senate. *Constitutional Amendments Relating to Abortion, Hearings before the Subcommittee on the Constitution of the Committee on the Judiciary.* 2 vols. 97th Cong., 1st. sess., 1981.

U.S. Congress. Senate. *Constitutional Restraints upon the Judiciary, Hearings before the Subcommittee on the Constitution of the Committee on the Judiciary.* 97th Cong., 1st sess., 1981.

U.S. Congress. Senate. *Court-Ordered School Busing, Hearings before the Subcommittee on the Separation of Powers of the Committee on the Judiciary.* 97th Cong., 1st. sess., 1981 (with appendix).

U.S. Congress. Senate. *The Human Life Bill, Hearings before the Subcommittee on Separation of Powers of the Committee on the Judiciary.* 97th Cong., 1st. sess., 1981.

U.S. Congress. Senate. *The Human Life Bill—S. 158; Report together with Additional and Minority Views, to the Committee on the Judiciary, U.S. Senate, by its Subcommittee on the Separation of Powers.* 97th Cong., 1st sess., 1981.

U.S. Congress. Senate. *Proposed Constitutional Amendment to Permit Voluntary Prayer, Hearings before the Committee on the Judiciary on S. J. Res. 199.* 97th Cong., 2d. sess., 1982.

U.S. News and World Report., various issues, 1954–1987.

Wasby, Stephen L.; D'Amato, Anthony; and Metrailer, Rosemary. *Desegregation from Brown to Alexander: An Exploration of Supreme Court Strategies.* Carbondale: Southern Illinois University Press, 1977.

The Washington Post, various issues, 1954–1987.

Wechsler, Herbert. "The Courts and the Constitution." *Columbia Law Review* 65 (1965): 1001–14.

White, Theodore H. *The Making of the President, 1968.* New York: Atheneum, 1969.

Bibliography

Wilkinson, J. Harvie III. *From Brown to Bakke: The Supreme Court and School Integration, 1954–1978.* New York: Oxford University Press, 1979.

Witt, Elder. *A Different Justice: Reagan and the Supreme Court.* Washington, D.C.: Congressional Quarterly, 1986.

Wolters, Raymond. *The Burden of Brown: Thirty Years of School Desegregation.* Knoxville: University of Tennessee Press, 1984.

Woodward, C. Vann. *The Strange Career of Jim Crow.* New York: Oxford University Press, 1955.

Workman, W. D. *The Case for the South.* New York: Devin-Adair, 1960.

Yarbrough, Tinsley E. *Judge Frank Johnson and Human Rights in Alabama.* University: University of Alabama Press, 1981.

Index

Index

Index